THE
HYMNS OF THE ATHARVA-VEDA

THE
HYMNS OF THE ATHARVA-VEDA

Translated

with a Popular Commentary

BY

RALPH T. H. GRIFFITH

VOL. II

GYAN

Published by

Gyan Publishing House
5, Ansari Road
Daryaganj, New Delhi-110002
Phone: 011-47034999, 9811692060
E-mail: books@gyanbooks.com

Distribution Network
gyanbooks.com
India, USA, Canada, UK, Australia, France

ISBN : 978-81-212-9944-2 (Set)
ISBN : 978-81-212-9942-8 (PB)
First Published, 1896

2nd Impression 2021

Printed at: Gyan Press, Delhi.

The Hymns of the Atharva-Veda, Vol. II
Author: Ralph T. H. Griffith

THE

HYMNS OF THE ATHARVA-VEDA

TRANSLATED

WITH A POPULAR COMMENTARY

BY

RALPH T. H. GRIFFITH

FORMERLY PRINCIPAL OF BENARES COLLEGE

VOL. II

Benares

E. J. LAZARUS AND CO.

1896.

CONTENTS.

THE

HYMNS OF THE ATHARVA-VEDA.

BOOK THE TENTH.

HYMN I.

Afar let her depart: away we drive her whom, made with hands, all-beautiful,
Skilled men prepare and fashion like a bride amid her nuptial train.

2 Complete, with head and nose and ears, all-beauteous, wrought with magic skill,
Afar let her depart: away we drive her.

3 Made by a Śûdra or a Prince, by priests or women, let her go
Back to her maker as her kin, like a dame banished by her lord.

4 I with this salutary herb have ruined all their magic arts,
The spell which they have cast upon thy field, thy cattle, or thy men.

5 Ill fall on him who doeth ill, on him who curseth fall the curse!
We drive her back that she may slay the man who wrought the witchery.

The hymn is a charm against witchcraft.

1 *Her:* Kṛityâ or Witchcraft embodied: a beautiful female form, created for malevolent purposes, like Spenser's false Duessa, by the magic power of some hostile sorcerer.

6 Against her comes the Ângirasa, the Priest whose eye is over us.
Turn back all witcheries, and slay those practisers of magic arts.

7 Whoever said to thee, Go forth against the foeman up the stream,
To him, O Krityâ, go thou back. Pursue not us, the sinless ones.

8 He who composed thy limbs with thought as a deft joiner builds a car,
Go to him: thither lies thy way. This man is all unknown to thee.

9 The cunning men, the sorcerers who fashioned thee and held thee fast,—
This cures and mars their witchery, this, repellent, drives it back the way it came. With this we make thee swim.

10 When we have found her ducked and drenched, a hapless cow whose calf hath died,
Let all my woe depart and let abundant riches come to me.

---

6 *The Ângirasa, the Priest:* Brihaspati, the Purohita of the Gods and the type of priestly rank, regarded as a descendant of, or devoted to, the great Rishi Angiras.

7 *Up the stream: uddpiam;* Professor Ludwig takes the word to mean unrelated, not akin (from *âpi*, an associate or kinsman, instead of from *ap*, water), with a play on the meaning 'up or against the stream.'

8 *Composed thy limbs:* as Archimago (Faery Queene, I. 1. 45) 'fram'd of liquid ayre' Duessa's 'tender partes.'

9 *Repellent:* or, amulet; made of the 'salutary herb' of stanza 4. *Make thee swim:* the favourite test of the infamous 'witch-finder' Matthew Hopkins in the middle of the seventeenth century, a test to which he himself was finally subjected. Even in recent times, in Europe as well as in India, reputed witches have been ducked in the nearest stream by superstitious villagers. 'We make thee swim (away).'—Ludwig.

10 *Ducked and drenched:* 'that she has swum away,' according to Ludwig.

11 If, as they gave thy parents aught, they named thee; or at sacrifice,
From all their purposed evil let these healing herbs deliver thee.

12 From mention of thy name, from sin against the Fathers or the Gods,
These herbs of healing shall by prayer release thee, by power, by holy texts, the milk of Ṛishis.

13 As the wind stirs the dust from earth and drives the rain-cloud from the sky,
So, chased and banished by the spell, all misery departs from me.

14 Go with a resonant cry, depart, like a she-ass whose cords are loosed.
Go to thy makers : hence ! away ! Go driven by the potent spell.

15 This, Kṛityâ, is thy path, we say, and guide thee. We drive thee back who hast been sent against us.
Go by this pathway, breaking loose for onslaught even as a host complete with cars and horses.

16 No path leads hitherward for thee to travel. Turn thee from us : far off, thy light is yonder.
Fly hence across the ninety floods, the rivers most hard to pass. Begone, and be not wounded.

17 As wind the trees, so smite and overthrow them : leave not cow, horse, or man of them surviving.
Return, O Kṛityâ, unto those who made thee. Wake them from sleep to find that they are childless.

---

11 *As they gave thy parents aught:* on the occasion of some ceremony in honour of the infant or youth. *Named thee:* uttered thy name in order to make thee the object of a solemn curse or incantation.

12 *The milk of Ṛishis:* the beneficial influence of the Sages to whom the holy texts were revealed.

16 *The ninety floods:* indefinitely for all the rivers between us and the place whence thou camest.

18 The charm or secret power which they have buried for thee in sacred grass, field, cemetery,
Or spell in household fire which men more cunning have wrought against thee innocent and simple,—

19 That tool of hatred, understood, made ready, stealthy and buried deep, have we discovered.
Let that go back to whence it came, turn thither like a horse and kill the children of the sorcerer.

20 Within our house are swords of goodly iron. Kṛityâ, we know thy joints and all their places.
Arise this instant and begone! What, stranger! art thou seeking here?

21 O Kṛityâ, I will cut thy throat and hew thy feet off. Run, begone!
Indra and Agni, Guardian Lords of living creatures, shield us well!

22 May Soma, gracious friend, imperial Sovran, and the world's Masters look on us with favour.

23 Bhava and Ṣarva cast the flash of lightning, the weapon of the Gods, against the sinner who made the evil thing, who deals in witchcraft!

24 If thou hast come two-footed or four-footed, made by the sorcerer, wrought in perfect beauty,
Become eight-footed and go hence. Speed back again, thou evil one.

---

18 *Secret power: valagá*, charms consisting of bones, nails, hair, etc., tied up in a piece of old matting or cloth, and buried arm-deep in the ground to injure enemies. See Ṣatapatha Brâhmaṇa, III. 5. 4. In connexion with this stanza cf. V. 31. 4, 5, 8. *Cemetery:* or burning-ground; a favourite place for the preparation of magical incantations and destructive charms. Cf. Horace, Epod. XVII. 47.

23 *Bhava and Ṣarva:* see IV. 28, and VI. 93.

24 *Become eight-footed:* that is, twice as swift as a swift quadruped.

25 Anointed, balmed, and well adorned, bearing all trouble with thee, go.
Even as a daughter knows her sire, so know thy maker, Kṛityâ, thou.

26 Kṛityâ, begone, stay not. Pursue as 'twere the wounded creature's track.
He is the chase, the hunter thou : he may not slight or humble thee.

27 He waits, and aiming with his shaft smites him who first would shoot at him,
And, when the foeman deals a blow before him, following strikes him down.

28 Hearken to this my word ; then go thither away whence thou hast come : to him who made thee go thou back.

29 The slaughter of an innocent, O Kṛityâ, is an awful deed. Slay not cow, horse, or man of ours.
In whatsoever place thou art concealed we rouse thee up therefrom : become thou lighter than a leaf.

30 If ye be girt about with clouds of darkness, bound as with a net,
We rend and tear all witcheries hence and to their maker send them back.

31 The brood of wizard, sorcerer, the purposer of evil deed,
Crush thou, O Kṛityâ ; spare not, kill those practisers of magic arts.

32 As Sûrya frees himself from depth of darkness, and casts away the night and rays of morning,
So I repel each baleful charm which an enchanter hath prepared ;
And, as an elephant shakes off the dust, I cast the plague aside.

---

26 *He* : the sorcerer who made thee.

The hymn has been translated by Ludwig, Der Rigveda, III. p. 520.

HYMN II.

WHO framed the heels of Pûrusha? Who fashioned the flesh of him? Who formed and fixed his ankles?
Who made the openings and well-moulded fingers? Who gave him foot-soles and a central station?

2 Whence did they make the ankles that are under, and the knee-bones of Pûrusha above them?
What led them onward to the legs' construction? Who planned and formed the knees' articulations?

3 A fourfold frame is fixt with ends connected, and up above the knees a yielding belly.
The hips and thighs, who was their generator, those props whereby the trunk grew firmly stablished?

4 Who and how many were those Gods who fastened the chest of Pûrusha and neck together?
How many fixed his breasts? Who formed his elbows? How many joined together ribs and shoulders?

5 Who put together both his arms and said, Let him show manly strength?
Who and what God was he who set the shoulder-blades upon the trunk?

6 Who pierced the seven openings in the head? Who made these ears, these nostrils, eyes, and mouth,
Through whose surpassing might in all directions bipeds and quadrupeds have power of motion?

The subject of the hymn is Purusha or Pûrusha, the Primeval Man, or Humanity personified, and in stanzas 16, 18, 28 identified with the Supreme Being.

1 *Foot-soles : uchchhlakhau ;* the word does not occur elsewhere, and its precise meaning is uncertain. I adopt Professor Ludwig's conjectural interpretation. *Central :* in the centre of the world.

2 *They :* the agents in his creation, whoever they were.

4 *Elbows : kaphauḍau ;* the meaning of the word is uncertain. Several other words also in the enumeration of the parts of Purusha's body are not found elsewhere and are conjecturally rendered.

7 He set within the jaws the tongue that reaches far, and thereon placed Speech the mighty Goddess.
He wanders to and fro mid living creatures, robed in the waters. Who hath understood it?

8 Who was he, first, of all the Gods who fashioned his skull and brain and occiput and forehead,
The pile that Pûrusha's two jaws supported? Who was that God who mounted up to heaven?

9 Whence bringeth mighty Pûrusha both pleasant and unpleasant things
Of varied sort, sleep, and alarm, fatigue, enjoyments and delights?

10 Whence is there found in Purusha want, evil, suffering, distress?
Whence come success, prosperity, opulence, thought, and utterance?

11 Who stored in him floods turned in all directions, moving diverse and formed to flow in rivers,
Hasty, red, copper-hued, and purple, running all ways in Purusha, upward and downward?

12 Who gave him visible form and shape? Who gave him magnitude and name?
Who gave him motion, consciousness? Who furnished Pûrusha with feet?

---

7 *He*: Purusha's creator.

11 *Red . . . . purple*: distinguishing arterial and venous blood.

12 *Form . . . . name*: 'Here,' Muir observes (O. S. Texts, V. 376, note), 'we have the *nāma* and *rūpa* of the Vedantists. Compare Taittirîya Brâhmaṇa, ii. 2, 7, 1: "Prajāpati created living beings. They, however, were in a shapeless state. He entered into them with form. Hence, men say 'Prajāpati is form.' He entered into them with name. Hence men say 'Prajāpati is name.'" On 'Nâma-rûpe the Connecting-link between Brahman and the World,' see Professor Max Müller's Three Lectures on the Vedânta Philosophy, pp. 151 sqq.

13 Who wove the vital air in him, who filled him with the downward breath?
What God bestowed on Pûrusha the general pervading air?

14 What God, what only Deity placed sacrifice in Pûrusha?
Who gave him truth and falsehood? Whence came Death and immortality?

15 Who wrapped a garment round him? Who arranged the life he hath to live?
Who granted him the boon of speech? Who gave this fleetness to his feet?

16 Through whom did he spread waters out, through whom did he make Day to shine?
Through whom did he enkindle Dawn and give the gift of eventide?

17 Who set the seed in him and said, Still be the thread of life spun out?
Who gave him intellect besides? Who gave him voice and gestic power?

18 Through whom did he bedeck the earth, through whom did he encompass heaven?
Whose might made Pûrusha surpass the mountains and created things?

19 Through whom seeks he Parjanya out, and Soma of the piercing sight?
Through whom belief and sacrifice? Through whom was spirit laid in him?

---

13 *General pervading air: vyânâ;* one of the five vital airs, that which is diffused throughout the body and assists digestion.

14 *Truth and falsehood:* or (the knowledge of) right and wrong.

15 *Arranged:* determined the duration of.

16 *Waters:* according to Ludwig *ápas* here is the neuter noun signifying work, sacrificial or holy work. Purusha appears in this stanza to be identified with the phenomenal Creator.

20 What leads him to the learned priest? What leads him to this Lord Supreme?
How doth he gain this Agni? By whom hath he measured out the year?

21 He, Brahma, gains the learned priest, he, Brahma, gains this Lord Supreme.
As Brahma, Man wins Agni here. Brahma hath measured out the year.

22 Through whom doth he abide with Gods? Through whom with the Celestial Tribes?
Why is this other called a star? Why is this called the Real Power?

23 Brahma inhabits with the Gods, Brahma among the Heavenly Tribes.
Brahma this other star is called, Brahma is called the Real Power.

24 By whom was this our earth disposed? By whom was heaven placed over it?
By whom was this expanse of air raised up on high and stretched across?

25 By Brahma was this earth disposed: Brahma is sky arranged above.
Brahma is this expanse of air lifted on high and stretched across.

---

20 *Learned priest: ṣrótriyam;* the Brahman versed in *ṣrúti* or the revealed doctrine of the Veda. Perhaps, as Dr. Scherman suggests, the rank and dignity of a Ṣrotriya is meant. *Lord Supreme:* Parameshṭhin.

21 *He, Brahma:* that is, becoming, or being identified with, Brahma or Brahman the phenomenal Creator.

22 The meaning of the second line of the stanza is unintelligible to me. The point appears to lie in using *nákshatram*, a star, as though it were *ná-kshatrám*, non-power, in opposition to *kshatrám*, power.

23 *Brahma inhabits with the Gods:* or, He dwells as Brahma with the Gods.

26 Together, with his needle hath Atharvan sewn his head and heart,
And Pavamâna hovered from his head on high above his brain.

27 That is indeed Atharvan's head, the well-closed casket of the Gods.
Spirit and Food and Vital Air protect that head from injury.

28 Stationed on high, Purusha hath pervaded all regions spread aloft and stretched transversely.
He who knows Brahma's castle, yea, the fort whence Purusha is named,

29 Yea, knows that fort of Brahma girt about with immortality,
Brahma and Brâhmas have bestowed sight, progeny, and life on him.

30 Sight leaves him not, breath quits not him before life's natural decay,
Who knows the fort of Brahma, yea, the fort whence Purusha is named.

31 The fort of Gods, impregnable, with circles eight and portals nine,
Contains a golden treasure-chest, celestial, begirt with light.

32 Men deep in lore of Brahma know that Animated Being which

---

26 *Pavamâna:* here, probably, meaning Wind. The word is also applied to Agni. Dr. Scherman takes it to be an epithet of Atharvan, 'shining.'

28 *Brahma's castle:* the human body. *Whence Purusha is named:* referring to the fanciful derivation of *púrusha* from *púr*, a fort or castle.

29 *Brâhmas:* Godlike Beings, the Gods.

31 *Portals nine:* the orifices of the human body, seven in the head and two below. Cf. Bhagavad-gitâ, V. 13. *Golden treasure-chest:* the heart.

32 *Animated Being: yakshám;* cf. X. 7. 38.

Dwells in the golden treasure-chest that hath three spokes and three supports.

33 Brahma hath passed within the fort, the golden castle, ne'er subdued,
Bright with excessive brilliancy, compassed with glory round about.

HYMN III.

Here is my charm the Varaṇa, slayer of rivals, strong in act.
With this grasp thou thine enemies, crush those who fain would injure thee.

2 Break them in pieces; grasp them and destroy them. This Amulet shall go before and lead thee.
With Varaṇa the Gods, from morn to morning, have warded off the Asuras' enchantment.

3 This charm, this Varaṇa healeth all diseases, bright with a thousand eyes and golden glister.
This charm shall conquer and cast down thy foemen. Be thou the first to slay the men who hate thee.

4 This will stay witchcraft wrought for thee, will guard thee from the fear of man:
From all distress and misery this Varaṇa will shield thee well.

The hymn has been translated by Ludwig, Der Rigveda, III. p. 398; partially by Muir, O. S. Texts, V. p. 375; and, with the omission of some stanzas and the addition of valuable annotations, by Scherman, Philosophische Hymnen aus der Rig-und Atharva-Veda-Sanhitâ, p. 41.

The hymn is a charm to secure health, long life, prosperity and fame.

1 *Varaṇa:* a plant or small tree (Crataeva Roxburghii), used in medicine and supposed to possess magical virtues. See IV. 7. 1. note, and VI. 85. 1.

The name is derived from the root *vṛi* or *var*, to repel or ward off.

5 Guard against ill of varied kind is Varaṇa this heavenly Plant.
The Gods have stayed and driven off Consumption which had seized this man.

6 If in thy sleep thou see an evil vision, oft as the beast repeats his loathed approaches,
This Amulet, this Varaṇa will guard thee from sneeze, and from the bird's ill-omened message.

7 From Mischief, from Malignity, from incantation, from alarm,
From death, from stronger foeman's stroke the Varaṇa will guard thee well.

8 Each sinful act that we have done,—my mother, father, and my friends,—
From all the guilt this heavenly Plant will be our guard and sure defence.

9 Affrighted by the Varaṇa let my rivals near akin to me
Pass to the region void of light: to deepest darkness let them go.

10 Safe are my cattle, safe am I, long-lived with all my men around.
This Varaṇa, mine Amulet, shall guard me well on every side.

---

6 *From sneeze:* The use of the benediction, God bless you! after sneezing is attributed to St. Gregory. Aristotle mentions a similar custom among the Greeks, and Cicero says (de Div. 2. 40), Sternutamenta erunt observanda. The same superstition has been observed also among natives of Africa and Indian tribes of North America. *The bird's ill-omened message:* the *śakúni*, or bird, here is probably the raven. The owl and the dove also were regarded as birds of ill omen. See Ṛigveda X. 165.

7 *The Varaṇa will guard: varaṇó vârayishyate.*

9 *Rivals: bhrấtṛivyấḥ;* primarily, father's brother's sons, cousins; then hostile cousins, rivals, enemies, which is almost exclusively the meaning of the word in the Veda. *The region void of light:* the Indian Tartarus or place of departed sinners, the *nấraka loká* or world of hell of XII 4. 36, the opposite in every respect of the bright and blissful world of Yama.

11 This Varaṇa is on my breast, the sovran, the celestial Plant.
Let it afflict my foemen as Indra quelled fiends and Asuras.

12 Through hundred autumn seasons, long to live, I wear this Varaṇa.
May it bestow on me great strength, cattle, and royalty, and power.

13 As with its might the wind breaks down the trees, the sovrans of the wood,
So break and rend my rivals, born before me and born after. Let the Varaṇa protect thee well.

14 As Agni and the wind devour the trees, the sovrans of the wood,
Even so devour my rivals, born before me and born after. Let the Varaṇa protect thee well.

15 As, shattered by the tempest, trees lie withering ruined on the ground,
Thus overthrow my rivals thou, so crush them down and ruin them, those born before and after. Let this Varaṇa protect thee well.

16 Cut them in pieces, Varaṇa! before their destined term of life,
Those who would hurt his cattle, those who fain would harm the realm he rules.

17 As Sûrya shines with brightest sheen, as splendour hath been stored in him,
So may the Charm, the Varaṇa, give me prosperity and fame. With lustre let it sprinkle me, and balm me with magnificence.

18 As glory dwelleth in the Moon and in the Sun who vieweth men,
So may the Charm, etc.

19 As glory dwelleth in the Earth, and in this Jâtavedas here,
So may the Charm, etc.

20 As glory dwelleth in a maid, and in this well-constructed car,
So may the Charm, etc.

21 As glory dwelleth in the draught of Soma and the honeyed drink,
So may the Charm, etc.

22 As glory dwells in sacrifice to Agni, and the hallowing word,
So may the Charm, etc.

23 As glory is bestowed upon the patron and this sacrifice,
So may the Charm, etc.

24 As glory dwelleth in the Lord of Life and in this God Supreme,
So may the Charm, etc.

25 As immortality and truth have been established in the Gods,
So may the Charm, the Varaṇa, give me prosperity and fame. With lustre let it sprinkle me, and balm me with magnificence.

HYMN IV.

THE first of all is Indra's car, next is the chariot of the Gods, the third is Varuṇa's alone.
The last, the Serpents' chariot, struck the pillar and then sped away.

2 Their lustre is the Darbha-grass, its young shoots are their horse's tail: the reed's plume is their chariot-seat.

---

20 *As glory dwelleth in a maid*: cf. 'The splendid energy of maids' (XII. 1. 25).

22 *The hallowing word*: the sacrificial exclamation Vashaṭ. See I. 11. 1, note.

A charm for the destruction of venomous serpents.

1 The imaginary chariot-race represents the weakness of serpents compared with the power of the Gods who are to be invoked to destroy them.

2 *Their*: the serpents'. The meaning of the line appears to be that their chariot and horses are the grass and reeds among which they live.

3 Strike out, white courser! with thy foot, strike both with fore and hinder foot.
Stay the dire poison of the Snakes, and make it weak as soaking wood.

4 Loud neighing he hath dived below, and rising up again replied,
Stayed the dire poison of the Snakes, and made it weak as soaking wood.

5 Paidva kills Kasarṇîla, kills both the white Serpent and the black.
Paidva hath struck and cleft in twain Ratharvî's and the Viper's head.

6 Go onward, horse of Pedu! go thou first: we follow after thee.
Cast thou aside the Serpents from the pathway whereupon we tread.

7 Here was the horse of Pedu born: this is the way that takes him hence.
These are the tracks the courser left, the mighty slayer of the Snakes.

8 Let him not close the opened mouth, nor open that which now is closed.
Two snakes are in this field, and both, female and male, are powerless.

---

3 *White courser*: the reference is to the white serpent-slaying or Ahi-destroying horse given by the Asvins to their devotee the royal Rishi Pedu (Rigveda I. 116. 6; 117. 9). This horse, according to M. Bergaigne (La Religion Védique, II. 452), symbolized the Sun and Soma. Cf. 'Like Pedu's horse who killed the brood of serpents, thus thou, O Soma, slayest every Dasyu' (R. V. IX. 88. 4). *Stay the dire poison*: I adopt Prof. Geldner's interpretation of this line (Vedische Studien, II. p. 75).

4 *Loud-neighing*: *aranghushâh*. Prof. Ludwig retains this word as the name of the horse.

5 *Paidva*: (the horse) belonging to Pedu. *Kasarṇîla*: an unidentified venomous serpent. *Ratharvî*: another species of serpent, so called on account of its rapid motion.

8 The first line is repeated from VI. 56. 1.

9 Powerless are the serpents here, those that are near and those afar.
I kill the scorpion with a club, and with a staff the new-come snake.

10 This is the remedy against Aghâṣva and the adder, both:
Indra and Paidva have subdued and tamed the vicious snake for me.

11 We fix our thoughts on Pedu's horse, strong, offspring of a stedfast line.
Behind our backs the vipers here crouch down and lie in wait for us.

12 Bereft of life and poison they lie slain by bolt-armed Indra's hand. Indra and we have slaughtered them.

13 Tiraṣchirâjis have been slain, and vipers crushed and brayed to bits.
Slay Darvi in the Darbha-grass, Karikrata, and White and Black.

14 The young maid of Kirâta race, a little damsel, digs the drug,
Digs it with shovels wrought of gold on the high ridges of the hills.

15 Hither the young unconquered leech who slays the speckled snake hath come.
He verily demolishes adder and scorpion, both of them.

16 Indra, Mitra and Varuṇa, and Vâta and Parjanya both have given the serpent up to me.

---

10 *Aghâṣva*: here, apparently, the name of a serpent. In Ṛigveda I. 116. 6 Aghâṣva (having bad or vicious horses) is another name or an epithet of Pedu.

13 *Tiraṣchirâjis*: serpents with transverse streaks. *Darvi*, *Karikrata*, *White*, and *Black* are other venomous snakes.

14 *Of Kirâta race*: the Kirâtas (the Kirrhadae of Arrian) were a barbarous non-Âryan or degraded race who inhabited woods and mountains and supported themselves by hunting.

17 Indra hath given him up to me, the female viper and the male,
The adder, him with stripes athwart, Kasarṇîla, Daṣonasi.

18 O Serpent, Indra hath destroyed the sire who first engendered thee:
And when these snakes are pierced and bored what sap and vigour will be theirs?

19 Their heads have I seized firmly as a fisher grasps the spotted prey,
Waded half through the stream and washed the poison of the serpents off.

20 Let the floods hurry on and bear the poison of all snakes afar.
Tiraṣchirâjis have been slain and vipers crushed and brayed to bits.

21 As from the salutary plants I deftly pick the fibres out,
And guide them skilfully like mares, so let thy venom, Snake! depart.

22 All poison that the sun and fire, all that the earth and plants contain,
Poison of most effectual power—let all thy venom pass away.

23 Serpents which fire or plants have generated, those which have sprung from waters or the lightning,
Whose mighty broods are found in many places, these serpents we will reverently worship.

24 Thou art a maid called Taudî, or Ghṛitâchî is thy name. Thy place
Is underneath my foot. I take the poison-killing remedy.

---

17 *Him with stripes athwart:* Tiraṣchirâji. *Daṣonasi:* another unidentified snake.

24 *Taudî:* the meaning of the word is uncertain. *Ghṛitâchî:* shining with or like butter or fat; the name of a species of snake.

The hymn has been translated by Ludwig, Der Rigveda, III. p. 502.

25 From every member drive away the venom, and avoid the heart.
Then let the poison's burning heat pass downward and away from thee.

26 The bane hath fled afar. It wept, and asked the poison how it fared.

27 Agni hath found the venom of the serpent, Soma drawn it out.
Back to the biter hath returned the poison, and the snake hath died.

HYMN V.

Ye are the power of Indra, ye the force and strength of Indra, ye his hero might and manliness.
I join you with the bonds of Prayer to the victorious enterprise.

6 For the victorious enterprise let all creation stand by me. For me ye, Waters, are prepared.

7 Ye are the share of Agni. Grant, O heavenly Waters unto us the Waters' brilliant energy.
By statute of Prajâpati I set you down for this our world.

The hymn, which is a mixture—sometimes even in the same stanza—of verse and prose, is a charm to secure the overthrow of an enemy and the acquisition of strength, dignity, long life, children, wealth and general prosperity.

1 *Ye:* the srcrificial Waters used in the ceremony which the hymn accompanies. *Bonds of Prayer:* the binding efficacy of devotion.

Stanza 1 is repeated in 2—5, with the substitution of Sway (royal power), Indra, Soma, and Waters respectively in the place of Prayer.

7 This stanza is repeated in 8—14 with the substitution, in the place of Agni, of Indra, Soma, Varuṇa, Mitra-Varuṇa, Yama, the Fathers, and God Savitar respectively. The verses in the original are in prose.

15 Waters, your ceremonial share of Waters which the Waters hold, which aids our sacrifice to Gods,
This as a remnant here I leave. Do not thou wash it clean away.
With this we let the man go by who hates us and whom we abhor.
Him would I fain o'erthrow and slay with this our ceremonial act, with this our prayer, our thunderbolt.

22 Whatever evil I have done within this last triennium,
From all that woe and misery let the Waters shield and guard me well.

23 Onward I urge your gathered floods: enter your own abiding-place,
Uninjured and with all your strength. Let nothing bend or bow us down.

24 May the pure Waters cleanse us from defilement,
Fair to behold, remove our sin and trouble, and bear away ill-dream and all pollution.

25 Thou art the step of Vishṇu, rival-slayer, sharpened by earth, aglow with fire of Agni.
Earth have I ranged: from earth we bar him who hates us and whom we hate.

---

15 *Thunderbolt*: see VI. 134. 1, note. This verse is repeated in 16—21, wave, calf, bull, Hiraṇyagarbha (Germ of Golden Light), and the speckled heavenly stone (the thunderbolt) being substituted, respectively, for 'ceremonial share.' The second, third, and fourth of these represent Agni who dwells, like the thunderbolt, in the form of lightning in the waters of the ocean of air.

25 *The step of Vishṇu*: referring to Vishṇu's three strides through the three worlds, or the rising, culmination, and setting of the Sun, which are to be symbolized in the performance of the ceremony by the officiator taking three steps between the altar and the Âhavanîya fire. See Kauçika-Sûtra VI. 14.

26 Ours is superior place and ours is conquest: may I in all fights tread down spite and malice.
Let him not live, let vital breath desert him.

36 With this I here invest the power and splendour, the life of that man and his vital breathing, the son of such a sire and such a woman, here do I overthrow and cast him downward.

37 I follow Sûrya's course in heaven, the course that takes him to the South.
May that bestow upon me wealth and glory of a Brâhman's rank.

38 I turn me to the regions bright with splendour.
May they bestow upon me wealth and glory of a Brâhman's rank.

39 I turn me to the Ṛishis Seven. May they, etc.

40 I turn me unto Prayer. May that, etc.

41 I turn me unto Brâhmans. May they, etc.

42 We hunt that man, we beat him down and slay him with our murderous blows.
We with the spell have hurried him to Parameshṭhin's opened jaws.

43 Let the shot missile catch him with Vaiṣvânara's two mighty fangs.
This offering, and the mightiest Goddess, the Fuel, eat him up!

---

26 *Him:* the enemy for whose destruction the ceremony is performed. This verse is repeated in 27—35, with the substitution, for Earth (thrice) and Agni, of Heaven and Sûrya in 27; the Quarters and Mind in 28; the Regions and Vâta in 29; the Ṛichas and Sâmans in 30; Sacrifice and Brahma or Prayer in 31; Plants and Soma (the Moon) in 32; Waters and Varuṇa in 33; Agriculture and Food in 34; Vital Breath and Man in 35.

36 *That man . . . such a sire . . . such a woman:* when the ceremony is performed, the names of the object of the imprecation and of his father and mother are to be substituted.

42 *Parameshṭhin,* Lord Supreme, in this place is Agni, as in I. 7. 2.

44 Thou art the bond of Varuṇa the King.
Bind, such an one, the son of such a woman, in vital breath and in the food that feeds him.

45 All food of thine, O Lord of Life, that lies upon the face of earth,
Thereof bestow thou upon us, O Lord of Life, Prajâpati!

46 Celestial Waters have I sought: with juice have I besprinkled them.
With milk, O Agni, have I come: bestow upon me splendid strength.

47 Give me the boon of splendid strength; give, Agni! progeny and life.
May the Gods know this prayer of mine, may Indra with the Ṛishis know.

48 What curse soever couples launch against us, whatever bitter speech the chatterers utter,
With Manyu's arrow, offspring of the spirit, transfix thou to the heart the Yâtudhânas.

49 Destroy the Yâtudhânas with thy fervour, consume the demons with thy wrath, O Agni.
Destroy the fools' gods with thy fiery splendour, destroy the blazing ones, the insatiable.

50 Well-skilled, against this man I hurl the Waters' bolt with four spikes, to cleave his head asunder.
May it destroy all members of his body. Let the whole host of Gods approve my purpose.

HYMN VI.

WITH power I cut away the head of my malignant rival, of mine evil-hearted enemy.

---

48 *Couples:* sacrificers and their wives. *Manyu:* Passion or Ardour personified. See IV. 31 and 32. *Yâtudhânas:* demons or sorcerers; see I. 7. 1, note.

50 *Waters' bolt:* the thunderbolt from the watery clouds.

The hymn is the glorification of an all-powerful amulet.

2 This Amulet of citron-wood shall make for me a trusty shield:
Filled with the mingled beverage, with sap and vigour hath it come.

3 What though the strong-armed carpenter have cleft thee with his hand and axe,
Pure animating waters shall cleanse thee and make thee bright again.

4 This Amulet, decked with chain of gold, shall give faith, sacrifice, and might, and dwell as guest within our house.

5 To this we give apportioned food, clarified butter, wine, and meath.
May it provide each boon for us as doth a father for his sons,
Again, again, from morn to morn, having approached the deities.

6 The Charm Bṛihaspati hath bound, the fatness-dropping citron-wood, the potent Khadira, for strength,
This Agni hath put on: it yields clarified butter for this man,
Again, again, from morn to morn. With this subdue thine enemies.

7 The Charm Bṛihaspati hath bound, the fatness-dropping citron-wood, the potent Khadira, for strength,
This Charm hath Indra put on him for power and manly puissance.
It yieldeth strength to strengthen him, again, again, from morn to morn, having approached the deities.

---

2 *Mingled beverage: manthá*, gruel; parched barley-meal stirred round in milk.

5 *Having approached the deities:* worn by the worshipper when he sacrifices.

6 *Khadira:* the Acacia Catechu; a tree with very hard wood from which the *sruva* or sacrificial ladle and axle-pins are made. The Khadira is mentioned together with the Aṣvattha or Sacred Fig Tree in III. 6. 1 and V. 5. 5. See also XII. 3. 1.

8 The Charm Bṛihaspati, etc.
This Charm hath Soma put on him for might, for hearing, and for sight.
This yields him energy indeed, again, again, etc.

9 The Charm Bṛihaspati, etc.
This Sûrya put on him, with this conquered the regions of the sky.
This yieldeth him ability, again, etc.

10 The Charm Bṛihaspati, etc.
This Charm did Chandra wear, with this conquered the forts of Asuras, the golden forts of Dânavas.
This yields him glory and renown, again, etc.

11 The Amulet Bṛihaspati bound on the swiftly-moving Wind.
This yieldeth him a vigorous steed, again, etc.

12 The Aṣvins with this Amulet protect this culture of our fields.
This yields the two Physicians might, again, etc.

13 Savitar wore this Amulet: herewith he won this lucid heaven.
This yields him glory and delight, again, etc.

14 Wearing this Charm the Waters flow eternally inviolate.
This yieldeth them ambrosia, again, etc.

15 King Varuṇa assumed and wore this salutary Amulet.
This yieldeth him his truthfulness, again, etc.

16 Wearing this Amulet the Gods conquered in battle all the worlds.
This yieldeth victory for them, again, etc.

17 The Amulet Bṛihaspati formed for the swiftly-moving Wind,
This salutary Amulet the Deities assumed and wore.
This yieldeth them the universe, again, again, from morn to morn. With this subdue thine enemies.

---

12 *The Aṣvins:* regarded as the protectors of agriculture which they first taught men to practise (Ṛigveda I. 117. 21 ; VIII. 22. 6). They are also the *Physicians* of the Gods : see A. V. VII. 53. 1; ṚV. VIII. 18. 8.

18 The Seasons formed that Amulet, the Groups of Seasons fashioned it.
The Year having constructed it preserveth everything that is.

19 The regions of the heaven, the points that lie between them fashioned it.
Created by Prajâpati, may the Charm cast my foemen down.

20 Atharvan made the Amulet, Atharvan's children fashioned it.
With them the sage Angirases brake through the Dasyus' fortresses. With this subdue thine enemies.

21 Dhâtar bound on this Amulet: he ranged and ordered all that is. With this do thou subdue thy foes.

22 The Amulet Brihaspati formed for the Gods, that slew the fiends,
That Amulet here hath come to me combined with sap and energy.

23 The Amulet, etc.
That Amulet here hath come to me, hath come with cows, and goats, and sheep, hath come with food and progeny.

24 The Amulet, etc.
That Amulet here hath come to me with store of barley and of rice, with greatness and prosperity.

25 The Amulet, etc.
That Amulet here hath come to me with streams of butter and of mead, with sweet delicious beverage.

---

22 *Combined with sap*: the Khadira, of which the amulet was in part composed, is said to have sprung from the *rasa*, sap or essence of the Gâyatrî. Another legend (Śatapatha-Brâhmaṇa III. 6. 2. 12) says that Suparṇî 'took possession (*â-chakâda*) of Soma by means of (a stick of) Khadira wood, whence (the name) Khadira.

26 The Amulet, etc.
That Amulet here hath come to me with power and abundant strength, hath come with glory and with wealth.

27 That Amulet, etc.
That Amulet here hath come to me with splendour and a blaze of light, with honour and illustrious fame.

28 The Amulet Bṛihaspati made for the Gods, that slew the fiends,
That Amulet here hath come to me combined with all prosperities.

29 That Amulet may the Deities bestow on me to win success,
The conquering, strength-increasing Charm, the damager of enemies.

30 I bind on me my happy fate with holy prayer and energy.
Foeless, destroyer of the foe, it hath subdued mine enemies.

31 May this Charm, offspring of the Gods, make me superior to my foe.
So may this Charm whose milk expressed these three worlds longingly await,
Be fastened on me here, that it may crown me with surpassing power.

32 The Charm to which men, Fathers, Gods look ever for their maintenance,
May this be fastened on me here, to crown me with surpassing power.

33 As, when the plough hath tilled the soil, the seed springs up in fertile land,
Let cattle, progeny, and food of every kind spring up with me.

34 Charm, forwarder of sacrifice, who hast a hundred priestly fees,

Speed to preëminence him to whom I have attached thy happy fate.

35 Love thou, O Agni, pleased with burnt oblations, this sacred fuel that is ranged in order.
In him may we find grace and loving-kindness, happiness, progeny, and sight, and cattle, in Jâtavedas kindled with devotion.

HYMN VII.

WHICH of his members is the seat of Fervour? Which is the base of Ceremonial Order?
Where in him standeth Faith? Where Holy Duty? Where, in what part of him is Truth implanted?

2 Out of which member glows the light of Agni? From which proceeds the breath of Mâtarisvan?
From which doth Chandra measure out his journey, travelling over Skambha's mighty body?

3 Which of his members is the earth's upholder? Which gives the middle air a base to rest on?
Where, in which member is the sky established? Where hath the space above the sky its dwelling?

4 Whitherward yearning blazeth Agni upward? Whitherward yearning bloweth Mâtarisvan?
Who out of many, tell me, is that Skambha to whom with longing go the turning pathways?

The hymn is a glorification of the Supreme Deity embodied, under the name of Skambha, the Pillar, Support, or Fulcrum of all existence.

1 *Fervour: tápas* (from *tap*, to be hot); warmth, pain, penance; religious austerity, fervent devotion. *Ceremonial Order: ṛitám;* Divine Law; divinely appointed sacrifice.

2 *Mâtariṣvan:* Wind; see V. 2. 9, note; 10. 8; 17. 1. *Chandra:* the Moon. *Skambha:* the word is the same as *stambha*, a pillar or buttress. So Sûrya (Ṛ. V. IV. 13. 5) and Soma (Ṛ. V. IX. 74. 2; 86. 46) are called the pillars or supports of heaven.

3 *The space above the sky:* the highest of the three heavens (see IV. 20. 2, and Ṛ. V. V. 60. 6); the Heaven of heavens, of the Hebrews, above the air and the starry firmament.

5 Whitherward go the half-months, and, accordant with the full year, the months in their procession?
Who out of many, tell me, is that Skambha to whom go seasons and the groups of seasons?

6 Whitherward yearning speed the two young Damsels, accordant, Day and Night, of different colour?
Who out of many, tell me, is that Skambha to whom the Waters take their way with longing?

7 Who out of many, tell me, is that Skambha
On whom Prajâpati set up and firmly stablished all the worlds?

8 That universe which Prajâpati created, wearing all forms, the highest, midmost, lowest,
How far did Skambha penetrate within it? What portion did he leave unpenetrated?

9 How far within the past hath Skambha entered? How much of him hath reached into the future?
That one part which he set in thousand places,—how far did Skambha penetrate within it?

10 Who out of many, tell me, is that Skambha in whom men recognize the Waters, Brahma,
In whom they know the worlds and their enclosures, in whom are non-existence and existence?

11 Declare that Skambha, who is he of many,
In whom, exerting every power, Fervour maintains her loftiest vow;
In whom are comprehended Law, Waters, Devotion and Belief?

---

7 *Prajâpati:* Lord of Life, Creator; here represented as inferior to Skambha whose commands he executes.

9 *That one part:* or, member. See stanza 25.

10 *Brahma:* the meaning here may be Prayer: 'divine thought.'—Muir. *Non-existence and existence:* all that possesses the poteutiality of existence as well as all that actually exists.

11 *Devotion:* or, and Brahma: 'divine science.—Muir.

12 **Who out of many, tell me, is that Skambha**
On whom as their foundation earth and firmament and sky are set;
In whom as their appointed place rest Fire and Moon and Sun and Wind?

13 **Who out of many, tell me, is that Skambha,**
He in whose body are contained all three-and-thirty Deities?

---

13 *Three-and-thirty Deities:* in the Ṛigveda the number of the Gods is frequently said to be thirty-three: 'Come, O Nâsatyas, with the thrice-eleven Gods' (I. 34. 11); 'Bring thou those three-and-thirty Gods' (I. 45. 2); 'O ye eleven Gods whose home is heaven, O ye eleven who make earth your dwelling, Ye, who with might, eleven, live in waters, accept this sacrifice, O Gods, with pleasure' (I. 139. 11); 'Bring, with their Dames, the Gods, the three-and-thirty' (III. 6. 9); see also Ṛ. V. VIII. 28. 1; 30. 2; 35. 3; Vâlakhilya 9. 2. The late Professor Haug remarks on an ancient Vaiṣvadeva Nivid or invoking prayer cited in his Aitareya Brâhmaṇam, Vol. II. p. 212: 'It is, however, highly interesting, as perhaps one of the most ancient accounts we have of the number of Hindu deities. They are here stated at 3 times 11, then at 33, then at 303, then at 3003. It appears from this statement that only the number 3 remained unchanged, whilst the number 30 was multiplied by 10 or 100. Similarly the number of gods is stated at 3339 in a hymn ascribed to the Ṛishi Visvámitra, Rigveda III. 9. 9. This statement appears to rely on the Vaiṣvadeva Nivid. For if we add 33 + 303 + 3003 we obtain exactly the number 3339. This coincidence can hardly be fortuitous, and we have strong reasons to believe that Visvâmitra perfectly knew this Visve Devâḥ Nivid.' But, as Professor Max Müller observes (Three Lectures on the Vedânta Philosophy, p. 26), 'we find the incipient reasoners postulating One God behind all the deities of the earliest pantheon. As early a writer as Yâska about 500 B. C. has formed to himself a systematic theology, and represents all the Vedic deities as really three, those like the Fire, whose place is on earth, those like Indra, whose place is in the air, and those like the Sun, whose place is in the sky; nay he declares that it is owing to the greatness of the deity that the one Divine Self is celebrated as if it were many. The same ideas are

14 Who out of many, tell me, is that Skambha
In whom the Sages earliest born, the Ṛichas, Sâman, Yajus, Earth, and the one highest Sage abide?

15 Who out of many, tell me, is that Skambha
Who comprehendeth, for mankind, both immortality and death,
He who containeth for mankind the gathered waters as his veins?

16 Who out of many, tell me, is that Skambha,
He whose chief arteries stand there, the sky's four regions, he in whom Sacrifice putteth forth its might?

17 They who in Purusha understand Brahma know Him who is Supreme.
He who knows Him who is Supreme, and he who knows the Lord of Life,
These know the loftiest Power Divine, and thence know Skambha thoroughly.

18 Who out of many, tell me, is that Skambha
Of whom Vaiṣvânara became the head, the Angirases his eye, and Yâtus his corporeal parts?

---

well summed up in one of the Upanishads (Bṛih. Âr. Up. III. 9), where we are told that there were at first more than three thousand and three hundred gods, but that they were reduced to 33, to 6, to 3, to 2, to 1½, and at last to one, which One is the breath of life, the Self, and his name is That.'

17 *Purusha*: man. *Brahma*: 'the divine essence.'—Muir. *Him who is Supreme*: Parameshṭhin. *The Lord of Life*: Prajâpati. *Power Divine*: *brâhmaṇam*; 'divine mystery.'—Muir.

18 *Yâtus*: evil spirits, demons. Professor Ludwig suggests the substitution of Yatis, a mythical race of ascetics connected with the Bhrigus; the malicious character of the Yâtus (Dr. Scherman remarks) not being in accordance with their identification with the members of the All-God.

19 Who out of many, tell me, is that Skambha
Whose mouth they say is Holy Lore, his tongue the
Honey-sweetened Whip, his udder is Virâj, they say?

20 Who out of many, tell me, is that Skambha
From whom they hewed the Ṛichas off, from whom
they chipped the Yajus, he
Whose hairs are Sâma-verses and his mouth the
Atharvângirases?

21 Men count as 'twere a thing supreme nonentity's
conspicuous branch;
And lower men who serve thy branch regard it as
an entity.

22 Who out of many, tell me, is that Skambha
In whom Âdityas dwell, in whom Rudras and Vasus
are contained,
In whom the future and the past and all the worlds
are firmly set;

---

19 *Holy Lore: bráhma*; 'divine knowledge.'—Muir. *The Honey-sweetened Whip:* the Madhukaśâ or Honey-whip (a symbol, perhaps, of creative and invigorating power) of the Aşvins: see IX. 1 sqq. *Virâj:* a divine being, the result of speculation: see VIII. 10.

20 *The Atharvângirases:* the Songs or Hymns of the Atharvans and Angirases; see Vol. I., Preface, p. vi.

21 The stanza may be rendered, in accordance with Professor Goldstücker's interpretation (O. S. Texts, V. p. 384): Some count as 'twere supreme this branch existing, non-reality; But some, inferior, deeming it reality, adore thy branch: that is, in Professor Goldstücker's words: 'Some people think that the *existing* branch (*i. e.* the existing Vedas—compare verse 20), which is not *the* reality (*asat*), is, as it were (*iva*), the highest (*paramam*) Veda; on the other hand, those (people) inferior (to the former), who believe that it is *the* reality (*sat*), worship thy branch (*i. e.* those later Vedas).' Professor Ludwig suggests the reading *ápare*, other, instead of *ávare*, inferior; in which case the meaning would be that different men entertain different opinions regarding the relative priority of the existent and the non-existent. My version in the text follows Muir's rendering which was partly suggested by Professor Aufrecht.

23 Whose secret treasure evermore the three-and thirty Gods protect?
Who knoweth now the treasure which, O Deities, ye watch and guard?

24 Where the Gods, versed in Sacred Lore, worship the loftiest Power Divine—
The priest who knows them face to face may be a sage who knows the truth.

25 Great, verily, are those Gods who sprang from non-existence into life.
Further, men say that that one part of Skambha is nonentity.

26 Where Skambha generating gave the Ancient World its shape and form,
They recognized that single part of Skambha as the Ancient World.

27 The three-and-thirty Gods within his body were disposed as limbs:
Some, deeply versed in Holy Lore, some know those three-and-thirty Gods.

28 Men know Hiraṇyagarbha as supreme and inexpressible:
In the beginning, in the midst of the world, Skambha poured that gold.

---

23 *Secret treasure:* according to Professor Goldstücker, the primitive, preaeval Veda, identified with Skambha.

24 *The priest:* 'the Atharva-veda priest (brahmâ), who has a knowledge of those god-guardians of the preaeval Veda has *the* knowledge (or, he who has such a knowledge is a (true) Atharva-veda priest).'—Goldstücker.

25 *Further:* Ludwig suggests *purâ*, of old, instead of *parâs* of the text. *Nonentity*: cf. stanza 10.

27 *Were disposed as limbs:* so Ludwig; 'found their several bodies.'—Muir; 'distributed the limbs among them.'—Scherman.

28 *Hiraṇyagarbha:* the Germ of Golden Light; here meaning Prajâpati, Lord of Creation. See IV. 2. 7. *That gold:* out of which Hiraṇyagarbha sprang to life. *Inexpressible: anatyudhyám:* Ludwig's 'über den hinaus sich nichts sagen lässt' and Scherman's 'Unübertönbaren' give more accurately the full meaning of the word.

29 On Skambha Fervour rests, the worlds and Holy Law repose on him.
Skambha, I clearly know that all of thee on Indra is imposed.

30 On Indra Fervour rests, on him the worlds and Holy Law recline.
Indra, I clearly know that all of thee on Skambha findeth rest.

31 Ere sun and dawn man calls and calls one Deity by the other's name.
When the Unborn first sprang into existence he reached that independent sovran lordship, than which aught higher never hath arisen.

32 Be reverence paid to him, that highest Brahma, whose base is Earth, his belly Air, who made the sky to be his head.

33 Homage to highest Brahma, him whose eye is Sûrya and the Moon who groweth young and new again, him who made Agni for his mouth.

34 Homage to highest Brahma, him whose two life-breathings were the Wind,
The Angirases his sight; who made the regions be his means of sense.

35 Skambha set fast these two, the earth and heaven,
Skambha maintained the ample air between them.
Skambha established the six spacious regions: this whole world Skambha entered and pervaded.

---

29 *On Indra is imposed:* or, in Indra is contained. In this and the following stanza Skambha is identified with Indra.

30 *One Deity by the other's name:* that is, the worshipper who invokes Indra is really invoking Skambha. *The Unborn:* Brahma, with whom Skambha is identified.

35 *Established the six spacious regions:* cf. 'What was that ONE who in the Unborn's image hath stablished and fixed firm these worlds' six regions?' (R. V. I. 164. 6).

36 Homage to highest Brahma, him who, sprung from Fervour and from toil,
Filled all the worlds completely, who made Soma for himself alone.

37 Why doth the Wind move ceaselessly? Why doth the spirit take no rest?
Why do the Waters, seeking truth, never at any time repose?

38 Absorbed in Fervour, is the mighty Being, in the world's centre, on the waters' surface.
To him the Deities, one and all betake them. So stands the tree-trunk with the branches round it.

39 Who out of many, tell me, is that Skambha
To whom the Deities with hands, with feet, and voice, and ear, and eye
Present unmeasured tribute in the measured hall of sacrifice?

40 Darkness is chased away from him: he is exempt from all distress.
In him are all the lights, the three abiding in Prajâpati.

41 He verily who knows the Reed of Gold that stands amid the flood, is the mysterious Lord of Life.

---

37 *Seeking truth:* following the natural law of their being.

38 *The mighty Being:* cf. X. 2. 32, and 8. 15; Brahma with whom Skambha is identified.

40 *The lights, the three:* Sun, lightning, and fire; or light manifested in heaven, the firmament, and on earth.

41 *The Reed of Gold:* meaning Agni. Cf. 'I look upon the streams of oil descending, and lo! the Golden Reed is there among them' (Ṛ. V. IV. 58. 5); where the *Golden Reed* is Agni produced as lightning in the streams of oil or fatness, the fertilizing waters which descend from the ocean of air. See Muir's note.

42 Singly the two young Maids of different colours approach the six-pegged warp in turns and weave it.
The one draws out the threads, the other lays them: they break them not, they reach no end of labour.

43 Of these two, dancing round as 'twere, I cannot distinguish whether ranks before the other.
A Male inweaves this web, a Male divides it: a Male hath stretched it to the cope of heaven.

44 These pegs have buttressed up the sky. The Sâmans have turned them into shuttles for the weaving.

HYMN VIII.

WORSHIP to loftiest Brahma, Lord of what hath been and what shall be,
To him who rules the universe, and heavenly light is all his own!

2 Upheld by Skambha's power these two, the heaven and the earth, stand fast.
Skambha is all this world of life, whatever breathes or shuts an eye.

---

42 *Two young Maids:* Ushas or Dawn and Night. *Six-pegged:* stretched over the six regions of the world. Dawn weaves the luminous weft of Day, and Night removes it from the loom.

43 *A Male:* the first Man or Male; Purusha, Âdipurusha, Prajâpati. *This web:* meaning here the mysterious primeval sacrifice which constitutes creation. Cf. 'The Man extends it, and the Man unbinds it: even to the vault of heaven hath he outspun it. These pegs are fastened to the seat of worship: they made the Sâma-hymns their weaving-shuttles' (Ṛ. V. X. 130. 2.)

The hymn has been translated by Ludwig, Der Rigveda, III. p. 400; nearly in full, by Muir, O. S. Texts, V. 380; and (omitting stanzas 42—44) by Scherman, with an excellent and almost exhaustive commentary, in his Philosophische Hymnen aus der Ṛig-und Atharva-veda-Sanhitâ.

The hymn consists of speculations, somewhat fragmentary and unconnected, on the Supreme Being and cosmogonical and theological subjects.

2 *Skambha's power:* see the preceding hymn.

3 Three generations have gone by and vanished, and others near have entered into sunlight.
There stood on high he who metes out the region: into green plants hath passed the Golden-coloured.

4 One is the wheel, the tires are twelve in number, the naves are three. What man hath understood it?
Three hundred spokes have thereupon been hammered, and sixty pins set firmly in their places.

5 Discern thou this, O Savitar. Six are the twins, one singly born.
They claim relationship in that among them which is born alone.

6 Though manifest, it lies concealed in the vast place they call the old:
Therein is firmly stationed all the moving, breathing universe.

7 Up, eastward, downward in the west, it rolleth, with countless elements, one-wheeled, single-fellied.
With half it hath begotten all creation. Where hath the other half become unnoticed?

---

3 *Three generations:* according to the legend (Śatapatha-Brâhmaṇa, II. 5. 1), Prajâpati produced in succession three kinds of creatures, birds, small reptiles, and serpents, all of which died. The fourth generation (mammalia) lived and enjoyed the light of the sun. *He who metes out the regions:* Agni as the Sun. *The Golden-coloured:* Agni, who as lightning enters into plants with the falling rain. The stanza is found, with variations, in Ṛ. V. VIII. 90. 14.

4 *The wheel:* the Sun in his annual course; the year. *The tires:* the months. *The naves:* the three chief seasons, Summer, Rains, and Winter. *Spokes . . . pins:* the days.

5 *Twins:* the seasons, consisting each of two months. *One:* the intercalary month.

6 *It:* the wheel, that is, the Sun. *Concealed:* at night. *Vast place:* the mysterious place to which both Day and Night alternately retire. Cf. Ṛ. V. III. 55. 15.

7 *With half:* the light and heat of day. *The other half:* the Sun during the night.

8 In front of these the five-horsed car moves onward: side-horses, harnessed with the others draw it.
No one hath seen its hither course untravelled; the height sees it more near, the depth more distant.

9 The bowl with mouth inclined and bottom upward holds stored within it every form of glory.
Thereon together sit the Seven Rishis who have become this mighty One's protectors.

10 The Verse employed at opening and conclusion, the Verse employed in each and every portion;
That by which sacrifice proceedeth onward, I ask thee which is that of all the Verses.

11 That which hath power of motion, that which flies, or stands, which breathes or breathes not, which, existing, shuts the eye—
Wearing all forms that entity upholds the earth, and in its close consistence still is only one.

12 The infinite to every side extended, the finite and the infinite around us,—
These twain Heaven's Lord divides as he advances, knowing the past hereof and all the future.

13 Within the womb Prajâpati is moving: he, though unseen, is born in sundry places.
He with one half engendered all creation. What sign is there to tell us of the other?

---

8 *These:* all living creatures. *The five horsed car:* the chariot of the Sun drawn by the five seasons, the Dewy and the Cold being counted as one. *Side-horses:* perhaps the quarters of the sky.

9 *The bowl:* the hemispherical sky, the earth being regarded as another bowl: 'The two great meeting bowls hath he united: each of the pair is laden with his treasure' (Ṛ. V. III. 55. 20). *This mighty One's protectors:* guardians of the universe.

10 *Opening and conclusion:* of a sacrificial ceremony.

12 *Hereof:* or, of this (universe).

13 *Is born in sundry places:* every birth that occurs being in reality a re-birth of the Creative Power Prajâpati. *With one half:* cf. stanza 7.

14 All men behold him with the eye, but with the mind they know not him
Holding aloft the water as a water-bearer in her jar.

15 With the full vase he dwells afar, is left far off what time it fails,
A mighty Being in creation's centre: to him the rulers of the realms bring tribute.

16 That, whence the Sun arises, that whither he goes to take his rest,
That verily I hold supreme: naught in the world surpasses it.

17 Those who in recent times, midmost, or ancient, on all sides greet the sage who knows the Veda,
One and all, verily, discuss Âditya, the second Agni, and the threefold Hańsa.

18 This gold-hued Hańsa's wings, flying to heaven, spread o'er a thousand days' continued journey.
Supporting all the Gods upon his bosom, he goes his way beholding every creature.

19 By truth he blazes up aloft, by Brahma he looks down below:
He breathes obliquely with his breath, he on whom what is highest rests.

---

15 The first line is obscure. Ludwig suggests that *vase* or pitcher here may mean the Moon. *A mighty Being : mahád yakshám ;* a supernatural animated Being (cf. X. 2. 32; 7. 38), apparently regarded as the First Cause of creation. *The rulers of the realms :* the Gods.

16 *That :* the mysterious place: cf. stanza 6.

17 *Âditya :* the Sun. Agni and Hańsa also are names of the Sun. The latter is called *threefold* from his three strides as Vishṇu, or from pervading heaven, firmament, and earth.

18 *Thousand :* 'For the heavenly world is at a distance of about 1000 days' travelling on horseback from here (this earth).'—Haug's Aitareya Brâhmaṇa, II. 2. 17.

20 The sage who knows the kindling-sticks whence by attrition wealth is drawn,
Will comprehend what is most high, will know the mighty Bráhmaṇa.

21 Footless at first was he produced, footless he brought celestial light.
Four-footed grown, and meet for use, he seized each thing enjoyable.

22 Useful will he become, and then will he consume great store of food —
The man who humbly worshippeth the eternal and victorious God.

23 Him too they call eternal; he may become new again to-day.
Day and Night reproduce themselves, each from the form the other wears.

24 A hundred, thousand, myriad, yea a hundred million stores of wealth that passes count are laid in him.
This wealth they kill as he looks on, and now this God shines bright therefrom.

25 One is yet finer than a hair, one is not even visible.
And hence the Deity who grasps with firmer hold is dear to me.

---

20 *Kindling-sticks:* the fire-drill, whence Agni, the great giver of riches, is produced. See Ṛ. V. III. 29.

21 *Footless:* moving unsupported in the sky. The epithet is applied to This Maid (Ushas or Dawn) in the Ṛigveda (VI. 59. 6). *Four-footed:* so in the Chhândogya-Upanishad, III. 18. 2: 'This Brahma has four feet: Speech is one foot, Breath is one foot, the Eye is one foot, the Ear is one foot.'—Scherman.

23 *Him:* the Sun.

24 *They kill:* men consume by enjoying. *Shines bright therefrom:* or, is glad thereat.

25 The Moon is the subject. *One:* the new moon when it first appears. *Not even visible:* when hidden 'in the vacant interlunar cave.' *The Deity:* the Sun.

26 This fair one is untouched by age, immortal in a mortal's house.
He for whom she was made lies low, and he who formed her hath grown old.

27 Thou art a woman, and a man; thou art a damsel and a boy.
Grown old thou totterest with a staff, new-born thou lookest every way.

28 Either the sire or son of these, the eldest or the youngest child,
As sole God dwelling in the mind, first born, he still is in the womb.

29 Forth from the full he lifts the full, the full he sprinkles with the full.
Now also may we know the source from which that stream is sprinkled round.

30 Brought forth in olden time, the everlasting, high over all that is was she, the Ancient.
The mighty Goddess of the Morn, refulgent with one eye, looketh round with one that winketh.

31 Known by the name of Guardian Grace the Deity sits girt by Right.
The trees have taken from her hue, green-garlanded, their robe of green.

32 When he is near she leaves him not, she sees him not though he is near.
Behold the wisdom of the God: he hath not died, he grows not old.

---

26 *This fair one:* or blissful one; Ushas or Dawn. *In a mortal's house:* Dawn is the friend of men and the constant visitor of their dwellings. *He:* in both places the setting Sun; Dawn being sometimes called the daughter of Prajâpati or the Sun.

27 The Moon is again the subject.

29 The Moon, regarded as the sender of rain, appears to be the subject of this stanza which, like the preceding stanza, is purposely enigmatical.

32 *He:* the Sun.

33 Voices that never were before emitted speak as fitteth them.
Whither they go and speak, they say there is the mighty Brâhmaṇa.

34 I ask thee where the waters' flower by wondrous magic art was placed,
Thereon the Gods and men are set as spokes are fastened in the nave.

35 Who gave command unto the wind that bloweth? Who ranged the five united heavenly regions?
Who were the Gods who cared not for oblations? Which of them brought the sacrificial waters?

36 One God inhabiteth the earth we live on; another hath encompassed air's mid-region.
One, the Supporter, takes the heaven and bears it: some keeping watch guard all the quarters safely.

37 The man who knows the drawn-out string on which these creatures all are strung,
The man who knows the thread's thread, he may know the mighty Brâhmaṇa.

38 I know the drawn-out string, the thread whereon these creatures all are strung.
I know the thread's thread also, thus I know the mighty Brâhmaṇa.

---

34 *The waters' flower:* meaning, apparently, the central point of the Universe with reference to the creative power attributed to the waters.

36 *One God:* Agni who dwells on earth as domestic and sacrificial fire. *Another:* Indra, God of the firmament. *The Supporter:* Vidhartar; Sûrya or Soma may be meant. *Guard all the quarters:* the Âṣâpalas or Lokapâlas are Agni, Yama, Varuṇa and others. See I. 31. 1, note.

37 *String:* the thread or chain of sacrifice connecting men with the Gods, on which all creation depends.

39 When Agni passed between the earth and heaven, devouring with his flame, the all-consumer,
Where dwelt afar the spouses of one husband, where at that moment, where was Mâtariṣvan?

40 Into the floods had Mâtariṣvan entered, the deities had past into the waters.
There stood the mighty measurer of the region: into the verdant plants went Pavamâna.

41 Over the Gâyatrî, above the immortal world he strode away.
Those who by Song discovered Song—where did the Unborn see that thing?

42 Luller to rest, and gatherer-up of treasures, Savitar like a God whose laws are constant, hath stood like Indra in the war for riches.

43 Men versed in sacred knowledge know that living Being that abides
In the nine-portalled Lotus Flower, enclosed with triple bands and bonds.

---

39 *The spouses of one husband:* perhaps the regions of the sky may be intended, personified as Goddesses each of whom is faithful to one lord and protector. *Mâtariṣvan:* the Wind-God.

40 *Measurer of the region:* Agni as the Sun: cf. stanza 3. *Pavamâna:* a name or epithet of Agni; Brilliant. This fourth pâda is taken from Ṛ. V. VIII. 90. 14, and Sâyaṇa in his Commentary on the passage explains *harítaḥ* (verdant plants) as the quarters of the sky, and *pávamânaḥ* as Vâyu or the Wind. Prof. Grassmann takes *pávamânaḥ* to be the Soma, and *harítaḥ* to be the horses of the Sun. This and the preceding stanza describe the descent of Agni in the form of lightning into the plants.

42 The stanza is found, with a variation, in Ṛ. V. X. 139. 3.

43 *That living Being: yakshám âtmanvát;* the Supreme Self or Soul. *Nine-portalled Lotus Flower:* the human body. Cf. X. 2. 31. *Enclosed with triple bands and bonds:* or, which the Three Qualities enclose. 'It is possible . . . that these may be here a first reference to the three *guṇas* [Fundamental Qualities] afterwards so celebrated in Indian philosophical speculation.'—Muir. The word *guṇa* meaning both rope or bond and quality.

44 Desireless, firm, immortal, self-existent, contented with the essence, lacking nothing,
Free from the fear of Death is he who knoweth that Soul courageous, youthful, undecaying.

HYMN IX.

BINDING the mouths of those who threaten mischief, against my rivals cast this bolt of thunder.
Indra first gave the Hundredfold Oblation, welfare of him who worships, foe-destroying.

2 Thy skin shall be the Altar ; let thine hair become the Sacred Grass.
This cord hath held thee firmly : let this pressing-stone dance round on thee.

3 The holy water be thy hair : let thy tongue make thee clean, O Cow.
Go, Hundredfold Oblation, made bright and adorable. to heaven.

This extremely abstruse and obscure hymn has been translated by Ludwig, Der Rigveda, III. p. 395, and in part by Muir, O. S Texts, V. p. 386, and Scherman, Philosophische Hymnen, p. 60. The latter scholar has added an excellent commentary on the portion which he has translated.

The hymn is a glorification of the Śataudanâ, the sacrificial Cow accompanied with a hundred *odanas,* messes of boiled rice or other grain mashed and cooked with milk.

1 *Binding the mouths* · addressed to the priest who is binding the mouth of the victim before immolation. *Hundredfold Oblation* : Śataudanâ. Cf. the sacrifice of the Pañchaudana goat in IX. 5.

2 The Cow is addressed *Dance round on thee* : part of the skin is laid on the ground for the Soma press to stand on.

Go . . . to heaven : the victim is *ipso facto* deified and goes straight to the Gods. Cf. VI. 122. 4.

4 He who prepares the Hundredfold Oblation gains each wish thereby:
For all his ministering priests, contented, move as fitteth them.

5 He rises up to heaven, ascends to yonder third celestial height,
Whoever gives the Hundredfold Oblation with the central cake.

6 That man completely wins those worlds, both of the heavens and of the earth,
Whoever pays the Hundredfold Oblation with its golden light.

7 Thine Immolators, Goddess! and the men who dress thee for the feast, all these will guard thee, Hundredfold Oblation! Have no fear of them.

8 The Vasus from the South will be thy guards, the Maruts from the North,
Âdityas from the West: o'ertake and pass the Agnishṭoma, thou!

9 The Gods, the Fathers, mortal men, Gandharvas, and Apsarases,
All these will be thy guards: o'ertake and pass the Atirâtra, thou!

10 The man who pays the Hundredfold Oblation winneth all the worlds,
Air, heaven, and earth, Âdityas, and Maruts, and regions of the sky.

---

4 *With the central cake: apûpánâbhim;* literally, having a navel which consists of, or is decorated with a cake of flour.

6 *Golden light:* the priests' honorarium paid in gold.

7 *Goddess:* the Cow is addressed.

8 *Agnishṭoma:* meaning Praise of Agni; a liturgical rite, the simplest form of Soma sacrifice.

9 *Atirâtra:* a form of the Soma sacrifice requiring three nocturnal recitations. See Satapatha-Brâhmaṇa (Sacred Books of the East) Part II. p. 398.

11 Sprinkling down fatness, to the Gods will the beneficent Goddess go.
Harm not thy dresser, Cow! To heaven, O Hundredfold Oblation, speed!

12 From all the Gods enthroned in heaven, in air, from those who dwell on earth,
Draw forth for evermore a stream of milk, of butter, and of mead.

13 Let thy head, let thy mouth, let both thine ears, and those two jaws of thine
Pour for the giver mingled curd, and flowing butter, milk, and mead.

14 Let both thy lips, thy nostrils, both thy horns, and those two eyes of thine
Pour for the giver, etc.

15 Let heart and pericardium, let thy lungs with all the bronchial tubes, etc.

16 Let liver, and let kidneys, let thine entrails, and the parts within, etc.

17 Let rectum and omentum, let thy belly's hollows, and thy skin, etc.

18 Let all thy marrow, every bone, let all thy flesh, and all thy blood, etc.

19 Let both thy shoulders and thy hump, thy forelegs, and their lower parts, etc.

20 Let neck and nape and shoulder-joints, thy ribs and inter-costal parts, etc.

21 So let thy thighs and thy knee-bones, thy hinder quarters, and thy hips, etc.

22 So let thy tail and all the hairs thereof, thine udder, and thy teats, etc.

23 Let all thy legs, the refuse of thy feet, thy heel-ropes, and thy hooves

---

23 *Refuse of thy feet* : *kúshṭhikâḥ*; scraps or parts of the feet of a victim generally considered unfit for sacrificial purposes. According to Sâyaṇa, the contents of the entrails.

Pour for the giver mingled curd, and flowing butter, milk, and mead.

24 Let all thy skin, Śataudanâ! let every hair thou hast, O Cow,
Pour for the giver mingled curd, and flowing butter, milk, and mead.

25 Sprinkled with molten butter, let the two meal-cakes be sport for thee.
Make them thy wings, O Goddess, and bear him who dresses thee to heaven.

26 Each grain of rice in mortar or on pestle, all on the skin or in the winnowing-basket,
Whatever purifying Mâtariśvan, the Wind, hath sifted, let the Hotar Agni make of it an acceptable oblation.

27 In the priest's hands I lay, in separate order, the sweet celestial Waters, dropping fatness.
As here I sprinkle them may all my wishes be granted unto me in perfect fulness. May we have ample wealth in our possession.

HYMN X.

Worship to thee springing to life, and worship unto thee when born!
Worship, O Cow, to thy tail-hair, and to thy hooves, and to thy form!

2 The man who knows the Seven Floods, who knows the seven distances,

---

Details of the sacrificial procedure are given in the Kauśika-Sûtra, LXV. 1, 2, 3, 8, 9, and LXVI. 5, 20.

The hymn has been translated in part by Ludwig, Der Rigveda, III. p. 270.

The hymn is a glorification of the sacred Cow.

2 *Seven Floods:* the Celestial Rivers, corresponding to the Seven Rivers of the country occupied by the Âryan immigrants. *Seven distances:* more usually three distances or vast distant spaces, corres-

Who knows the head of sacrifice, he may receive the holy Cow.

3 I know the Seven Water-floods, I know the seven distances,
I know the head of sacrifice, and Soma shining bright in her.

4 Hitherward we invite with prayer the Cow who pours a thousand streams,
By whom the heaven, by whom the earth, by whom these waters are preserved.

5 Upon her back there are a hundred keepers, a hundred metal bowls, a hundred milkers.
The Deities who breathe in her all separately know the Cow.

6 Her foot is sacrifice, her milk libation, Svadhâ her breath, Mahîlukâ the mighty:
To the God goes with prayer the Cow who hath Parjanya for her lord.

7 Agni hath entered into thee; Soma, O Cow, hath entered thee.
Thine udder is Parjanya, O blest Cow; the lightnings are thy teats.

8 Thou pourest out the Waters first, and corn-lands afterward, O Cow.
Thirdly thou pourest princely sway. O Cow, thou pourest food and milk.

---

ponding to the three worlds of heaven, firmament, and earth, are spoken of (A. V. VI. 75 3; R. V. VIII. 5. 8; 32. 22). Here seven is used to correspond with the rivers; the distant spaces beyond them; the secrets of furthest heaven. *The head of sacrifice:* the most important part; sacrifice being regarded as an animated being.

5 *Metal bowls:* to serve as milk-pails.

6 *Svadhâ:* food offered to the Fathers or Manes; or the sacrificial benediction used at such presentations. *Mahîlukâ:* a name or an epithet of the sacred Cow. *Parjanya:* specially the protector of the Cow as God of the rainy cloud which makes grass grow to feed her.

7 *Thine udder is Parjanya:* and pours out fatness like the raincloud.

9 When, Holy One, thou camest nigh invited by the Âdityas' call,
Indra gave thee to drink, O Cow, a thousand bowls of Soma juice.

10 The Bull, what time thou followedst the way of Indra, summoned thee;
Thence the Fiend-slayer, angered, took thy water and thy milk away.

11 O Cow, the milk which in his wrath the Lord of Riches took from thee,
That same the vault of heaven now preserveth in three reservoirs.

12 The Cow Celestial received that Soma in three vessels, where
Atharvan, consecrated, sate upon the Sacred Grass of gold.

13 Come hither with the Soma, come with every footed thing; the Cow
With Kalis and Gandharvas by her side hath stepped upon the sea.

14 Come hither with the Wind, yea, come with every creature borne on wings.
Laden with holy verse and song the Cow hath leapt into the sea.

15 Come with the Sun, come hitherward with every creature that hath eyes,
Bearing auspicious lights with her the Cow hath looked across the sea.

---

10 *The Bull:* the mighty Vṛitra, the obstructer of the seasonable rain, conquered by Indra. Cf. the dragon-fights of the Greek Apollo and the Scandinavian Sigmund. Similarly, 'Am I a sea or a whale that thou settest a watch over me?' (Job. 7. 12); where the allusion is to the sea of air and Jehovah's struggle with one of its monsters. 'By his understanding he smiteth through the proud' (the dragon of the upper ocean).—Job. 26. 12.

13 *Kalis:* a class of mythical beings connected with the Gandharvas, and supposed to be addicted to gambling. Cf. VII. 103. 1.

16 When, covered round about with gold, thou stoodest there, O Holy One,
The ocean turned into a horse and mounted on thy back, O Cow.

17 Then came and met the Blessèd Ones, Deshṭrî, the Cow, and Svadhâ, where
Atharvan, consecrated, sate upon the Sacred Grass of gold.

18 The Kshatriya's mother is the Cow, thy mother, Svadhâ! is the Cow.
Sacrifice is the weapon of the Cow: the thought arose from her.

19 From Brahma's summit there went forth a drop that mounted up on high:
From that wast thou produced, O Cow, from that the Hotar sprang to life.

20 Forth from thy mouth the Gáthâs came, from thy neck's nape sprang strength, O Cow.
Sacrifice from thy flanks was born, and rays of sunlight from thy teats.

21 From thy fore-quarters and thy thighs motion was generated, Cow!
Food from thine entrails was produced, and from thy belly came the plants.

22 When into Varuṇa's belly thou hadst found a passage for thyself,
The Brahman called thee thence, for he knew how to guide and lead thee forth.

23 All trembled at the babe that came from him who brings not to the birth.
He hath produced her—thus they cried—He is a cow, and, formed by spells, he hath become akin to her.

---

16 *Deshṭrî*: a divine female; the Instructress, who points out the path of duty.

20 *Gáthâs*: religious non-Vedic verses.

24 He only joineth battle, yea, he who alone controlleth her.
Now sacrifices have become victories, and the Cow their eye.

25 The Cow hath welcomed sacrifice: the Cow hath held the Sun in place.
Together with the prayer the mess of rice hath passed into the Cow.

26 They call the Cow immortal life, pay homage to the Cow as Death.
She hath become this universe, Fathers, and Ṛishis, hath become the Gods, and men, and Asuras.

27 The man who hath this knowledge may receive the Cow with welcoming.
So for the giver willingly doth perfect sacrifice pour milk.

28 Within the mouth of Varuṇa three tongues are glittering with light.
That which shines midmost of them is this Cow most difficult to hold.

29 Four-parted was the Cow's prolific humour.
One-fourth is Water, one-fourth life eternal, one-fourth is sacrifice, one-fourth are cattle.

30 The Cow is Heaven, the Cow is Earth, the Cow is Vishṇu, Lord of Life.
The Sâdhyas and the Vasus have drunk the out-pourings of the Cow.

31 When these, Sâdhyas and Vasus, have drunk the out-pourings of the Cow,
They in the Bright One's dwelling-place pay adoration to her milk.

32 For Soma some have milked her: some worship the fatness she hath poured.

---

31 *In the Bright One's dwelling-place:* in the home of the Sun.

32 A home in highest heaven will reward the man who gives a cow as sacrificial fee to Brâhmans.

They who have given a cow to him who hath this knowledge have gone up to the third region of the sky.

33 He who hath given a Cow unto the Brâhmans winneth all the worlds.
For Right is firmly set in her, devotion, and religious zeal.

34 Both Gods and mortal men depend for life and being on the Cow.
She hath become this universe: all that the Sun surveys is she.

In this hymn the word for cow is *vaśá*, meaning, according to the Commentators, a barren cow: 'Ours art thou, Agni, Bhârata, honoured by us with barren cows (*vaśábhiḥ*),' (R. V. II. 7. 5): but frequently used as synonymous with *gó*, *gaús* in the feminine.

The hymn has been translated by Ludwig, Der Rigveda, III. p. 534.

BOOK XI.

HYMN I.

Agni, spring forth! Here Aditi, afflicted, cooks a Brahmaudana, yearning for children.
Let the Seven Ṛishis, world-creators, rub thee into existence here with gift of offspring.

2 Raise, as I bid, the smoke, my strong companions, lovers of freedom from deceit and malice!
Victor in fight, heroic, here is Agni by whom the Gods subdued the hostile demons.

3 Thou, Agni, wast produced for mighty valour, to cook Brahmaudana, O Jâtavedas.
Seven Ṛishis, makers of the world, begat thee. Grant to this woman wealth with store of heroes.

The hymn is an accompaniment to the preparation and presentation of a Brahmaudana (a mess of rice pap boiled in milk and partly distributed to Brâhmans, especially to priests who officiate at the sacrifice), which is to ensure children, prosperity, and happiness to the institutor of the sacrifice and his wife: 'Brahmaudana that winneth all things' (A. V. IV. 35. 7).

1 *Spring forth:* be born; spring into life from the fire-drill and burn brilliantly, so that the sacrifice may be effectually performed. *Aditi:* see I. 9. 1, note; here regarded as the type of motherhood (*Âdityâḥ vai prajâḥ*, men are Aditi's children.—Taittirîya-Brâhmaṇa, I. 8. 8. 1), and representing the sacrificer's wife. Cf. A. V. VI. 81. 3. *A Brahmaudana:* as an offering to the Gods, the Sâdhyas (see IX. 10. 24) according to the Taittirîya-Brâhmaṇa, III. 3. 10. 4. *World-creators:* see III. 28. 1; IV. 1. 2, note. *Rub thee into existence:* produce thee by agitation of the fire-drill. *With gift of offspring:* children being especially the gift of Agni. Cf. Ṛ. V. I. 66. 4; III. 1. 23.

2 *Companions:* priests who are associated with the chief performer of the sacrifice.

4 Burn up, O Agni, kindled with the fuel. Knowing the Gods who merit worship, bring them.
Cooking, for these, oblation, Jâtavedas! lift up this man to heaven's most lofty summit.

5 Your portion from of old is triply parted, portion of Gods, of Fathers, and of mortals.
Know, all, your shares. I deal them out among you. The portion of the Gods shall save this woman.

6 Strong art thou, Agni, conquering, all-surpassing. Crush down our foemen, ruin those who hate us.
So let this measure, measured, being measured, make all our kin thy tributary vassals.

7 Increase with kinsmen and with all abundance: to mighty strength and power lift up this woman.
Erect, rise upward to the sky's high station, rise to the lofty world which men call Svarga.

8 May this great Earth receive the skin, this Goddess Pṛithivî, showing us her love and favour. Then may we go unto the world of virtue.

9 Fix on the skin these two joined press-stones, duly rending the fibres for the sacrificer.
Strike down and slay those who assail this woman, and elevating raise on high her offspring.

---

4 *To heaven's most lofty summit:* to the highest human felicity on earth, and eventually to bliss in heaven.

5 *Triply parted:* here the rice is deposited in three heaps; the share of the Fathers to be offered as an obsequial oblation, and that of men to be given as food to the Brâhmans.

8 *The skin:* of a black antelope, on which the pressure of the Soma and the bruising and husking of the rice used in oblations are performed. This skin is one of the symbols of Brâhmanical worship and civilization. See Ṣatapatha-Brâhmaṇa, I. 1. 4. 1 (Sacred Books of the East, XII. p. 23).

9 *Fibres: anṣûn;* portions of the stalks of the plant; perhaps, as has been suggested, the internodes or parts between the knots.

10 Grasp with thy hand, O man, the well-formed press-stones: the holy Gods have come unto thy worship.
Three wishes of thy heart which thou electest, these happy gains for thee I here make ready.

11 Here thy devotion is, here is thy birthplace. Aditi, Mother of brave sons, accept thee!
Wipe away those who fight against this woman: with wealth and store of goodly sons endow her.

12 Rest in the roaring frame of wood: be parted from husk and chaff, ye Sacrificial Fibres.
May we surpass in glory all our rivals. I cast beneath my feet the men who hate us.

13 Go, Dame, and quickly come again: the waters, enclosed, have mounted thee that thou mayst bear them.
Take thou of these such as are fit for service: skilfully separating leave the others.

14 Hither these Dames have come in radiant beauty. Arise and seize upon thy strength, O woman.
To thee hath sacrifice come: take the pitcher, blest with a good lord, children, children's children.

15 Instructed by the Ṛishis, bring those waters, the share of strength which was of old assigned you.
Let this effectual sacrifice afford you protection, fortune, offspring, men, and cattle.

16 Agni, on thee the sacrificial caldron hath mounted: shining, fiercely flaming, heat it.
May hottest flames, divine, sprung from the Ṛishis, gathering with the Seasons, heat this portion.

---

10 *Three wishes:* one for each of the offerings or shares mentioned in stanza 5.

12 *Wooden frame:* the Soma press, made partly of wood.

13 *Go, Dame:* to bring the water required for the preparation of the offering. *The waters, enclosed:* literally, the pen or fold of the waters. *Have mounted:* have willingly allowed themselves to be taken up.

14 *These Dames:* the waters personified. Cf. stanza 17.

17 Purified, bright, and holy, let these Women, these lucid waters, glide into the caldron.
Cattle and many children may they give us. May he who cooks the Odana go to heaven.

18 Ye, Sacrificial Rice and Soma Fibres, cleansed and made pure by prayer and molten butter,
Enter the water: let the caldron take you. May he who dresses this ascend to heaven.

19 Expand thyself abroad in all thy greatness, with thousand Prishṭhas, in the world of virtue.
Grandfathers, fathers, children, and descendants, fifteenth am I to thee when I have dressed it.

20 With thousand streams and Prishṭhas, undecaying, Brahmaudana is celestial, God-reaching.
Those I give up to thee with all their children. Force them to tribute, but to me be gracious.

21 Rise to the altar: bless this dame with offspring. Promote this woman; drive away the demons.
May we surpass in glory all our rivals. I cast beneath my feet the men who hate us.

22 Approach this woman here with store of cattle: together with the deities come to meet her.
Let not a curse or imprecation reach thee: in thine own seat shine forth exempt from sickness.

23 Fashioned at first by Right, set by the spirit, this altar of Brahmaudana was appointed.
Place the pure boiler on it, woman! set thou therein the rice-mess of Celestial Beings.

---

17 *Odana:* the general word for the mess of mashed rice, differentiated by composition with words signifying the peculiar character or object of the oblation, as Pañchaudana (IX. 5. 8 sqq.), Ṣataudanâ (X. 9. 3 sqq.), qualifying, respectively goat and cow.

19 *Expand thyself:* addressed to the Odana. *Prishṭhas:* Stotras or lauds, consisting of several Sâmans and employed at the mid-day libation.

Fifteenth: meaning, perhaps, ensurer of children to the fifteenth generation. The stanza is spoken by the priest who cooks the rice.

20 *Those:* unfriendly men. *Force them to tribute:* cf. stanza 6.

24 This second hand of Aditi, this ladle which the Seven Rishis, world-creators, fashioned,
May this scoop deftly pile upon the altar, therein, the members of the rice-oblation.

25 Let the dressed offering and divine Ones serve thee: creep from the fire again, own these as masters.
Made pure with Soma rest within the Brahmans: let not thine eaters, Rishis' sons, be injured.

26 Give understanding unto these, King Soma! all the good Brâhmans who attend and serve thee.
Oft, in Brahmaudana, and well I call on Rishis, their sons, and those who sprang from Fervour.

27 Here I set singly in the hands of Brahmans these cleansed and purified and holy Women.
May Indra, Marut-girt, grant me the blessing which, as I sprinkle you, my heart desireth.

28 Here is my gold, a light immortal: ripened grain from the field this Cow of Plenty give me!
This wealth I place among the Brâhmans, making a path that leads to heaven among the Fathers.

29 Lay thou the chaff in Agni Jâtavedas: remove the husks and drive them to a distance.
That, we have heard, that is the House-Lord's portion: we know the share allotted to Destruction.

---

24 *Ladle*: *srûch*; offering-spoon. *Scoop*: or, spoon; *dárvi*, used especially in fire-oblations.

25 *Creep from the fire*: addressed to the Odana. *These*: the priests. *Rishis' sons*: or ancestral Sages.

26 *Who sprang from Fervour*: whose element is religious asceticism and devotion; of pious nature.

27 *Women*: sacrificial waters.

28 *My gold, a light immortal*: a piece of gold presented with the oblation at the recitation of the text, 'This (butter) is thy body, O Shining (Agni)! this (gold) is thy light' (Sacred Books of the East, XXVI. p. 54).

29 *The House-Lord's portion*: the share allotted to Agni God of the Homestead.

30 Mark him who toils and cooks and pours oblation: make this man climb the path that leads to heaven,
That he may mount and reach life that is highest, ascending to the loftiest vault above us.

31 Adhvaryu, cleanse that face of the Supporter. Make room, well knowing, for the molten butter.
Purify duly all the limbs with fatness. I make a path to heaven amid the Fathers.

32 Supporter, send to those men fiends and battle, to all non-Brâhmans who attend and serve thee.
Famous and foremost, with their great possessions, let not these here, the Ṛishis' sons, be injured.

33 I set thee, Odana, with Ṛishis' children: naught here belongs to men not sprung from Ṛishis.
Let Agni my protector, all the Maruts, the Viṣve Devas guard the cooked oblation.

34 May we adore thee, Sacrifice that yieldeth an everlasting son, cow, home of treasures,
Together with increasing store of riches, long life and immortality of children.

35 Thou art a Bull that mounts to heaven: to Ṛishis and their offspring go.
Rest in the world of pious men: there is the place prepared for us.

36 Level the ways: go thitherward, O Agni. Make ready thou the Godward-leading pathways.
By these our pious actions may we follow sacrifice dwelling in the seven-rayed heaven.

Destruction: Nirṛiti, who is propitiated with a portion of the offering.

31 *The Supporter:* the Odana, which maintains the prosperity of those who offer it.

35 *The Bull:* the powerful Odana.

36 *Seven-rayed:* bright with the seven rays of the Sun. Cf. VII. 107. 1. 'Mahidhara remarks that four of them lie in, or point to, the four quarters; one pointing upwards and another downwards; and the seventh and best being the disc of the sun itself, called Hiraṇyagarbha' (Dr. J. Eggeling, Sacred Books of the East, XII. p. 271).

37 May we invested with that light go upward, ascending to the sky's most lofty summit,
Wherewith the Gods, what time they had made ready Brahmaudana, mounted to the world of virtue.

HYMN II.

Bhava and Ṣarva, spare us, be not hostile. Homage to you, twin Lords of beasts and spirits!
Shoot not the arrow aimed and drawn against us: forbear to harm our quadrupeds and bipeds.

2 Cast not our bodies to the dog or jackal, nor, Lord of Beasts! to carrion-kites or vultures.
Let not thy black voracious flies attack them; let not thy birds obtain them for their banquet.

3 We offer homage to thy shout, Bhava! thy breath, thy racking pains:
Homage, Immortal One! to thee, to Rudra of the thousand eyes.

4 We offer reverence to thee from eastward, and from north and south,
From all the compass of the sky, to thee and to the firmament.

5 Homage, O Bhava, Lord of Beasts, unto thy face and all thine eyes,
To skin, and hue, and aspect, and to thee when looked at from behind!

6 We offer homage to thy limbs, thy belly, and thy tongue, and mouth, we offer homage to thy smell.

7 Never may we contend with him, the mighty archer, thousand-eyed,
Rudra who wears black tufts of hair, the slaughterer of Ardhaka.

A hymn of praise and prayer to Bhava, Ṣarva, and Rudra.

1 *Bhava and Ṣarva:* see IV. 28. 1, note; VI. 93. 1. 2; VIII. 2. 7; XI. 6. 9; XII. 4. 17; XIII. 4. 4; XV. 5. 1, 2.

7 *Ardhaka:* the name of a demon which does not occur elsewhere. It may be the same as Andhaka; son of Kaṣyapa and Diti, who was

8 May he, may Bhava from all sides avoid us, avoid us even as fire avoids the waters. Let him not threaten us. To him be homage.

9 Four times, eight times be homage paid to Bhava, yea, Lord of Beasts, ten times be reverence paid thee!
Thine are these animals, five several classes, oxen, and goats, and sheep, and men, and horses.

10 Thine the four regions, thine are earth and heaven, thine, Mighty One, this firmament between them;
Thine everything with soul and breath here on the surface of the land.

11 Thine is this ample wealth-containing storehouse that holds within it all these living creatures.
Favour us, Lord of Beasts, to thee be homage! Far from us go ill-omens, dogs, and jackals, and wild-haired women with their horrid shrieking!

12 A yellow bow of gold thou wieldest, slaying its hundred, tufted God! smiting its thousand.
Weapon of Gods, far flies the shaft of Rudra: wherever it may be, we pay it homage.

13 Thou, Rudra, followest close the foe who lies in wait to conquer thee,
Even as a hunter who pursues the footsteps of the wounded game.

14 Accordant and allies, Bhava and Rudra, with mighty strength ye go to deeds of valour. Wherever they may be, we pay them homage.

15 Be homage, Rudra, unto thee approaching and departing hence!
Homage to thee when standing still, to thee when seated and at rest!

---

slain by Rudra when he attempted to carry off the tree of Paradise: 'So, burnt by Rudra, Andhak fell in Svetâranya's flowery dell' (Râmâyaṇa, III. 30).

9 *Five several classes*: cf. II. 34. 1, note.

11 *Wild-haired women*: mourners with dishevelled hair at funerals.

16 Homage at evening and at morn, homage at night, homage by day:
To Bhava and to Sarva, both, have I paid lowly reverence.

17 Let us not outrage with our tongue far-seeing Rudra, thousand-eyed,
Inspired with varied lore, who shoots his arrows forward, far away.

18 Foremost we go to meet his car, the chariot of the long-haired God,
Drawn by brown horses, dusky, black, o'erthrowing, slaying, terrible. Let reverence be paid to him.

19 Cast not thy club at us, thy heavenly weapon. Lord of Beasts, be not wroth with us. Let reverence be paid to thee.
Shake thy celestial branch above some others elsewhere, not o'er us.

20 Do us no harm, but comfort us: avoid thou us, and be not wroth. Never let us contend with thee.

21 Covet not thou our kine or men, covet not thou our goats or sheep.
Elsewhither, strong One! turn thine aim: destroy the mockers' family.

22 Homage to him whose weapon, Cough or Fever, assails one like the neighing of a stallion; to him who draws one forth and then another!

23 Homage be paid him with ten Sakvarî verses who stands established in the air's mid-region, slaying non-sacrificing God-despisers!

---

19 *Branch:* meaning missile.

22 *Like the neighing of a stallion:* which the incessant cough and cries of the sufferers are supposed to resemble.

Who draws one forth: one arrow from his quiver.

23 *Sakvarî verses:* hymns of praise in the Sakvarî metre, consisting of 8 × 7 syllables, or four pâdas of fourteen syllables each.

24 For thee were forest beasts and sylvan creatures placed in the wood, and small birds, swans, and eagles.
Floods, Lord of Beasts! contain thy living beings: to swell thy strength flow the celestial Waters.

25 Porpoises, serpents, strange aquatic monsters, fishes, and things unclean at which thou shootest.
Nothing is far for thee, naught checks thee, Bhava! The whole earth in a moment thou surveyest. From the east sea thou smitest in the northern.

26 O'erwhelm us not with Fever or with poison, nor, Rudra! with the fire that comes from heaven. Elsewhere, and not on us, cast down this lightning.

27 Ruler of heaven and Lord of earth is Bhava: Bhava hath filled the spacious air's mid-region. Where'er he be, to him be paid our homage!

28 King Bhava, favour him who offers worship, for thou art Paśupati, Lord of victims.
Be gracious to the quadruped and biped of the believer in the Gods' existence.

29 Harm thou among us neither great nor little, not one who bears us, not our future bearers.
Injure no sire among us, harm no mother. Forbear to injure our own bodies, Rudra.

30 This lowly reverence have I paid to Rudra's dogs with mighty mouths,
Hounds terrible with bark and howl, who gorge unmasticated food.

---

28 *Lord of victims*: or of beasts in general.

29 The stanza is taken, with variants, from Ṛ. V. I. 114. 7, addressed to Rudra. *Not one who bears us*: according to the Ṛ. V. reading the meaning of this *pâda* is '(harm) neither the growing boy nor the full-grown man.' Muir translates: 'neither him who is growing nor those who are to grow;' but there seems to be no authority for giving this meaning to the verb *vah* (*veh-o*), to bear, or carry.

31 Homage to thy loud-shouting hosts and to thy long-haired followers!
Homage to hosts that are adored, homage to armies that enjoy!
Homage to all thy troops, O God. Security and bliss be ours!

HYMN III.

Of that Odana Bṛihaspati is the head, Brahma the
mouth. 2 Heaven and Earth are the ears, the Sun
and Moon are the eyes, the Seven Ṛishis are the
vital airs inhaled and exhaled. 3 Vision is the
pestle, Desire the mortar. 4 Diti is the winnowing
basket, Aditi is she who holds it, Vâta is the sifter.
5 Horses are the grains, oxen the winnowed rice-
grains, gnats the husks. 6 Kabru is the husked grain,
the rain-cloud is the reed. 7 Grey iron is its flesh,
copper its blood. 8 Tin is its ashes, gold its colour,
the blue lotus flower its scent. 9 The threshing-
floor is its dish, the wooden swords its shoulders, the
car-shafts its backbones. 10 Collar-bones are its

---

31 *Enjoy:* devour their prey.

The hymn has been translated by Muir, O. S. Texts, IV. 335, and by Ludwig, Der Rigveda, III. p. 549.

The hymn which, with the exception of four lines is in prose, is a glorification of the Odana or oblation of boiled rice or pap.

3 *Desire:* or Kâma. See IX. 2.

4 *Diti:* a Goddess or personification usually associated with Aditi as her antithesis or complement; the name and idea being evolved from the elder Aditi in the same way as Sura, a God, is from the ancient Vedic Asura, a demon. See VII. 7. In later times Diti, wife of Kaṣyapa, was regarded as the mother of the Daityas who were, like the Greek Titans, enemies of the Gods whose mother was Aditi, Kaṣyapa's other wife. See Râmâyaṇa, I. XLV.

6 *Kabru:* there is no clue to the meaning of this word.

9 *Wooden swords:* sacrificial implements used for stirring the boiled rice, for trimming the mound used as an altar, and for other purposes calculated to assure the proper performance of the rite.

entrails, straps its intestines. 11 This earth, verily
becomes the jar, and heaven the cover of the Odana
as it is cooking. 12 Furrows are its ribs, sandy soils
the undigested contents of its stomach. 13 Law is
its water for the hands and family custom its asper-
sion. 14 The jar covered with the Ṛich has been
solemnly directed by the priestly office. 15 Receiv-
ed by the Brahman, it has been carried round. 16
The Bṛihat is the stirring-spoon, the Rathantara the
ladle. 17 The Seasons are the dressers, the Groups
of Seasons kindle the fire. 18 The caldron flames
round the oblation (*charu*) whose mouth consists of
five openings.

19 The sacrificial word, all worlds are to be won with Odana;

20 Whereon in order rest the three, the ocean, and the heaven, and earth.

21 Within the residue whereof the Gods arranged six eightieth parts—

22 I ask thee, of this Odana what is the mighty magnitude.

23 He who may know the magnitude of the Odana
24 Would say, Not small, nor devoid of moistening
sauce; not this, nor anything whatever. 25 He
would not declare it to be greater than the giver
imagines it to be. 26 The theologians say, Thou
hast eaten the averted Odana and the Odana turned
hitherward. 27 Thou hast eaten the Odana, and the

---

16 *Bṛihat:* the name of a most highly valued Sâman in Bṛihatî metre (8 + 8 + 12 + 8), found in Sâmaveda II. ii. i. 12, reproduced from Ṛigveda VI. 46. 1, 2. *Rathantara:* another most important Sâman in the same metre, found in Sâmaveda II. i. i. 11, taken from Ṛigveda VII. 32. 22, 23.

18 *Charu:* a sacrificial caldron; also boiled rice, or oblation of grain boiled in milk, butter or water.

The grotesquely fantastic character of the hymn precludes attempts at serious explanation.

Odana will eat thee. 28 Thou hast eaten this averted; thy inward breath will leave thee; so he said to this one. 29 Thou hast eaten this turned hitherward; thy downward breath will leave thee; so he said to this one. 30 I indeed have not eaten the Odana, nor has the Odana eaten me. 31 The Odana has just eaten the Odana.

2

32 And thence he said to this one, Thou hast eaten this with a different head from that with which the ancient Rishis ate: thy offspring, reckoning from the eldest, will die. I have eaten it neither turned downward, nor turned away, nor turned hitherward. With Brihaspati as head: with him I have eaten, with him have I come to it. Now this Odana is complete with all members, joints, and body. Complete, verily, with all his members, joints, and body is he who possesses this knowledge. 33 And thence he said to him, Thou hast eaten this with other ears than those with which the ancient Rishis ate it. Thou wilt be deaf. I have eaten it neither, etc. (as in verse 32). With Heaven and Earth as ears, with these I have eaten it, with these I have come to it. Now this Odana, etc. (as in 32). 34 And thence he said to him, Thou hast eaten this with other eyes . . . thou wilt be blind. With Sun and Moon, etc. 35 And thence, etc. . . . with other mouth. Thy offspring will die, reckoning from the head . . . With Brahma as mouth. 36 And thence, etc. . . . with other tongue . . . Thy tongue will die . . . With the tongue of Agni. 37 And thence, etc. . . . With other teeth . . . Thy teeth will fall out . . . . With the Seasons as teeth. 38 And thence, etc. . . . with other vital airs . . . . Thy vital airs will leave thee . . . With the Seven Rishis as the vital airs. 39 And thence, etc. . . . with other expanse . . . . Consumption will destroy thee . . . With the firmament as expanse.

40 And thence, etc. . . . with other back . . . Lightning will slay thee . . . . With the heaven as back.
41 And thence, etc. . . . with other breast . . . Thou wilt fail in agriculture . . . . With the earth as breast.
42 And thence, etc. . . . . with other belly . . . colic will destroy thee . . . . With truth as belly. 43
And thence, etc. . . . with other abdomen . . . Thou wilt die in the water . . . With the sea as abdomen.
44 And thence, etc . . . with other thighs . . . Thy thigh will perish . . . . With Mitra-Varuṇa as thighs.
45 And thence, etc. . . . with other knees . . . . Thou wilt become a sick man . . . . With the knees of Tvashṭar. 46 And thence, etc. . . . with other feet . . . Thou wilt become a wanderer . . . . . With the feet of the Aṣvins. 47 And thence, etc . . . . with other fore-parts of the feet . . . . A serpent will kill thee . . . . With the fore-parts of Savitar's feet.
48 And thence, etc. . . . . with other hands . . . The Brâhmaṇa (divine power) will kill thee . . . . With the hands of Right. 49 And thence, etc . . . . with other basis . . . . Without standing-ground and resting-place thou wilt die . . . . . . Having taken my stand on truth. With this I ate it, with this I came to it. Now this Odana is complete with all members, joints, and body. Complete, verily, with all his members, joints, and body is he who possesses this knowledge.

HYMN IV.

HOMAGE to Prâṇa, him who hath dominion o'er the universe,
Who hath become the Sovran Lord of all, on whom the whole depends!

The hymn is a glorification of Prâṇa, Breath, Vital Spirit, Life, regarded as a deity and apparently identified with Prajâpati the Lord of Creation.

2 Homage, O Prâṇa, to thy roar, to thunder-peal and lightning-flash!
Homage, O Prâṇa, unto thee what time thou sendest down thy rain!

3 When Prâṇa with a thunderous voice shouts his loud message to the plants,
They straightway are impregnate, they conceive, and bear abundantly.

4 When the due season hath arrived and Prâṇa shouteth to the herbs,
Then all is joyful, yea, each thing upon the surface of the earth.

5 When Prâṇa hath poured down his flood of rain upon the mighty land,
Cattle and beasts rejoice thereat: Now great will be our strength, they cry.

6 Watered by Prâṇa's rain the plants have raised their voices in accord:
Thou hast prolonged our life, they say, and given fragrance to us all.

7 Homage to thee when coming nigh, homage to thee departing hence!
Homage, O Prâṇa, be to thee when standing and when sitting still.

8 Homage to thee at every breath thou drawest in and sendest forth!
Homage to thee when turned away, homage to thee seen face to face! This reverence be to all of thee!

9 Prâṇa, communicate to us thy dear, thy very dearest form.
Whatever healing balm thou hast, give us thereof that we may live.

---

2 In this and the four following stanzas Prâṇa is invested with the attributes of Parjanya the God of the Rain-cloud. Cf. Ṛ. V. V. 83.

10 Prâṇa robes living creatures as a father his belovèd son.
Prâṇa is sovran Lord of all, of all that breathes not, all that breathes.

11 Prâṇa is Fever, he is Death. Prâṇa is worshipped by the Gods.
Prâṇa sets in the loftiest sphere the man who speaks the words of truth.

12 Prâṇa is Deshṭrî, and Virâj. Prâṇa is reverenced by all.
He is the Sun, he is the Moon. Prâṇa is called Prajâpati.

13 Both breaths are rice and barley, and Prâṇa is called the toiling ox:
In barley is the inbreath laid, and rice is named the outward breath.

14 The human infant in the womb draws vital breath and sends it out:
When thou, O Prâṇa, quickenest the babe it springs anew to life.

15 The name of Prâṇa is bestowed on Mâtariṣvan and on Wind.
On Prâṇa, past and future, yea, on Prâṇa everything depends.

16 All herbs and plants spring forth and grow when thou, O Prâṇa, quickenest,
Plants of Atharvan, Angiras, plants of the deities and men.

17 When Prâṇa hath poured down his flood of rain upon the mighty earth,
The plants are wakened into life, and every herb that grows on ground.

18 The man who knows this truth of thee, O Prâṇa, and what bears thee up—
To him will all present their gift of tribute in that loftiest world.

---

12 *Deshṭrî:* the divinity who shows men the path of duty. *Virâj:* see VIII. 10.

19 As all these living creatures are thy tributaries, Prâṇa, so
Shall they bring tribute unto him who hears thee with attentive ears.

20 Filled with a babe, mid deities he wanders: grown near at hand, he springs again to being.
That Father, grown the present and the future, hath past into the son with mighty powers.

21 Haṅsa, what time he rises up, leaves in the flood one foot unmoved.
If he withdrew it there would be no more to-morrow or to-day,
Never would there be night, no more would daylight shine or morning flush.

22 It rolleth on, eight-wheeled and single-fellied, and with a thousand eyes, forward and backward.
With one half it engendered all creation. What sign is there to tell us of the other?

23 Homage, O Prâṇa, unto thee armed with swift bow among the rest,
In whose dominion is this All of varied sort that stirs and works!

24 May he who rules this Universe of varied sort, that stirs and works,
Prâṇa, alert and resolute, assist me through the prayer I pray.

25 Erect among the sleepers he wakes, and is never laid at length.
No one hath ever heard that he hath been asleep while others slept.

---

20 *He springs again to being:* every birth that occurs being in reality a rebirth of Prâṇa. The same is said of Prajâpati.

21 *Haṅsa:* the Sun: see X. 8. 17.

22 *It:* the chariot of the Sun. The stanza is repeated, with a variant, from X. 8. 7.

23 *Armed with swift bow:* like Rudra, Bhava, and Sarva.

26 Thou, Prâṇa, never shalt be hid, never shalt be estranged from me.
I bind thee on myself for life, O Prâṇa, like the Waters' germ.

HYMN V.

STIRRING both worlds the Brahmachârî moveth: in him the deities are all one-minded.
He hath established firmly earth and heaven: he satisfies his Master with his Fervour.

2 After the Brahmachârî go the Fathers, the heavenly hosts, all Gods in separate order.
After him too have the Gandharvas followed, thirty and three, three hundred, and six thousand. He satisfies all Gods with his devotion.

3 The Master, welcoming his new disciple, into his bowels takes the Brahmachârî.
Three nights he holds and bears him in his belly. When he is born, the Gods convene to see him.

---

26 *The Waters' germ:* Agni, offspring in his lightning form of the waters or watery clouds of the ocean of air.

The hymn has been translated, with the omission of a few stanzas, by Muir, O. S. Texts, V. p. 394, and, in its entirety and with annotations, by Scherman, Philosophische Hymmen, p. 69.

The hymn is a glorification of the Brahmachârî or religious student.

1 *Brahmachârî:* a young Brâhman in the first *Âṣrama*, stage or period, of his religious life from the time of his *upanayanam*, confirmation or initiation by investiture of the sacrificial cord, till he marries and enters the second stage as a householder. *Master:* Âchârya; religious teacher. *Fervour: tapas;* religious austerity and fervent devotion.

3 The Âchârya performs for the disciple the part of a spiritual second mother; and by the initiation ceremony the youth is regenerate or born anew. Details of a Brahmachârî's initiation are given in Âṣvalâyana—Gṛihya-Sûtra, I. 20. 2 sqq., and in other Gṛihya-Sûtras, translated in Sacred Books of the East, Vols. XXIX and XXX.

4 This log is earth, the second log is heaven: he fills the air's mid region with the fuel.
With fuel, with his zone the Brahmachârî contents the worlds, with labour and with Fervour.

5 The Brahmachârî, earlier born than Brahma, sprang up through Fervour, robed in hot libation.
From him sprang heavenly lore, the highest Brahma, and all the Gods, with life that lasts for ever.

6 Lighted by fuel goes the Brahmachârî, clad in black-buck skin, consecrate, long-bearded.
Swiftly he goes from east to northern ocean, grasping the worlds, oft bringing them anear him.

7 The Brahmachârî, fathering Prayer, world, Waters, Virâj, Prajâpati and Parameshṭhin,
Lay as a germ within the Immortal's bosom, then became Indra and destroyed the demons.

8 The Master fashioned both these cloudy regions, profound and spacious pair, the earth and heaven.
The Brahmachârî guards them with his Fervour. In him the deities are all one-minded.

9 The Brahmachârî first of all brought hither this ample earth as alms, and heaven above it.
He makes these twain two fuel-logs, and worships. On these supported rest all living creatures.

---

4 *This log:* part of the ceremony consists in the Brahmachâri's placing fuel on the sacrificial fire. *Zone:* the sacrificial cord or girdle first assumed at initiation.

5 *Earlier born than Brahma:* that is, than the Personal Deity.

6 *Black-buck skin:* as prescribed for religious students. Cf. XI. 1. 8, note.

7 *Within the Immortal's bosom:* 'in the womb of immortality.'—Muir.

8 *The Master:* the Âchârya, as the cause of the Brahmachâri's spiritual birth.

9 *As alms:* with reference to the poverty of the Brahmachâri who lives on the gifts of the pious.

10 Both treasuries of sacred lore lie hidden, one hitherward, beyond heaven's ridge the other.
The Brahmachârî with his Fervour guards them.
He makes this all his own as knowing Brahma.

11 Hitherward one, hence from the earth the other, two Agnis meet between these cloudy regions.
Close to these two firm rays of light are clinging.
The Brahmachârî enters them through Fervour.

12 Thundering, shouting, ruddy-hued, and pallid, he bears along the earth great manly vigour.
Down on the ridge of earth the Brahmachârî pours seed, and this gives life to heaven's four regions.

13 The Brahmachârî stores with fuel Waters, and Fire, and Sun, and Moon, and Mâtarisvan.
The Waters' lights move separate in the rain-cloud.
Man, rain, and water are their molten butter.

14 The Master is Death, Varuṇa, Soma, the plants of earth, and milk.
The thunder-clouds were men of war. By these this heavenly light was brought.

15 Varuṇa, made a Master, takes at home the butter to himself.
Whatever with Prajâpati he sought, the Brahmachârî gave like Mitra from his loftiest soul.

16 The pupil is the Master, yea, the pupil is Prajâpati.
Prajâpati shines bright; the bright Virâj grew potent Indra's self.

17 By Fervour and by self-restraint the King protects the realm he rules.
By self-restraint the Master seeks a Brahmachârî to instruct.

---

10 *He makes this all his own as knowing Brahma*: 'wise, he appropriates that divine knowledge as his exclusive portion.'—Muir.

11 *Two Agnis*: apparently, lightning and terrestrial fire; but the sense is not clear.

17 *Self-restraint*: *Brahmachárya*: religious study in general, and

18 By self-restraint a maiden finds a youth to be her wedded lord.
By self-restraint the ox and horse seek to win fodder for themselves.

19 By Fervour and by self-restraint the Gods drave Death away from them,
And Indra brought by self-restraint heaven's lustre to the deities.

20 The plants, what is and what shall be, day, night, the tall tree of the wood,
The year with seasons of the year, all from the Brahmachârî sprang.

21 All creatures of the earth and heaven, tame animals and sylvan beasts,
Wingèd and wingless creatures, from the Brahmachârî sprang to life.

22 All children of Prajâpati have breath distinctly in themselves.
The Brahma that is stored within the Brahmachârî guards them all.

23 Piled up on high, but never yet ascended, that power of deities is brightly shining.
From that sprang heavenly lore, the loftiest Brahma, and all the Gods with life that lasts for ever.

---

specially the self-restraint and purity enjoined upon all religious students and regarded as preëminent virtues.

'The Taittirîya Brâhmaṇa, iii. 10, 11, 3, tells a story illustrative of the great virtue ascribed to brahmacharyya, or religious self-restraint:—Bharadvâja practised brahmacharyya during three lives. Indra, approaching him when he was lying decayed and old, said: 'Bharadvâja, if I give thee a fourth life, what wilt thou do with it?' He answered: 'I will use it only to practise brahmacharyya.'—Muir.

The hymn has been translated by Ludwig, Der Rigveda, III. p. 452, and, in part, by Muir, O. S. Texts, V. p. 400. According to Prof. Alfred Hillebrandt, the Vedic poet's fancy has represented the mutual relations of the sun and moon in those of the Âchârya and the Brahmachârî. Especially in stanza 3, the Âchârya is the Sun who devours the dying Moon and keeps him within him during three nights. See Vedische Mythologie, I. p. 471.

24 The Brahmachârî wields the radiant Brahma wherein all Gods are woven close together;
Creating breath, inhaling and exhaling, voice, mind, and heart, Brahma and holy wisdom.

25 Bestow on us the power of sight and hearing, glory and food and seed and blood and belly.

26 These, standing on the flood, the Brahmachârî formed, practising in sea his hot devotion.
When he hath bathed, brown, yellow-hued, he shines exceedingly on earth.

HYMN VI.

We call on Agni, on the trees lords of the forest, herbs and plants,
Indra, Sûrya, Bṛihaspati: may they deliver us from woe.

2 We call on Vishṇu, Bhaga, on Mitra and Varuṇa the King,
Aṅsa, Vivasvân we address: may they deliver us from woe.

3 We call on Savitar the God, on Pûshan the establisher,
Tvashṭar the foremost we address: may they deliver us from woe.

4 Gandharvas and Apsarases, the Aṣvins, Brahmaṇaspati,
Aryaman, God, by name we call: may they deliver us from woe.

5 This word of ours to Day and Night, and to the Sun and Moon we speak,
All the Âdityas we address; may they deliver us from woe.

The hymn is a prayer to all Divinities and Sanctities for deliverance from distress.

2 *Aṅsa:* the Distributer; one of the Âdityas. This deity is not mentioned again in the Atharva-veda, and his name occurs only twice in the Ṛigveda hymns.

6 Vâta, Parjanya we address, the Quarters, and the Firmament,
And all the Regions of the sky: may they deliver us from woe.

7 From all that brings a curse may Day and Night and Dawn deliver me.
May Soma free me, God to whom they give the name of Chandramâs.

8 All creatures both of heaven and earth, wild beasts and sylvan animals,
And wingèd birds of air we call: may they deliver us from woe.

9 Bhava and Ṣarva we address, and Rudra who is Lord of Beasts,
Their arrows which we feel and know: may they be ever kind to us.

10 We speak to Constellations, Heaven, to Earth, to Genii, and to Hills,
To Seas, to Rivers, and to Lakes: may they deliver us from woe.

11 Or the Seven Ṛishis we address, Waters divine, Prajâpati,
Fathers with Yama at their head: may they deliver us from woe.

12 Gods whose abode is in the heaven and those who dwell in middle air,
And Mighty Ones who rest on earth: may they deliver us from woe.

13 Âdityas, Rudras, Vasus, Gods aloft in heaven, Atharvan's sons,
The sages, sons of Angiras: may they deliver us from woe.

---

7 *Chandramâs:* the Moon as measurer of time, compounded of *chandra*, bright, Moon, and *mas*, from *mâ*, to measure, the root also of moon (the measure or measurer).

9 *Bhava and Ṣarva:* see XI. 2.

14 To sacrifice, to worshipper, hymns, songs, and healing charms, we speak,
To priestly acts and Yayus texts : may they deliver us from woe.

15 To the five kingdoms of the plants which Soma rules as Lord we speak:
Darbha, hemp, barley, mighty power: may these deliver us from woe.

16 To demons and fierce fiends we speak, to Holy Genii, Fathers, Snakes,
And to the hundred deaths and one: may these deliver us from woe.

17 We speak to Seasons, Season-Lords, to years and sections of the year,
To Months, half-months, and years complete: may they deliver us from woe.

18 Come hither from the south, ye Gods, rise and come forward from the west,
Gathered together, all ye Gods, ye mighty Ones, from east and north : may they deliver us from woe.

19 This we address to all the Gods, faithful, maintainers of the Right,
With all their Consorts by their side: may they deliver us from woe.

20 We speak to the collected Gods, faithful, maintainers of the Right.
Present with their collective Dames: may these deliver us from woe.

---

15 *Soma:* see VI. 15. 3, note. *Darbha:* Kuśa grass (Poa Cynosuroides), used in sacred ceremonies and deified on account of its sanctifying virtues.

Hemp: bhangá; Cannabis Sativa : from which the intoxicating drug is produced. *Barley:* cf. 'Thou art barley, thou art the king of grain' (Baudhâyana, Srauta-Sûtra, III. 6. 5).

16 *Hundred deaths and one:* see I. 30. 3; II. 28. 1; VIII. 2. 27.

17 *Season-Lords:* Agni and other Gods who preside over the several Seasons.

21 The spirit, yea, the spirits' Lord, ruler of spirits, we address.
Together let all spirits meet: may these deliver us from woe.

22 The five Sky regions, Goddesses, and the twelve Seasons which are Gods,
The teeth of the completed year, may these deliver us from woe.

23 The deathless balm that Mâtalî knows, purchased at a chariot's price,
Indra effused into the floods. Waters, give us that healing balm!

HYMN VII.

The Residue of Sacrifice containeth name, and form, and world:
Indra and Agni and the whole universe are compris-ed therein.

2 The Residue of Sacrifice holdeth Earth, Heaven, and all that is:
The Residue of Sacrifice holdeth sea, waters, Moon, and Wind.

3 Real, non-real, both are there, Prajâpati, and Death, and strength:
Thereon depend the worldly ones: in me are glory, Dra and Vra.

---

21 *Spirits' Lord:* Bhûtapati; Lord of Creatures, especially of ghosts and evil spirits. The name is applied to Agni, Rudra, Bhava and Ṣarva.

23 *Mâtalî:* a divine being associated with Yama and the Fathers. Cf. X. 13. 3. The legend referred to cannot be traced.

The hymn is a glorification of the Uchchhishṭa or Residue of the Sacrifice.

1 *Name and form:* the connecting links between Brahman and the world. See X. 2. 12, note.

3 *Real, non-real:* 'both the existent and the non-existent.'—Muir. The participles are in the masculine gender. *Worldly ones:* meaning, apparently, all human beings. *Dra and Vra:* these words are absolutely meaningless, and probably corrupt. *In me:* that is, in the Residue: cf. stanza 14, line 2.

4 The firm, the fast, the strong, the hard, Brahma, the All-creating Ten,
Gods, as a wheel about the nave, are fixed all round the Residue.

5 Verse, Song, and Sacrificial Text, chanting, the prelude, and the laud,
The hum is in the Residue, the tone, the murmur of the psalm.

6 Within the Residue, like babes unborn, the parts of sacrifice,
Aindrâgna, Pâvamâna lie, Mahânâmnî, Mahâvrata.

7 The Vâjapeya, Royal Rite, the Agnishṭoma and its forms,
Hymns, joyfullest with living grass the Aṣvamedha, are therein.

---

4 *The All-creating Ten:* probably, as Muir suggests, the ten Maharshis or Great Ṛishis mentioned by Manu, I. 34 sqq., who are called Lords of living creatures. 'Reference to rishis or to seven rishis as "formers of existing things" (*bhûta-kṛitaḥ*), is also found in the Atharva-veda, VI. 108. 4; VI. 133. 4. 5; XI. 1. 1, 3, 24; XII. 1. 39; and the word *bhûtakṛitaḥ*, without the addition of rishis, is found in the same work iii. 28. 1; iv. 35. 2, and xix. 16. 2.'—O. S. Texts, I. p. 37.

5 *Verse, Song, and Sacrificial Text:* ṛich, sâman, and yâjus. *Chanting:* of the hymns of the Sâma-veda by the Udgâtar-priest. *The hum:* the sound *him*, or *hiṅg* in the chanting, commencing each Sâman.

6 *Aindrâgna:* the due of Indra and Agni. *Pâvamâna:* the due of Soma Pavamâna. *Mahânâmnî:* certain verses of the Sâma-veda. *Mahâvrata:* a ceremony forming part of a Sattra or year-long sacrificial Session.

7 *The Vâjapeya:* an important Soma sacrifice. *Royal rite:* the Râjasûya, a great sacrifice or religious ceremony performed at the coronation of a supreme sovereign or universal monarch by the king himself and his tributary princes. *Agnishṭoma:* a protracted ceremony or sacrifice (literally, Praise of Agni), extending over several days in spring, and forming an essential part of the Jyotishṭoma. *Aṣvamedha:* the Horse-Sacrifice. See Ṛ. V. I. 162 and 163.

8 Dîkshâ and Agnyâdheya, rite that sates the wish, with magic hymn,
Suspended rites, long sessions, are contained within the Residue.

9 Faith, fire-oblation, fervent zeal, service, and sacrificial cry,
Guerdon, good works and their reward, are stored within the Residue.

10 Sacrifice of one night, or two, Sadyaḥkrî, Ukthya, and Prakrî,
Call, deep-toned summons are therein, fine parts, through lore, of sacrifice.

11 Sacrifice of four nights, of five, of six nights, day and night conjoined,
Shoḍaṣî, seven-night sacrifice, all these sprang from the Residue, these which the Immortal One contains.

12 Pratîhâra and Nidhanam, the Viṣvajit, the Abhijit,
The two Sâhnâtirâtras and the Twelve-day rite are stored therein.

---

8 *Dîkshâ:* a ceremony preliminary to a sacrifice; an initiatory rite. See Aitareya Brâhmaṇa, I. 1. 1. *Agnyâdheya:* the ceremony of setting the fire on the sacrificial fire-place or ground prepared for its reception.

9 *Fire-oblation:* or, Agnihotra; a burnt oblation to Agni, chiefly of milk, oil, and sour gruel. *Sacrificial cry:* exclamation of Vashaṭ, when the offering is thrown into the fire. *Guerdon:* the Dakshiṇâ, or honorarium presented to the officiating priests. *Good works:* sacrifice. *Reward:* in heaven.

10 *Sadyaḥkrî:* the name of a certain Ekâha or one-day sacrifice, within which, by shortening the procedure, three several ceremonies are performed. *Ukthya:* a Soma sacrifice supplementary to, or a modification of, the Agnishṭoma. *Prakrî:* a sacrifice named, similarly to Sadyaḥkrî, from the purchase of Soma. *Call:* invocation.

11 *Shoḍaṣî:* a sacrifice almost identical with the Ukthya. See Aitareya Brâhmaṇa, IV. 1. 1.

12 *Pratîhâra:* the response in the Sâman, chanted by the Pratihartar priest who assists the Udgâtar. *Nidhanam:* the finale of the Sâman. *Viṣvajit:* (all-conquering) the name of an Ekâha or one-day sacrifice in the Gavâmayana ceremony. *Abhijit:* (victorious) an Ekâha in tch Gavâmayana, eight days before the Viṣvajit. *Sâhnâtirâtras:* certain ceremonies performed during a night and the following day.

13 Pleasantness, reverence, peace, and power, strength, vigour, immortality—
All forward wishes are with love satisfied in the Residue.

14 Nine several oceans, earths, and skies are set within the Residue.
Bright shines the Sun therein, in me, the Residue, are Day and Night.

15 The Residue, the Father's sire, who bears this universe, supports
Vishûvân, Upahavya, and all worship offered secretly.

16 The Father's sire, the Residue, grandson of Spirit, primal Sire,
Lord of the universe, the Bull, dwells on the earth victorious.

17 Right, truth, dominion, fervent zeal, toil, duty, action, future, past,
Valour, prosperity, and strength dwell in the Residue, in strength.

18 Welfare, resolve and energy, the six expanses, kingship, sway,
Prayer, and direction, and the year, oblation, planets, are therein;

19 And the four Hotars, Âprî hymns, the Nivids, and Four-monthly rites,
Oblations, sacrifices, and animal offerings, and their forms.

---

14 *Nine:* the usual number of three oceans of air, etc. multiplied by three.

15 *Vishûvân:* or Vishuvân; the day exactly in the middle of a Sattra or sacrificial session. *Upahavya:* oblation.

16 *The Bull:* the Mighty One.

18 *Six Expanses:* the four quarters of the sky with the spaces above and below. *Direction:* a liturgical order given during the performance of a sacrifice.

19 *Âprî hymns:* certain propitiatory hymns of the Rigveda addressed to Agni. *Nivids:* invocations of the Gods inserted in certain parts of the liturgy.

20 Months, half-months, sections of the year, seasons, are in the Residue,
The waters resonant afar, the thunder, and the mighty noise.

21 Pebbles, sand, stones, and herbs, and plants, and grass are in the Residue.
Closely embraced and laid therein are lightnings and the clouds and rain.

22 Gain, acquisition, and success, fulness, complete prosperity,
Great gain and wealth, are laid, concealed and treasured, in the Residue.

23 All things that breathe the breath of life, all creatures that have eyes to see,
All the celestial Gods whose home is heaven sprang from the Residue.

24 Verses, and songs, and magic hymns, Purâṇa, sacrificial text,
All the celestial Gods whose home is heaven sprang from the Residue.

25 Inbreath and outbreath, eye and ear, decay and freedom from decay,
All the celestial Gods whose home is heaven sprang from the Residue.

26 All pleasures and enjoyments, all delights and rapturous ecstasies,
All the celestial Gods whose home is heaven sprang from the Residue.

27 The Deities, the Fathers, men, Gandharvas, and Apsarases,
All the celestial Gods whose home is heaven sprang from the Residue.

---

24 *Verses and songs:* ṛichas and sâmans; hymns of the Ṛigveda and Sâmaveda. *Magic hymns:* like those of the Atharva-veda. *Purâṇa:* ancient legend. *Sacrificial text:* the Yajurveda.

The hymn has been translated, with the omission of some stanzas, by Muir, O. S. Texts, V. 396—398, and by Scherman, Philosophische Hymnen, p. 87.

HYMN VIII.

WHEN Manyu brought his consort home forth from Saṅkalpa's dwelling-place,
Who were the wooers of the bride, who was the chief who courted her?

2 Fervour and Action were the two, in depths of the great billowy sea:
These were the wooers of the bride; Brahma the chief who courted her.

3 Ten Gods before the Gods were born together in the ancient time.
Whoso may know them face to face may now pronounce the mighty word.

4 Inbreath and outbreath, eye and ear, decay and freedom from decay,
Spiration upward and diffused, voice, mind have brought us wish and plan.

5 As yet the Seasons were unborn, and Dhâtar and Prajâpati,
Both Aṣvins, Indra, Agni. Whom then did they worship as supreme?

6 Fervour and Action were the two, in depths of the great billowy sea;
Fervour sprang up from Action: this they served and worshipped as supreme.

7 He may account himself well versed in ancient time who knows by name
The earth that was before this earth, which only wisest Sages know.

Concerning the origin of some Gods and the creation of man.

1 *Manyu:* Ardour personified. *Saṅkalpa:* Resolution. *Wooers of the bride:* the bridegroom's friends who arranged the marriage, and took part in the ceremony as paranymphs or bridemen. *Chief:* or, first.

2 *Fervour:* *tápas*; religious devotion or austerity. *Action:* *kárma.* *Brahma:* here the Personal Deity.

3 *Ten Gods:* perhaps the 'All-creating Ten' mentioned in XI. 7. 4.

6 *Billowy sea:* the aerial ocean of watery cloud.

8 From whom did Indra spring? from whom sprang Soma? whence was Agni born?
From whom did Tvashṭar spring to life? and whence is Dhâtar's origin?

9 Indra from Indra, Soma from Soma, from Agni Agni sprang.
Tvashṭar from Tvashṭar was produced, Dhâtar was Dhâtar's origin.

10 Those Gods who were of old, the Ten begotten earlier than the Gods,
What world do they inhabit since they gave the world unto their sons?

11 When he had brought together hair, sinew and bone, marrow and flesh,
And to the body added feet, then to what world did he depart?

12 Whence, from what region did he bring the hair, the sinews, and the bones,
Marrow and limbs, and joints, and flesh? Who was the bringer, and from whence?

13 Casters, those Gods were called who brought together all the elements:
When they had fused the mortal man complete, they entered into him.

14 The thighs, the knee-bones, and the feet, the head, the face, and both the hands,
The ribs, the nipples, and the sides—what Ṛishi hath constructed that?

15 Head, both the hands, and face, and tongue, and neck, and intercostal parts,
All this, investing it with skins, Mahî conjoined with bond and tie.

---

10 *Unto their sons:* 'Thus by my appointment, and by the force of devotion, was all this world both motionless and moving created by those great beings [the ten Maharshis].'—Manu, I. 41. See Muir, O. S. Texts, I. p. 37.

11 *He:* the Creator.

15 *Mahî:* a Goddess usually associated with Iḍâ and Sarasvatî.

16 What time the mighty body lay firmly compact with tie and bond,
Who gave its colour to the form, the hue wherewith it shines to-day?

17 All Deities had lent their aid: of this a noble Dame took note,
Îṣâ, the Consort of Command. She gave its colour to the form.

18 When Tvashṭar, Tvashṭar's loftier Sire, had bored it out and hollowed it,
Gods made the mortal their abode, and entered and possessed the man.

19 Sleep, specially, Sloth, Nirṛiti, and deities whose name is Sin,
Baldness, old age, and hoary hairs within the body found their way.

20 Theft, evil-doing, and deceit, truth, sacrifice, exalted fame,
Strength, princely power, and energy entered the body as a home.

21 Prosperity and poverty, kindnesses and malignities,
Hunger and thirst of every kind entered the body as a home.

22 Reproaches, freedom from reproach, all blamable, all blameless deeds,
Bounty, belief, and unbelief entered the body as a home.

23 All knowledge and all ignorance, each other thing that one may learn,
Entered the body, prayer, and hymns, and songs, and sacrificial texts.

24 Enjoyments, pleasures, and delights, gladness, and rapturous ecstasies,

---

17 *Îṣâ:* Power or Faculty; a creative abstraction.

18 *Tvashṭar's loftier sire:* apparently, as Hillebrandt says, a mere abstraction (V. Mythologie, I. 528). Cf. stanza 9, line 2.

Laughter and merriment and dance entered the body as a home.

25 Discourse and conversation, and the shrill-resounding cries of woe,
All entered in, the motives and the purposes combined therewith.

26 Inbreath and outbreath, ear and eye, decay and freedom from decay,
Breath upward and diffused, voice, mind, these quickly with the body move.

27 All earnest wishes, all commands, directions, and admonishments,
Reflections, all deliberate plans entered the body as a home.

28 They laid in the abhorrent frame those waters hidden, bright, and thick,
Which in the bowels spring from blood, from mourning or from hasty toil.

29 Fuel they turned to bone, and then they set light waters in the frame.
The molten butter they made seed: then the Gods entered into man.

30 All Waters, all the Deities, Virâj with Brahma at her side:
Brahma into the body passed: Prajâpati is Lord thereof.

31 The Sun and Wind formed, separate, the eye and vital breath of man.
His other person have the Gods bestowed on Agni as a gift.

32 Therefore whoever knoweth man regardeth him as Brahma's self:
For all the Deities abide in him as cattle in their pen.

---

28 *Waters:* in the shape of tears and sweat.

30 *Brahma:* in line 1 the Personal Deity is probably understood.

32 Here there is a pantheistic identification of Purusha or Man with Brahma the Supreme Self or Soul.

33 At his first death he goeth hence, asunder, in three separate parts.
He goeth yonder with one part, with one he goeth yonder: here he sinketh downward with a third.

34 In the primeval waters cold the body is deposited.
In this there is the power of growth: from this is power of growth declared.

HYMN IX.

ALL arms and every arrow, all the power and might that bows possess,
The warlike weapon, axes, swords, the plan and purpose in the heart,
All this, O Arbudi, make thou visible to our enemies, and let them look on mist and fog.

2 Arise ye and prepare yourselves: ye, the celestial hosts, are friends.
Let your mysterious natures be seen by our friends, O Arbudi.

3 Rise both of you: begin your work with fettering and binding fast.
Assail, both of you, Arbudi, the armies of our enemies.

---

33 *Three separate parts:* one part goes to heaven, one to the sun and wind, and one to earth.

34 *The power of growth:* when, after decomposition, it has been changed into earth.

The hymn has been translated by Ludwig, Der Rigveda, III. p. 402. See also Muir, O. S. Texts, V. 387; and Scherman, Philosophische Hymnen, p. 67.

The hymn is an incantation for the defeat and destruction of a hostile army.

1 *Arms:* of the body. *Arbudi:* Arbuda was a serpentlike demon of the air, conquered by Indra (Ṛ. V. II. 11. 20; VIII. 3. 19); and Arbudi seems to have been originally a kindred being of similar nature and powers, but willing and able to assist those who invoke his aid. *Mist and fog:* which are under the control of the dragonish deity of air.

3 *Both of you:* Arbudi and Nyarbudi, a similar supernatural being.

4 The God whose name is Arbudi, and Nyarbudi the Mighty One,
The two by whom the air and this great earth are compassed and possessed,
With these two friends of Indra I go forth to conquer with the host.

5 Rise, with our army stand thou up, O Godlike Being, Arbudi.
Breaking the hosts of enemies, surround them with thy winding coils.

6 Exhibiting, O Arbudi, seven children of the mist and fog,
When butter hath been offered, rise with all of these and with the host.

7 Beating her breast, with tearful face, let the short-eared, the wild-haired hag
Shriek loudly when a man is slain, pierced through by thee, O Arbudi;

8 Snatching away the vertebra, while with her thought she seeks her son,
Her husband, brother, kin, when one, Arbudi! hath been pierced by thee.

9 Let vultures, ravens, kites, and crows, and every carrion-eating bird
Feast on our foes, and show where one, Arbudi! hath been pierced by thee.

10 Then let each greedy beast of prey, and fly and worm regale itself
Upon the human corpse where one, Arbudi, hath been pierced by thee.

11 Attack them, both of you; bear off their vital breath, O Nyarbudi.
Let mingled shouts and echoing cries of woe amid our foemen show where thou, O Arbudi, hast pierced.

12 Shake them, and let them sink with fear: o'erwhelm our enemies with dread.

With widely-grasping bends of arm, O Arbudi, crush down our foes.

13 Let those mens' arms grow faint and weak, dull be the purpose of their heart;
And let not aught of them be left when thou, O Arbudi, hast pierced.

14 Self-smiting, beating breast and thigh, careless of unguent, with their hair dishevelled, weeping, hags shall run together, when a man is slain, when thou, O Arbudi, hast pierced.

15 Apsarases with dog-like mates, and Rûpakâs, O Arbudi,
And her who licks the cup inside, and seeks to wound in ill-kept place,
All these, O Arbudi, do thou make visible to our enemies, and let them look on mists and fog.

16 The fiend who creeps upon the sword, maimed, dwelling where the wounded lie,
The misty shapes that lurk concealed, Gandharvas and Apsarases, demons, and snakes, and Other Folk;

17 Armed with four fangs and yellow teeth, deformed, with faces smeared with blood, the terrible and fearless ones,

18 Make thou, O Arbudi, those wings of hostile armies quake with dread.
Let Conqueror and Victor, friends of Indra, overcome our foes.

---

15 *With dog-like mates:* wedded to Gandharvas who are described as hairy like dogs and monkeys. See IV. 37. 11; XIX. 36. 6. *Rûpakâs;* appearing in agreeable forms. *The cup inside:* 'the interior of the body.'—Ludwig.

16 *Upon the sword:* the meaning of *khadûre* is uncertain. I adopt Ludwig's interpretation which seems plausible. *Other Folk;* a euphemistic expression for certain supernatural beings regarded as spirits of darkness. See VIII. 10. 28.

19 Stifled and crushed, O Nyarbudi, low let the smitten foeman lie.
With tongue of fire and crest of smoke go conquering maidens with our host!

20 May Indra, Lord of Might, strike down each bravest warrior of the foes
Whom this our band hath put to flight: let not one man of those escape.

21 Let their hearts burst asunder, let their breath fly up and pass away.
Let dryness of the mouth o'ertake our foemen, not the friendly ones.

22 The clever and the foolish ones, those who are twisted round, the deaf,
The dusky-hued, the hornless goats, and those whose voice is like the buck's,
All these, O Arbudi, do thou make visible to our enemies: cause them to look on mists and fog.

23 Arbudi and Trishandhi fall upon our foes and scatter them,
So that, O Indra, Lord of Might, Slayer of Vṛitra, we may kill thousands of these our enemies!

24 Tall trees, and those who live in woods, the herbs and creeping plants of Earth,
Gandharvas, and Apsarases, Snakes, Holy Beings, Fathers, Gods,
All these do thou, O Arbudi, make visible to our enemies: cause them to look on mists and fog.

25 High sway have Maruts, and the God Âditya, Brahmaṇaspati,
High sway have Indra, Agni, and Dhâtar, Mitra, Prajâpati,
High sway have Ṛishis given to you, showing upon our enemies where thou, O Arbudi, hast pierced.

---

23 *Trishandhi*: the name of a battle-loving demon. See the following hymn.

The hymn has been translated by Ludwig, Der Rigveda, III. p. 530.

26 With full dominion over these, rise, stand ye up, prepare yourselves.
Ye are our friends, celestial hosts. When ye have won this battle, go, each to his several sphere, apart.

HYMN X.

Rise up, with all your banners rise; prepare your strength, ye vapoury Forms!
Serpents and fiends and Other Folk, charge and pursue our enemies!

2 Let those who bear an evil name, in air, in heaven, on earth, and men,
After Trishandhi's will, revere your power, the sway that Knowledge gives, together with your ruddy flags.

3 Let those with iron faces, with faces like needles or like combs,
Flesh-eaters, rapid as the wind, cling closely to our foemen with Trishandhi for their thunderbolt.

4 Omniscient Âditya, make full many a corpse to disappear.
Let this devoted army of Trishandhi be in my control.

5 Rise up, O Godlike Being, rise, Arbudi, with thine army: this
Tribute is sacrificed to thee, Trishandhi's welcome offering.

The hymn is an incantation for the destruction of the enemy.

1 *Vapoury Forms:* or Mists and Fogs, personified. Cf. XI. 9. 1. *Other Folk:* spirits of darkness. See XI. 9. 16, note.

2 *Trishandhi:* literally, composed of three parts or members; a personification of an arrow consisting of shaft, steel, and point (see Aitareya Brâhmaṇa, I. 25), and regarded as a warlike Power associated with Arbudi.

6 May this four-footed White-foot, may this arrow brace and bind thee fast:
Together with Trishandhi's host, be thou, O Witchcraft, meant for foes.

7 Down let the dim-eyed demon fly, and let her short-eared sister shriek:
Red be the banners when the host of Arbudi hath won the day.

8 Let all the birds that move on wings come downward, all fowls that roam the heavens and air's mid-region.
Let beasts of prey and flies attack, and vultures that eat raw flesh mangle and gnaw the carcase.

9 By that same binding treaty which thou madest, Bṛihaspati! with Indra and with Brahma,
By Indra's pledge I bid the Gods come hither. Conquer on this side, not on their side yonder.

10 Bṛihaspati Ângirasa, Ṛishis made strong and keen by prayer
Have set Trishandhi in the heaven, dire weapon that destroys the fiends.

11 The Gods enjoyed Trishandhi for the sake of energy and power,
Him under whose protection, both, Indra and yon Âditya, stand.

12 The Gods, victorious, won themselves all worlds by this oblation, which
Bṛihaspati Ângirasa effused, a very thunderbolt, a weapon to destroy the fiends.

13 That fiend-destroying weapon which Bṛihaspati Ângirasa poured out and made a thunderbolt,

---

6 *Four-footed White-foot:* the personified arrow, consisting of shaft, steel, point, and feathers, (Aitareya Brâhmaṇa, I. 25) with a white foot or notch.

10 *Angirasa:* descendant of, or devoted to the ancient sage Angiras and his family; a common epithet of Bṛihaspati, the type of the priesthood.

11 *Yon Âditya:* the Sun.

Even therewith, Bṛihaspati, I brush that hostile armament, and strike the foemen down with might.

14 Over to us come all the Gods who eat the hallowed sacrifice.
With this oblation be ye pleased: conquer on this side, not on that.

15 Over to us let all Gods come: dear is Trishandhi's offering.
Keep the great pledge through which, of old, the Asuras were overthrown.

16 Let Vâyu bend the arrow-points of those who are our enemies.
Let Indra break their arms away: no power to lay the shaft be theirs!
Âditya utterly destroy their missile! Chandramâs bar the path of him who lingers!

17 If they have issued forth strongholds of Gods, and made their shields of prayer,
Gaining protection for their lives, protection round about, make all their instigation powerless.

18 With the Flesh-eater and with Death, following the Purohita,
On! forward with Trishandhi's host! conquering enemies advance!

19 Do thou, Trishandhi, with the gloom of darkness compass round our foes;
Let none escape of them expelled with speckled butter mixt with curds.

20 Let White-foot fall upon those wings of our opponents' armament;

---

17 The stanza is repeated from V. 8. 6.

18 *The Flesh-eater:* Agni in his most terrible form as the fire of the funeral pile. See III. 21. 9. *The Purohita:* Bṛihaspati, Priest of the Gods.

19 *Speckled butter mixt with curds:* the oblation called Pṛishadâjyá. See XIX. 6. 14.

20 *White-foot:* the arrow. See stanza 6.

The hymn has been translated by Ludwig, Der Rigveda, III. p. 531.

Mazed and bewildered be those bands of foes this day, O Nyarbudi.

21 Mazed are the foemen, Nyarbudi! Slay thou each bravest man of them: with this our army slaughter them.

22 Low lie the warrior, mailed, unmailed, each foeman in the rush of war,
Down-smitten with the strings of bows, the fastenings of mail, the charge!

23 The armour-clad, the armourless, enemies clothed with coats of mail,
All these struck down, O Arbudi, let dogs devour upon the earth.

24 Car-borne and carless fighting men, riders and those who go on foot,
All these, struck down, let vultures, kites, and all the birds of air devour.

25 Low let the hostile army lie, thousands of corpses, on the ground,
Pierced through and rent to pieces where the deadly weapons clash in fight.

26 With eagles let them eat the evil-hearted, pierced in the vitals, lying crushed and howling,
The foe whoe'er will fight against this our protecting sacrifice.

27 With this which Gods attend, with this which never fails to gain its end,
Let Indra, Vritra-slayer, smite, and with Trishandhi as a bolt.

BOOK XII.

HYMN I.

TRUTH, high and potent Law, the Consecrating Rite,
Fervour, Brahma, and Sacrifice uphold the Earth.
May she, the Queen of all that is and is to be, may
Pṛithivî make ample space and room for us.

2 Not over-crowded by the crowd of Manu's sons, she
who hath many heights and floods and level plains;
She who bears plants endowed with many varied powers,
may Pṛithivî for us spread wide and favour us.

3 In whom the sea, and Sindhu, and the waters, in
whom our food and corn-lands had their being,
In whom this all that breathes and moves is active,
this Earth assign us foremost rank and station!

4 She who is Lady of the earth's four regions, in whom
our food and corn-lands had their being,
Nurse in each place of breathing, moving creatures,
this Earth vouchsafe us kine with milk that fails
not!

5 On whom the men of old before us battled, on whom
the Gods attacked the hostile demons,
The varied home of bird, and kine and horses, this
Pṛithivî vouchsafe us luck and splendour!

A hymn of praise and prayer to Pṛithivî or deified Earth.

1 *Law:* the established Order of the universe. *Consecrating Rite:* *dîkshâ*; for details of this ceremony see Aitareya Brâhmaṇa, I. 1. 3. *Pṛithivî:* literally, the wide, the extended.

2 *Manu's sons:* human beings, descendants of Manu, primeval Man, the Old German Mannus.

3 *Sindhu:* the Indus. Greek 'Ινδός; from the Iranian Hindu. 'Indus incolis Sindus appellatus' (Pliny, Hist. Nat. 6. 20. 71).

6 Firm standing-place, all-bearing, store of treasures, gold-breasted, harbourer of all that moveth,
May Earth who bears Agni Vaiśvânara, Consort of mighty Indra, give us great possessions.

7 May Earth, may Pṛithivî, always protected with ceaseless care by Gods who never slumber,
May she pour out for us delicious nectar, may she bedew us with a flood of splendour.

8 She who at first was water in the ocean, whom with their wondrous powers the sages followed,
May she whose heart is in the highest heaven, compassed about with truth, and everlasting,
May she, this Earth, bestow upon us lustre, and grant us power in loftiest dominion.

9 On whom the running universal waters flow day and night with never-ceasing motion,
May she with many streams pour milk to feed us, may she bedew us with a flood of splendour.

10 She whom the Aśvins measured out, o'er whom the foot of Vishṇu strode,
Whom Indra, Lord of Power and Might, freed from all foemen for himself,
May Earth pour out her milk for us, a mother unto me her son.

11 O Pṛithivî, auspicious be thy woodlands, auspicious be thy hills and snow-clad mountains.

---

8 *Water in the ocean:* cf. 'heavenly Floods, first-born by holy Order (Ṛ. V. X. 109. 1). 'In the beginning waters alone formed this universe' (Śatapatha-Brâhmaṇa, XIV. 8. 6. 1); 'And the earth was without form and void . . . . And the Spirit of God moved upon the face of the waters' (Genesis, I. 2).

10 *Whom the Aśvins measured out:* the formation or manifestation by light, of heaven and earth is ascribed to the Aśvins in Ṛ. V. X. 24. 5, 6. *The foot of Vishṇu:* when, as the Sun, he made the first of his three strides through the three worlds.

11 *Every-coloured:* 'with the variation of each soil.'

Unslain, unwounded, unsubdued, I have set foot upon the Earth,
On earth, brown, black, ruddy and every-coloured, on the firm earth that Indra guards from danger.

12 O Pṛithivî, thy centre and thy navel, all forces that have issued from thy body—
Set us amid those forces; breathe upon us. I am the son of Earth, Earth is my Mother. Parjanya is my Sire; may he promote me.

13 Earth on whose surface they enclose the altar, and all-performers spin the thread of worship;
In whom the stakes of sacrifice, resplendent, are fixed and raised on high before the oblation, may she, this Earth, prospering, make us prosper.

14 The man who hates us, Earth! who fights against us, who threaten us with thought or deadly weapon, make him our thrall as thou hast done aforetime.

15 Produced from thee, on thee move mortal creatures: thou bearest them, both quadruped and biped.
Thine, Pṛithivî, are these Five human Races, for whom, though mortal, Sûrya as he rises spreads with his rays the light that is immortal.

16 In concert may these creatures yield us blessings. With honey of discourse, O Earth, endow me.

17 Kind, ever gracious be the Earth we tread on, the firm Earth, Pṛithivî, borne up by Order, mother of plants and herbs, the all-producer.

18 A vast abode hast thou become, the Mighty. Great stress is on thee, press and agitation, but with unceasing care great Indra guards thee.
So make us shine, O Earth, us with the splendour of gold. Let no man look on us with hatred.

---

12 *Parjanya:* see M. Müller, India, What can it Teach us? p. 183.

15 *Five human Races:* the Five Tribes, frequently mentioned in the hymns of the Rigveda and Atharva-veda. See III. 21. 5; 24. 3; IV. 23. 1; V. 17. 9; VI. 75. 3; VIII. 6. 1.

19 Agni is in the earth, in plants; the waters hold Agni in them, in the stones is Agni.
Agni abideth deep in men: Agnis abide in cows and steeds.

20 Agni gives shine and heat in heaven: the spacious air is his, the God's.
Lover of fatness, bearer of oblation, men enkindle him.

21 Dark-kneed, invested with a fiery mantle, Pṛithivî sharpen me and give me splendour!

22 On earth they offer sacrifice and dressed oblation to the Gods. Men, mortals, live upon the earth by food in their accustomed way.
May that Earth grant us breath and vital power. Pṛithivî give me life of long duration!

23 Scent that hath risen from thee, O Earth, the fragrance which growing herbs and plants and waters carry,
Shared by Apsarases, shared by Gandharvas, therewith make thou me sweet: let no man hate me.

24 Thy scent which entered and possessed the lotus, the scent which they prepared at Sûryâ's bridal,
Scent which Immortals, Earth! of old collected, therewith make thou me sweet: let no man hate me.

25 Thy scent in women and in men, the luck and light that is in males,
That is in heroes and in steeds in sylvan beasts and elephants,

---

19 *Cf.* III. 21. 1, 2, and note.

23 *Scent that hath risen from thee:* a philosophical definition of earth is *gandhavatî*, she who is endowed with fragrance or odour, which is regarded as its peculiar characteristic as *rasa*, taste, is of water. *Apsarases:* the names of the Apsarases in IV. 37. 3 are all derived from fragrant plants or sweet scents. *Gandharvas:* their name being fancifully derived from *gandha*, scent.

24 *Sûryâ's bridal:* the typical marriage ceremony. See XIV. 1. 6 sqq.

25 *Of maids;* cf. X. 3. 20.

The splendid energy of maids, therewith do thou unite us, Earth! Let no man look on us with hate.

26 Rock, earth, and stone, and dust, this Earth is held together, firmly bound.
To this gold-breasted Pṛithivî mine adoration have I paid.

27 Hither we call the firmly held, the all-supporting Pṛithivî,
On whom the trees, lords of the wood, stand evermore immovable.

28 Sitting at ease or rising up, standing or going on our way,
With our right foot and with our left we will not reel upon the earth.

29 I speak to Pṛithivî the purifier, to patient Earth who groweth strong through Brahma.
O Earth, may we recline on thee who bearest strength, increase, portioned share of food, and fatness.

30 Purified for our bodies flow the waters: we bring distress on him who would attack us.
I cleanse myself, O Earth, with that which cleanseth.

31 Earth, be thine eastern and thy northern regions, those lying southward and those lying westward,
Propitious unto me in all my movements. Long as I tread the ground let me not stumble.

32 Drive us not from the west or east, drive us not from the north or south.
Be gracious unto us, O Earth: let not the robbers find us; keep the deadly weapon far away.

---

30 *Him who would attack us:* the meaning of *syéduḥ* is uncertain. I follow Ludwig's interpretation of the word which according to the S. P. Dictionary probably means slime: 'our slime (the dirt on our bodies) in place unwelcome we deposit.'

31 *Let me not stumble:* cf. stanza 28.

33 Long as, on thee, I look around, possessing Sûrya as a friend,
So long, through each succeeding year, let not my power of vision fail.

34 When, as I lie, O Earth, I turn upon my right side and my left,
When stretched at all our length we lay our ribs on thee who meetest us,
Do us no injury there, O Earth who furnishest a bed for all.

35 Let what I dig from thee, O Earth, rapidly spring and grow again.
O Purifier, let me not pierce through thy vitals or thy heart.

36 Earth, may thy summer, and thy rains, and autumn, thy winter, and thy dewy frosts, and spring-time,
May thy years, Pṛithivî! and ordered seasons, and day and night pour out for us abundance.

37 The purifier, shrinking from the Serpent, she who held fires that lie within the waters,
Who gives as prey the God-blaspheming Dasyus, Earth choosing Indra for her Lord, not Vṛitra, hath clung to Ṣakra, to the Strong and Mighty.

38 Base of the seat and sheds, on whom the sacrificial stake is reared,
On whom the Yajus-knowing priests recite their hymns and chant their psalms,
And ministers are busied that Indra may drink the Soma juice;

---

37 *The Serpent:* the dragon Vṛitra, the malevolent demon who obstructs the rain. *Ṣakra:* the Mighty One; Indra.

38 *Base of the seat and sheds:* the *seat* is the lodge or place of the Soma, erected in the sacrificial enclosure near the Agnîdhrîya hearth; and the two *sheds* or *havirdhânas* shelter the Soma carts and sacrificial offerings. See plan of the sacrificial enclosure in Vol. I. of Haug's Aitareya Brâhmaṇa, or in Mrs. Manning's Ancient and Mediæval

39 On whom the ancient Ṛishis, they who made the world, sang forth the cows,
Seven worshippers, by session, with their fervent zeal and sacrifice;

40 May she, the Earth, assign to us the opulence for which we yearn.
May Bhaga share and aid the task and Indra come to lead the way.

41 May she, the Earth, whereon men sing and dance with varied shout and noise,
Whereon men meet in battle, and the war-cry and the drum resound,
May she drive off our foemen, may Pṛithivî rid me of my foes.

42 On whom is food, barley and rice, to whom these Races Five belong,
Homage to her, Parjanya's wife, to her whose marrow is the rain!

43 Whose castles are the work of Gods, and men wage war upon her plain—
The Lord of Life make Pṛithivî, who beareth all things in her womb, pleasant to us on every side!

44 May Earth the Goddess, she who bears her treasure stored up in many a place, gold, gems, and riches,

---

India, Vol. I. p. 89. *Sacrificial stake:* or Yûpa, erected close to the eastern gate of the enclosure, just beyond the Uttarâ Vedi. It is a lofty post of Khadira, Bilva, or Palâśa wood, anointed with clarified butter, adorned with ribbons, and surmounted by a flag. It is then deified and regarded as a form of Agni. See the hymn addressed to the Sacrificial Post, Ṛ. V. III. 8.

39 *They who made the world:* see XI. 7. 4, note. *Sang forth the cows:* called forth by the power of their hymns the heavenly cows or beams of light that had been imprisoned in the massive cloud by the demon of darkness. *By session:* with long-continued sacrifice.

42 *Races Five:* see III. 25. 5, note. *Parjanya's wife:* wedded to, and impregnated by, the God of the Rain-cloud. See M. M., India, What can it Teach us? p. 183.

Giver of opulence, grant great possessions to us bestowing them with love and favour.

45 Earth, bearing folk of many a varied language with divers rites as suits their dwelling-places,
Pour, like a constant cow that never faileth, a thousand streams of treasure to enrich me!

46 Thy snake, thy sharply-stinging scorpion, lying concealed, bewildered, chilled with cold of winter,
The worm, O Pṛithivî, each thing that in the Rains revives and stirs,
Creeping, forbear to creep on us! With all things gracious bless thou us.

47 Thy many ways on which the people travel, the road for car and wain to journey over,
Thereon meet both the good and bad, that pathway may we attain without a foe or robber. With all things gracious bless thou us.

48 Supporting both the foolish and the weighty she bears the death both of the good and evil.
In friendly concord with the boar, Earth opens herself for the wild swine that roams the forest.

49 All sylvan beasts of thine that love the woodlands, man-eaters, forest-haunting, lions, tigers,
Hyena, wolf, Misfortune, evil spirit, drive from us, chase the demons to a distance.

50 Gandharvas and Apsarases, Kimîdins, and malignant sprites,
Piṣâchas all, and Râkshasas, these keep thou, Earth! afar from us.

51 To whom the wingèd bipeds fly together, birds of each various kind, the swans, the eagles;
On whom the Wind comes rushing, Mâtariṣvan, rousing the dust and causing trees to tremble, and flame pursues the blast hither and thither;

52 Earth, upon whom are settled, joined together, the night and day, the dusky and the ruddy, Pṛithivî compassed by the rain about her,

Happily may she stablish us in each delightful dwelling place.

53 Heaven, Earth, the realm of Middle Air have granted me this ample room,
Agni, Sun, Waters, all the Gods have joined to give me mental power.

54 I am victorious, I am called the lord superior on earth,
Triumphant, all-o'erpowering, the conqueror on every side.

55 There, when the Gods, O Goddess, named thee, spreading thy wide expanse as thou wast broadening eastward,
Then into thee passed many a charm and glory: thou madest for thyself the world's four regions.

56 In hamlets and in woodland, and in all assemblages on earth,
In gatherings, meetings of the folk, we will speak glorious things of thee.

57 As the horse scattereth the dust, the people who dwelt upon the land, at birth, she scattered,
Leader and head of all the world, delightful, the trees' protectress and the plants' upholder.

58 Whate'er I say I speak with honey-sweetness, whatever I behold for that they love me.
Dazzling, impetuous am I: others who fiercely stir I slay.

59 Mild, gracious, sweetly odorous, milky, with nectar in her breast,
May Earth, may Pṛithivî bestow her benison, with milk, on me.

60 Whom Viṣvakarman with oblation followed, when she was set in mid-air's billowy ocean—

---

60 *Viṣvakarman:* the Omnific; the Architect of the Universe, resembling Prajâpati and often not distinguished from him. *Those with mothers:* all living creatures.

A useful vessel, hid, when, for enjoyment, she was made manifest to those with mothers.

61 Thou art the vessel that containeth people, Aditi, granter of the wish, far-spreading.

Prajâpati, the first-born Son of Order, supplieth thee with whatsoe'er thou lackest.

62 Let thy breasts, free from sickness and Consumption, be, Pṛithivî, produced for our advantage.

Through long-extended life wakeful and watching still may we be thy tributary servants.

63 O Earth, my Mother, set thou me happily in a place secure.

Of one accord with Heaven, O Sage, set me in glory and in wealth.

HYMN II.

This is no place to hold thee; mount the Naḍa: this lead is thine appointed share. Come hither.

Together with Consumption in the cattle, Consumption in our men, go hence, go southward.

2 With this we chase and banish all consumptive malady and Death,

With sinner and malicious man, with helper and with minister.

---

61 *Aditi*: here meaning Pṛithivî or Earth.

The hymn has been translated by Ludwig, Der Rigveda, III. p. 544.

A composite funeral hymn and deprecation of Agni Kravyâd or the fire that consumes the bodies of the dead.

1 *Thee*: Agni of the funeral pile whose task is finished. *The Naḍa*: literally, the reed; a name of the Anvâhâryapachanâgni or fire used for cooking the monthly Srâddha or commemorative repast in honour of the Manes or spirits of the Departed. See Sacred Books of the East, XII. p. 338 (Ṣatapatha-Brâhmaṇa II. 3. 2). *Lead*: used in incantations as a charm to drive away malevolent spirits. See I. 16. 2; XIX. 20. 52. *Southward*: to the home of Yama and the Departed in the southern region.

2 *With this*: by the power of this charm.

3 Death and Misfortune we expel, Malignity we drive away.
O Agni, thou who eatest not the corpse, eat him who hateth us: him whom we hate we send to thee.

4 If the corpse-eating Agni, or a tiger leaving his lair, hath entered this our homestead,
With beans prepared in butter I expel him: far let him go to fires that lie in waters.

5 When, angered that a man hath died, we in our wrath have banished thee,
That deed is easily set right through thee: we kindle thee again.

6 Again have the Âdityas, Rudras, Vasus, the Brahman, bringer of good things, O Agni,
Again hath Brahmaṇaspati disposed thee for long life lasting through a hundred autumns.

7 I sweep afar, for sacrifice to Fathers, corpse-eating Agni who hath come among us
Although he saw this other, Jâtavedas: in loftiest space let him inflame the caldron.

8 I drive corpse-eating Agni to a distance: sin-laden let him go to Yama's vassals.
Here let this other, Jâtavedas, carry oblation to the Deities, foreknowing.

9 I quickly sweep away corpse-eating Agni, Death, with his bolt depriving men of motion.
From household fire, well-knowing, I divide him: so in the world of Fathers be his portion.

10 Corpse-eating Agni, toil-worn, meet for praises, I send away by paths used by the Fathers.
Stay there; keep watch among the Fathers: come not again to us by ways whereon Gods travel.

---

3 *Who eatest not the corpse: akravyâd:* Agni in his friendly form as distinguished from the terrible fire of the funeral pile.

7 *For sacrifice to Fathers:* cf. stanza 1. *This other, Jâtavedas:* the ordinary sacrificial and domestic fire.

8 *Yama's vassals:* the Departed.

11 They being cleansed and bright, the purifiers, kindle Saṅkasuka for our well-being.
Impurity leaveth us and sin departeth: lighted by the good cleanser Agni cleanseth.

12 Agni the God, the Breaker-up, hath mounted to the heights of heaven.
Released from all transgression, he hath from the curse delivered us.

13 On Agni here, the Breaker-up, we wipe impurities away.
Cleansed, fit for sacrifice have we become: may he prolong our lives.

14 The Breaker-up, the Burster, the Destroyer, and the Silent One,
These have expelled Consumption far, far off from thee and all thou hast.

15 Corpse-eating Agni we expel, the Agni who bewilders men,
Him who is in our horses, in our heroes, cows, and goats, and sheep:

16 We drive thee forth to other folk, to alien cattle, alien steeds,
Thee the corpse-eating Agni, thee the Agni who bewilders men.

17 Whereon the Deities, whereon men too have purified themselves,
Exalting fatness, cleanse thyself, Agni, therein and mount to heaven.

18 O Agni, kindled and adored, turn not away to visit us.
Shine brightly even there in heaven, so that we long may see the Sun.

---

11 *Saṅkasuka:* the breaker-up and destroyer (of corpses); the funeral fire.

14 The four names are euphemistic expressions denoting the dreaded fire.

19 Wipe all away on lead and reed, on Agni, him who breaketh up,
Then on a black-hued sheep, and on a cushion pain that racks the head.

20 Wipe off pollution, lay it in the lead and in the black-hued sheep,
And headache in the cushion; then be cleansed and fit to sacrifice.

21 Go onward, Death, pursue thy special pathway apart from that which Gods are wont to travel.
To thee I say it who hast eyes and hearest: great grow the number of these men around us!

22 Divided from the dead are these, the living: now is our calling on the Gods successful.
We have gone forth for dancing and for laughter: may we with brave sons speak to the assembly.

23 Here I erect this rampart for the living: let none of these, none other, reach this limit.
May they survive a hundred lengthened autumns, and may they bury Death beneath this mountain.

---

19 *Lead:* cf. stanza 1. *Reed:* that is, in the fire called Naḍa (reed) in stanza 1.

21 This stanza, taken with the last pâda varied from Ṛ. V. X. 18. 1, is recited with the two following stanzas when the burial of the remains of the cremated corpse has been completed, and the log separating the dead from the living (stanza 23) has been laid down. *Death:* Mṛityu, the God of Death; distinct from Yama the Regent of the Departed.

22 Taken, with the last pâda varied, from Ṛ. V. X. 18. 3. *We have gone forth:* from the burial-ground after completion of our duties there. *For dancing and for laughter:* to return to our usual joyous life. So, with us, after a military funeral, the band returns playing lively airs.

23 Taken from Ṛ. V. X. 18. 4. *This rampart:* represented by a log of wood and a stone deposited by the Adhvaryu as a line of demarcation between the dead and the living, limiting, as it were, the jurisdiction of Death until the natural time for his approach. *This mountain:* represented by the stone, or by a newly-raised mound of earth.

24 Live your full lives and find old age delightful, all of you striving, one behind the other.
May Tvashṭar, maker of fair things, be gracious, and lead your whole lives on to full existence.

25 As the days follow days in close succession, as with the seasons duly come the seasons,
As each successor fails not his foregoer, so constitute the lives of these, Ordainer!

26 Gather your strength, my friends; the stream flows stony: acquit yourselves as men, and cross the river.
Abandon here the powers that were malignant, and let us cross to powers exempt from sickness.

27 Rise up erect, cross over, my companions: the stream is stony that flows here before us.
Abandon here the powers that were ungracious, and let us cross to powers benign and friendly.

28 Becoming pure and bright and purifying begin the Vaiṣvadevî strain for splendour.
May we rejoice, o'erpassing troublous places, with all our heroes through a hundred winters.

29 On pathways swept by wind, directed upward, passing beyond the lower, on the higher,
Thrice seven times have the Ṛishis, the Departed, forced Mṛityu backward with the fastened fetter.

---

24 Taken from Ṛ. V. X. 18. 5. *One behind the other:* in natural order, the oldest first reaching the end of the journey of life.

25 Taken from Ṛ. V. X. 18. 5. *So constitute:* that they may pass away in due order of seniority. *Ordainer:* a Divine Being, the arranger, maintainer, and manager of all things He is associated with Tvashṭar and Prajâpati, and sometimes identified with the latter.

26 Taken from Ṛ. V. X. 53. 8. This stanza and that which follows it appear to be out of place here. Taken literally, they are words of encouragement to the bearers who with the funeral procession are crossing a stream. But, according to stanza 23, the funeral ceremony in the burial-ground has already been completed by laying down the log and stone to form a rampart or boundary.

28 *The Vaiṣvadevî strain:* a sacred verse addressed to all the Gods or to the Viṣve Devas.

29 *Fetter:* see V. 19. 12, note.

30 Effacing Mṛityu's footstep ye came hither, to further times prolonging your existence.
Seated, drive Mṛityu to his proper dwelling: then may we, living, speak to the assembly.

31 Let these unwidowed dames with goodly husbands adorn themselves with fragrant balm and unguent.
Decked with fair jewels, tearless, sound and healthy, first let the dames go up to where he lieth.

32 I with oblation separate both classes, and with my prayer dispart their several portions.
I offer food that wastes not to the Fathers, and to these men give life of long duration.

33 That Agni, Fathers! who, himself immortal, hath entered and possessed our mortal bosoms,
Even him I grasp and hold the God within me. Let him not hate us, may we never hate him.

34 When ye have left the household fire, with the Corpse-eater southward go.
Do that which is delightful to the Fathers, Brahmans, and yourselves.

35 Agni, the banqueter on flesh, not banished, for the eldest son
Taketh a double share of wealth and spoileth it with poverty.

36 What man acquires by plough, by war, all that he wins by toil of hand,
He loses all if Agni the Carnivorous be not set aside.

---

30 The first line is taken from Ṛ. V. X. 18. 2. *Effacing Mrityu's footstep:* preventing the premature return of the God of Death. 'Avoiding the path of Death.'—Wilson; 'That your way may avoid the house of Death.'—Max Müller. Cf. A. V. 19. 12, note.

31 Taken from Ṛ. V. X. 18. 7. *He:* the corpse.

32 *Both classes:* the Fathers or Manes and the living mourners.

34 *Southward:* to the realm of Yama and the Departed. Cf. stanza1.

35 The meaning seems to be, that if the rites are not duly performed the eldest son of the departed, though he receives a double share of the property, will be eventually ruined.

37 Unholy, splendour-reft is he, his sacrifice unfit to eat.
Kravyâd deprives of tilth, of cow, of riches him whom he pursues.

38 Oft as a greedy beggar speaks the mortal who has brought distress,
Those whom Carnivorous Agni close at hand runs after and detects.

39 When a dame's husband dies the house is tangled fast in Grâhi's net.
A learned Brahman must be sought to drive Carnivorous Agni forth.

40 From any evil we have done, act of impurity or sin,
Let waters purge me and from all that comes from Agni Breaker-up.

41 By pathways travelled by the Gods these waters, well-knowing, from below have mounted upward.
High on the summit of the raining mountain the ancient rivers fresh and new are flowing.

42 Drive off Carnivorous Agni, thou Agni who eatest not the flesh; carry oblation paid to Gods.

43 The Flesh-eater hath entered him: he hath pursued the Flesh-eater.
Making two tigers different-wise, I bear away the ungracious one.

44 He who holds Gods within himself, the rampart and defence of men,
Agni, the sacred household fire, hath come and stands between them both.

---

38 *Brought distress:* on his family, by omitting to perform the necessary rites.

40 *From all:* defilement.

42 *Who eatest not the flesh:* or, the corpse. Cf. stanza 3, note.

43 *Him:* the dead man. *Two tigers:* the sacrificial and the funeral fire.

44 *Them both:* Agni Gârhapatya or the Householder's Fire stands between the sacrificial fire and Agni Kravyâd.

45 Prolong the lives of those who live, O Agni. Let the dead go unto the world of Fathers.
As goodly household fire burn up Arâti; give this man dawn brighter than all the mornings.

46 Subduing all our adversaries, Agni, give us their food, their strength and their possessions.

47 Grasp ye this Indra, furtherer, satisfier: he will release you from disgrace and trouble.
With him drive back the shaft that flies against you, with him ward off the missile shot by Rudra.

48 Seize with firm hold the Ox who boundeth forward: he will uplift you from disgrace and trouble.
Enter this ship of Savitar: let us flee from poverty over all the six expanses.

49 Thou followest the day and night, supporting, standing, at peace, promoting, rich in heroes.
Long, bearing undiseased and happy sleepers, be ours, O Bed, with smell of man about thee.

50 They sever from the Gods, they live in sin and misery evermore,
Those whom from very near at hand Carnivorous Agni casteth down as a horse tramples down the reeds.

51 The faithless, who from lust of wealth abide with him who feeds on flesh,
For ever set upon the fire an alien caldron, not their own.

---

45 *Arâti*: Malignity personified.

48 *The Ox*: Indra. *Ship of Savitar*: sacrifice to that God. Cf. 'Bhaga's ship' (II. 36. 5.)

49 Addressed to the Bed. *Followest day and night*: art idle during the day and occupied at night. The stanza is out of place.

51 *Abide with him who feeds on flesh*: get their living by officiating at the cremation of corpses.

52 Forward in spirit would he fly, and often turns he back again,
Whomso Carnivorous Agni from anear discovers and torments.

53 Among tame beasts the black ewe is thy portion, and the bright lead is thine, they say, Flesh-eater!
Mashed beans have been assigned thee for oblation: go, seek the dark wood and the wildernesses.

54 I sought the rustling sugar-cane, white Sesamum, and cane and reed,
I made this Indra's fuel, and the Fire of Yama I removed.

55 Against the sinking western Sun I set them; each sundered path, knowing my way, I entered.
I have warned off the ghosts of the Departed: to these I give the boon of long existence.

HYMN III.

Mount, male from male, the skin. Go thither: summon those whom thou lovest, one and all, to meet thee.
Strong as ye were when first ye met each other, still be your strength the same in Yama's kingdom.

---

54 *Fire of Yama:* fire of the funeral pile.

55 *Sinking western Sun:* regarded as a type of Yama.

The hymn has been translated by Ludwig, Der Rigveda, III. p. 479.

The hymn is an accompaniment to the preparation and presentation of sacrificial offerings to the Gods by a householder and his wife, with prayer for prosperity and happiness on earth and in heaven.

1 *Male from male:* Aṣvattha (Ficus Religiosa) with a masculine name, that has grown on a Khadira (Acacia Catechu) which is also a masculine word; its somewhat unusual birth increasing the magical virtue of the holy wood. Cf. III. 6. 1, note. Here, as in Ṛ. V. I. 135. 8, the vessel for holding the Soma juice, made of the wood of this Asvattha, is intended. *The skin:* of a black antelope. See XI. 1. 8. *Go thither:* the householder who institutes the sacrifice is addressed. The first ten stanzas are recited by the officiating priest.

2 So strong your sight, so many be your powers, so great your force, your energies so many.
When fire attends the body as its fuel, then may ye gain full chargers, O ye couple.

3 Together in this world, in God-ward pathway, together be ye in the realms of Yama.
Invite, made pure with means of purifying, whatever seed of yours hath been developed.

4 Do ye, O sons, unite you with the waters, meeting this living man, ye life-sustainers.
Allot to them the Odana your mother is making ready, which they call immortal.

5 That which your mother and your sire, to banish sin and uncleanness from their lips, are cooking,
That Odana with hundred streams, sky-reaching, hath in its might pervaded earth and heaven.

6 Live with your sons, when life on earth is ended, live in the sphere most rich in light and sweetness.
In skies that have been won by sacrificers make both the worlds, earth, heaven, your habitation.

7 Approach the eastern, yea, the eastern region: this is the sphere to which the faithful turn them.
Your cooked oblation that in fire was offered, together, wife and husband, meet to guard it.

---

2 *Gain full chargers*: meet your oblation in heaven, and be rewarded for the pious offerings which you are now preparing.

3 *In God-ward pathway*: on your journey to heaven.

4 *Allot to them*: allow the sacrificial waters to share the task of preparing the oblation of mashed rice.

7 The couple walk round the Soma vessel, beginning on the east side and moving round from left to right. See Sacred Books of the East, XII. p. 37, note. *To which the faithful turn them*: 'For the east is the quarter of the gods, and from the east westwards the gods approach men: that is why one offers to them while standing with his face towards the east' (Ṣatapatha-Brâhmaṇa, III. 1. 1. 7; S. B. of the East, XXVI. 3).

8 Now, as your steps approach the southern quarter, move in your circling course about this vessel.
Herein, accordant with the Fathers, Yama shall mightily protect your cooked oblation.

9 Best of the regions is indeed this western wherein the King and gracious Lord is Soma.
Thither resort for rest, follow the pious. Then gain the laden chargers, O ye couple.

10 Ever victorious is the northern region : may the east quarter set us first and foremost.
The Man became the five-divisioned metre. May we abide with all our members perfect.

11 This stedfast realm is Queen. To her be homage! To me and to my sons may she be gracious.
Guard thou, O Goddess Aditi, all-bounteous, our cooked oblation as an active warder.

12 Embrace us as a father clasps his children. Here on the Earth let kindly breezes fan us.
Let the rice-mess these two cook here, O Goddess, know this our truthfulness and zealous fervour.

13 If the dark bird hath come to us and, stealing the hanging morsel, settled in his dwelling,
Or if the slave-girl hath, wet-handed, smearing the pestle and the mortar, cleansed the waters,

---

8 *Yama:* as Regent of the south.

9 *Western:* according to the Shadviṅśa-Brâhmaṇa, Varuṇa is Regent of the west, and Soma of the north. *Laden chargers:* cf. stanza 2.

10 *The five-divisioned metre:* Paṅkti consisting of five pâdas or divisions, and Purusha or representative Man being *pâṅktah*, or composed of five parts, hair, skin, flesh, bones, and marrow (Aitareya-Brahmaṇa, II. 14).

11 *Stedfast region:* lower space; Earth, with whom Aditi is identified.

13 *Dark bird:* probably a crow, which is still regarded as a bird of ill omen. Mr. T. D. Broughton says (Letters written in a Mahratta camp, during the year 1809) 'I remember the whole Durbar being thrown into confusion by a *crow* flying through the tent: it was said to predict some fatal event; and to avert it, the Muha Ráj (Scindiah) was enjoined to construct a crow of gold, with a chain of pearls round its neck, and present it to the Brahmans—an injunction with which he literally complied.'

14 This pressing-stone, broad-based and strength-bestowing, made pure by cleansing means, shall chase the demon.
Mount on the skin : afford us great protection. Let not the sons' sin fall on wife and husband.

15 Together with the Gods, banning Piśâchas and demons, hath Vanaspati come hither.
He shall rise up and send his voice out loudly. May we win all the worlds with him to help us.

16 Seven victims held the sacrificial essence, the bright one and the one that hath grown feeble.
The three-and-thirty Deities attend them. As such, conduct us to the world of Svarga.

17 Unto the world of Svarga shalt thou lead us : there may we dwell beside our wife and children.
I take thy hand. Let not Destruction, let not Malignity come hither and subdue us.

Slave-girl : or, Dâsî ; a non-Âryan woman of the country whose duty is to husk and pound the rice when the mistress of the house does not do the work herself.

15 *Vanaspati :* literally, lord of the forest ; tree ; wood ; meaning here the wooden pestle used for pounding out the rice.

16 *Seven victims :* the following legend (found also, slightly different, in Aitareya-Brâmaṇa, II 8 is recorded in Śatapatha-Brâhmaṇa, I. 2. 3. 6, 7 : 'At first, namely, the gods offered up a man as a victim. When he was offered up, the sacrificial essence went out of him. It entered into the horse. They offered up the horse. When it was offered up, the sacrificial essence went out of it. It entered into the ox. When it was offered up, the sacrificial essence went out of it. It entered into the sheep. When it was offered up, the sacrificial essence went out of it. It entered into the goat. They offered up the goat. When it was offered up, the sacrificial essence went out of it. It entered into this earth. They searched for it by digging. They found it (in the shape of) those two (substances) the rice and barley : therefore even now they obtain these two by digging ; and as much efficacy as all those sacrificed animal victims would have for him, so much efficacy has this oblation (of rice &c.) for him who knows this' (Sacred Books of the East, XII. p. 50). See also Muir, O. S. Texts, IV. p. 289, note. *Bright . . . . feeble :* apparently the Moon in two different phases. See Hillebrandt, Vedische Mythologie, I. 328.

17 *Thy hand :* the handle of the pestle.

18 We have subdued that sinful-hearted Grâhi. Thou shalt speak sweetly having chased the darkness.
Let not the wooden gear made ready fail us, nor harm the grain of rice that pays due worship.

19 Soon to be, decked with butter, all-embracing, come to this world wherewith one birth unites thee.
Seize thou the winnowing-fan which rains have nourished, and let this separate the chaff and refuse.

20 Three worlds hath Power Divine marked out and measured, heaven yonder, and the earth, and air's mid-region.
Grasp ye the stalks and in your hands retain them: let them be watered and again be winnowed.

21 Manifold, various are the shapes of victims. Thou growest uniform by great abundance.
Push thou away this skin of ruddy colour: the stone will cleanse as one who cleanses raiment.

22 Earth upon earth I set thee. This thy body is consubstantial, but in form it differs.
Whate'er hath been worn off or scratched in fixing, leak not thereat: I spread a charm to mend it.

23 Thou for thy son shalt yearn as yearns a mother. I lay thee down and with the earth unite thee.
Conjoined with sacrificial gear and butter may pot and jar stand firmly on the altar.

---

18 *Grâhi:* the female demon who seizes and destroys men.

19 The first line is apparently addressed to the coming Soma juice. *Which rains have nourished:* made of reeds which grow chiefly in the rainy season.

20 *Stalks:* or joints: the pieces between the knots of the Soma plants. *Be watered:* sprinkled with water to strengthen and swell them before the juice is extracted. The process is called âpyâyanam.

21 *Victims:* animal victims. Cf. stanza 16. *Thou:* the Soma plant, *Of ruddy colour:* dyed red for sacrificial purposes.

22 *Earth upon earth I set thee:* I place the earthen pitcher on the ground.

23 *Thy son:* the rice which will be brought forth in the shape of an Odana.

24 Eastward may Agni as he cooks preserve thee.
Southward may Indra, girt by Maruts, guard thee.
Varuṇa strengthen and support thee westward, and
Soma on the north hold thee together.

25 Drops flow, made pure by filters, from the rain-cloud:
to heaven and earth and to the worlds they travel.
May Indra light them up, poured in the vessel, live-
ly and stedfast, quickening living creatures.

26 From heaven they come, they visit earth, and rising
from earth unite themselves with air's mid-region.
Purified, excellent, they shine in beauty. Thus may
they lead us to the world of Svarga.

27 Yea, and supreme, alike in conformation, and brilli-
ant and refulgent and immortal,
As such, enjoined, well-guarding, water-givers, dress
ye the Odana for wife and husband.

28 Numbered, they visit earth, these drops of moisture,
commensurate with plants and vital breathings.
Unnumbered, scattered, beautiful in colour, the bright
ones have pervaded all refulgence.

29 Heated, they rage and boil in agitation, they cast
about their foam and countless bubbles—
Like a fond woman when she sees her husband—
what time ye waters and these rice-grains mingle.

30 Take up these rice-grains lying at the bottom: let
them be blent and mingled with the waters.
This water I have measured in the vessel, if as mid-
points the rice-grains have been meted.

31 Present the sickle: quickly bring it hither. Let
them cut plants and joints with hands that harm not.
So may the plants be free from wrath against us,
they o'er whose realm Soma hath won dominion.

---

24 *Soma on the north:* cf. stanza 9, note.

30 *Mid-points:* the intermediate points of the compass.

31 *The sickle:* to cut and trim the sacred grass which is to be spread on the altar and the floor of the sacrificial enclosure.

32 Strew ye fresh grass for the boiled rice to rest on: fair let it be, sweet to the eye and spirit.
Hither come Goddesses with Gods, and sitting here taste in proper season this oblation!

33 On the strewn grass, Vanaspati, be seated; commensurate with Gods and Agnishṭomas
Let thy fair form, wrought as by Tvashṭar's hatchet, mark these that yearn for thee within the vessel.

34 In sixty autumns may the Treasure-Guardian seek to gain heavenly light by cooked oblation.
On this may sons and fathers live dependent. Send thou this mess to Fire that leads to heaven.

35 On the earth's breast stand firmly as supporter: may Deities stir thee who ne'er hast shaken.
So living man and wife with living children remove thee from the hearth of circling Agni.

36 All wishes that have blessed those with fulfilment, having won all the worlds have met together.
Let them plunge in both stirring-spoon and ladle: raise this and set it in a single vessel.

37 Pour out the covering butter, spread it eastward: sprinkle this vessel over with the fatness.
Greet this, ye Deities, with gentle murmur, as lowing cows welcome their tender suckling.

---

33 *Vanaspati:* meaning here the *yûpa* or sacrificial stake which, according to the Vaitâna-Sûtra, X. 7, is laid upon the Barhis or sacred grass when this stanza is recited.

34 *Treasure-Guardian:* meaning, apparently, the master of the house who in *sixty autumns* more will have reached the natural term of his life.

35 *Stand firmly:* the stake is now raised, and the lower end is sunk into a hole (Vaitâna-Sûtra, X. 9). *Circling Agni:* the fire which is carried round the oblation from left to right in order to protect it from the attacks of Râkshasas and evil spirits. See Sacred Books of the East, XII. 45, note.

36 *Raise this:* the cooked rice.

38 Thou hast poured oil and made the worlds: let heaven, unequalled, be spread out in wide extension.
Herein be cooked the buffalo, strong-pinioned: the Gods shall give the Deities this oblation.

39 Whate'er thy wife, away from thee, makes ready, or what, O wife, apart from thee, thy husband,
Combine it all: let it be yours in common while ye produce one world with joint endeavour.

40 All these now dwelling on the earth, mine offspring, these whom this woman here, my wife, hath borne me,
Invite them all unto the vessel: knowing their kinship have the children met together.

41 Swollen with savoury meath, the stream of treasures, sources of immortality blent with fatness—
Soma retains all these: in sixty autumns the Guardian Lord of Treasures may desire them.

42 The Lord of Treasures may desire this treasure: lordless on every side be all the others.
Our mess, presented, seeking heaven, hath mounted in three divisions all three realms of Svarga.

43 May Agni burn the God-denying demon: let no carnivorous Piśâcha drink here.
We drive him off, we keep him at a distance. Âdityas and Angirases pursue him!

44 This meath do I announce, mingled with butter, to the Angirases and the Âdityas.
With pure hands ne'er laid roughly on a Brahman go, pious couple, to theworld of Svarga.

---

38 *Made the worlds:* sacrifice being the all-powerful element in creation. *The buffalo, strong-pinioned:* the mighty Odana which, when offered to the Gods, flies up to heaven.

41 *Sources of immortality:* the streams of Soma juice which bestow upon the worshippers eternal life in heaven. *Sixty autumns:* cf. stanza 34.

42 *All the others:* our enemies. *In three divisions:* one for the Gods, one for the Fathers, and one given to the Brâhmans. Cf. X. 1. 5.

45 Of this have I obtained the noblest portion from that same world whence Parameshṭhin gained it.
Pour forth, besprinkle butter rich in fatness: the share of Angiras is here before us.

46 To Deities, to Truth, to holy Fervour this treasure we consign, this rich deposit.
At play, in meeting let it not desert us, never give out to anyone besides me.

47 I cook the offering, I present oblation: only my wife attends the holy service.
A youthful world, a son hath been begotten. Begin a life that brings success and triumph.

48 There is no fault in this, no reservation, none when it goes with friends in close alliance.
We have laid down this vessel in perfection: the cooked mess shall re-enter him who cooked it.

49 To those we love may we do acts that please them. Away to darkness go all those who hate us!
Cow, ox, and strength of every kind approach us! Thus let them banish death of human beings.

50 Perfectly do the Agnis know each other, one visitor of plants and one of rivers,
And all the Gods who shine and glow in heaven. Gold is the light of him who cooks oblation.

51 Man hath received this skin of his from nature: of other animals not one is naked.
Ye make him clothe himself with might for raiment. Odana's mouth is a home-woven vesture.

---

46 *Give out:* yield its blessings.

48 *In this:* oblation.

50 *Visitor of plants:* entering them, in the shape of the lightning contained in rain. *Of rivers:* the waters of the ocean of air, the clouds in which Agni dwells in the form of lightning. *Gold is the light:* see XI. 1. 28.

51 *Ye:* the sacrificer and his wife. Man is born naked, but the offering of an Odana supplies him with strength and clothing.

52 Whatever thou may say at dice, in meeting, whatever falsehood through desire of riches,
Ye two, about one common warp uniting, deposit all impurity within it.

53 Win thou the rain: approach the Gods. Around thee thou from the skin shalt make the smoke rise upward.
Soon to be, decked with butter, all-embracing, come to this world wherewith one birth unites thee.

54 In many a shape hath heaven transformed its body, as in itself is known, of varied colour.
Cleansing the bright, the dark form hath it banished: the red form in the fire to thee I offer.

55 To the eastern region, to Agni the Regent, to Asita the Protector, Âditya the Archer, we present thee, this offering of ours. Do ye preserve it from aggression.
To full old age may Destiny conduct us; may full old age deliver us to Mṛityu. Then may we be with our prepared oblation.

56 To the southern region, to Indra the Regent, to Tiraşchirâji the Protector, to Yama the Archer, we present, etc. (as in stanza 55).

57 To the western region, to Varuṇa the Regent, to Pṛidâku the Protector, to Food the Archer, we present, etc.

---

52 *One common warp:* the sacrifice in the performance of which the husband and wife are associated.

53 The second line is repeated from stanza 19.

55 The rest of the hymn is almost entirely non-metrical, reproduced, with slight alterations from III. 27, in honour of the regents, warders, and arrows of the six regions. No ritual procedure is prescribed in the Kauşika-Sûtra for this portion of the hymn which may have found its way into the text after the composition of that work.

The hymn is very obscure in parts, and occasionally unintelligible to me.

58 To the northern region, to Soma the Regent, to Svaja the Protector, to Thunderbolt the Archer, we present, etc.

59 To the stedfast region, to Vishṇu the Regent, to Kalmâshagrîva the Protector, to Plants the Archers, we present, etc.

60 To the upper region, to Brihaspati the Regent, to Ṣvitra the Protector, to Rain the Archer, we present thee, this offering of ours. Do ye preserve it from aggression.

To full old age may Destiny conduct us, may full old age deliver us to Mṛityu. Then may we be with our prepared oblation.

HYMN IV.

I GIVE the gift, shall be his word: and straightway they have bound the Cow

For Brahman priests who beg the boon. That bringeth sons and progeny.

2 He trades and traffics with his sons, and in his cattle suffers loss

Who will not give the Cow of Gods to Ṛishis' children when they beg.

3 They perish through a hornless cow, a lame cow sinks them in a pit.

Through a maimed cow his house is burnt: a one-eyed cow destroys his wealth.

4 Fierce fever where her droppings fall attacks the master of the kine.

So have they named her Vaṣâ, for thou art called uncontrollable.

On the imperative duty of giving cows to Brahmans, and the sin and danger of withholding the gift.

2 *The Cow of Gods:* that belongs to holy priests.

4 *Vaṣâ:* a barren cow; a cow; the word being fancifully connected with *vaṣa*, power, authority, control.

5 The malady Viklindu springs on him from ground whereon she stands,
And suddenly, from fell disease, perish the men on whom she sniffs.

6 Whoever twitches up her ears is separated from the Gods.
He deems he makes a mark, but he diminishes his wealth thereby.

7 If to his own advantage one applies the long hair of her tail,
His colts, in consequence thereof, die, and the wolf destroys his calves.

8 If, while her master owneth her, a carrion crow hath harmed her hair,
His young boys die thereof, Decline o'ertakes them after fell disease.

9 What time the Dâsî woman throws lye on the droppings of the Cow,
Misshapen birth arises thence, inseparable from that sin.

10 For Gods and Brâhmans is the Cow produced when first she springs to life,
Hence to the priests must she be given: this they call guarding private wealth.

11 The God-created Cow belongs to those who come to ask for her.

---

5 *Viklindu:* the meaning is uncertain; perhaps, dissolution, general decay.

6 *Twitches up her ears:* in order to brand them and mark the cow as his own property.

9 *Dâsî:* of barbarous or indigenous race; or slave-girl. Ludwig translates the first line differently: 'wenn ihren reinigenden laugenartigen [palyûlanam?] mist die Dâsî zusammenfegt:' What time the Dâsi girl collects alkaline droppings of the cow; but this could hardly be considered a sinful act, unless the owner was robbed thereby.

They call it outrage on the priests when one retains
her as his own.

12 He who withholds the Cow of Gods from Ṛishis'
sons who ask the gift
Is made an alien to the Gods, and subject to the
Brâhmans' wrath.

13 Then let him seek another Cow, whate'er his profit
be in this.
The Cow, not given, harms a man when he denies
her at their prayer.

14 Like a rich treasure stored away in safety is the
Brâhmans' Cow.
Therefore men come to visit her, with whomsoever
she is born.

15 So when the Brâhmans come unto the Cow they
come unto their own.
For this is her withholding, to oppress these in
another life.

16 Thus after three years may she go, speaking what
is not understood.
He, Nârada! would know the Cow, then Brâhmans
must be sought unto.

17 Whoso calls her a worthless Cow, the stored-up
treasure of the Gods,
Bhava and Ṣarva, both of them, move round and
shoot a shaft at him.

---

16 *Speaking what is not understood:* that is, giving warnings which are disregarded. Ludwig, taking *gadâ* in *ávijñâtagadâ* as coming from *gadam*, poison, instead of from *gada*, speech, translates: 'an der man das gift nicht hat erkannt:' whose poison [deadly danger of retaining her] none hath recognized. *Nârada:* a *devarshi* or Ṛishi of the celestial class who acts as a reporter between heaven and earth. His name is introduced as an imaginary auditor to make a warning or speech more solemn and authoritative. Cf. V. 19. 9. The meaning of the stanza seems to be that the cow must not be retained beyond three years.

18 The man who hath no knowledge of her udder and the teats thereof,
She yields him milk with these, if he hath purposed to bestow the Cow.

19 If he withholds the Cow they beg, she lies rebellious in his stall.
Vain are the wishes and the hopes which he, withholding her, would gain.

20 The Deities have begged the Cow, using the Brâhman as their mouth:
The man who gives her not incurs the enmity of all the Gods.

21 Withholding her from Brâhmans, he incurs the anger of the beasts,
When mortal man appropriates the destined portion of the Gods.

22 If hundred other Brâhmans beg the Cow of him who owneth her,
The Gods have said, She, verily, belongs to him who knows the truth.

23 Whoso to others, not to him who hath this knowledge, gives the Cow,
Earth, with the Deities, is hard for him to win and rest upon.

24 The Deities begged the Cow from him with whom at first she was produced:
Her, this one, Nârada would know: with Deities he drove her forth.

25 The Cow deprives of progeny and makes him poor in cattle who
Retains in his possession her whom Brâhmans have solicited.

---

18 The cow which the owner intends to bestow on a Brahman will give him milk without the trouble of milking her.

26 For Agni and for Soma, for Kâma, Mitra and Varuṇa,
For these the Brâhmans ask: from these is he who giveth not estranged.

27 Long as her owner hath not heard, himself, the verses, let her move
Among his kine: when he hath heard, let her not make her home with him.

28 He who hath heard her verses and still makes her roam among his kine,
The Gods in anger rend away his life and his prosperity.

29 Roaming in many a place the Cow is the stored treasure of the Gods.
Make manifest thy shape and form when she would seek her dwelling-place.

30 Her shape and form she manifests when she would seek her dwelling-place:
Then verily the Cow attends to Brahman priests and their request.

31 This thought he settles in his mind, This surely goeth to the Gods.
Then verily the Brahman priests approach that they may beg the Cow.

32 By Svadhâ to the Fathers, by sacrifice to the Deities,
By giving them the Cow, the Prince doth not incur the mother's wrath.

33 The Prince's mother is the Cow: so was it ordered from of old.
She, when bestowed upon the priests, cannot be given back, they say.

---

27 *The verses:* the holy texts recited by the Brahmans who ask for her as their fee.

29 *Would seek: jighâṅsati* (as suggested by Whitney, Index Verborum) instead of *jighâṅsati* of the text.

32 *Svadhâ:* sacrificial libation offered to the Manes.

34 As molten butter, held at length, drops down to Agni from the scoop,
So falls away from Agni he who gives no Cow to Brahman priests.

35 Good milker, with rice-cake as calf, she in the world comes nigh to him,
To him who gave her as a gift the Cow grants every hope and wish.

36 In Yama's realm the Cow fulfils each wish for him who gave her up;
But hell, they say, is for the man who, when they beg, bestow her not.

37 Enraged against her owner roams the Cow when she hath been impregned.
He deemed me fruitless, is her thought; let him be bound in snares of Death!

38 Whoever looking on the Cow as fruitless, cooks her flesh at home,
Bṛihaspati compels his sons and children of his sons to beg.

---

35 *Rice-cake: puroḍâṣa*; a sacrificial cake of ground rice usually divided into pieces and offered in one or more cups.

37 *Fruitless: vehátam*; a cow which habitually miscarries, and which may therefore be slaughtered 'when a king or another man who deserves high honour is to be received' (Aitareya-Brâhmaṇa I. 15). Prof. Haug observes in his note: 'That cows were killed at the time of receiving a most distinguished guest is stated in the Smṛitis. But, as Sâyaṇa observes, (which entirely agrees with the opinions held now-a-days) this custom belongs to former Yugas (periods of the world). Thence the word *goghna*, i. e. cow-killer, means in the more ancient Sanskrit books "a guest" (See the commentators on Pâṇini 3, 4, 73); for the reception of a high guest was the death of the cow of the house.' According to Âpastamba's Aphorisms on the Sacred Law of the Hindus, the Snâtaka or student who has completed his course of religious study, when he speaks of a cow that is not a milch-cow is not to say 'She is not a milch-cow,' but 'this is a cow which will become a milch-cow.' See Sacred Books of the East, II. p. 95.

39 Downward she sends a mighty heat, though amid kine a Cow she roams.
Poison she yields for him who owns and hath not given her away.

40 The animal is happy when it is bestowed upon the priests;
But happy is the Cow when she is made a sacrifice to Gods.

41 Nârada chose the terrible Viliptî out of all the cows
Which the Gods formed and framed when they had risen up from sacrifice.

42 The Gods considered her in doubt whether she were a Cow or not.
Nârada spake of her and said, The veriest Cow of cows is she.

43 How many cows, O Nârada, knowest thou, born among mankind?
I ask thee who dost know, of which must none who is no Brâhman eat?

44 Viliptî, cow, and she who drops no second calf, Bṛihaspati!
Of these none not a Brâhman should eat if he hope for eminence.

45 Homage, O Nârada, to thee who hast quick knowledge of the cows.
Which of these is the direst, whose withholding bringeth death to man?

46 Viliptî, O Bṛihaspati, cow, mother of no second calf—
Of these none not a Brâhman should eat if he hope for eminence.

47 Threefold are kine, Viliptî, cow, the mother of no second calf:
These one should give to priests, and he will not offend Prajâpati.

---

41 *Viliptî*: literally, besmeared or anointed.

48 This, Brâhmans! is your sacrifice: thus should one think when he is asked,
What time they beg from him the Cow fearful in the withholder's house.

49 He gave her not to us, so spake the Gods, in anger, of the Cow.
With these same verses they addressed Bheda: this brought him to his death.

50 Solicited by Indra, still Bheda refused to give this Cow.
In strife for victory the Gods destroyed him for that sin of his.

51 The men of evil counsel who advise refusal of the Cow,
Miscreants, through their foolishness, are subjected to Indra's wrath.

52 They who seduce the owner of the Cow and say, Bestow her not,
Encounter through their want of sense the missile shot by Rudra's hand.

53 If in his home one cooks the Cow, sacrificed or not sacrificed,
Wronger of Gods and Brâhmans, he departs, dishonest, from the world.

HYMN V.

Created by toil and holy fervour, found by devotion, resting in right; 2 Invested with truth, surrounded with honour, compassed about with glory; 3 Girt round with inherent power, fortified with faith, protected by consecration, installed at sacrifice,

---

49 *Bheda*: nothing further appears to be known of this man who refused to give his cow to Indra.

This hymn, which is unintelligible in parts, has been translated by Ludwig, Der Rigveda, III. p. 448.

The hymn, which is partly in prose, is a continuation of Hymn 4, inculcating, still more forcibly, the sin and danger of robbing a Brâhman of his cow.

the world her resting-place; 4 Brahma her guide,
the Brâhman her lord and ruler; 5 Of the Ksha-
triya who taketh to himself this Brâhman's cow and
oppresseth the Brâhman

6 The glory, the heroism, and the favouring fortune
depart. 7 The energy and vigour, the power and might,
the speech and mental strength, the glory and duty;
8 Devotion and princely sway, kingship and people,
brilliance and honour, and splendour and wealth;
9 Long life and goodly form, and name and fame, in-
breathing and expiration, and sight, and hearing;
10 Milk and flavour, and food and nourishment, and
right and truth, and action and fulfilment, and
children and cattle; 11 All these blessings of a
Kshatriya depart from him when he oppresseth the
Brâhman and taketh to himself the Brâhman's cow.
12 Terrible is she, this Brâhman's cow, and fearfully
venomous, visibly witchcraft. 13 In her are all hor-
rors and all deaths. 14 In her are all dreadful deeds,
all slaughters of mankind. 15 This, the Brâhman's
cow, being appropriated, holdeth bound in the fetter
of Death the oppressor of the Brâhman, the blas-
phemer of the Gods.

16 A hundred-killing bolt is she: she slays the
Brâhman's injurer.

17 Therefore the Brâhmans' cow is held inviolable
by the wise.

18 Running she is a thunderbolt, when driven away
she is Vaiṣvânara; 19 An arrow when she draweth
up her hooves, and Mahâdeva when she looketh
around; 20 Sharp as a razor when she beholdeth,
she thundereth when she belloweth. 21 Death is
she when she loweth, and a fierce God when she
whisketh her tail; 22 Utter destruction when she

---

12 *Visibly witchcraft*: an epithet follows, *kilbijârrita*, invested with *kilbuja*, the meaning of the compound being uncertain. Cf. stanza 53, note.

moveth her ears this way and that, Consumption when she droppeth water; 23 A missile when milking, pain in the head when milked; 24 The taking away of strength when she approacheth, a hand-to-hand fighter when roughly touched; 25 Wounding like an arrow when she is fastened by her mouth, contention when she is beaten; 26 Fearfully venomous when falling, darkness when she hath fallen down.

27 Following him, the Brâhman's cow extinguisheth the vital breath of the injurer of the Brâhman; 28 Hostility when being cut to pieces, woe to children when the portions are distributed; 29 A destructive missile of Gods when she is being seized, misfortune when carried away; 30 Misery while being additionally acquired, contumely and abuse while being put in the stall; 31 Poison when in agitation, fever when seasoned with condiments; 32 Sin while she is cooking, evil dream when she is cooked; 33 Uprooting when she is being turned round, destruction when she hath been turned round; 34 Discord by her smell, grief when she is being eviscerated; a serpent with poison in its fang when drawn; 35 Loss of power while sacrificially presented, humiliation when she hath been offered; 36 Wrathful Ṣarva while being carved, Ṣimidâ when cut up; 37 Poverty while she is being eaten, Destruction when eaten. 38 The Brâhman's cow when eaten cuts off the injurer of Brâhmans both from this world and from the world yonder. 39 Her slaughter is the sin of witchcraft, her cutting-up is a thunderbolt, her undigested grass is a secret spell. 40 Homelessness is she when denied her rights. 41 Having become Flesh-eating Agni the Brâhman's cow entereth into and devoureth the

---

36 *Ṣimidâ:* apparently a female demon, or a disease attributed to her influence. 'May all the rivers keep us free from Simidâ' (Ṛ. V. VII. 50.). Cf. A. V. IV. 25. 4.

oppressor of Brâhmans. 42 She sunders all his members, joints, and roots. 43 She cuts off relationship on the father's side and destroys maternal kinship. 44 The Brâhman's cow, not restored by a Kshatriya, ruins the marriages and all the kinsmen of the Brâhman's oppressor. 45 She makes him houseless, homeless, childless : he is extinguished without posterity to succeed him. 46 So shall it be with the Kshatriya who takes to himself the cow of the Brâhman who hath this knowledge.

47 Quickly, when he is smitten down by death, the clamorous vultures cry :

48 Quickly around his funeral fire dance women with dishevelled locks,
Striking the hand upon the breast and uttering their evil shriek.

49 Quickly the wolves are howling in the habitation where he lived :

50 Quickly they ask about him, What is this ? What thing hath happened here ?

51 Rend, rend to pieces, rend away, destroy, destroy him utterly.

52 Destroy Ângirasî ! the wretch who robs and wrongs the Brâhmans, born

53 Of evil womb, thou witchcraft hid, for Vaiṣvadevî is thy name,

54 Consuming, burning all things up, the thunderbolt of spell and charm.

55 Go thou, becoming Mṛityu sharp as razor's edge, pursue thy course :

---

52 *Ângirasî:* (the cow) belonging to Angiras and his representatives the Atharva-priests.

53 *Born of evil womb: kûlbajam* = ku-ulba-jam.—Ludwig. Cf. stanza 12. *Vaiṣvadevî:* belonging to all the Gods or to the Viṣve Devas.

The metrical portions of the hymn (47—93) have been translated by Ludwig, Der Rigveda, III. p. 5:9.

56 Thou bearest off the tyrants' strength, their store of merit, and their prayers.

57 Bearing off wrong, thou givest in that world to him who hath been wronged.

58 O Cow, become a tracker through the curse the Brâhman hath pronounced,

59 Become a bolt, an arrow through his sin, be terribly venomous.

60 O Cow, break thou the head of him who wrongs the Brâhmans, criminal, niggard, blasphemer of the Gods.

61 Let Agni burn the spiteful wretch when crushed to death and slain by thee.

62 Rend, rend to bits, rend through and through, scorch and consume and burn to dust,

63 Consume thou, even from the root, the Brâhmans' tyrant, godlike Cow!

64 That he may go from Yama's home afar into the worlds of sin.

65 So, Goddess Cow, do thou from him, the Brâhmans' tyrant, criminal, niggard, blasphemer of the Gods,

66 With hundred-knotted thunderbolt, sharpened and edged with razor-blades,

67 Strike off the shoulders and the head.

68 Snatch thou the hair from off his head, and from his body strip the skin:

69 Tear out his sinews, cause his flesh to fall in pieces from his frame.

70 Crush thou his bones together, strike and beat the marrow out of him.

71 Dislocate all his limbs and joints.

72 From earth let the Carnivorous Agni drive him, let Vâyu burn him from mid-air's broad region,

73 From heaven let Sûrya drive him and consume him.

BOOK XIII.

HYMN I.

RISE, Mighty One, who liest in the waters, and enter this thy fair and glorious kingdom.
Let Rohita who made this All uphold thee carefully nurtured for supreme dominion.

2 The strength that was in waters hath ascended. Mount o'er the tribes which thou hast generated.
Creating Soma, waters, plants and cattle, bring hitherward both quadrupeds and bipeds.

3 Ye Maruts, strong and mighty, sons of Pṛiṣni, with Indra for ally crush down our foemen.
Let Rohita, ye bounteous givers, hear you, thrice-seven Maruts who delight in sweetness!

4 Up to the lap of births, to lofty places, hath Rohita, the germ of Dames, ascended.

This Book is almost entirely devoted to the glorification of Rohita, the Red, a form of Fire and of the Sun, but distinguished from both those deities. The whole Book has been translated and elucidated with an excellent commentary by M. Victor Henry (Les Hymnes Rohitas. Livre XIII de l' Atharva-véda, Traduit et Commenté par Victor Henry, Chargé de Cours à la Faculté des Lettres de Paris. Paris: J. Maisonneuve, 1891).

1 *Mighty One*: *vâjin*; 'winner of the spoil.'—Henry. *Liest in the waters*: in which thou, as the Sun, hast set. *Rohita*: thyself as the rising Sun.

2 *The tribes*: celestial as well as terrestrial; Rohita being the great source from which all life has sprung.

3 *Thrice-seven*: a fanciful expression for an indefinite number. In Ṛ. V. VIII. 85. 8. the number of the Maruts or Storm-Gods is said to be thrice-sixty, or, according to Sâyaṇa, sixty-three, that is nine bands or companies consisting of seven each. Cf. A. V. I. 1, 1, note.

4 *The lap of births*: the place whence all creation springs. There is a play of words in the original: *rûho ruroha róhita â ruroha*. Dames; the Dawns.

Conjoined with these he found the six realms : seeing his way in front here he received the kingship.

5 For thee hath Rohita obtained dominion, scattered thine enemies, become thy safeguard.
So by the potent Sakvarîs let Heaven and Earth be milked to yield thee all thy wishes.

6 Rohita gave the Earth and Heavens their being. There Parameshṭhin held the cord extended.
Thereon reposeth Aja Ekapâda. He with his might hath stablished Earth and Heaven.

7 Rohita firmly stablished Earth and Heaven : by him was ether fixt, by him the welkin.
He measured out mid-air and all the regions : by him the Gods found life that lasts for ever.

8 Arranging shoots, springs, Rohita considered this Universe in all its forms and phases.
May he, gone up to heaven with mighty glory, anoint thy sovranty with milk and fatness.

9 Thy risings up, thy mountings and ascensions wherewith thou fillest heaven and air's mid-region—
By prayer for these, by milk of these, increasing, in Rohita's kingdom watch, among his people.

---

5 *For thee:* for thyself, Rohita. *Scattered:* M. Henry reads *vyâsyan* = *ví âsyat* for *ví âsthan* of the text which is marked as doubtful in the Index Verborum. *Ṣakvarîs:* (from *ṣak*, to be strong) verses in the Ṣakvarî metre consisting of 56 (7 × 8) syllables; here the stanzas of the two Sâmans or psalms called Raivata (Wealthy) and Ṣâkvara (Potent), the former of which is identified with the Bṛihat, in Aitareya Brâhmaṇa, IV. 13., and the latter with the Rathantara. See XI. 3. 16, note.

6 *Parameshṭhin:* the Supreme Being. *Aja Ekapâda:* the Unborn or Eternal One-footed; a personification of the Sun and here identified with Rohita.

7 *Ether: svár;* the highest heaven, the empyrean, the abode of the Sun, supported by the vault of *nâka*, the firmament or welkin. *Life that lasts for ever:* or Amrita, the ambrosia, Soma that makes them immortal.

8 *Shoots, springs: prarúho rúhás;* the 'risings up' and 'mountings' of the next stanza.

10 The tribes thy heat produced have followed hither the Calf and Gâyatrî, the strain that lauds him.
With friendly heart let them approach to serve thee, and the Calf Rohita come with his mother.

11 Erected, Rohita hath reached the welkin, wise, young, creating every form and figure.
Agni, refulgent with his heightened lustre, in the third realm hath brought us joy and gladness.

12 Thousand-horned Bull, may Jâtavedas, worshipped with butter, balmed with Soma, rich in heroes,
Besought, ne'er quit me: may I ne'er forsake thee. Give me abundant men and herds of cattle.

13 Rohita is the sire and mouth of worship: to him with voice, ear, heart I pay oblation.
To Rohita come Gods with joyful spirit. May he by risings raise me till I join him.

14 Rohita ordered sacrifice for Viṣvakarman: thence have I obtained this strength and energy.
May I proclaim thee as my kin over the greatness of the world.

---

10 *The tribes:* cf. stanza 2. Here the Celestials are meant. *Thy heat:* there is a play on the word *tápas* which means both heat and fervent devotion or religious austerity. *The Calf:* Agni or Rohita as the young Sun. *Gâyatrî:* the personification of the metre which is especially sacred to Agni identified here with Rohita. *His mother:* Dawn, who precedes and may be said to produce the Sun.

11 *Agni:* as the Sun, identified with Rohita.

12 *Thousand-horned Bull:* the mighty one with his countless rays of light.

13 *Till I join him:* I adopt M. Henry's reading *samítyaí*, infinitive dative, for *sámityai* of the text which appears to be corrupt.

14 *Viṣvakarman:* the Omnific; 'the mythical being who has arranged in heaven all the phases of the first sacrifice whence all creation sprang, phases of which those of the earthly sacrifice are the image and the copy.'—Henry. Creation typified and originated by the mysterious primeval sacrifice is the subject of R̥. V. X. 130. 'Indra after having slain Vṛitra became Viṣvakarman. Prajâpati after having produced the creatures became (also) Visvakarman' (Haug's Aitareya Brâhmana, IV. 22). See also R̥. V. X. 81 and 82.

15 On thee have mounted Brihatî and Pankti, and
Kakup with great splendour, Jâtavedas!
The cry of Vashaṭ with the voice uplifted, and
Rohita with seed on thee have mounted.

16 He goes into the womb of earth, he robes himself in
heaven and air.
He on the Bright One's station hath reached heavenly light and all the worlds.

17 To us, Vâchaspati, may Earth be pleasant, pleasant
our dwelling, pleasant be our couches.
Even here may Prâṇa be our friend: may Agni, O
Parameshṭhin, give thee life and splendour.

18 And those, Vâchaspati, our own five seasons, sacred
to Viṣvakarman their creator.
Even here our friend be Prâṇa: Parameshṭhin, may
Rohita vouchsafe thee life and splendour.

---

15 *With the voice uplifted*: 'What is the exact meaning of the strange epithet *ushṇihâkshará* applied to the cry vashaṭ? Of course it would be very simple to correct *ushṇíhâkshâro* and to translate ". . . . the *ushṇih* and the imperishable vashaṭ;" but this would require three changes of accent against which the pada text protests . . . . One resource is left, to admit that the poet (?), after having expressly enumerated several metres, has added the ushṇih by means of a pun on the word *ushṇihâ* "nape of the neck" and "ushṇih." In this case *ushṇihâkshará* might signify "that which is pronounced on the top," because the vashaṭ is a sort of crowning of the sacrifice, or still rather it would be a refined substitute for the adjective *uchchairghosha*, which is found in two places in the A. V., and would naturally be rendered by "uttered with a high voice." This latter interpretation appears to me to be almost certainly correct.'—Henry. Prof. Ludwig translates: 'Ushṇihâ, Om.'

16 *The Bright One's station*: the abode of the Sun, the empyrean. Stanzas 16—20 form part of the Godânam ceremony (see II. 13.), and appear to have been inserted in the hymn solely on account of the mention of Rohita in stanza 18.

17 *Vâchaspati*: Lord of Speech, a Genius presiding over human life; an epithet of Soma, Viṣvakarman, Prajâpati, and Brihaspati. See I. 1. 1, note. *Prâṇa*: Vital Breath personified. See XI. 4. *Parameshṭhin*: meaning, apparently, both the Supreme Being and the youth who has obtained complete sanctification by the initiatory ceremony.

18 *Our own five seasons*: that is, may they be propitious to the youth.

19 Breed, O Vâchaspati, joy and understanding, kine in our stall and children in our consorts.
Even here may Prâṇa be our friend: may Agni, O Parameshṭhin, give thee life and splendour.

20 With splendour let God Savitar, and Agni, with splendour Mitra, Varuṇa invest thee.
Treading down all Malignities, come hither. Pleasant and glorious hast thou made this kingdom.

21 Rohita, car-borne by a speckled leader, thou, pouring water, goest on in triumph.

22 Golden, refulgent, lofty is the Lady, Rohiṇî, Rohita's devoted Consort.
Through her may we win various spoil and booty, through her be conquerors in every battle.

23 Rohita's seat is Rohiṇî before us: that is the path the speckled Mare pursueth.
Kaṣyapas and Gandharvas lead her upward, and heavenly sages ever watch and guard her.

24 Sûrya's bay steeds refulgent and immortal draw the light-rolling chariot on for ever.
Drinker of fatness, Rohita, resplendent, hath entered into various-coloured heaven.

25 Rohita, Bull whose horns are sharply pointed, superior of Agni and of Sûrya,
He who supports the sundered earth and heaven,—from him the Gods effect their own creations.

---

20 *This kingdom*: cf. stanza 1, line 1.

22 *Rohiṇî*: feminine of Rohita; the Red (cow or mare): here meaning Ushas or Dawn. In later times Rohiṇî was the name of a lunar asterism personified as a daughter of Daksha and regarded as the favourite wife of the Moon.

23 *Speckled Mare*: cf. stanza 21. *Kaṣyapas*: a class of semi-divine genii or spirits who regulate the course of the Sun. *Gandharvas*: celestial beings who dwell in the sky and govern the course of the heavenly bodies.

25 *Horns*: rays of light. *Superior of Agni*: see introductory note.

26 Rohita rose to heaven from mighty ocean, Rohita rose and clomb all steeps and rises.

27 Prepare the Milky One who teems with fatness : she is the Gods' never-reluctant milch-cow.
Indra drink Soma : ours be peace and safety. Let Agni lead the laud, and chase our foemen.

28 Both kindling and inflamed, adored with butter and enhanced thereby,
May conquering Agni, conqueror of all, destroy mine enemies.

29 Let him smite down in death and burn the foeman who attacketh me.
Our adversaries we consume through Agni the Carnivorous.

30 Beat them down, Indra, with thy bolt, beat them down, mighty with thine arm.
I through the energy and force of Agni have secured my foes.

31 Cast down our foes beneath our feet, O Agni. Bṛihaspati, oppress our rebel kinsman.
Low let them fall, O Indra-Agni, Mitra-Varuṇa, powerless to show their anger.

32 Ascending up on high, O God, O Sûrya, drive my foes away.
Yea, beat them backward with the stone : to deepest darkness let them go.

33 Calf of Virâj, the Bull of prayers and worship, white-backed, he hath gone up to air's mid-region.

---

27 *Prepare:* or, mete out. *The Milky One:* the altar, the source of all prosperity. The stanza is addressed to the priest whose duty is to measure it out and prepare it for sacrifice.

32 *The stone:* the thunderbolt. 'Are there no stones in heaven But what serve for the thunder?'—Othello, V. 2.

33 *Calf of Virâj:* here the divine being Virâj (see X. 10. 1.) appears as a personification of Ushas or Dawn, both the mother and the consort of the Sun. *Brahma:* used in two senses, the Supreme Being, the Sun, and prayer.

Singing, they hymn the Calf, with gifts of butter him who is Brahma they exalt with Brahma.

34 Rise up to earth, rise up to heaven above it; rise up to opulence, rise up to kingship.
Rise up to offspring, rise to life immortal; rise, and with Rohita unite thy body.

35 With all the Gods who circle round the Sun, upholding royal sway,
With all of these may Rohita accordant, give sovranty to thee with friendly spirit.

36 Cleansed by prayer, sacrifices bear thee upward: bay coursers, ever travelling, convey thee. Thy light shines over sea and billowy ocean.

37 Rohita, conqueror of cows and riches and gathered spoil, is heaven's and earth's upholder.
Over earth's greatness would I tell my kinship with thee who hast a thousand births and seven.

38 A glorious sight to beasts and men, thou goest glorious to the regions and mid-regions.
On earth's, on Aditi's bosom, bright with glory. Fain would I equal Savitar in beauty.

39 Thou, yonder, knowest all things here, when here thou knowest what is there.
From here men see the sphere of light, Sûrya profoundly wise in heaven.

40 A God, thou injurest the Gods: thou movest in the ocean's depth.
Men kindle common Agni: him only the higher sages know.

---

36 *Sea and billowy ocean:* the ocean of air; a hendiadys.

37 *Hast a thousand births and seven;* art re-born day after day for ever. The numbers are fanciful.

40 *Thou injurest the Gods:* dimmest their glory with thy surpassing brightness. *Common Agni:* whose blessings all men enjoy, although only sages can really understand the nature of the Deity.

41 Beneath the upper realm, above this lower, bearing her Calf at foot, the Cow hath risen.
Whitherward, to what place hath she departed? Where doth she calve? Not in this herd of cattle.

42 She hath become one-footed or two-footed, four-footed, or eight-footed or nine-footed,
This universe's thousand-syllabled Paṅkti. Oceans flow forth from her in all directions.

43 Rising to heaven, immortal, hear my calling. Cleansed by prayer, sacrifices bear thee upward. Bay coursers, ever on the road, convey thee.

44 This, O Immortal One, I know of thee, thy progress to the sky, thy dwelling-place in loftiest heaven.

45 Beyond the sky, beyond the Earth looks Sûrya, and beyond the floods.
The single eye of all that is, to mighty heaven hath he arisen.

46 The earth was made his altar, and the wide expanses were the fence.
There Rohita established both these Agnis, fervent heat and cold.

47 He stablished heat and cold, he made the mountains sacrificial posts.

---

41 The stanza is taken from Ṛ. V. I. 164. 17. Cf A. V. IX. 9. 17. Ushas or Dawn hath risen between heaven and earth, carrying with her the young Sun her offspring. *Calve:* produce the Sun. *This herd of cattle:* this world.

42 Taken partly from Ṛ. V. I. 164. 41: see A. V. IX. 10. 21. According to M. Henry, the feet of the cow are the beams of Dawn which multiply as she advances. 'In another sense the "feet" are rhythmic unities, which leads up to the introduction of the *paṅkti*,' a metre consisting of forty syllables. The thousand-syllabled *paṅkti* represents, according to this explanation, the spread of the light over the universe. See M. Henry's note.

46 *Expanses:* the quarters of the sky and the spaces above and below. *The fence:* the paridhis or enclosing-sticks surrounding the sacrificial fire. See Sacred Books of the East, XII. p. 87. *Both these Agnis:* the Sun of Summer and the Sun of Winter.

Then both the Agnis, Rohita's who found celestial light, with rain for molten butter, sacrificed.

48 Rohita's Agni—his who found heaven's light—is kindled with the prayer.

From him the heat, from him the cold, from him the sacrifice was born.

49 Both Agnis—Rohita's who found the light of heaven—made strong by prayer,

Waxing by prayer, adored with prayer, by prayer enkindled, sacrificed.

50 One is deposited in Truth, one kindled in the waters: both

Agnis of Rohita who found the light are set aflame with prayer.

51 That decked by Wind, and that prepared by Indra Brahmaṇaspati,

Agnis of Rohita who found light, prayer-enkindled, sacrificed.

52 Rohita made the earth to be his altar, heaven his Dakshiṇâ.

Then heat he took for Agni, and with rain for molten butter he created every living thing.

53 The earth became an altar, heat was Agni, and the butter rain.

There Agni made, by song and hymn, these mountains rise and stand erect.

54 Then, having made the hills stand up, Rohita spake to Earth and said:

In thee let every thing be born, what is and what is yet to be.

---

48 *Agni:* here representing the two Agnis of stanza 46.

50 *One:* the Sun. *One:* lightning springing from the watery clouds.

52 *Dakshiṇâ:* or, priestly fee.

55 This sacrifice, the first of all, the past, the present, had its birth.
From that arose this universe, yea, all this world of brightness, brought by Rohita the heavenly Sage.

56 If thou should kick a cow, or by indecent act offend the Sun,
Thy root I sever: nevermore mayst thou cast shadow on the ground.

57 Thou who, between the fire and me, passest across the line of shade,
Thy root I sever: nevermore mayst thou cast shadow on the ground.

58 Whoe'er he be who, Sûrya, God! comes between thee and me to-day,
On him we wipe away ill-dream, and troubles, and impurity.

59 Let us not, Indra, leave the path, the Soma-presser's sacrifice.
Let not malignities dwell with us.

60 May we obtain, completely wrought, the thread spun out to reach the Gods,
That perfecteth our sacrifice.

---

55 *This sacrifice:* typifying and originating creation. See Ṛ. V. X. 82. 7, 88. 9; 130. 1, notes.

56 Directed against demoniacal beings.

57 M. Henry observes: 'These three stanzas [56—58] seem to refer to a solar eclipse, and it is very probable that they figured among the "rohitas" recited at such an occurrence (Kauṣika Sûtra, XCIX. 4).'

59 Taken from Ṛ. V. X. 57. 1.

60 From Ṛ. V. X. 57. 2. *The thread:* the long line of heavenly light.

The hymn has been translated also by Ludwig, Der Rigveda, III. p. 536. See also Muir, O. S. Texts, V. 395: and Scherman. Philosophische Hymnen, p. 73.

HYMN II.

RADIANT, refulgent in the sky are reared the banners of his light,
Âditya's, who beholdeth man, mighty in act and bountiful.

2 Let us laud him, the whole world's Herdsman, Sûrya, who with his rays illumines all the regions,
Mark of the quarters, brightening them with lustre, swift, mighty-pinioned, flying in the ocean.

3 From west to east thou speedest freely, making by magic day and night of diverse colours.
This is, Âditya, thy transcendent glory, that thou alone art born through all creation.

4 Victorious, inspired, and brightly shining, whom seven strong tawny-coloured coursers carry,
Whom Atri lifted from the flood to heaven, thus men behold thee as thy course thou runnest.

5 Let them not snare thee speeding on thy journey: pass safely, swiftly places hard to traverse,—
While measuring out the day and night thou movest—O Sûrya, even Heaven and Earth the Goddess.

The hymn is a glorification of the Sun as Âditya, Sûrya, and Rohita.

2 *Mark of the quarters:* (*prajñânam*, as corrected by von Roth, instead of *prajñânâm* of the text) the sign according to which the position of the cardinal points is fixed.

4 *Atri:* a celebrated Ṛishi, said to have been thrown into a fiery pit by the Asuras and delivered by the Asvins (Ṛ. V. I. 112. 7; 116. 8; 118. 7). In later times he was regarded as one of the ten Prajâpatis or Lords of Creation engendered by Manu for the purpose of creating the universe. In Ṛ. V. V. 40. 8 Atri is said to have 'established in the heaven the eye of Sûrya,' eclipsed or darkened by the magic arts of the demon Svarbhâṇu, the Râhu of later times. In stanza 9 of the same hymn the Atris or descendants of Atri are said to have 'found the Sun again.'

5 *Let them not snare thee:* the Sun being regarded as a bird. See XVII. 1. 8, note.

6 Hail to thy rapid car whereon, O Sûrya, thou circlest in a moment both the limits,
Whirled by thy bay steeds, best of all at drawing, thy hundred horses or seven goodly coursers!

7 Mount thy strong car, O Sûrya, lightly rolling, drawn by good steeds, propitious, brightly gleaming,
Whirled by thy bays, most excellent at drawing, thy hundred horses or seven goodly coursers.

8 Sûrya hath harnessed to his car to draw him seven stately bay steeds gay with golden housings.
The Bright One started from the distant region: dispelling gloom the God hath climbed the heavens.

9 With lofty banner hath the God gone upward, and introduced the light, expelling darkness.
He hath looked round on all the worlds, the Hero, the son of Aditi, Celestial Eagle.

10 Rising, thou spreadest out thy rays, thou nourishest all shapes and forms.
Thou with thy power illumest both the oceans, encompassing all spheres with thy refulgence.

11 Moving by magic power to east and westward, these two young creatures, sporting, circle ocean.
One of the pair beholds all living creatures: with wheels of gold the bay steeds bear the other.

12 Atri established thee in heaven, O Sûrya, to create the month.
So on thou goest, firmly held, heating, beholding all that is.

---

6 *Both the limits:* the eastern and western horizons.

10 *Both the oceans:* celestial and terrestrial.

11 The stanza is taken, with variations, from R. V. X. 85. 18, and is found also, with variants, in A. V. VII. 81. 1. *To east and westward:* or, forward and backward. *Two young creatures:* Sûrya and Soma; Sun and Moon.

13 As the Calf both his parents so thou joinest both the distant bounds.
Surely the Gods up yonder knew this sacred mystery long ago.

14 Sûrya is eager to obtain all wealth that lies along the sea.
Great is the course spread out for him, his eastward and his westward path.

15 He finishes his race with speed and never turns his thought aside.
Thereby he keeps not from the Gods enjoyment of the Drink of Life.

16 His heralds bear him up aloft, the God who knoweth all that live,
Sûrya, that all may look on him.

17 The Constellations pass away, like thieves, departing in the night,
Before the all-beholding Sun.

18 His herald rays are seen afar refulgent o'er the world of men,
Like flames of fire that burn and blaze.

19 Swift and all-beautiful art thou, O Sûrya, maker of the light,
Illuming all the radiant realm.

20 Thou goest to the hosts of Gods, thou comest hither to mankind,
Hither, all light to be behold.

---

13 *The Calf:* Agni. *His parents:* the upper and lower parts of the fire-drill. *Both the distant bounds:* cf. stanza 6. The force of the comparison is not very obvious. See M. Henry's note.

16 Stanzas 16—24 are taken from Ṛ. V. I. 50. 1—9, and appear again in A. V. XX. 47. 13—21. *Heralds:* or, banners; the rays of light or luminous clouds that announce his approach. *The God who knoweth all that live:* *jâtávedasam;* here an epithet of Sûrya.

21 With that same eye of thine wherewith thou seest, brilliant Varuṇa,
The active one among mankind,

22 Traversing sky and wide mid-air, thou metest with thy beams our days,
Sun, seeing all things that have life.

23 Seven bay steeds harnessed to thy car bear thee, O thou far-seeing One,
God, Sûrya, with the radiant hair.

24 Sûrya hath yoked the pure bright seven, the daughters of the car, with these,
His own dear team, he travelleth.

25 Devout, aflame with fervent heat, Rohita hath gone up to heaven.
He is re-born, returning to his birthplace, and hath become the Gods' imperial ruler.

26 Dear unto all men, facing all directions, with hands and palms on every side extended,
He, the sole God, engendering earth and heaven, beareth them with his wings and arms together.

27 The single-footed hath outstepped the biped, the biped overtakes the triple-footed.
The biped hath outstridden the six-footed: these sit around the single-footed's body.

---

21 *Varuṇa:* used here as an appellative (the Encompasser) of Sûrya. Sâyaṇa explains the word as *unishṭanivâraka*, averter of evil.

24 *The pure bright seven:* the seven steeds that draw his chariot; the number having reference to the sun's seven rays. See XI. 1. 36, note. *His own dear team:* or, yoked of themselves.

26 Taken, with variations, from Ṛ. V. X. 81. 3. *Beareth:* the Ṛ. V. reading is *dhámati*, weldeth, that is, fuses the matter which he forms into heaven and earth.

27 Taken, with variations, from Ṛ. V. X. 117. 8. *The single-footed:* the Sun appears to be meant, whose motion is swifter than that of the biped, the ordinary man, who, again, walks faster than the triple-footed or old man who moves with the assistance of a staff. Cf. the Sphinx's enigma solved by Oedipus. The second line is less easy to explain.

28 When he, unwearied, fain to go, hath mounted his bays, he makes two colours, brightly shining.
Rising with banners, conquering the regions, thou sendest light through all the floods, Âditya.

29 Verily, Sûrya, thou art great: truly, Âditya, thou art great.
Great is thy grandeur, Mighty One: thou, O Âditya, thou art great.

30 In heaven, O Bird, and in mid-air thou shinest: thou shinest on the earth and in the waters.
Thou hast pervaded both the seas with splendour: a God art thou, O God, light-winner, mighty.

31 Soaring in mid-course hither from the distance, fleet and inspired, the Bird that flies above us,
With might advancing Vishṇu manifested, he conquers all that moves with radiant banner:

32 Brilliant, observant, mighty Lord, an Eagle illuming both the spheres and air between them.
Day and the Night, clad in the robes of Sûrya, spread forth more widely all his hero powers.

33 Flaming and radiant, strengthening his body, bestowing floods that promptly come to meet us,
He, luminous, winged, mighty, strength-bestower, hath mounted all the regions as he forms them.

34 Bright presence of the Gods, the luminous herald, Sûrya hath mounted the celestial regions.
Day's maker, he hath shone away the darkness, and radiant, passed o'er places hard to traverse.

The Ṛ. V. version is different: 'Four-footed creatures (dogs) come when bipods (men) call them and stand and look where five (several men) are met together,' being uncertain at first whether their masters are among them or not. See A. V. XIII. 3. 25. There are many traces of similar riddles in the Veda. The riddles propounded by Samson are recorded in the Bible; there is a large collection of enigmas in the Icelandic Herverar Saga; and old English and Scottish ballads abound in them. See Baring-Gould's Strange Survivals, pp. 220—237.

29 Taken, with variations, from Ṛ. V. VIII. 90. 11.

35 He hath gone up on high, the Gods' bright presence, the eye of Mitra, Varuṇa, and Agni.
The soul of all that moveth not or moveth, Sûrya hath filled the earth and air and heaven.

36 High in the midst of heaven may we behold thee whom men call Savitar, the bright red Eagle,
Soaring and speeding on thy way, refulgent, unwasting light which Atri erst discovered.

37 Him, Son of Aditi, an Eagle hasting along heaven's height, I supplicate in terror.
As such prolong our lengthened life, O Sûrya: may we, unharmed, enjoy thy gracious favour.

38 This gold-hued Hańsa's wings, soaring to heaven, spread o'er a thousand days' continued journey.
Supporting all the Gods upon his bosom, he goes his way beholding every creature.

39 Rohita, in primeval days Prajâpati, was, after, Time.
Mouth of all sacrifices, he, Rohita, brought celestial light.

40 He, Rohita, became the world: Rohita gave the heaven its heat.
Rohita with his beams of light travelled along the earth and sea.

41 To all the regions Rohita came, the imperial Lord of heaven.
He watches over ocean, heaven, and earth and all existing things.

42 Mounting the lofty ones, he, bright, unwearied, splendidly shining, makes two separate colours,

---

35 Taken from Ṛ. V. I. 115. 1.

36 *Atri*: cf. stanza 4.

38 The stanza occurs in A. V. X. 8. 18, and is repeated in 3. 14 of this Book.

39 *Time*: Kâla, personified and deified. See XIX. 53.

42 *The lofty ones*: the quarters of the sky and the intermediate spaces. *Two separate colours*: light when he is present, and darkness when he is absent. *Wind-approacher*: it seems impossible to get any

While through all worlds that are he sends his lustre,
radiant, observant, mighty, wind-approacher.

43 One form comes on, the other is reverted: to day
and night the Strong One shapes and fits him.
With humble prayer for aid we call on Sûrya, who
knows the way, whose home is in the region.

44 The suppliant's way, filling the earth, the Mighty
circleth the world with eye that none deceiveth.
May he, all-seeing, well-disposed and holy, give ear
and listen to the word I utter.

45 Blazing with light his majesty hath compassed ocean
and earth and heaven and air's mid-region.
May he, all-seeing, well-disposed and holy, give ear
and listen to the word I utter.

46 Agni is wakened by the people's fuel to meet the
Dawn who cometh like a milch-cow.
Like young trees shooting up on high their branches,
his flames are mounting to the vault of heaven.

---

meaning out of *vâtamâyás*, *vâtam âyáḥ* of the Pada text. The S. P. Dictionary considers it to be an interpolation. Prof. Ludwig translates it by 'der windzauber' the wind-spell, as though it were *vâta + mâyâ*. M. Henry changes the word into *vâtam âpo*, '(over) wind and waters.' The pâda would then run 'bright, strong, observant, over wind and waters.'

43 'The sun does never set nor rise. When people think the sun is setting (it is not so). For after having arrived at the end of the day it makes itself produce two opposite effects, making night to what is below and day to what is on the other side.' Similarly, *mutatis mutandis*, for day.—Haug's Aitareya Brâhmaṇa, III. 44.

44 *The suppliant's way:* the refuge and help of the distressed; Rohita, the Sun.

46 The stanza is taken from Ṛ. V. V. 1. 1. The second line is difficult:—'and then his irradiations proceed aloft to the heavens, like the flocks of moving birds.'—Stevenson. 'Like birds (?) flying up to a branch, the flames of Agni went up to heaven, (or like strong men reaching up to).'—Max Müller.

The hymn has been translated also by Ludwig, Der Rigveda, III. p. 540.

HYMN III.

He who engendered these, the earth and heaven, who made the worlds the mantle that he weareth,
In whom abide the six wide-spreading regions through which the Bird's keen vision penetrateth,
This God is wroth offended by the sinner who wrongs the Brâhman who hath gained this knowledge.
Agitate him, O Rohita; destroy him: entangle in thy snares the Brâhman's tyrant.

2 He from whom winds blow pure in ordered season, from whom the seas flow forth in all directions,
This God, etc.

3 He who takes life away, he who bestows it; from whom comes breath to every living creature,
This God, etc.

4 Who with the breath he draws sates earth and heaven, with expiration fills the ocean's belly,
This God, etc.

5 In whom Virâj, Prajâpati, Parameshṭhin, Agni Vaiṣvânara abide with Pankti,
He who hath taken to himself the breathing of the Supreme, the vigour of the Highest,
This God, etc.

6 On whom rest six expanses and five regions, four waters, and three syllables of worship,
He who hath looked between both spheres in anger,
This God, etc.

The hymn is a glorification of Rohita, with a malediction on the man who wrongs a Brâhman.

1 *The Bird's:* the Sun's. *This knowledge:* of the nature of Rohita as enunciated in lines 1 and 2 of the stanza. *This God:* this refrain of two lines concludes every stanza except the last.

2 *Seas:* collections of waters. *With Pankti:* that is, with the whole series or company of divine beings. Cf. XIII. 1. 42, note.

6 *Three syllables of worship:* the three mystical words *bhûr, bhuvaḥ svar*, Earth, Air, Heaven. M. Henry calls attention to the regular decrease in the numbers from six to two.

7 He who, consuming food, became its master, the Lord of Prayer, the Regent of Devotion,
The world's Lord, present and to be hereafter, This God, etc.

8 He who metes out the thirteenth month, constructed with days and nights, containing thirty members, This God, etc.

9 Dark the descent; the strong-winged birds are golden: they fly aloft to heaven, enrobed in waters.
They have come hither from the seat of Order, This God, etc.

10 What silver, Kasyapa, thou hast refulgent, what brightly-shining lotus-flower collected,
Wherein are gathered seven Suns together, This God, etc.

11 In front the Bṛihat-Sâman is his mantle, and from behind Rathantara enfolds him,
Ever with care robing themselves in splendour. This God, etc.

12 One of his wings was Bṛihat, and the other Rathantara, vigorous with one same purpose,
What time the Gods gave Rohita his being. This God, etc.

13 At evening he is Varuṇa and Agni, ascending in the morning he is Mitra.

---

7 *Present and to be hereafter: bhūtó*, present, is masculine, and *bhavishyád*, future, neuter.

8 The creation of the thirteenth or intercalary month is here especially ascribed to Rohita or the Sun, the Moon being the creator of the ordinary months of the year.

9 The stanza, taken from Ṛ. V. I. 164. 47, is found also in A. V. VI. 22. 1 and IX. 10. 22.

10 *Kaśyapa:* as regulator of the course of the Sun.

11 *Rathantara:* 'The two (principal) Sâmans at the Sattra are the Bṛihat and Rathantaram. These are the two boats of the sacrifice, landing it on the other shore (in the celestial world) . . . . Bṛihat and Rathantaram are two wings.'—Haug's Aitareya Brâhmaṇa, IV. 13.

13 *Varuṇa:* the God who especially presides over the night; the starry heaven deified.

As Savitar, he moves through air's mid region, as
Indra warms the heavens from the centre. This
God, etc.

14 This gold-hued Haṅsa's wings, soaring to heaven
spread o'er a thousand days' continued journey.
Supporting all the Gods upon his bosom, he goes his
way beholding every creature. This God, etc.

15 This is the God who dwells within the waters, the
thousand-rooted, many-powered Atri,
He who brought all this world into existence. This
God, etc.

16 With flying feet his tawny coursers carry the bright
God through the sky, aglow with splendour,
Whose limbs uplifted fire and heat the heavens: hither
he shines with beams of golden colour. This God, etc.

17 He beside whom his bay steeds bear the Âdityas,
by whom as sacrifice go many knowing
The sole light shining spread through various places.
This God, etc.

18 The seven make the one-wheeled chariot ready:
bearing seven names the single courser draws it.
The wheel, three-naved, is sound and undecaying:
thereon these worlds of life are all dependent.
This God, etc.

19 Eight times attached the potent Courser draws it,
Sire of the Gods, father of hymns and praises.
So Mâtarisvan, measuring in spirit the thread of
Order, purifies all regions. This God, etc.

20 The thread that goes through all celestial quarters
within the Gâyatrî, womb of life eternal. This
God, etc.

---

14 This stanza is repeated from XIII. 2. 38.

15 *Atri*: cf. XIII. 2. 4, note.

18 See IX. 9. 2.

20 *The thread*: the uninterrupted chain of sacrifice, reaching from earth to heaven, uniting men with the Gods and producing all earthly blessings and happiness hereafter.

21 Three are the settings, three the upward risings, three are the spaces, yea, and three the heavens.
We know thy triple place of birth, O Agni, we know the deities' triple generations.

22 He who, as soon as born, laid broad earth open, and set the ocean in the air's mid-region, This God, etc.

23 Thou, Agni, kind with lights and mental powers, hast up in heaven shone as the Sun, enkindled.
The Maruts, sons of Pṛisni, sang his praises what time the Gods gave Rohita his being. This God, etc.

24 Giver of breath, giver of strength and vigour, he whose commandment all the Gods acknowledge,
He who is Lord of this, of man and cattle, This God, etc.

25 The single-footed hath outstepped the biped, the biped overtakes the triple-footed.
The quadruped hath wrought when bipeds called him, standing and looking on the five collected.
This God is wroth offended by the sinner that wrongs the Brâhman who hath gained this knowledge.
Agitate him, O Rohita; destroy him: entangle in thy snares the Brâhman's tyrant.

---

21 *Three are the settings:* as M. Henry observes, the idea of the triple birth of Agni, from Heaven as the Sun, from men as Sacrificial Fire, and from the waters of the firmament as lightning (see Ṛ. V. X. 45. 1), is at the bottom of these arithmetical speculations. *Triple place of birth:* 'Three several places of his birth they honour, in mid-air, in the heaven, and in the waters' (Ṛ. V. I. 95. 3).

24 This stanza is the second verse of the Hymn to Prajâpati, Ṛ. V. X. 121, which appears, with variations, in A. V. IV. 2. The original refrain is, 'What God (other than Prajâpati, according to Prof. Ludwig) shall we adore with our oblation?'

25 The first line is repeated from XIII. 2. 27; and line 2, which is taken, with variations, from the same stanza of the original hymn (Ṛ. V. X. 117. 8) is explained in the note thereon. According to M. Henry, *the quadruped* is the Sun, often represented under the form of a bull or horse, who comes at the prayer of men and from his station in heaven looks down on the five human races.

26 Born is the darksome Mother's Son, the whitely shining Calf of Night.
He, Rohita, ascendeth up to heaven, hath mounted to the heights.

HYMN IV.

Down looking, on the ridge of sky Savitar goes to highest heaven.
2 To misty cloud filled with his rays Mahendra goes encompassed round.
3 Creator, and Ordainer, he is Vâyu, he is lifted cloud.
4 Rudra, and Mahâdeva, he is Aryaman and Varuṇa.
5 Agni is he, and Sûrya, he is verily Mahâyama.
6 Calves, joined, stand close beside him, ten in number, with one single head
7 From west to east they bend their way: when he mounts up he shines afar.

---

26 There is a play of words in this stanza: *rohati rúho ruroha róhitaḥ.* Cf. XIII. 1. 4, note.

The hymn has been translated also by Ludwig, Der Rigveda, III p. 543.

This hymn, which is partly in prose, is a glorification of the Sun who, identified with, or comprehending in himself, other divine personages, is the one only Deity.

1 *Savitar:* (from *sû*, to beget) the Sun regarded as a stimulating, vivifying, generative Power, sometimes identified with, and sometimes distinguished from, Sûrya.

2 *Mahendra:* 'Indra is called *mahendra*, *i. e.*, the great Indra, because he had become great (greater than all the other gods).' (Haug's Aitareya Brâhmaṇa, III. 21).

4 *Mahâdeva:* the great God; the name is now appropriated to Ṣiva.

5 *Mahâyama:* the great Yama. These three names with *mahâ* prefixed are unknown to the bards of the Ṛigveda.

6 *Calves:* the sunbeams. *Ten:* used indefinitely for many, with reference, perhaps, to the ten regions of the world, the four quarters, the intermediate points, and the upper and lower spaces. *With one single head:* all emanating from the Sun.

8 His are these banded Maruts: they move gathered close like porters' thongs.

9 To misty cloud filled with his rays Mahendra goes encompassed round.

10 His are the nine supports, the casks set in nine several places here.

11 He keepeth watch o'er creatures, all that breatheth and that breatheth not.

12 This conquering might hath entered him. He is the sole, the simple One, the One alone.

13 In him these Deities become simple and One.

14 Renown and glory, and force and cloud, the Brâhman's splendour, and food, and nourishment,

15 To him who knoweth this God as simple and One.

16 Neither second, nor third, nor yet fourth is he called;

17 He is called neither fifth, nor sixth, nor yet seventh;

18 He is called neither eighth, nor ninth, nor yet tenth.

19 He watcheth over creatures, all that breatheth and that breatheth not.

---

8 *Gathered close like porters' thongs:* the reading of the text, *ṣikyâkṛitaḥ*, is absolutely unintelligible. M. Henry suggests that for *âsṛitaḥ* we should read *âkṛiti* or *âkṛitiḥ*, which in Vedic language means a constituent part; the luminous rays, often likened to reins, being here compared to the loops or swings fastened to the ends of a pole or yoke to receive a load: 'elle va, et ses parties constituantes sont [comme] des courroies de porte-faix.'

10 *Casks:* as there is a cask or bucket in heaven (cf. 'The bucket which the bounteous heroes [the Maruts] shook down from heaven for their worshipper.'—Ṛ. V. V. 53. 6. Vedic Hymns, Part I. p 319), so there is one for mid-air and one for earth, and these, in accordance with Vedic custom, are multiplied by three.

12 *This conquering might:* power derived from the sacrifice which men are performing on earth.

14 *And cloud: nábhaṣcha*, out of place here, and probably an interpolation suggested by the second meaning (water) of *ámbhas*, force. See S. P. Dictionary, under *ámbhas*.

20 This conquering might hath entered him. He is the sole, the simple One, the One alone.

21 In him these Deities become simple and One.

22 Devotion and Religious Fervour, and renown and glory, and force and cloud, the Brâhman's splendour, and food and nourishment,

23 And past and future, and Faith and lustre, and heaven and sweet oblation, 24 To him who knoweth this God as simple and One. 25 He, verily, is death, he is immortality, he is the monster, he is the fiend.

26 He is Rudra, winner of wealth in the giving of wealth, in uttering homage he is the sacrificial exclamation Vashaṭ duly employed.

27 All sorcerers on earth obey with reverence his high behest.

28 All constellations yonder, with the Moon, are subject to his will.

29 He was brought forth from Day: and Day derives his origin from him.

30 He was brought forth from Night: and Night derives her origin from him.

---

22 *And cloud:* see note on stanza 14.

25 *The monster . . . the fiend:* 'Doubtlessly one of the manifold incarnations of the Sun, one of the aspects under which Vedic mythology represents him. So the Asvins have a "wolf" [Vṛika] whom they succour (Ṛ. V. VII. 68. 8., cf. Ṛ. V. VI. 13. 5.) and a "demon," a "miser" (á-râ-van = he who gives not) who succours their protégés (Ṛ. V. VII. 68. 7., X. 40. 7.); and these two appear to be one (Ṛ. V. VI. 13. 5.). The "wolf" of the story of *Little Red Ridinghood* is indubitably also the Sun inasmuch as he devours the Dawn; people have as yet no idea of all the folk-lore that is scattered about in the Vedas.'—Henry. The Ṛigveda passages referred to are somewhat differently rendered and explained in my Hymns of the Ṛigveda.

29—39 Cf. 'From him (Purusha) Virâj was born; again Purusha from Virâj was born' (Ṛ. V. X. 90. 5); and 'Daksha was born of Aditi, and Aditi was Daksha's child' (Ṛ. V. X 72. 4); 'on which Yâska remarks (Nirukta, XI. 23): How can this be possible? They

31 He was produced from Air: and Air derives its origin from him.
32 He was produced from Wind: and Wind derives his origin from him.
33 From Heaven was he produced: and Heaven derives his origin from him.
34 He sprang from regions of the sky: from him the heavenly regions sprang.
35 He is the offspring of the Earth: Earth hath her origin from him.
36 He was produced from fire: and fire derives its origin from him.
37 He is the waters' offspring: and from him the waters were produced.
38 From holy verses was he born: from him the holy verses sprang.
39 He is the son of sacrifice: and sacrifice was born from him.
40 Sacrifice, sacrifice's Lord, he was made head of sacrifice.
41 He thundereth, he lighteneth, he casteth down the thunder-stone
42 For misery or happiness, for mortal man or Asura.
43 Whether thou formest growing plants, or sendest rain for happiness, or hast increased the race of man,
44 Such is thy greatness, liberal Lord! A hundred bodily forms are thine.
45 Millions are in thy million, or thou art a billion in thyself.

---

may have had the same origin; or, according to the nature of the gods, they may have been born from each other,—have derived their substance from one another.'—Muir, O. S. Texts, IV. p. 13. See also O. S. T., I. p. 9, note 20.

45 *Millions are in thy million: bádve bádvāni*, Prof. Whitney's correction for *báddhe báddhāni* which is unintelligible. 'et dans ton milliard [il y a] des milliards [de corps].'—Henry. According to Sâyaṇa, a *bádva* is a hundred *koṭis*, that is, a billion; but it seems to mean indefinitely a very large number.

46 Stronger than immortality is Indra: stronger thou than deaths;

47 Yea, stronger than Malignity art thou, O Indra, Lord of Might. Calling thee Master, Sovran Chief, we pay our reverence to thee.

48 Worship to thee whom all behold! Regard me, thou whom all regard,

49 With food, and fame, and vigour, with the splendour of a Brâhman's rank.

50 We pay thee reverence calling thee strength, power, and might, and conquering force.

51 We pay thee reverence calling thee red power, the silvery expanse.

52 We pay thee reverence calling thee vast, wide, the good, the universe.

53 We pay thee reverence calling thee extension, compass, width, and world.

54 We pay thee reverence, calling thee rich, opulent in this and that, with wealth unceasing and secure.

55 Worship to thee whom all behold! Regard me, thou whom all regard,

56 With food, and fame, and vigour, with the splendour of a Brâhman's rank.

---

46 *Than immortality:* the word *namurâd* is doubtful. M. Henry would read *naro 'surâd:* than the fiend, O men.

47 *Lord of Might:* or, perhaps, here, Consort of Ṣachî, Indra's power personified.

BOOK XIV.

HYMN I.

TRUTH is the base that bears the earth; by Sûrya are the heavens upheld.
By Law the Âdityas stand secure, and Soma holds his place in heaven.

This Book which contains only two hymns, concerning nuptial ceremonies and formulas, has been translated and exhaustively elucidated by Professor Albrecht Weber in Indische Studien, V. pp. 178—217; and the stanzas which are not taken from the Ṛigveda have been translated by Professor Ludwig, Der Rigveda, III. pp. 470—476.

The greater portion of Hymn I. is taken, with many transpositions and variations, from Ṛigveda X. 85, which is itself a composite hymn and evidently one of the latest of that collection. Its main subject is the ceremony of marriage in general, and more especially the wedding of Sûryâ, the daughter of the Sun, who is regarded as the typical bride whose nuptial ceremonies are to be the pattern of marriages on earth.

1 *Truth:* or reality; *satyám* is used interchangeable with *ṛitám*, the natural and moral Law and Order by which the Universe is regulated. Professor Max Müller interprets differently:—'It sounds, no doubt, very well to translate Satyena uttabhitâ bhûmi*h* by 'the earth is founded on truth;' and I believe every translator has taken satya in that sense here. Ludwig translates, 'Von der Wahrheit ist die Erde gestützt.' But such an idea, if it contains any tangible meaning at all, is far too abstract for those early poets and philosophers. They meant to say 'the earth, such as we see it, is held up, that is, rests upon something real, though we may not see it, on something which they called the Real, 'Sometimes they trace even this Satya or *Ri*ta, the Real or Right, to a still higher cause and say (Rig-veda X. 190, 1): 'The Right and Real was born from the Lighted Heat; from thence was born Night, and thence the billowy sea. From the sea was born Saṃvatsara, the year, he who Ordereth day and night, the Lord of all that moves (winks). The Maker (dhâtri) shaped Sun and Moon in order; he shaped the sky, the earth, the welkin, and the highest heaven.' And to which, in course of time, they gave many more names, such as *Ri*ta, the right, Brahman,' etc.—India, What can it Teach us? p. 65. According to this view, the first three words of the hymn may be rendered:

2 By Soma are the Âdityas strong, by Soma mighty is the earth:
Thus Soma in the lap of all these constellations hath his home.

3 One thinks, when men have brayed the plant, that he hath drunk the Soma's juice.
Of him whom Brahmans truly know as Soma never mortal eats.

4 When they begin to drink thee, then, O God, thou swellest out again.
Vâyu is Soma's sentinel. The month is that which shapes the years.

5 Soma, preserved by covering rules, guarded by hymns in Bṛihatî,
Thou standest listening to the stones: none tastes of thee who dwells on earth.

The Real holdeth up the earth; or, Earth resteth on Reality. *The Âdityas*: 'die Ewigen,' the Eternal Ones.—Weber. *Soma*: the Moon. He is prominently mentioned as being the consort of Sûryâ or Sunlight.

2 *By Soma*: by the power of the deified Soma juice whose influence pervades, quickens, and supports all existence. In the second line *Soma* apparently means the Moon; but perhaps there is an allusion also to the other sense of the word. *These constellations*: the nakshatras or lunar mansions. 'In the centre of these stars.'—Muir.

3 *Know as Soma*: know to be the Moon, regarded as the food of the Gods and the Fathers or Manes. The Moon wanes while it is being eaten, and waxes while being filled with the souls of the Departed who enter it. Soma, from *su*, to squeeze, pour out, means the rainer, the source of rain, and is primarily the Moon, its identification with the Soma plant being a secondary phase in the development of lunar mythology.

4 *They*: the Gods and Fathers. *Then*: when they have eaten or drunk. *Vâyu is Soma's sentinel*: the wind keeps the terrestrial Soma fresh, and the Wind-God may be regarded as one of the warders of the celestial Soma. Soma, the Moon, also, who floats upon the bosom of the air, is watched and guarded by Vâyu. *The years*: or, half years, formed by the month, that is, Soma the Moon.

5 *Covering rules*: arrangements for protection. *Hymns in Bṛihatî*: Sâma songs composed in the Bṛihatî metre. But the meaning of *bârhataiḥ* is uncertain. According to Sâyaṇa, the Bârhatas are the seven

6 Thought was her coverlet, the power of sight was unguent for her eyes:
Her treasure-chest was earth and heaven, when Sûryâ went unto her lord.

7 Raibhî was her dear bridal friend, and Nârâṣansî led her home.
Lovely to see was Sûryâ's robe: by Gâthâ beautified she moves.

8 Songs were the cross-bars of the pole, Kurîra metre decked her head.
Both Aṣvins were the paranymphs: Agni was leader of the train.

9 Soma was he who wooed the maid: the groomsmen were both Aṣvins, when
The Sun-God Savitar bestowed his willing Sûryâ on her lord.

---

guardians of the celestial Soma, Svâna, Bhrâja, Kṛiṣânu, and others; and Professor Weber is of opinion that they appear here as warders of the Moon. The meaning appears to be that the Moon, secure in heaven, is not disturbed by the sound of the press-stones employed in the preparation of the Soma juice on earth. *None tastes of thee:* cf. stanza 3.

6 Soma the Moon is the deity or deified subject of the preceding five stanzas. Sûryâ's Bridal is the subject of stanzas 6—17. *Treasure-chest: kóṣaḥ*; meaning, probably, trousseau or bridal outfit. According to some, the box or body of the chariot is intended.

7 *Raibhî:* (from *rebha*, a bard or panegyrist) a ritualistic verse; praise of the bride personified as the friend who is to accompany her to her husband's house and live with her until she has become accustomed to the change. *Nârâṣansî:* a song that celebrates the glory of men; that is, here, the excellence of the bridegroom. *Gâthâ:* song in general. All three are personified as attendants and friends of the bride in the nuptial procession.

8 *Kurîra:* according to Sâyaṇa, the name of a certain metre. *Decked her head:* or, perhaps, her car, as its canopy. The meaning of *opaṣáḥ* here is uncertain. 'Kurira metre was the thong of the whip.'—Wilson; 'Verflochtnes Lied ihr Haargeflecht.'—Weber. See Geldner, Vedische Studien, I. p. 137. *Both Aṣvins were the paranymphs:* in Ṛ. V. I. 116. 17; 117. 13; and 119. 5, the Aṣvins appear to be Sûryâ's husbands. Here they are the interceders or match-makers who had asked her in marriage for Soma. Cf. A. V. II. 30. 2, and V. 25. 3.

10 Her spirit was the bridal car, the canopy thereof was heaven:
Two radiant oxen formed the team when Sûryâ came unto her lord.

11 Steadily went the steers upheld by holy verse and song of praise.
Thy chariot-wheels were listening ears: thy path was tremulous in the sky.

12 Pure, as thou wentest, were thy wheels, breath was the axle piercing them.
Sûryâ advancing to her lord rode on the chariot of her heart.

13 The bridal pomp of Sûryâ, which Savitar started, moved along.
In Maghâ days are oxen slain, in Phalgunîs they wed the bride.

14 When on your three-wheeled chariot, O ye Asvins, ye came as suitors unto Sûryâ's bridal,
Where was one chariot-wheel of yours? Where stood ye for the sire's command?

15 Twin Lords of Lustre, at the time when ye to Sûryâ's wooing came,
Then all the Gods agreed to your proposal. Pûshan as son elected you as father.

---

13 *In Maghâ days:* when the moon is in the lunar mansion Maghâ. *Slain:* only on especially festive occasions such as weddings. 'Are whipped along.'—Wilson (following Sâyaṇa). *Phalgunîs:* two asterisms or lunar mansions, called Arjunîs in the corresponding stanza of the Ṛigveda. *They wed the bride:* she is escorted to her husband's home.

14 *Three-wheeled chariot:* see Ṛ. V. I. 34. 3. The three wheels represent heaven, middle air, and earth, pervaded by the Asvins as heralds of sunlight. *For the sire's command:* to receive Savitar's invitation to take part in the bridal procession. According to Sâyaṇa, 'to offer your gift.'

15 *Pûshan:* here meaning Savitar. *Son.....father:* intended to express close relationship, and Savitar's obligation to the Asvins who had arranged the marriage.

16 Two wheels of thine the Brahmans know, Sûryâ! according to their times.
That which is hidden only those who know the highest truths have learned.

17 Worship we pay to Aryaman, finder of husbands, kindly friend.
As from its stalk a cucumber, from here I loose thee, not from there.

18 Hence and not thence I send her free. I make her softly fettered there,
That, bounteous Indra! she may live blest in her fortune and her sons.

19 Now from the noose of Varuṇa I free thee, wherewith the blessèd Savitar hath bound thee.
May bliss be thine together with thy wooer in Order's dwelling, in the world of virtue.

20 Let Bhaga take thy hand and hence conduct thee: let the two Asvins on their car transport thee.
Go to the house to be the household's mistress, and speak as lady to thy gathered people.

---

16 The *two wheels* are probably heaven and earth, and the third, *that which is hidden*, may be the year, as Sâyaṇa explains. Or, perhaps, the ascending and descending course of the Sunlight, and its passage during the night from west to east may be intended by the three wheels.

17 This stanza, which is not found in the Ṛigveda, is the beginning of a series of formulas (17—21) for general use in wedding ceremonies, to be recited when the bride mounts her chariot or litter, while she is travelling to her husband's house, and when she enters her new home. *Aryaman*: regarded as the typical intimate friend (which is the meaning of the name) who asks and obtains a woman in marriage for another. See II. 36. 2. *From here*: from thy father's house. *From there*: from thy new home where thy whole life is to be spent.

19 *The noose of Varuṇa*: the girdle with which the bride is girded after she has been bathed, combed, and dressed for the marriage ceremony. See Prof. Max Müller's Ṛigveda-Sanhitâ, Vol. VI. Preface, p. 14. A noose, for a different purpose, is one of Varuṇa's usual accompaniments. *Wooer*: husband.

20 *Bhaga*: as the God of good fortune and the institutor of marriage. The Ṛigveda in the corresponding stanza has Pûshan, the God of Prosperity.

21 Happy be thou and prosper with thy children here: be vigilant to rule thy household in this home.
Closely unite thy body with this man thy lord. So shalt thou, full of years, address thy company.

22 Be not divided; dwell ye here; reach the full time of human life.
With sons and grandsons sport and play, rejoicing in your happy home.

23 Moving by magic power from east to westward, these children twain go sporting round the ocean.
The one beholds all creatures: thou, the other, art born anew, duly arranging seasons.

24 Thou, born afresh, art new and new for ever; ensign of days, before the Dawns thou goest.
Coming, thou orderest for Gods their portion. Thou lengthenest, Moon, the days of our existence.

25 Give thou the woollen robe away: deal treasure to the Brahman-priests.
This Witchery hath got her feet: the wife attendeth on her lord.

26 It turneth dusky-red: the witch who clingeth close is driven off.
Well thrive the kinsmen of this bride: the husband is bound fast in bonds.

27 Unlovely is his body when it glistens with that wicked fiend,
What time the husband wraps about his limbs the garment of his wife.

---

23 In this stanza and the following one, which are but loosely connected with the rest of the hymn, the *children twain*, or two youths or young creatures, are Sûrya and Soma, the Sun and Moon. The stanzas are found also in A. V. VII. 81. 1, 2, and XIII. 2. 11, 12.

25 The formulas that follow are recited on the morning following the consummation of the marriage. *The woollen robe:* 'the garment soiled by the body.'—Wilson. *This Witchery:* or, female fiend, who lay in wait for the bride. *The wife attendeth on her lord:* the fiend returns to her originator as a wife to her husband. This is Prof. Ludwig's interpretation. Prof. Weber takes *wife* and *lord* or husband here to be the wedded pair.

28 The butchering, the cutting-up, the severing of limb and joint,—
Behold the forms which Sûryâ wears: yet these the Brahman purifies.

29 Pungent is this, bitter is this, filled as it were with arrow barbs, empoisoned and not fit for use.
The Brahman who knows Sûryâ well deserves the garment of the bride.

30 The Brahman takes away the robe as a fair thing that brings good luck.
He knows the expiating rite whereby the wife is kept unharmed.

31 Prepare, ye twain, happy and prosperous fortune, speaking the truth in faithful utterances.
Dear unto her, Bṛihaspati, make the husband, and pleasant be these words the wooer speaketh.

32 Remain ye even here and go no farther: strengthen this man, ye Cows, with plenteous offspring.
May Dawns that come for glory, bright with Soma, here may all Gods fix and enchant your spirits.

33 Come, O ye Cows, with offspring dwell around him: he doth not stint the Gods' alloted portion.
To him, your friend, may Pûshan, all the Maruts, to him may Dhâtar, Savitar send vigour.

---

28 Prof. Weber and the St. Petersburg Lexicon explain the first line as referring to the carcass of the animal that has been slaughtered for the festivity. The meanings of *âśasanam*, *viśasanam*, and *adhivikártanam* are uncertain. Prof. Wilson, following Sâyaṇa, translates them by 'border-cloth,' 'head-cloth,' and 'divided skirt;' and in Hymns of the Ṛigveda I have translated somewhat similarly: 'The fringe, the cloth that decks her head, and then the triply-parted robe,—Behold the hues which Sûryâ wears.' *These the Brahman purifies:* as the Brahman who slaughters the animals is not made impure by their blood he is the fittest person to cleanse and purify the soiled garments.

29 *This:* garment. *Not fit for use:* literally, not fit to eat. *Sûryâ:* meaning here the song of Sûryâ's Bridal.

30 The rest of the hymn, with the exception of some five stanzas, is peculiar to the Atharva-veda and not borrowed from the Ṛ. V.

34 Straight in direction be the paths, and thornless, whereby our fellows travel to the wooing.
With Bhaga and with Aryaman Dhâtar endue the pair with strength!

35 Whatever lustre is in dice, whatever lustre is in wine,
Whatever lustre is in cows, Asvins, endue this dame therewith.

36 With all the sheen that balmeth wine, or thigh of female paramour,
With all the sheen that balmeth dice, even with this adorn the dame.

37 He who in water shines unfed with fuel, whom sages worship in their sacrifices,
May he, the Waters' Child, send us sweet waters, those that enhanced the power of mighty Indra.

38 I cast away a handful here, hurtful, injurious to health.
I lift another handful up, sparkling and bringing happiness.

39 Hither let Brâhmans bring her bathing water; let them draw such as guards the lives of heroes.
Aryaman's fire let her encircle, Pûshan! Fathers-in-law stand, with their sons, expectant.

40 Blest be the gold to thee, and blest the water, blest the yoke's opening, and blest the pillar.

---

34 Stanza 23 in the Ṛ V. hymn. *To the wooing:* according to Sâyaṇa's explanation, to the father, to whom the interceders are to apply for his daughter's hand on behalf of their friend. The stanza is out of place at this advanced stage of the proceedings.

37 *He:* Agni. The following formulas are recited when water is brought for the bride's morning bath.

38 *Handful:* of water.

39 *Aryaman's fire:* the husband's household fire, round which the bride walks sprinkling the floor of the room with holy water. *Expectant:* waiting for the bride to come.

40 *Gold:* in the shape of female ornaments. *Yoke's opening:* the yoke being symbolical of ploughing and agricultural operations. *The pillar:* a post in the middle of the threshing-floor to which oxen are

Blest be the waters with their hundred cleansings: blest be thy body's union with thy husband.

41 Cleansing Apâlâ, Indra! thrice, thou gavest sun-bright skin to her
Drawn, Śatakratu! through the hole of car, of wagon, and of yoke.

42 Saying thy prayer for cheerfulness, children, prosperity, and wealth,
Devoted to thy husband, gird thyself for immortality.

43 As vigorous Sindhu won himself imperial lordship of the streams,
So be imperial queen when thou hast come within thy husband's home.

---

tied; symbolical of treading out corn. Prof. Weber suggests that the bride may have been fastened to the pillar as a symbol of stedfast loyalty; and drawn through the yoke to signify that she comes to her husband in perfect health (cf. stanza 41); and adduces instances of somewhat similar popular customs in parts of Germany.

41 The stanza is taken from Ṛ. V. VIII. 80. 7. Apâlâ, it is said, was afflicted with some cutaneous disease and was consequently repudiated by her husband. She sacrificed and prayed to Indra who restored her to health by the procedure mentioned in the verse. 'Sâyaṇa says that Indra dragged her through the wide hole of his chariot, the narrower hole of the cart, and the small hole of the yoke, and she cast off three skins. The first skin became a hedgehog, the second an alligator, and the third a chameleon. I suppose, with Prof. Aufrecht, that the hole or space of the chariot and cart represents the opening between the four wheels; the hole of the yoke seems to me to be the opening through which the animal's head passed, corresponding to Homer's ζεύγλη, Il. 19. 406.'—E. B. Cowell. The rack or frame of the cart is used in the procedure mentioned by Prof. Weber (stanza 40), and the custom of creeping through a gap in a wall, or a hole in a rock or tree, for the cure of certain diseases, was formerly, and is still well known in various parts of Europe. See Simrock's Handbuch der Deutschen Mythologie, p. 538, and Kelly's Folk-Lore, pp. 154—157. In English villages, children were sometimes drawn through the arch made by a strong blackberry shoot in order to free them from whooping-cough. The process was, it seems, supposed to symbolize the regeneration or new birth of the patient.

42 The following formulas (42—46) are recited while the bride is being dressed after her bath.

44 Over thy husband's fathers and his brothers be imperial queen.
Over thy husband's sister and his mother bear supreme control.

45 They who have spun, and woven, and extended, Goddesses who have drawn the ends together,
May they invest thee for full long existence. Heiress of lengthened life, endue this garment.

46 They mourn the living, they arrange the sacred rite: the men have set their thoughts upon a distant cast;
They who have brought the Fathers this delightful gift, when wives allowed their lords the joy of their embrace.

47 I place upon the lap of Earth the Goddess, a firm auspicious stone to bring thee children.
Stand on it, thou, greeted with joy, resplendent: a long long life may Savitar vouchsafe thee.

48 As Agni in the olden time took the right hand of this our Earth,
Even so I take and hold thy hand: be not disquieted, with me, with children and with store of wealth.

---

44 *Fathers*: meaning, probably, father, uncles, and grandfather. This is stanza 46 in the Ṛigveda hymn.

45 Here the bride puts on her upper garment.

46 The stanza is taken, with variations, from R. V. X. 40. 10. *They mourn the living: jîvám rudanti*; according to Sâyaṇa, 'they weep for the life (of their wives);' 'by their very weeping they desire (to pray for) their wives' lives.'—Wilson. According to Prof. Weber, 'they raise loud shouts of joy.' According to Sâṅkhâyana-Gṛihya-Sûtra, I. 15. 2, the stanza is recited if the bride begins to cry on leaving her father's house. *A distant cast*: of the noose or snaring-net: apparently meaning, they have taken thought for the distant future and for the children who will live after them. *This delightful gift*: the sons who will perpetuate the service of the Fathers or ancestral Manes.

47 The bride now treads upon a stone placed for the purpose; and the bridegroom takes her by the hand (48—52).

48 The bridegroom speaks.

49 God Savitar shall take thy hand, and Soma the King shall make thee rich in goodly offspring.

Let Agni, Lord Omniscient, make thee happy, till old old age a wife unto thy husband.

50 I take thy hand in mine for happy fortune that thou mayst reach old age with me thy consort.

Gods, Aryaman, Bhaga, Savitar, Purandhi, have given thee to be my household's mistress.

51 Bhaga and Savitar the God have clasped that hand of thine in theirs.

By rule and law thou art my wife : the master of thy house am I.

52 Be it my care to cherish her : Bṛihaspati hath made thee mine.

A hundred autumns live with me thy husband, mother of my sons!

53 Tvashṭar, by order of the holy sages, hath laid on her Bṛihaspati's robe for glory.

By means of this let Savitar and Bhaga surround this dame, like Sûryâ, with her children.

54 May Indra-Agni, Heaven-Earth, Mâtarisvan, may Mitra-Varuṇa, Bhaga, both the Asvins,

Bṛihaspati, the host of Maruts, Brahma, and Soma magnify this dame with offspring.

55 It was Bṛihaspati who first arranged the hair on Sûryâ's head,

And therefore, O ye Asvins, we adorn this woman for her lord.

---

50 Taken from stanza 36 of the Ṛigveda hymn. *Purandhi*: the God of Intelligence, or, perhaps, of Plenty.

53 This and the following stanza contain benedictions on the bride.

54 *Indra-Agni*, *Heaven-Earth*: regarded as dual deities. *Mitra-Varuṇa*: as a dual deity. *Brahma*: in the neuter gender; the Divine Essence.

56 This lovely form the maiden wears in spirit I long to look on as my wife approaching.
Her will I follow with my nine companions. Who is the sage that loosed the bonds that held her?

57 I free her: he who sees, within my bosom, my heart's nest knows how her fair form hath struck me.
I taste no stolen food: myself untying Varuṇa's nooses I am freed in spirit.

58 Now from the bond of Varuṇa I loose thee, wherein the blessèd Savitar hath bound thee.
O bride, I give thee here beside thy husband fair space and room and pleasant paths to travel.

59 Lift up your weapons. Drive away the demons. Transport this woman to the world of virtue.
Dhâtar, most wise, hath found for her a husband. Let him who knows, King Bhaga, go before her.

60 Bhaga hath formed the four legs of the litter, wrought the four pieces that compose the framework.
Tvashṭar hath decked the straps that go across it. May it be blest, and bring us happy fortune.

61 Mount this, all-hued, gold-tinted, strong-wheeled, fashioned of Kiṇsuka, this chariot lightly rolling,
Bound for the world of life immortal, Sûryâ! Make for thy lord a happy bride's procession.

---

56 In this and the following stanzas the bridegroom expresses his rapture at the sight of his bride apparelled to meet him. It will be observed that in this and other places the order of the stanzas does not correspond with the stages of the actual procedure of the ceremony. *Nine companions:* the friends who attended the bridegroom. Prof. Weber suggests the possibility of a comparison with the ten witnesses in the Roman Confarreatio (Rossbach, röm. Ehe, pp. 117—119). *That held her:* in her father's house.

58 The first line is repeated from stanza 19. The second line begins the address to the bride as she leaves home (58—61).

61 The stanza is taken from the Ṛigveda hymn, verse 20. *Kiṇsuka:* the wood of the Butea Frondosa. *Sûryâ:* the girl is addressed by the name of the typical bride Sûryâ the daughter of the Sun.

62 To us, O Varuṇa, bring her, kind to brothers; bring her, Bṛihaspati, gentle to the cattle.
Bring her, O Indra, gentle to her husband: bring her to us, O Savitar, blest with children.

63 Hurt not the girl, ye Pillars twain upon the path which Gods have made.
The portal of the heavenly home we make the bride's auspicious road.

64 Let prayer be offered up before and after, prayer in the middle, lastly, all around her.
Reaching the Gods' inviolable castle shine in thy lord's world gentle and auspicious.

HYMN II.

For thee with bridal train they first escorted Sûryâ to her home.
Give to the husband in return, Agni, the wife with future sons.

---

62 This and the two following stanzas contain the prayers of the friends and relatives of the bridegroom who are awaiting the arrival of the nuptial procession.

63 *Pillars twain:* the main door-posts of the bridegroom's house. So with the Romans: 'When the procession arrived at the house of the bridegroom, the door of which was adorned with garlands and flowers, the bride was carried across the threshold . . . . that she might not knock against it with her foot, which would have been an evil omen.'—Smith's Dictionary of Antiquities—Matrimonium.

64 *The God's inviolable castle:* the bridegroom's house in which the Gods are duly honoured; the *heavenly home* of the preceding stanza.

A full account of the marriage ceremonies of the Hindus, derived from the ritual of Brâhmans who use the Sâmaveda, will be found in Colebrooke's Miscellaneous Essays, No. III. Prof. Ludwig's Commentary on the Ṛigveda portion of the hymn is full and excellent; and the portion of the original hymn describing Sûryâ's Bridal has been exhaustively discussed by Prof. J. Ehni, Zeitschrift der Deutschen Morgenländischen Gesellschaft, XXXIII. pp. 166—176.

The hymn is a continuation of hymn I. and contains, though not in the exact order in which they are to be performed, the rest of the most important nuptial ceremonies.

1 Stanzas 1—4 are taken from Ṛigveda X. 85. 38—41. *Thee:* Agni, represented by the sacred fire in the house of the bride's father, round which she is now led by the bridegroom. *They:* the Gandharvas, according to Sâyaṇa.

2 Agni hath given the bride again with splendour and a lengthened life.
Long-lived be he who is her lord: a hundred autumns let him live.

3 She was the wife of Soma first: next the Gandharva was thy lord.
Agni was thy third husband: now one born of woman is thy fourth.

4 Soma to the Gandharva, and to Agni the Gandharva gave.
Now, Agni hath bestowed on me riches and sons and this my bride.

5 Your favouring grace hath come, ye who are rich in spoil! Asvins, our longings are stored up within your hearts.
Ye, Lords of Splendour, have become our twofold guard: may we as dear friends reach the dwelling of the friend.

6 Thou, Dame, rejoicing, take with kindly spirit wealth worthy to be famed, with all thy heroes.
Give, Lords of Light, a fair ford, good to drink at: remove the spiteful stump that blocks the pathway.

---

2 Stanzas 2—11 are benedictive formulas to be recited while the procession is on its way to the bridegroom's house. *Long-lived:* with reference to the belief that the husband's life was in danger on the wedding night. Ludwig refers to the advice given by Hermes to Odysseus (Homer, Od. X. 297—301) in case the goddess should invite him to share her couch.

3 As the typical bride Sûryâ was married to Soma [and probably also for other reasons], the young maid originally belongs to him; then to the Gandharva as the guardian of virginity; then to Agni as the sacred fire round which she walks in the marriage ceremony; and fourthly to her human husband.—Grassmann.

5 *Ye who are rich in spoil:* the exact meaning of *vâjinîvasû* is uncertain. Weber translates it by Opferreiche, rich in sacrifice; others by riders or drivers of fleet mares or horses; lords of noble mares. *Of the friend: aryamnâh;* meaning, here, of the bridegroom. The stanza is taken from Ṛ. V. X. 40. 12.

6 *With all thy heroes:* with brave sons to come hereafter. *Lords of Light:* Asvins, heralds of the dawn. The stanza is taken, with variations, from Ṛ. V. X. 40. 13

7 May all the Rivers, all the Plants, may all the Forests, all the Fields,
O Bride, protect thee from the fiend, guard his sons' mother for her lord.

8 Our feet are on this pleasant path, easy to travel, bringing bliss,
Whereon no hero suffers harm, which wins the wealth of other men.

9 Hear these my words, ye men, the benediction through which the wedded pair have found high fortune.
May the divine Apsarases, Gandharvas, all they who are these fruitful trees' protectors,
Regard this bride with their auspicious favour, nor harm the nuptial pomp as it advances.

10 Consumptions, which, through various folk, attack the bride's resplendent train,
These let the holy Gods again bear to the place from which they sprang.

11 Let not the highway thieves who lie in ambush find the wedded pair.
Let wicked men's malignities go elsewhere by an easy path.

12 I look upon the house and bride's procession with prayer and with the gentle eye of friendship.
All that is covered there in perfect beauty may Savitar make pleasant to the husband.

13 She hath come home, this dame come home to bless us this her appointed world hath Dhâtar shown her.
So may Prajâpati, and both the Asvins, Aryaman, Bhaga gladden her with offspring.

---

10 This and the following stanza are taken from R. V. X. 85. 31, 32.

12 Stanzas 12—18 contain formulas to be recited when the procession arrives at the bridegroom's house. *I:* perhaps, as Weber suggests, the bridegroom's father who is awaiting the bride's arrival. *All that is covered there:* the charms of the bride seated in her litter.

13 *Dhâtar:* the Supporter or Establisher, regarded as the special Upholder of marriage. Cf. VI. 60. 3; VII. 17. 1—3. *Bhaga* and *Prajâpati* also are deities presiding over marriage and the production of children.

14 This dame hath come, an animated corn-field: there sow, thou man, the seed of future harvest.
She from her teeming side shall bear thee children, and feed them from the fountain of her bosom.

15 Take thou thy stand, a Queen art thou, like Vishṇu here, Sarasvatî!
O Sinîvâlî, let her bear children, and live in Bhaga's grace.

16 So let your wave bear up the pins, and ye, O Waters, spare the thongs;
And never may the holy pair, sinless and innocent, suffer harm.

17 Not evil-eyed no slayer of thy husband, be strong, mild, kind, and gentle to thy household.
Mother of heroes, love thy husband's father: be happy, and through thee may we too prosper.

18 No slayer of thy husband or his father, gentle and bright, bring blessing on the cattle.
Loving thy husband's father, bring forth heroes. Tend well this household fire: be soft and pleasant.

19 Up and begone! What wish hath brought thee hither from thine own house? Thy mightier, I conjure thee.

---

14 *Thou man:* the text has *naraḥ*, ye men! the pluralis excellentiae, used honorificially for the singular.

15 *A Queen:* or, splendid *Sarasvatî:* the bride is complimentarily addressed as an incarnation of the Goddess of Fertility. *Sinîvâlî:* Goddess of the day of New Moon, and presiding over fecundity and easy childbirth like the Latin Lucina. Cf. Herrick's 'midwife moon.' See Vol. I., Index of Names, etc.

16 The stanza is a later addition to Ṛ. V. III. 33 which is an address by the great Ṛishi Viṣvâmitra to the rivers Vipâṣ and Ṣutudrî which he is about to cross. *Pair:* here meaning the bride and bridegroom; but in the Ṛ. V. hymn the bullocks that drew Viṣvâmitra's car. The verse is out of place here, and should come between stanzas 11 and 12, while the procession is yet on its way.

17 Cf. Ṛ. V. X. 85. 44. *Evil-eyed:* see A. V. II. 7. 5, note.

19 Stanzas 19—27 contain exorcising formulas and benedictions on the new household. *Nirṛiti:* Destruction personified. *Malignity:* *Arâti.*

Vain is the hope, O Nirṛiti, that brought thee. Fly off, Malignity; stay here no longer.

20 As first of all this woman hath adored the sacred household fire,
So do thou, Dame, pay homage to the Fathers and Sarasvatî.

21 Take thou this wrapper as a screen, to be a covering for the bride.
O Sinîvâlî, let her bear children, and live in Bhaga's grace.

22 Let her who shall be blest with sons, the maid who finds a husband, step
Upon the rough grass that ye spread and on the skin ye lay beneath.

23 Over the ruddy-coloured skin strew thou the grass, the Balbuja.
Let her, the mother of good sons, sit there and serve this Agni here.

24 Step on the skin and wait upon this Agni: he is the God who drives away all demons.
Here bear thou children to this man thy husband: let this thy boy be happy in his birthright.

25 Let many babes of varied form and nature spring in succession from this fruitful mother.
Wait on this fire, thou bringer of good fortune. Here with thy husband serve the Gods with worship.

---

20 *Household fire:* similarly among the Romans the husband received the bride with fire and water which she had to touch by way of introduction to her new household duties.

22 *The skin:* so after entering her new home the Roman bride was seated on a sheep-skin, and then the keys of the house were put into her hand.

23 *Balbuja:* a common coarse species of grass (Eleusine Indica) found growing in large tufts on pasture ground, road sides, etc. The *ruddy-coloured skin*, as Weber observes, probably symbolizes the household fire.

24 *This thy boy:* a little boy is introduced, as a representative of her future children.

25 *Babes:* the text has *paśávaḥ*; literally, domestic animals.

26 Bliss-bringer, furthering thy household's welfare, dear, gladdening thy husband and his father, enter this home, mild to thy husband's mother.

27 Be pleasant to thy husband's sire, sweet to thy household and thy lord.
To all this clan be gentle, and favour these men's prosperity.

28 Signs of good fortune mark the bride. Come all of you and look at her.
Wish her prosperity : take on you her evil luck and go your way.

29 Ye youthful maidens, ill-disposed, and all ye ancient women here,
Give all your brilliance to the bride, then to your several homes depart!

30 Sûryâ the child of Savitar mounted for high felicity
Her litter with its cloth of gold, wearing all forms of loveliness.

31 Rise, mount the bridal bed with cheerful spirit. Here bring forth children to this man thy husband.
Watchful and understanding like Indrâṇî wake thou before the earliest light of Morning.

32 The Gods at first lay down beside their consorts; body with body met in close embracement.
O Dame, like Sûryâ perfect in her grandeur, here rich in future children, meet thy husband.

---

27 *To thy husband's sire: çváçurebhyaḥ*; the honorific plural.

28 This and the two following stanzas are out of place here. They are recited while the procession is on its way.

31 Stanzas 31—40 contain the epithalamium. *Indrâṇî*: Indra's Consort. Among the Romans 'the bride was conducted by matrons who had not had more than one husband *(pronubae)* to the lectus genialis in the atrium, which was on this occasion magnificently adorned and strewed with flowers.'—Smith's Dictionary of Greek and Roman Antiquities: Matrimonium.

33 Rise and go hence, Viṣvâvasu : with reverence we worship thee.
Steal to her sister dwelling with her father : this is the share—mark this—of old assigned thee.

34 Apsarases rejoice and feast together between the sun and place of sacrificing.
These are thy kith and kin : go thou and join them: I in due season worship thee, Gandharva.

35 Homage we pay to the Gandharva's favour, obeisance to his eye and fiery anger.
Viṣvâvasu, with prayer we pay thee homage. Go hence to those Apsarases thy consorts.

36 May we be happy with abundant riches. We from this place have banished the Gandharva.
The God is gone to the remotest region, and we have come where men prolong existence.

37 In your due season, Parents! come together. Mother and sire be ye of future children.
Embrace this woman like a happy lover. Raise ye up offspring here : increase your riches.

38 Send her most rich in every charm, O Pûshan, her who shall be the sharer of my pleasures ;
Her who shall twine her eager arms about me, and welcome all my love and soft embraces.

39 Up, happy bridegroom ! with a joyous spirit caress thy wife and throw thine arm around her.

---

33 *Viṣvâvasu:* one of the Gandharvas, who is regarded as the protector of virginity. He is told to leave the bride who no longer requires his care, and to transfer his guardianship to her unmarried sister. The first line is taken from Ṛ. V. X. 85. 22, and the second, with variations, from verse 21 of the same hymn.

34 *Between the sun and place of sacrificing:* between heaven and earth; in mid-air. Cf. A. V. VII. 109. 3, where I have translated *havirdhânam* (receptacle of the offering; cart on which the Soma plants are carried) more literally by 'libation-holder.'

38 This stanza, addressed by the bridegroom to the bride, is taken from Ṛ. V. X. 85. 37.

Here take your pleasure, procreate your offspring.
May Savitar bestow long life upon you.

40 So may the Lord of Life vouchsafe you children,
Aryaman bind you, day and night, together.
Enter thy husband's house with happy omens, bring blessing to our quadrupeds and bipeds.

41 Sent by the Gods associate with Manu, the vesture of the bride, the nuptial garment,—
He who bestows this on a thoughtful Brahman, drives from the marriage-bed all evil demons.

42 The priestly meed wherewith ye twain present me, the vesture of the bride, the nuptial garment,—
This do ye both, Bṛihaspati and Indra, bestow with loving-kindness on the Brahman.

43 On your soft couch awaking both together, revelling heartily with joy and laughter,
Rich with brave sons, good cattle, goodly homestead, live long to look on many radiant mornings.

44 Clad in new garments, fragrant, well-apparelled, to meet refulgent Dawn have I arisen.
I, like a bird that quits the egg, am freed from sin and purified.

45 Splendid are Heaven and Earth, still near to bless us, mighty in their power;
The seven streams have flowed: may they, Goddesses, free us from distress.

---

40 This stanza, taken from Ṛ. V. X. 85. 43, is not, properly, part of the epithalamium, but is recited when the bridegroom has entered his home with the bride.

41 Stanzas 41—58 contain the ceremonial that follows the wedding night. *Associate with Manu:* with reference to the great antiquity of the custom. Cf. A. V. VII. 37. *The vesture of the bride:* cf. the preceding hymn, stanza 29. *All evil demons:* so in Spenser's Epithalamion the approach of 'the Pouke,' 'other evil sprights,' and 'mischivous witches with theyr charmes,' is deprecated.

44 Spoken by the husband.

45 *The seven streams have flowed:* said, probably, with reference to the morning ablutions of the wedded pair.

46 To Sûryâ and the Deities, to Mitra and to Varuṇa,
Who know aright the thing that is, this adoration have I paid.

47 He without ligature, before making incision in the neck,
Closed up the wound again, most wealthy Bounteous Lord who healeth the dissevered parts.

48 Let him flash gloom away from us, the blue, the yellow and the red.
I fasten to this pillar here the burning pest Pṛishâtakî.

49 All witcheries that hang about this garment, all royal Varuṇa's entangling nooses,
All failure of success and all misfortunes here I deposit fastened to the pillar.

50 My body that I hold most dear trembles in terror at this robe.
Tree, make an apron at the top. Let no misfortune fall on us.

51 May all the hems and borders, all the threads that form the web and woof,
The garment woven by the bride, be soft and pleasant to our touch.

---

46 Stanza 17 of Ṛ. V. X. 85.

47 The stanza is taken from Ṛ. V. VIII. 1. 12, where the reference is to Indra healing Etaṣa who had been wounded by Sûrya.

48 The colours are probably the amissae virginitatis signa. *Pṛishâtakî:* according to the St. Petersburg Lexicon, a certain disease or the female demon who causes it; according to Weber, the garment that the bride has worn, an interpretation which is supported by the following stanza.

50 *Tree:* the post on which the garment is hung. *Apron:* or encircling band, so as to form a pocket to confine the threatened misfortune.

51 The garment that the young husband is to wear on the first day of his wedded life, and that, apparently, has been made for him by the bride. Weber refers to a similar custom among peasants in Saxony, the garment so prepared being called 'das Brauthemde,' the bride-shirt.

52 These maids who from their father's house have come with longing to their lord have let the preparation pass. All hail!

53 Her whom Bṛihaspati hath loosed the Viṣve Devas keep secure.
With all the splendour that is stored in cows do we enrich this girl.

54 Her whom Bṛihaspati hath loosed the Viṣve Devas keep secure.
With all the vigour that is stored in cows do we enrich this girl.

55 Her whom Bṛihaspati, etc.
With all good fortune, etc.

56 Her whom Bṛihaspati, etc.
With all the glory, etc.

57 Her whom Bṛihaspati, etc.
With all the milky store possessed by cows do we enrich this girl.

58 Her whom Bṛihaspati hath freed the Viṣve Devas keep secure.
With all the store of sap that cows contain do we enrich this girl.

59 If, wearing long loose hair, these men have danced together in thy house, committing sin with shout and cry,
May Agni free thee from that guilt, may Savitar deliver thee.

---

52 The meaning and the application of the stanza are obscure. *These maids:* probably the honorific plural, as in other places of the hymn, and meaning only the bride. The word *dikshdm*, meaning usually consecration or preparation for some religious observance, appears in this place to mean the bride's dress or some portion of it; perhaps a loose wrapper to be thrown off when her ablutions are completed. *All hail!: svāhā;* the benedictive exclamation used at the close of invocations to the deities, and apparently out of place here.

53 *Her:* the bride. According to Ludwig, the *dikshā* (weihe). The following five stanzas are mere repetitions with the change of one word in each.

59 Stanzas 59—62 contain expiatory formulas to avert the evil consequences of riotous, foolish, or inauspicious doings in the house of the

60 If in thy house thy daughter here have wept, with wild dishevelled locks, committing sin with her lament,
May Agni, etc.

61 If the bride's sisters, if young maids have danced together in thy house, committing sin with shout and cry,
May Agni free thee from that guilt, may Savitar deliver thee.

62 If any evil have been wrought by mischief-makers that affects thy cattle, progeny or house,
May Agni free thee from the woe, may Savitar deliver thee.

63 This woman utters wish and prayer, as down she casts the husks of corn:
Long live my lord and master! yea, a hundred autumns let him live!

64 Join thou this couple, Indra! like the Chakravâka and his mate:
May they attain to full old age with children in their happy home.

65 Whatever magic hath been wrought on cushion, chair, or canopy,
Each spell to mar the wedding rites, all this we throw into the bath.

66 Whatever fault or error was in marriage or in bridal pomp,
This woe we wipe away upon the cloak the interceder wears.

---

bride's father after the departure of the nuptial procession. The remaining stanzas contain expiatory and benedictive formulas to be recited at various stages of the ceremony and afterwards.

63 *Down:* into the sacred fire as an oblation.

64 *The Chakravâka:* this bird (Anas Casarca, commonly called the Brahmany duck) and his mate—the Chakwâ and Chakwî—are regarded as emblems of conjugal love and constancy, and as such are very frequently mentioned in later Indian poetry.

66 *The interceder:* or match-maker, who found and wooed the bride for his friend. See A. V. VI. 60. 1. This 'is a familiar duty in the Isle of Man, and he who discharges it is known by a familiar name.

67 We, having laid the stain and fault upon the interceder's cloak,
Are pure and meet for sacrifice. May he prolong our lives for us.

68 Now let this artificial comb, wrought with a hundred teeth, remove
Aught of impurity that dims the hair upon this woman's head.

69 We take away Consumption from each limb and member of the bride.
Let not this reach Earth, nor the Gods in heaven, let it not reach the sky or air's wide region.
Let not this dust that sullies reach the Waters, nor Yama, Agni, nor the host of Fathers.

70 With all the milk that is in Earth I gird thee, with all the milk that Plants contain I dress thee.
I gird thee round with children and with riches. Do thou, thus girt, receive the offered treasure.

71 I am this man, that dame art thou: I am the psalm and thou the verse. I am the heaven and thou the earth.
So will we dwell together here, parents of children yet to be.

They call him the *Dooiney Molla*—literally, the 'man-praiser'; and his primary function is that of an informal, unmercenary, purely friendly and philanthropic match-maker, introduced by the young man to persuade the parents of the young woman that he is a splendid fellow with substantial possessions or magnificent prospects, and entirely fit to marry her.'—Hall Caine, *The Manxman*. The interceder or match-maker in India received a *kambala*, blanket, woollen cloth, or cloak for his trouble, and was accordingly held responsible for any short-comings in the arrangements. Weber refers to a somewhat similar German custom according to which the bride gives a handkerchief to the priest after the marriage ceremony and to the bridegroom's nearest male relative after the first dance that follows.

67 *He:* apparently the interceder, indirectly, by taking on himself all responsibility for fault and failure in the proceedings.

71 *I am this man, this dame art thou:* the Roman custom was somewhat similar; but the bride saluted her husband with the words: *ubi tu Caius, ego Caia. The psalm: sáman* or chanted song. *The verse: rich;* the recited verse, which is regarded as the mother or source of the *Sáman*.

72 Unmarried men desire to wed; bountiful givers wish for sons.
Together may we dwell with strength unscathed for high prosperity.

73 May they, the Fathers who, to view the bride, have joined this nuptial train,
Grant to this lady and her lord children and peaceful happiness.

74 Her who first guided by a rein came hither, giving the bride here offspring and possessions,
Let them convey along the future's pathway. Splendid, with noble children, she hath conquered.

75 Wake to long life, watchful and understanding, yea, to a life shall last a hundred autumns.
Enter the house to be the household's mistress. A long long life let Savitar vouchsafe thee.

---

74 *Guided by a rein:* the meaning of *raṣanâyámânâ* here is obscure. Weber translates the word by 'einen Gürtel bildend,' forming a girdle (central point for the whole marriage procession?); and Ludwig by '[wie] eine kette gleichsam nach sich ziehend,' drawing as it were a chain after her. *Them:* perhaps the Fathers mentioned in stanza 73.

For a very full and detailed account of marriage ceremonies and customs among the ancient Indians, see Dr. E. Haas, Indische Studien, V. pp. 267—412.

BOOK XV.

HYMN I.

THERE was a roaming Vrâtya. He rousèd Prajâpati to action. 2 Prajâpati beheld gold in himself and engendered it. 3 That became unique, that became distinguished, that became great, that became excellent, that became Devotion, that became holy Fervour, that became Truth: through that he was born. 4 He grew, he became great, he became Mahâdeva. 5 He gained the lordship

---

The purpose of this unique and obscure Book is the idealization and hyperbolical glorification of the Vrâtya, or perhaps as Professor Aufrecht conjectures, of the Vrâtya who by means of the prescribed ceremonies obtains investiture with the sacred cord and is permitted to share the duties and privileges of Brâhmanical Âryans. The Book has been transliterated and translated by Prof. Aufrecht in Indische Studien, I. pp. 121—140.

1 *Vrâtya*: from *vrâta*, a troop; the chief of a band of wanderers of Âryan extraction, but absolutely independent, free from the fetters of the Brâhmanical hierarchy, and not following the Âryan, i. e. Brâhmanist way of life. See Weber, Indische Studien, I. pp. 33, 51.

'The Tandya-Brâhmana of the Sâma Veda contains the Vrâtya-stomas by which the Vràtyas or *Aryans not living according to the Brahmanical system* could get admission to that community. Some of them are thus described: "They drive in open chariots of war, carry bows and lances, wear turbans, robes bordered with red and having fluttering ends and sheep skins folded double; their leaders are distinguished by brown robes and silver neck ornaments; they pursue neither agriculture nor commerce; their laws are in a state of confusion; they speak the same language as those who have received Brâhmanical consecration, but nevertheless call what is easily spoken hard to pronounce." '—R. Ch. Dutt's Ancient India, I. pp. 286, 287.

2 *Gold*: the meaning is obscure. 'Ist darunter das Om gemeint?'—Aufrecht.

4 *Mahâdeva*: the Great God; a title specially given in the Veda to Rudra or to one of the deities connected with him. In later literature and at the present day Mahâdeva (Hindî, Mahâdeo) means exclusively Ṣiva.

of the Gods. He became Lord. 6 He became
Chief Vrâtya. He held a bow, even that Bow of
Indra. 7 His belly is dark-blue, his back is red.
8 With dark-blue he envelops a detested rival,
with red he pierces the man who hates him: so
the theologians say.

II.

He arose and went his way to the eastern region. The Bṛihat, the Rathantara, the Âdityas and all the Gods followed him. That man is alienated from the Bṛihat, the Rathantara, the Âdityas, and all Gods who reviles the Vrâtya who possesses this knowledge. He who hath this knowledge becomes the beloved home of the Bṛihat, the Rathantara, the Âdityas, and all the Gods. In the eastern region Faith is his leman, the hymn his panegyrist, knowledge his vesture, day his turban, night his hair, Indra's two Bays his circular ornaments, the splendour of the stars his jewel. Present and Future are his running footmen, mind is his war-chariot, Mâtarisvan and Pavamâna are they who draw it, Vâta is his charioteer, Storm his goad,

---

6 *Bow of Indra:* the rainbow. Cf. Revelation, X. 1.

1 *Bṛihat . . . Rathantara:* two important Sâmans. See XI. 3. 16. *Panegyrist: mâgadháḥ;* the word meaning originally 'belonging to the Magadha country (south Behar)' means a professional bard, minstrel, or panegyrist of a king, whose duty it was to recite the praises of his lord with allusions to his genealogy and the deeds of his ancestors, or to attend his army on a march and animate the soldiers with martial songs. Prof. Weber (History of Indian Literature, p. 112) suggests another interpretation of the word in this place: 'Owing to the obscurity of the Vrátya book, the proper meaning of this passage is not altogether clear, and it is possible, therefore, that here also the dissolute minstrel might be intended.. Still the connection set forth in the Sáma-Sútras of Láṭyáyana and Dráhyáyaṇa, as well as in the corresponding passage of the Kátíya-Sútra, between the Vrátyas and the *magadhadeśíya brahmabandhu*, and the hatred with which the Magadhas are elsewhere (see Roth, p. 38) spoken of in the Atharva-Saṃhitá, both lead us to interpret the *mágadha* of the Vrátya book as an heretical teacher [or promulgator of Budhhist doctrine].'

Fame and Glory are his harbingers. Fame and Glory come to him who hath this knowledge. 2

2 He arose and went away to the southern region. Yajñâyajñiya and Vâmadevya and Sacrifice and Sacrificer and sacrificial victims followed him. The man who reviles the Vrâtya possessing this knowledge is alienated from Yajñâyajñiya and Vâmadevya, Sacrifice, Sacrificer and sacrificial victims. He who hath this knowledge becomes the beloved home of Yajñâyajñiya, Vâmadevya, Sacrifice, Sacrificer, and sacrificial victims. In the southern region Dawn is his leman, Mitra his panegyrist, knowledge his vesture, day his turban, night his hair, Indra's two Bays are his circular ornaments, New Moon Night and Full Moon Night are his running attendants, Mind, etc. as in stanza 1.

3 He arose and went away to the western region. Vairûpa and Vairâja, the Waters, and King Varuṇa followed him. He who reviles the Vrâtya possessing this knowledge is alienated from Vairûpa and Vairâja, the Waters, and Varuṇa the King. He who possesses this knowledge becomes the dear home of Vairûpa and Vairâja, the Waters and King Varuṇa. In the western region Irâ is his leman, Laughter his panegyrist, knowledge, etc., as above. Day and Night are his running attendants, Mind, etc., as above.

---

2 *Yajñâyajñiya :* the name of a Sâman containing the verse Ṛ. V. I. 168. 1, which begins with Yajñâ-yajñâ, 'At every sacrifice.' *Vâmadevya :* the name of several Sâmans, especially of one consisting of the three verses Ṛ. V. IV. 31. 1 ; VIII. 81. 7 ; I. 18. 6 = Sâma-veda I. ii. ii. 3. 5—7. Cf. A. V. IV. 34. 1 ; VIII. 10. 13.

3 *Vairûpa . . . Vairâja* : names of important Sâmans. See Haug's Aitareya Brâhmaṇam, II. p. 309. *Irâ :* closely connected with Iḍâ and Ilâ ; Recreation Enjoyment.

4 He arose and went away to the northern region. Syaita and Naudhasa, the Seven Rishis, and King Soma followed him. He who reviles the Vrâtya possessing this knowledge is alienated from Syaita, etc. He who hath this knowledge becomes the dear home of Syaita, etc. In the northern region Lightning is his leman, Thunder his panegyrist, etc. as above. Revelation and Tradition are his running attendants, Mind, etc., as above.

III.

For a whole year he stood erect. The Gods said unto him, Why standest thou, O Vrâtya? He answered and said, Let them bring my couch. 3 They brought the couch for that Vrâtya. 4 Two of its feet were Summer and Spring, and two were Autumn and the Rains. 5 Brihat and Rathantara were the two long boards, Yajñâyajñiya and Vâmadevya the two cross-boards. 6 Holy verses were the strings lengthwise, and Yajus formulas the cross-tapes. 7 Sacred lore was the blanket, Devotion the coverlet. 8 The Sâman was the cushion, and chanting the bolster. 9 The Vrâtya ascended that couch. 10 The hosts of Gods were his attendants, solemn vows his messengers, and all creatures his worshippers. 11 All creatures become the worshippers of him who possesses this knowledge.

IV.

For him they made the two Spring months protectors from the eastern region, and Brihat and

---

4 *Syaita and Naudhasa:* two important Sâmans. 'In the form of the Naudhasa Sâman the earth is wedded to heaven, and in the form of the Syaita Sâman heaven is wedded to the earth' (Haug's Ait. Brâhmaṇam, II. p. 308). *Revelation and Tradition:* *srutám cha vísrutam cha;* 'Ruf und Beruhmtheit,' Fame and Celebrity.'—Aufrecht.

6 *Holy verses:* *richas;* verses of the Rigveda.

1 *They:* the Gods. *Spring months:* Chaitra and Vaisakha; mid-March to mid-May. 2 *Summer months:* Suchi and Sukra (Pure and

Rathantara superintendents. The two Spring months protect from the eastern region, and Bṛihat and Rathantara superintend, the man who possesses this knowledge. For him they made the two Summer months protectors from the southern region, and Yajñâyajñiya and Vâmadevya superintendents. The two Summer months, etc. as in verse 1, *mutatis mutandis.* 3 They made the two Rain months his protectors from the western region, and Vairûpa and Vairâja superintendents. The two Rain months, etc. as above. 4 They made the two Autumn months his protectors from the northern region, and Ṣyaita and Naudhasa superintendents. The two Autumn months, etc. as above. 5 They made the two Winter months his protectors from the region of the nadir, and earth and Agni superintendents. The two Winter months, etc. 6 They made the two Dewy months his protectors from the region of the zenith, and Heaven and the Âdityas superintendents. The two Dewy months, etc.

V.

For him they made the Archer Bhava a deliverer from the intermediate space of the eastern region. Bhava the Archer, a deliverer, delivers him from the intermediate space of the eastern region. Neither Ṣarva nor Bhava nor Iṣâna slays him who

---

Bright), or Jyeshṭha and Âshâḍha; mid-May to mid-July. 3 *Rain months:* Srâvaṇa and Bhâdra; mid-July to mid-September. 4 *Autumn months:* Âṣvina and Kârttika; mid-September to mid-November. 5 *Winter months:* Agrahâyaṇa and Pausha; mid-November to mid-January. 6 *Dewy months:* Mâgha and Phâlguna; mid-January to mid-March. But the Indian seasons vary considerably according to geographical situation.

---

1 *Iṣâna:* Lord, Ruler; one of the older names of Rudra.

possesses this knowledge, or his cattle, or his kinsmen. 2 They made Sarva the Archer his deliverer from the intermediate space of the southern region, etc., as in verse 1, *mutatis mutandis.* 3 They made Pasupati the Archer his deliverer from the intermediate space of the western region, etc. 4 They made the Awful God, the Archer, his deliverer from the intermediate space of the northern region, etc., as above. 5 They made Rudra the Archer his deliverer from the intermediate space of the region of the nadir, etc. 6 They made Mahâdeva his deliverer from the intermediate space of the region of the zenith, etc. 7 They made Isâna the Archer his deliverer from all the intermediate regions. Isâna the Archer, a deliverer, delivers him from all the intermediate regions. Neither Sarva, nor Bhava, nor Isâna slays him who possesses this knowledge, or his cattle, or his kinsmen.

VI.

He went his way to the region of the nadir. Earth and Agni and herbs and trees and shrubs and plants followed him. He who possesses this knowledge becomes the dear home of Earth and Agni and herbs and trees and shrubs and plants. 2 He went his way to the region of the zenith. Right and Truth and Sun and Moon and Stars followed him. He who possesses this knowledge becomes, etc., as in verse 1, *mutatis mutandis.* 3 He went away to the last region. Richas, Sâmans Yajus formulas and Devotion followed him. He

---

Paṣupati: Lord of Beasts. See XI. 6. 9.

4 *The Awful God: ugrám devám ;* 'the God Ugra'—Muir. Rudra is meant.

The hymn has been translated by Muir, O. S. Texts, IV. 338.

who, etc., as above. 4 He went away to the great region. Itihâsa and Purâṇa and Gâthâs and Nârâśansîs followed him. He who, etc. 5 He went away to the supreme region. The Âhavanîya, Gârhapatya, and Southern Fires, and Sacrifice, and Sacrificer, and sacrificial victims followed him. He who, etc. 6 He went away to the unindicated region. The Seasons, groups of seasons, the worlds and their inhabitants, the months and half-months, and Day and Night followed him. He who, etc. 7 He went away to the unfrequented region. Thence he thought that he should not return. Diti and Aditi and Iḍâ and Indrâṇî followed him. He who, etc. 8 He went away to the regions. Virâj and all the Gods and all the Deities followed him. He who, etc. 9 He went away to all the intermediate spaces. Prajâpati and Parameshṭhin and the Father and the Great Father followed him. He who possesses this knowledge becomes the beloved home of Prajâpati and Parameshṭhin and the Father and the Great Father.

VII.

He, having become moving majesty, went to the ends of the earth. He became the sea. 2 Prajâpati and Parameshṭhin and the Father and the Great Father and the Waters and Faith, turned into rain, followed him. 3 The Waters, Faith, and rain approach him who possesses this knowledge. 4 Faith and Sacrifice and the world, having become

---

4 *Itihâsa and Purâṇa:* legendary and traditionary records, the forerunners of the two great epics and the many Purâṇas that have actually come down to us. *Gâthâs:* stanzas preserved by oral transmission among the people. *Nârâśansîs:* eulogistic legends of heroes. 5 *Âhavanîya:* the eastern of the three fires burning at a sacrifice. 7 *Diti:* see VII. 7.

9 *Parameshṭhin:* see VIII. 5. 9. *The Father:* perhaps Bṛihaspati. *The Great Father:* Brahmâ, the phenomenal Creator.

food and nourishment, turned toward him. 5 Faith, Sacrifice, the world, food and nourishment approach him who possesses this knowledge.

VIII.

He was filled with passion: from him sprang the Râjanya. 2 He came to the people, to kinsmen, food and nourishment. 3 He who possesses this knowledge becomes the dear home of the people, kinsmen, food and nourishment.

IX.

He went away to the people. 2 Meeting and Assembly and Army and Wine followed him. 3 He who hath this knowledge becomes the dear home of Meeting, Assembly, Army, and Wine.

X.

So let the King, to whose house the Vrâtya who possesses this knowledge comes as a guest, 2 Honour him as superior to himself. So he doth not act against the interests of his princely rank

---

Râjanya: the oldest designation of a Kshatriya or man of the military and royal class. In the Purusha-Sûkta (Ṛ. V. X. 90; A. V. XIX. 6) the Râjanya is said to have been (at creation) the arms of the sacrificed Purusha or Primal Man who is identified with the universe. In the Taittirîya-Sanhitâ (VII. 1. 1) and the Ṣatapatha-Brâhmaṇa (II. 1. 4) he is said to have been generated by Prajâpati, and in the Taittirîya-Brâhmaṇa (III. 12. 9) the Yajur-veda is said to be the womb from which he was born. See Muir, O. S. Texts, I. 16, 17. The word *râjanyàḥ*, which comes from the root *râj*, to rule, is here fancifully connected with the root *raj* (*sò 'rajyata*, he was filled with passion).

2 *Meeting: sabhấ;* of the people of the hamlet. *Assembly: sámitiḥ;* congregation of the clan for sacrificial, religious, or other important purpose. See Zimmer, Altindisches Leben, pp. 172—175. *Wine: súrâ;* the material from which this liquor was made was probably barley or rice. It may have been the *dhânyo rásaḥ* (juice of corn) of A. V. II. 26. 5, a sort of beer. In the Taittirîya-Brahmaṇa I. 3. 2. 2, Soma is said to be the best nourishment of the Gods, and Surâ of men. They are a pair, husband and wife. See Zimmer, Altindisches Leben, p. 280.

or his kingdom. 3 From him, verily, sprang Priesthood and Royalty. They said, Into whom shall we enter? 4 Let Priesthood enter into Bṛihaspati, and Royalty into Indra, was the answer. 5 Hence Priesthood entered into Bṛihaspati and Royalty into Indra. 6 Now this Earth is Bṛihaspati, and Heaven is Indra. 7 Now this Agni is Priesthood, and yonder Sun is Royalty. 8 Priesthood comes to him, and he becomes endowed with priestly lustre, 9 Who knows that Earth is Bṛihaspati and Agni Priesthood. 10 Great power comes to him and he becomes endowed with great power, 11 Who knows that Âditya is Royalty and that Heaven is Indra.

XI.

Let him to whose house the Vrâtya who possesses this knowledge comes as a guest, 2 Rise up of his own accord to meet him, and say, Vrâtya, where didst thou pass the night? Vrâtya, here is water. Let them refresh thee. Vrâtya, let it be as thou pleasest. Vrâtya, as thy wish is so let it be. Vrâtya, as thy desire is so be it. 3 When he says to his guest, Where didst thou pass the night? he reserves for himself thereby the paths that lead to the Gods. 4 When he says to him, Here is water, he secures thereby water for himself. 5 When he says to him, Let them refresh thee, he thereby

---

3 *Priesthood: bráhma. Royalty: kshatrám;* primarily, strength, power; secondarily, princely power, dominion, and the military or ruling class or order. 7 *Agni:* (or Fire) identified with Bṛihaspati. *Sun:* as representing Indra. 11 *Âditya:* the title is applicable to any son of Aditi, but especially to Varuṇa and, as in this place, to Sûrya or the Sun.

An abstract of XI.—XIII. is given in Âpastamba's Aphorisms on the Sacred Law of the Hindus, II. 3. 7. 13—17 (Sacred Books of the East, II. pp. 118, 119), where the Vrâtya (from *vrata*, a vow) is the Srotriya or religious student who has learnt one recension of the Veda; a faithful fulfiller of his vows.

wins vital breath to exceeding old age. 6 When he says to him, Vrâtya, let it be as thou pleasest, he secures to himself thereby what is pleasant. 7 That which is pleasant comes to him, and he is the beloved of the beloved, who is possessed of this knowledge. 8 When he says to him, Vrâtya, as thy will is so let it be, he secures to himself thereby the fulfilment of his will. 9 Authority comes to him who possesses this knowledge, and he becomes the controller of the powerful. 10 When he says to him, Vrâtya, as thy desire is so be it, he secures to himself thereby the attainment of his desire. 11 His desire comes to him who possesses this knowledge and he gains the complete satisfaction of his wish.

XII.

The man, to whose house, when the fires have been taken up from the hearth and the oblation to Agni placed therein, the Vrâtya possessing this knowledge comes as a guest, 2 Should of his own accord rise to meet him and say, Vrâtya, give me permission. I will sacrifice. 3 And if he gives permission he should sacrifice, if he does not permit him he should not sacrifice. 4 He who sacrifices when permitted by the Vrâtya who possesses this knowledge 5 Well knows the path that leads to the Fathers and the way that leads to the Gods. 6 He does not act in opposition to the Gods. It becomes his sacrifice. 7 The abode of the man who sacrifices when permitted by the Vrâtya who possesses this knowledge is long left remaining in this world. 8 But he who sacrifices without the

---

1 *Oblation to Agni: agnihotrám;* consisting chiefly of milk, oil, and sour gruel. The oblation is of two kinds, (1) of constant obligation, (2) occasional and optional.

6 *It becomes his sacrifice:* or, His sacrifice is accepted.

7 *Abode: âyátanam;* or, hearth whereon the householder's sacred fire is kept burning.

permission of the Vrâtya who possesses this knowledge 9 Knows not the path that leads to the Fathers nor the way that leads to the Gods. 10 He is at variance with the Gods. He hath offered no accepted sacrifice. 11 The abode of the man who sacrifices without the permission of the Vrâtya who possesses this knowledge is not left remaining in this world.

XIII.

He in whose house the Vrâtya who possesses this knowledge abides one night secures for himself thereby the holy realms that are on earth. 2 A second night . . . . the holy realms that are in the firmament (the rest as in verse 1) 3 A third night . . . the holy realms that are in heaven. 4 A fourth night . . . . the holy realms of the Holy. 5 Unlimited nights . . . . unlimited holy realms. 6 Now he to whose house a non-Vrâtya, calling himself a Vrâtya, and one in name only, comes as a guest, 7 Should punish him and not punish him. 8 He should serve him with food, saying to himself, To this Deity I offer water ; I lodge this Deity ; I wait upon this, this Deity. 9 To that Deity the sacrifice of him who has this knowledge is acceptable.

XIV.

He, when he went away to the eastern region, went away having become the Marut host, and having made Mind an eater of food. He who hath this knowledge eats food with Mind as food-eater. 2 He, when he went away to the southern region,

---

7 *Punish him and not punish him:* meaning perhaps, punish him quietly by letting him feel that his fraud is detected. 9 The meaning is that the merit of the host is as great as if he had honoured a real Godlike Vrâtya.

1 *Mind:* meaning here, will, resolution, an attribute of the impetuous Storm-Gods.

2 *Strength:* the preëminent attribute of Indra.

went away having become Indra, and having made Strength an eater of food. He who hath this knowledge eats food with strength as food-eater.
3 He, when he went away to the western region, went away having become King Varuṇa, and having made the Waters eaters of food. He who hath this knowledge eats food with the Waters as food-eaters. 4 He, when he went away to the northern region, went away having become King Soma and having made the Seven Ṛishis' oblation an eater of food. He who hath this knowledge eats food with oblation as food-eater. 5 He, when he went away to the stedfast region, went away having become Vishṇu and having made Virâj an eater of food. He who hath this knowledge eats food with Virâj as food-eater. 6 He, when he went away to animals, went away having become Rudra and having made herbs eaters of food. He who hath this knowledge eats food with herbs as food-eaters. 7 He, when he went away to the Fathers, went away having become King Yama and having made the exclamation Svadhâ an eater of food. He who hath this knowledge eats food with the exclamation Svadhâ as food-eater. 8 He, when he went away to men, went away having become Agni and having made the exclamation Svâhâ an eater of food. He who hath this know-

---

3 *Waters:* the special dominion of Varuṇa; originally, the waters of the celestial ocean.

5 *Stedfast region:* the nadir. *Virâj:* here feminine; sometimes regarded as the daughter of Vishṇu.

6 *Rudra:* as Paṣupati, or Lord of Beasts. *Herbs:* as the food of cattle.

7 *Svadhâ:* originally an oblation to the Fathers or Manes consisting of *ghṛitam* (clarified butter or sacrificial oil), attenuated to a mere exclamation taking the place of, or accompanying, the offering presented to those spirits.

8 *Svâhâ:* Benedictio sit; All hail! an auspicious exclamation uttered at the end of invocations of the Gods.

ledge eats food with the exclamation Svâhâ as food-eater. 9 He, when he went away to the upper region, went away having become Bṛihaspati and having made the exclamation Vashaṭ an eater of food. He who hath this knowledge eats food with the exclamation Vashaṭ as food-eater. 10 He, when he went away to the Gods, went away having become Îṣâna and having made Passion an eater of food. He who hath this knowledge eats food with Passion as food-eater. 11 He, when he went away to creatures, went away having become Prajâpati and having made vital breath an eater of food. He who hath this knowledge eats food with vital breath as food-eater. 12 He, when he went away to all the intermediate spaces, went away having become Parameshṭhin and having made Devotion an eater of food. He who hath this knowledge eats food with Devotion as food-eater.

HYMN XV.

Of that Vrâtya 2 There are seven vital airs, seven downward breaths, seven diffused breaths. 3 His first vital breath, called Upward, is this Agni. 4 His second vital breath, called Mature, is that

---

9 *Vashaṭ:* a sacrificial exclamation uttered by the Hotar at the end of the Yâjyâ or consecration verse, whereupon the oblation is cast into the fire by the Adhvaryu. The word *vashaṭ* probably stands for *vakshat*, a Vedic imperative of *vah*, to carry, and means, Let him (Agni) bear (the offering to the Gods). Bṛihaspati in this verse is a form of Agni.

10 *Îṣâna:* the Lord or Ruler. See XVI. 1. 5. *Passion:* or, Manyu; Anger, Wrath personified. See IV. 31 and 32.

11 *Vital breath:* or Prâṇa.

12 *Devotion:* or Brahma.

---

2 *Vital airs: prâṇâḥ;* meaning specially air inhaled. *Downward breaths: apânâḥ. Diffused breaths: vyânâḥ;* airs diffused through the whole body.

4 *Âditya:* the Sun.

Âditya 5 His third vital breath, called Approached, is that Moon. 6 His fourth vital breath. called Pervading, is this Pavamâna. 7 His fifth vital breath, called Source, are these Waters. 8 His sixth vital breath, called Dear, are these domestic animals. 9 His seventh vital breath, called Unlimited, are these creatures.

HYMN XVI.

His first downward breath is the time of Full Moon.
2 His second downward breath is the eighth day
after Full Moon. 3 His third downward breath is
the night of New Moon. 4 His fourth downward
breath is Faith. 5 His fifth downward breath is
Consecration. 6 His sixth downward breath is
Sacrifice. 7 His seventh downward breath are
these sacrificial fees.

HYMN XVII.

His first diffused breath is this Earth. 2 His second
diffused breath is that Firmament. 3 His third
diffused breath is that Heaven. 4 His fourth
diffused breath are those Constellations. 5 His
fifth diffused breath are the Seasons. 6 His sixth
diffused breath are the Season-groups. 7 His
seventh diffused breath is the year. 8 With one
and the same object the Gods go round the Year
and the Seasons follow round the Vrâtya. 9 When

---

6 *Pavamâna:* (from the root *pû*, to purify) the Wind personified.

8 *Domestic animals: paṣávaḥ;* including cows, horses, goats, sheep, oxen, and dogs.

---

1 *Time of Full Moon:* Paurṇamâsi.

2 *Eighth day after Full Moon:* Ashṭakâ.

3 *Night of New Moon:* Amâvâsyâ.

5 *Consecration:* Dîkshâ.

7 *Sacrificial fees:* Dakshiṇâs.

---

9 I find this verse and the following absolutely unintelligible.

they surround the Sun on the day of New Moon, and that time of Full Moon, 10 That one immortality of theirs is just an oblation.

HYMN XVIII.

OF that Vrâtya 2 The right eye is the Sun and the
left eye is the Moon. 3 His right ear is Agni and
his left ear is Pavamâna. 4 Day and Night are
his nostrils. Diti and Aditi are his head and skull.
5 By day the Vrâtya is turned westward, by night
he is turned eastward. Worship to the Vrâtya!

It is hard to understand, and I do not attempt to explain, the idealization and grotesquely extravagant glorification of the Vrâtya or heretical nomad who appears at one time to be a supernatural Being endowed with the attributes of all-pervading Deity, and at another as a human wanderer in need of food and lodging. In my Preface, p. VII., I have followed von Roth, in taking the Vrâtya to be the religious wandering mendicant, regarded as a being of peculiar sanctity. But this explanation of the word is of later origin than the compilation of the Songs of the Atharvans, and, as far as regards this Book, must be abandoned.

BOOK XVI.

HYMN I.

THE Bull of the Waters hath been let go; the
heavenly fires have been let go. 2 Breaking, break-
ing down, crushing, crushing to pieces, 3 Mroka,
mind-destroying, rooting up, consuming, ruiner of
the soul, ruiner of the body. 4 Here I let him go:
thou washest me clean of him. 5 With this we let
him loose who hates us and whom we hate. 6 Thou
art in front of the waters. I let loose your sea.
7 I let loose the Agni who is within the waters,
Mroka the uprooter, the destroyer of the body.
8 Your Agni who entered into the waters, even he
here is that very dread of yours. 9 May he anoint
you with Indra's own mighty power!

10 May stainless waters cleanse us from defilement.

11 May they carry sin away from us, may they carry away from us the evil dream.

The Book consists almost entirely of charms and conjurations for various purposes.

The subject of the hymn is the preparation and use of holy water, with a prayer for purification and freedom from sin.

1 *The Bull of the Waters*: the mighty Agni who dwells as lightning in the watery clouds of the sea of air.

3 *Mroka*: Agni in his most destructive and dreaded form; the fire of the funeral pile. All his hostile powers are here enumerated. Cf. Pâraskara-Gṛihya-Sútra, II. 6. 10. (Sacred Books of the East, XXIX. p. 313).

11 *May they carry sin away*: cf. Ṛ. V. I. 23. 22 and X. 9. 8: Whatever sin is found in me, whatever evil I have wrought, If I have lied or falsely sworn, Waters, remove it far from me.

The hymn is in prose with the exception of verses 10, 12, 13.

12 Look on me with a friendly eye, O Waters, and touch my skin with your auspicious body.

13 We call the gracious Fires that dwell in waters. Goddesses, grant me princely power and splendour.

HYMN II.

AWAY from distasteful food, strength and sweet
speech 2 Are pleasant. May I obtain a pleasant
voice. 3 I have invoked the Protector; I have
invoked his protection. 4 Quick of hearing are
mine ears; mine ears hear what is good. Fain
would I hear a pleasant sound. 5 Let not good
hearing and overhearing fail the Eagle's eye, the
undecaying light. 6 Thou art the couch of the
Ṛishis. Let worship be paid to the divine couch.

HYMN III.

I AM the head of riches. Fain would I be the head
of mine equals. 2 Let not Ruja and Vena desert
me. Let not the Head and the Preserver forsake
me. 3 Let not the Boiler and the Cup fail me:

The hymn is a charm to secure various blessings.

1 *Distasteful food:* I adopt the St. P. Lexicon's suggestion of *duradmanyaḥ* instead of the *durarmaṇyáḥ* of the text.

3 *The Protector:* or Herdsman; Agni.

4 *Hear a pleasant sound:* that is, be favourably spoken of.

5 *The Eagle's eye:* the vision of the all-seeing Sun.

6 *The couch of the Ṛishis* the *brahmâsanam:* or seat prepared for the Brahman priest is addressed.

The hymn is a charm to secure power and long life.

2 *Ruja:* a word of doubtful signification which does not occur elsewhere. It is apparently used here as a name of the Sun; perhaps the Breaker, he who breaks up and disperses the morning clouds, from the root *ruj*, to break or shatter. *Vena:* the Sun, as he rises in the mists of the morning. See II. 1, note.

3 *The Boiler and the Cup:* meaning, generally, sacrificial implements. I adopt the suggestion, given in the St. P. Lexicon, of *ukhaḥ*, boiler, instead of *urváḥ* of the text which is meaningless here.

let not the Supporter and the Sustainer abandon me. 4 Let not Unyoking and the Moist-fellied car desert me: let not the Sender of Moisture and Mâtarisvan forsake me. 5 Bṛihaspati is my soul, he who is called the Friend of man, dear to my heart. 6 My heart is free from sorrow; spacious is my dwelling-place. I am the sea in capacity.

HYMN IV.

I AM the centre of riches. Fain would I be the centre of mine equals. 2 Pleasant art thou to sit by one, a mother: immortal among mortals. 3 Let not inward breath desert me; let not outward breath depart and leave me. 4 Let Sûrya protect me from Day, Agni from Earth, Vâyu from Firmament, Yama from men, Sarasvatî from dwellers on the earth. 5 Let not outward and inward breath fail me. Be not thou destructive among the men. 6 Propitious to-day be dawns and evenings May I drink water with all my people safe around me. 7 Mighty are ye, domestic creatures. May Mitra-Varuṇa stand beside me. May Agni give me inward and outward breath. May he give me ability.

HYMN V.

WE know thine origin, O Sleep. Thou art the son of Grâhi, the minister of Yama. Thou art the

---

4 *Unyoking and the Moist-fellied car*: a periphrasis for the setting Sun as he sinks in the western waters. *Sender of Moisture*: the rain-cloud. *Mâtarisvan*: the wind.

The hymn is a charm to secure long life and success.

2 *Thou*: meaning, apparently, Agni.

5 *Thou*: Agni.

7 *Mighty*: *śákvarîḥ*; an epithet frequently applied to holy waters which are here addressed. Cf. A V. III. 13. 7; XI. 2. 23; XIII. 1. 5. *Mitra-Varuṇa*: *mitrâvâruṇau*; Mitra and Varuṇa regarded as a dual deity.

The hymn, an address to Sleep, is a charm against evil dreams.

1 *Grâhi*: a she-demon who seizes and kills men.

Ender, thou art Death. As such, O Sleep, we
know thee well. As such preserve us from the
evil dream. 2 We know thine origin, O Sleep.
Thou art the son of Destruction, the minister of
Yama, etc. (as in verse 1). 3 We know thine ori-
gin, O Sleep. Thou art the son of Misery, etc. 4
We know thine origin, O Sleep. Thou art the son
of Disappearance, etc. 5 We know thine origin,
O Sleep. Thou art the son of Defeat, etc. 6 We
know thine origin, O Sleep. Thou art the son of
the sisters of the Gods, the minister of Yama.
Thou art the Ender, thou art Death. As such, O
Sleep, we know thee well. As such, preserve us
from the evil dream.

HYMN VI.

Now have we conquered and obtained: we have been freed from sin to-day.

2 Let Morning with her light dispel that evil dream that frightened us.

3 Bear that away to him who hates, away to him who curses us.

4 To him whom we abhor, to him who hates us do we send it hence.

5 May the Goddess Dawn in accord with Speech, and
the Goddess Speech in accord with Dawn, 6 The
Lord of Dawn in accord with the Lord of Speech
and the Lord of Speech in accord with the Lord

---

2 *Destruction:* Nirṛiti.

The hymn has been translated by Ludwig, Der Ṛigveda, III. p. 468.

The hymn is a charm to avert evil dreams and transfer them and malignant spirits to an enemy.

1 This and the following line are taken from R. V. VIII. 47. 18.

6 *Lord of Dawn:* or Consort of Ushas; said to be Aniruddha, son of Kâma the God of Love. *Lord of Speech:* Vâchaspati; see A. V. I. 1. 1, note.

of Dawn, 7 Carry away to Such-an-one niggard fiends, hostile demons, and Sadânvas, 8 Kumbhîkas, Dushîkas, and Pîyakas, 9 Evil day-dream, evil dream in sleep, 10 Wishes for boons that will not come, thoughts of poverty, the snares of the Druh who never releases—11 This, O Agni, let the Gods bear off to Such-an-one that he may be a fragile good-for-nothing eunuch.

HYMN VII.

HEREWITH I pierce this man. With poverty I pierce him. With disappearance I pierce him. With defeat I pierce him. With Grâhi I pierce him. With darkness I pierce him. 2 I summon him with the awful cruel orders of the Gods. 3 I place him between Vaiṣvânara's jaws. 4 Thus or otherwise let her swallow him up. 5 Him who hates us may his soul hate, and may he whom we hate hate himself. 6 We scorch out of heaven and earth and firmament the man who hates us, 7 Suyâman son of Chakshus! 8 Here I wipe away the evil dream on the descendant of Such-an-one, son of Such-a-

---

7 *Such-an-one:* used like our *M.* or *N.* instead of the name of the person intended which is to be supplied when the incantation is employed. *Sadânvas:* ever-shrieking fiends. See II. 14. 1, note.

8 *Kumbhîkas, Dushîkas, Pîyakas:* various malignant demons.

9 *Druh:* a female spirit of mischief. See II. X. 1—10.

An imprecation on an enemy.

1 *Poverty:* or misery. The enemy is attacked with all the woes that are regarded as the parents of sleep that brings the evil dream. See XVI. 5. 1, 3—5.

3 *Her:* the female fiend Grâhi.

7 *Suyâman:* the charm is addressed as a human impersonation; *suyâman* meaning 'well-coming,' Benvenuto, and Chakshus meaning 'vision.'

8 *Such-an-one......Such-a-woman:* the actual names are to be supplied when the charm is employed. Cf. supra, Hymn VI. 7.

woman. 9 Whatsoever I have met with, whether
at dusk or during early night, 10 Whether wak-
ing or sleeping, whether by day or by night, 11
Whether I meet with it day by day, from that do
I bribe him away. 12 Slay him ; rejoice in this ;
crush his ribs. 13 Let him not live. Let the
breath of life forsake him.

HYMN VIII.

Whatever we have gained, whatever hath accrued to us, our Right, our energy, our Devotion, our heavenly light, our sacrifice, our domestic animals, our offspring, our men,—from all share herein we exclude Such-an-one, descendant of Such-an-one, son of Such-a-woman. Let him not be freed from the noose of Grâhi. Here I bind up his splendour, his energy, his vital breath, his life, and cast him down beneath me.

2 Whatever we have gained, etc. (as in verse 1). Let him not be freed from the noose of Nirṛiti, etc.

3 Whatever we have gained, etc. Let him not be freed from the noose of misery, etc.

4 Whatever we have gained, etc. Let him not be freed from the noose of disappearance, etc.

5 Whatever we have gained, etc. Let him not be freed from the noose of defeat, etc.

6 Whatever we have gained, etc. Let him not be freed from the noose of the sisters of the Gods, etc.

7 Whatever we have gained, etc. Let him not be freed from the noose of Bṛihaspati, etc.

8 Whatever we have gained, etc. Let him not be freed from the noose of Prajâpati, etc.

9 Whatever we have gained, etc. Let him not be freed from the noose of the Ṛishis, etc.

An imprecation on an enemy.

10 Whatever we have gained, etc. Let him not be freed from the noose of the Ṛishis' children, etc.

11 Whatever, etc. Let him not be freed from the noose of the Angirases, etc.

12 Whatever, etc. Let him not be freed from the noose of the Ângirases, etc.

13 Whatever, etc. Let him not be freed from the noose of the Atharvans, etc.

14 Whatever, etc. Let him not be freed from the noose of the Âtharvans, etc.

15 Whatever, etc. Let him not be freed from the noose of the Trees, etc.

16 Whatever, etc. Let him not be freed from the noose of Shrubs, etc.

17 Whatever, etc. Let him not be freed from the noose of the Seasons, etc.

18 Whatever, etc. Let him not be freed from the noose of the Season-groups, etc.

19 Whatever, etc. Let him not be freed from the noose of the Months, etc.

20 Whatever, etc. Let him not be freed from the noose of the Half-months, etc.

21 Whatever, etc. Let him not be freed from the noose of Day and Night, etc.

22 Whatever, etc. Let him not be freed from the noose of continued Day, etc.

23 Whatever, etc. Let him not be freed from the noose of Heaven and Earth, etc.

24 Whatever, etc. Let him not be freed from the noose of Indra-Agni, etc.

25 Whatever, etc. Let him not be freed from the noose of Mitra-Varuṇa, etc.

26 Whatever, etc. Let him not be freed from the noose of King Varuna, etc.

27 Whatever we have gained, whatever hath accrued to us, our Right, our energy, our Devotion, our heavenly light, our sacrifice, our domestic animals, our offspring, our men,—from all share herein we exclude Such-an-one, descendant of Such-an-one, son of Such-a-woman. Let him not be freed from the fetter and noose of Death. Here I bind up his splendour, his energy, his vital breath, his life, and cast him down beneath me.

HYMN IX.

OURS is superior place and ours is conquest: may I in all fights tread down spite and malice.

2 This word hath Agni, this hath Soma spoken. May Pûshan set me in the world of virtue.

3 We have come to the light of heaven; to the light of heaven have we come: we have united with the light of Sûrya.

4 Sacrifice is fraught with wealth for the increase of prosperity. I would win riches; fain would I be wealthy. Do thou bestow wealth upon me.

The hymn is a charm to secure wealth and felicity.

1 This line is repeated from A. V. X. 5. 36.

3 This verse is to be recited while looking at the Sun.

4 *Thou:* Sûrya.

BOOK XVII.

HYMN I.

VANQUISHING, overpowering, a conqueror, exceeding strong,
Victorious, winner of the light, winner of cattle and of spoil,
Indra by name, adorable, I call: a long, long life be mine!

2 Vanquishing, etc.
Indra by name, adorable I call: may I be dear to Gods.

3 Vanquishing, etc.
Indra by name, adorable I call: may creatures love me well.

4 Vanquishing, etc.
Indra by name, adorable, I call: may cattle hold me dear.

5 Vanquishing, etc.
Indra by name, adorable, I call: may equals love me well.

6 Rise up, O Sûrya, rise thou up; with strength and splendour rise on me.
Let him who hates me be my thrall; let me not be a thrall to him.
Manifold are thy great deeds, thine, O Vishṇu.
Sate us with cattle of all forms and colours: set me in happiness, in loftiest heaven.

The single hymn which constitutes this Book is a prayer to Indra, identified with Vishṇu and the Sun, for the love of Gods, men, and beasts, general protection and prosperity, and all earthly and heavenly blessings.

7 Rise up, O Sûrya, rise thou up; with strength and splendour rise on me.
Make me the favourite of all, of those I see and do not see.
Manifold are thy great deeds, thine, O Vishṇu.

8 Let not the fowlers who are standing ready injure thee in the flood, within the waters.
Ascend this heaven, leaving each curse behind thee. Favour us: let thy gracious love attend us.
Manifold are thy great deeds, thine, O Vishṇu.

9 Do thou, O Indra, for our great good fortune, with thine inviolable rays protect us.
Manifold are thy great deeds, thine, O Vishṇu.

10 Be thou most gracious unto us, Indra, with favourable aid,
Rising to heaven's third sphere, invoked with song to quaff the Soma juice, loving thy home to make us blest.
Manifold are thy great deeds, thine, O Vishṇu.

11 Thou art the vanquisher of all, O Indra, omniscient Indra, and invoked of many.
Indra, send forth this hymn that fitly lauds thee. Favour us: let thy gracious love attend us.
Manifold are thy great deeds, thine, O Vishṇu.

12 In heaven and on the earth thou art uninjured, none reach thy greatness in the air's mid region.
Increasing by inviolate devotion as such in heaven grant us protection, Indra.
Manifold are thy great deeds, thine, O Vishṇu.

---

8 The Sun is the Bird (Cf. A. V. IV. 6. 3), and the *fowlers* are the malignant fiends who would stay his flight through the watery clouds of the sea of air. Cf. 'Come hither, Indra, with bay steeds, joyous, with tails like peacock's plumes. Let no men check thy course as fowlers stay the bird: pass o'er them as o'er desert lands' (Ṛ. V. III. 45. 1).

10 *Heaven's third sphere*: the highest heaven, the abode of the Sun.

13 Grant us protection, Indra, with that body of thine that is on earth, in fire, in waters,
That dwells within light-finding Pavamâna, wherewith thou hast pervaded air's mid region.
Manifold are thy great deeds, thine, O Vishṇu.

14 Indra, exalting thee with prayer, imploring, Ṛishis have sat them down in holy Session.
Manifold are thy great deeds, thine, O Vishṇu.

15 Round Trita, round the spring with thousand currents thou goest, round the light-finding assembly.
Manifold are thy great deeds, thine, O Vishṇu.

16 Thou guardest well the four celestial regions, pervading heaven and earth with light and splendour.
Thou givest help to all these living creatures, and, knowing, followest the path of Order.
Manifold are thy great deeds, thine, O Vishṇu.

17 With five thou sendest heat: with one removing the curse thou comest in bright sunshine hither.
Manifold are thy great deeds, thine, O Vishṇu.

18 Indra art thou, Mahendra thou; thou art the world, the Lord of Life.
To thee is sacrifice performed: worshippers offer gifts to thee.
Manifold are thy great deeds, thine, O Vishṇu.

---

13 *Light-finding Pavamâna:* wind that reaches even the height of heaven.

15 *Trita:* a deity of the atmosphere, connected with Indra and the winds; here perhaps the representative of the whole expanse of heaven. *The spring:* the fountain of heaven; the rain-cloud. *The light-finding assembly:* the company of the Gods who dwell in the highest sphere.

17 *With five:* of thy seven beams. See XI. 1. 36, note.

18 *Mahendra:* Great Indra. Cf. A. V. XIII. 4. 2, 9. *The Lord of Life:* or, Prajâpati.

19 What is is based on what is not: the present lies on that which is.

Present on future is imposed and future on the present based.

Manifold are thy great deeds, thine, O Vishṇu.

Sate us with cattle of all varied colour. Set me in happiness, in loftiest heaven.

20 Bright art thou, and refulgent: as thou shinest with splendour so I fain would shine with splendour.

21 Lustre art thou, illuming: as thou glowest with lustre so I too would shine with cattle, with all the lustre of a Brâhman's station.

22 Glory to him when rising, when ascending! Glory to him when he hath reached the zenith!

To him far-shining, him the self-refulgent, to him the Sovran Lord and King be glory!

23 Worship to him when he is turning westward, to him when setting, and when set be worship!

To him far-shining, him the self-refulgent, to him the Sovran Lord and King be glory!

24 With all his fiery fervour this Âditya hath gone up on high,

Giving my foes into my hand. Let me not be my foeman's prey. Manifold are thy great deeds, thine, O Vishṇu.

Sate us with cattle of all varied colours. Set me in happiness, in loftiest heaven.

25 Thou for our weal, Âditya, hast mounted thy ship with hundred oars.

Thou hast transported me to day: so bear me evermore to night.

---

24 The stanza is taken from Ṛ. V. I. 50. 13, addressed to Surya.

25 *Ship:* with reference to the sea of air traversed by the Sun.

26 Thou for our weal, O Sûrya, hast mounted thy ship with hundred oars.
Thou hast transported me to night: so bear me evermore to day.

27 Encompassed by Prajâpati's devotion as shield, with Kaṣyapa's bright light and splendour,
Reaching old age, may I made strong and mighty live through a thousand years with happy fortune.

28 Compassed am I with prayer, my shield and armour; compassed with Kaṣyapa's bright light and splendour.
Let not shafts reach me shot from heaven against me, nor those sent forth by men for my destruction.

29 Guarded am I by Order and the Seasons, protected by the past and by the future.
Let not distress, yea, let not Death come nigh me: with water of my speech have I o'erwhelmed them.

30 On every side let Agni guard and keep me; the rising Sun drive off the snares of Mṛityu!
Let brightly flushing Mornings, firm-set mountains, and lives a thousand be with me united.

BOOK XVIII.

HYMN I.

FAIN would I win my friend to kindly friendship. So may the Sage, come through the air's wide ocean, Remembering the earth and days to follow, obtain a son the issue of his father.

The subjects of this Book are funeral rites and sacrificial offerings to the Fathers, the Manes or spirits of the dead.

The first sixteen stanzas of this funeral hymn, with the exception of one verse and with variations, constitute the tenth hymn of Book X. of the Ṛigveda, and are only indirectly connected with the main subject, being a dialogue between Yama and Yamî, the son and daughter of Vivasvân. Yama and Yami are, says Professor von Roth, as their names denote, twin brother and sister, and are the first human pair, the originators of the race. As the Hebrew conception closely connected the parents of mankind by making the woman formed from a portion of the body of the man, so by the Indian tradition they are placed in the relationship of twins. This thought is laid by the hymn in question in the mouth of Yamî herself when she is made to say; 'Even in the womb the creator made us for husband and wife.' Professor Müller, on the other hand, says (Lectures on the Science of Language, second series, p. 510): 'There is a curious dialogue between her (Yami) and her brother, where she (the night) implores her brother (the day) to make her his wife, and where he declines her offer 'because,' as he says 'they have called it a sin that a brother should marry his sister.'' Again, p. 521, 'There is not a single word in the Veda pointing to *Yama* and *Yamī* as the first couple of mortals, the Indian Adam and Eve......If Yama had been the first created of men, surely the Vedic poets, in speaking of him, could not have passed this over in silence.' See, however, the passage from the Atharva-veda, XVIII. 3. 13, to be quoted further on. [Reverence ye with an oblation Yama, the son of Vivasvat, the assembler of men, who was the first of men that died, and the first that departed to this (celestial) world].'—Muir, O. S. Texts, V. P. 288. This conception of Yama as the first man may be, as Prof. M. Müller holds, 'a later phase of religious thought.'

1 Yamî speaks. *The Sage: vedhâḥ;* the wise Yama. *Come:* Sâyaṇa explains the masculine participle *juganvân* by the feminine *gatavatî*, that is, I Yami who have come; and Ludwig takes it to be used for *jagmushî*, in a transitive sense, 'making him come.' *The earth:* which appears destined to remain without human inhabitants.

2 Thy friend loves not the friendship which considers her who is near in kindred as a stranger.
Sons of the mighty Asura, the heroes, supporters of the heaven, see far around them.

3 Yea, this the Immortals seek of thee with longing, a scion of the only man existing.
Then let thy soul and mine be knit together. Embrace thy consort as her loving husband.

4 Shall we do now what we ne'er did aforetime? we who spake righteously now talk impurely?
Gandharva in the floods, the Dame of Waters—such is our bond, such our most lofty kinship.

5 Even in the womb God Tvashṭar, vivifier, shaping all forms, Creator, made us consorts.
Ne'er are his holy statutes violated: that we are his the heaven and earth acknowledge.

6 Who yokes to-day unto the pole of Order the strong and passionate steers of checkless spirit,
With shaft-armed mouths, heart-piercing, joy-bestowing? Long shall he live who duly pays them service.

---

2 Yama replies. *A stranger:* of a different family, and so a lawful wife. *Sons of the mighty Asura:* the spies or sentinels spoken of in stanza 8 who are regarded as the sons of the Lord God.

3 Yamí speaks.

4 Yama replies. *Gandharva in the floods:* the Sun. God in the waters of the sea of air. *The Dame of Waters:* Saranyû, the consort of the Sun-God Vivasvân. 'His aqueous wife.'—Muir. She may represent the misty air of morning, heated and penetrated by the early sun. *Such is our bond:* this is the relationship between us; it does not go farther back, and is far too close to allow us to marry each other.

5 Yamí speaks; and argues that by making them of different sexes the Creator manifestly intended them for each other.

6 Yama replies. This stanza which does not occur in the original hymn (R. V. X. 10), and which seems to be altogether out of place here, is taken from R. V. I. 84. 16 which is addressed to Indra, and the passage refers to the institutor of a sacrifice to that God. *The strong and passionate steers:* the zealous and indefatigable priests who are yoked to the chariot-pole of Order or employed in the performance of sacrifice ordained by eternal Law. The words used by the priests in the discharge of their holy functions are the arrows with which their mouths are armed.

7 Who knows that earliest day whereof thou speakest?
Who hath beheld it? Who can here declare it?
Great is the law of Varuṇa and Mitra. What, wanton, wilt thou say to men to tempt them?

8 I Yamî am possessed by love of Yama, that I may rest on the same couch beside him.
I as a wife would yield me to my husband. Like car-wheels let us speed to meet each other.

9 They stand not still, they never close their eyelids, those sentinels of Gods who wander round us.
Not me—go quickly, wanton, with another, and hasten like a chariot-wheel to meet him.

10 May Sûrya's eye with days and nights endow him, and ever may his light spread out before him.
In heaven and earth the kindred pair commingle.
On Yamî be the unbrotherly act of Yama.

11 Sure there will come succeeding times when brothers and sisters will do acts unmeet for kinsfolk.
Not me, O fair one—seek another husband, and make thine arm a pillow for thy consort.

---

7 *Of Varuṇa and Mitra:* as the moral Governors of the world. *To tempt them:* the meaning of *víchyâ* is uncertain. The St. P. Lexicon explains it by 'deceitfully.' 'What sayest thou, who punishest men with hell?'—Wilson. Prof. Ludwig takes it to be an irregular indefinite participle of *vyach*, to embrace: when thou hast embraced the (other) men.

8 Yamî speaks. *Like car-wheels let us speed:* the words are difficult, and this is not the exact meaning. Cf. Solomon's Song, VI. 12: 'Or ever I was aware, my soul made me Like the chariots of Ammi-nadib'; or, according to the Septuagint: 'There I will give thee my breasts; my soul knew not; it made me the chariots of Aminadab.'

9 Yama replies. *Sentinels of Gods:* recording angels who observe and report the actions of men. Cf. A. V. IV. 16. 4, and note.

10 Yamî speaks. Her meaning is: if there be any guilt let me take it on myself, and let not Yama's life be shortened by way of punishment. *The kindred pair:* Day and Night.

11 Yama replies. *Make thine arm a pillow:* Ludwig interprets differently. See his Der Rigveda, V. p. 512.

12 Is he a brother when no help is left her? Is she a sister when Destruction cometh?
Forced by my love these many words I utter. Come near, and hold me in thy close embraces.

13 I am no help for thee, no refuge, Yamî. I will not clasp and press thee to my bosom.
This is abhorrent to my mind and spirit—a brother on the couch beside a sister.

14 I will not fold mine arms about thy body: they call it sin when one comes near a sister.
Not me—prepare thy pleasure with another. Thy brother seeks not this from thee, O fair one.

15 Alas! thou art indeed a weakling, Yama. We find in thee no trace of heart or spirit.
As round a tree the woodbine clings, another will cling about thee girt as with a girdle.

16 Embrace another, Yamî. Let some other, even as the woodbine rings a tree, enfold thee.
Win thou his heart and let him win thy fancy; so make with him a bond of blest alliance.

17 Three hymns the Sages have disposed in order, the many-formed, the fair, the all-beholding.
These in one single world are placed and settled—the growing plants, the breezes, and the waters.

---

12 Yami speaks. *Destruction:* the utter extinction of the human race.

13 Yama replies. This and the following stanza are the expansion of one verse of the Ṛigveda hymn.

15 Yami speaks. *Woodbine:* cf. A. V. VI. 8. 1.

16 Yama replies. Sâyaṇa's interpretation of the original hymn, which is many places obscure and difficult, differs, in many places from that which I have adopted, and Wilson's Translation should be consulted for the views of the great Indian Commentator and the Pandits of his time. The hymn has been transliterated, translated, and annotated by Muir, O. S Texts, V. 288—291, and translated by Geldner and Kaegi in their Siebenzig Lieder des Rigveda. Ludwig's translation and commentary, and Der Vedische Mythus des Yama by J. Ehni (Strassburg, 1890) should be consulted.

17 *The Sages:* the Fathers, to whose power many natural phenomena and many blessings enjoyed by men are referred.

18 The Bull hath yielded for the Bull the milk of heaven: inviolable is the Son of Aditi.
According to his wisdom Varuṇa knoweth all: he halloweth, the holy, times for sacrifice.

19 Gandharvî spake. May she, the Lady of the Flood amid the river's roaring leave my heart untouched.
May Aditi accomplish all that we desire, and may our eldest Brother tell us this as chief.

20 Yea, even this blessèd Morning, rich in store of food, splendid, with heavenly lustre, hath shone out for man,
Since they as was the wish of yearning Gods, brought forth that yearning Agni for the assembly as the Priest.

21 And the fleet Falcon brought for sacrifice from afar this flowing drop most excellent and passing wise,
Then when the Âryan tribes chose as invoking Priest Agni the wonder-worker, and the hymn rose up.

---

18 Stanzas 18—26 constitute, with occasional variations, the eleventh hymn of Book X. of the Ṛigveda, the subject being the origin and institution of sacrifice which was first established by Agni under the authority of Varuṇa. *The Bull:* or, the strong; the mighty Soma. *For the Bull:* for mighty Varuṇa. *The milk of heaven:* the divine Soma juice, to be used at sacrifice. *The Son of Aditi:* the great Âditya, Varuṇa. *According to his wisdom: yáthâ dhiyấ:* the two words being taken together as an adverbial phrase. *Knoweth all:* See A. V. IV. 16. According to Sâyaṇa it is Agni who milks the stream of prosperity from heaven for the worshipper or institutor of the sacrifice. I have generally followed Prof. Pischel's interpretation (Vedische Studien, I. pp. 188, 189) of stanzas 18—22.

19 *Gandharvî:* said to be the daughter of Surabhi one of the daughters of Daksha, and the mother of the race of horses. Here she appears to be an Apsaras or water-nymph, haunting the banks of rivers and practising the seductive arts of a siren. The meaning appears to be: let no disturbing influence unsettle my devout thoughts. *Our eldest Brother:* Varuṇa, regarded as the founder of society united by common religious observances.

20 The poet regards the coming of the dawn as a proof that the sacrifice is successful. *Since they:* the human priests.

21 *The fleet Falcon:* Agni in the form of lightning. *The flowing drop:* Soma. See A. V. VI. 48. 1, note.

22 Still art thou kind to him who feeds thee as with grass, and skilled in sacrifice offers thee holy gifts,
When thou having received the sage's strengthening food with lauds, after long toil comest with many more.

23 Urge thou thy Parents, as a lover, to delight: the lovely One desires and craves it from his heart.
As Priest he calls aloud, as Warrior shows his skill, as Asura tries his strength, and with the hymn is stirred.

24 Far famed is he, the mortal man, O Agni thou Son of Strength, who hath obtained thy favour.
He, gathering power, borne onward by his horses, makes his days lovely in his might and splendour.

25 Hear us, O Agni, in the great assembly: harness thy rapid car, the car of Amrit.
Bring Heaven and Earth, the Deities' Parents, hither: stay with us here, nor from the Gods be absent.

26 When, holy Agni, the divine assembly, the holy synod mid the Gods, is gathered,
And when thou, godlike One, dealest forth treasures, vouchsafe us too our portion of the riches.

27 Agni hath looked upon the van of Mornings, and on the days the earliest Jâtavedas.
After the Dawns, after their rays of brightness, Sûrya hath entered into earth and heaven.

---

22 *Thou:* Agni. *As with grass:* 'as pasture satisfies (the herds).'—Wilson. *With many more:* bringing many other Gods to the sacrifice.

23 *As a lover:* woos his mistress. Agni is called upon to entreat his parents, Heaven and Earth, to reproduce him perpetually. *The lovely one:* Agni.

25 *In the great assembly:* 'in the dwelling common to the deities.'—Wilson. *Rapid: dravitnúm,* taken by Sâyaṇa with *amṛitasya* and explained by 'distilling the drink of Gods.'

27 The first pâda is taken from Ṛ. V. IV. 13. 1.

28 Agni hath looked against the van of Mornings, against the days the earliest Jâtavedas:
In many a place against the beams of Sûrya, against the heavens and earth hath he extended.

29 Heaven and Earth, first by everlasting Order, speakers of truth, are near enough to hear us,
When the God, urging men to worship, sitteth as Priest, assuming all his vital vigour.

30 As God comprising Gods by Law eternal, bear, as the chief who knoweth, our oblation,
Smoke-bannered with the fuel, radiant, joyous, better to praise and worship, Priest for ever.

31 I praise your work that ye may make me prosper; hear, Heaven and Earth, twain worlds that drop with fatness!
While days and Gods go to the world of spirits, here let the Parents with sweet mead refresh us.

32 When the Cow's nectar wins the God completely, men here below are heaven's and earth's sustainers.
All the Gods came to this thy heavenly Yajus, which from the motley Pair milked oil and water.

---

29 Stanzas 29—35 and half of 36 are taken from Ṛ. V. X. 12. 1—8. *First:* most exalted as well as most ancient. *The God:* Agni. *As Priest*: as Hotar; sacrificing, or invoking priest.

30 *Better to praise:* more skilful than human priests in praising the Gods.

31 *Days and Gods:* in the Ṛ. V. hymn, nights and days. *World of spirits: ásunîtim;* 'ins jenseits.'—Ludwig.

32 This stanza is very obscure. The meaning appears to be that, by possessing the Amrit, ambrosia, or nectar contained in the milk of the sacrificial cow and in the Soma juice which wins and captivates Agni, men are enabled to offer acceptable sacrifices to the Gods, and thus to support the heavens and earth. *Heavenly Yajus;* divine sacrificial prayer or formula. But *divyám* by its position in the verse seems rather to belong to *ghṛitám*, butter or sacrificial oil. *Motley Pair: éni;* many-coloured heaven and earth. 'When the self-aggregated ambrosia of the divine Agni is generated from his radiance, then the products of it sustain both heaven and earth, all the worshippers

33 Hath the King seized us? How have we offended against his holy Ordinance? Who knoweth?
For even Mitra mid the Gods is angry. There are both song and wealth for those who come not.

34 'Tis hard to understand the Immortal's nature, where she who is akin becomes a stranger.
Guard ceaselessly, great Agni, him who ponders Yama's name easy to be comprehended.

35 They in the synod where the Gods rejoice them, where they are seated in Vivasvân's dwelling,
Have given the Moon his beams, the Sun his splendour: the two unweariedly maintain their brightness.

36 The counsel which the Gods meet to consider, their secret plan, of that we have no knowledge.
There let God Savitar, Aditi, and Mitra proclaim to Varuṇa that we are sinless.

37 Companions, let us learn a prayer to Indra whom the thunder arms,
To glorify your bold and most heroic Friend.

38 For thou by slaying Vṛitra art the Vṛitra-slayer, famed for might.
Thou, Hero, in rich gifts surpassest wealthy chiefs.

---

glorify this thy oblation, the celestial nutritious water which thy white radiance milks forth.'—Wilson. According to Sâyaṇa, *the products of it* are the plants and trees which spring from the *amṛita* or rain which rewards the oblations of men, and the *viśve devâḥ* of the text are *sarve stotâraḥ*, all the worshippers. Some meaning is apparent in this paraphrase, but it cannot be extracted from the words of the text.

33 *The King:* Varuṇa. *Even Mitra:* we must have committed some great sin, for even Mitra, the Friend, the gracious God, is wroth with us. *Wealth:* rich offerings. *For those who come not:* for the Gods who will not yet come to receive our worship and oblations.

34 The second half of the first line is repeated from line 1 of stanza 2, but its application here is not obvious. See Ludwig, Der Rigveda, IV. p. 405.

35 *Vivasvân's dwelling:* heaven, the abode of the Sun.

37 This and the following stanza are taken from Ṛ. V. IV. 24. 1. 2.

39 O'er the broad land thou goest like a Stega: here on vast earth let breezes blow upon us.
Here hath our dear Friend Varuṇa, united, like Agni in the wood, shot forth his splendour.

40 Sing praise to him the chariot-borne, the famous, Sovran of men, the dread and strong destroyer.
O Rudra, praised, be gracious to the singer: let thy darts spare us and smite down another.

41 The pious call Sarasvatî, they worship Sarasvatî while sacrifice proceedeth.
The virtuous call Sarasvatî to hear them. Sarasvatî send bliss to him who giveth!

42 Sarasvatî is called on by the Fathers who come right forward to our solemn worship.
Seated upon this sacred grass rejoice you. Give thou us strenthening food that brings no sickness.

43 Sarasvatî, who comest with the Fathers, joying in hymns, O Goddess, and oblations,
Give plenteous wealth to this the sacrificer, a portion, worth a thousand, of refreshment.

44 May they ascend, the lowest, highest, midmost, the Fathers who deserve a share of Soma.
May they who have attained to life, the Fathers, righteous and gentle, aid us when we call them.

---

39 *Stega:* said to be a certain biting or stinging insect. According to Sâyaṇa, 'the aggregation of rays, the Sun.' Prof. Ludwig suggests that the ploughshare may be meant, which turns up the soil and exposes it to the influence of the sun. *Varuṇa:* here, apparently, representing the Sun whose rays penetrate even the thick wood. Cf. Ṛ. V. V. 48. 5, where Sâyaṇa explains *várunaḥ* as an adjective = *tamovârakaḥ*, darkness-repelling, and an epithet of Agni.

40 Taken, with variations, from Ṛ. V. II. 33. 11.

41 This and the two following stanzas are taken, with variations, from Ṛ. V. X. 17. 7—9.

42 *Rejoice you:* the Fathers are included in the invitation.

44 This and the two following stanzas are taken from Ṛ. V. X. 15. 1, 3. 2. *Ascend:* rise to higher rank; obtain the best oblation, according to Sâyaṇa. *Lowest, highest, midmost:* the Fathers being classified in heaven according to their degrees of merit acquired on earth.

45 I have attained the gracious-minded Fathers, I have gained son and progeny from Vishṇu.
They who enjoy pressed juices with oblation, seated on sacred grass, come oftenest hither.

46 Now be this homage offered to the Fathers, to those who passed of old and those who followed,
Those who have rested in the earthly region, and those who dwell among the happy races.

47 Mâtalî prospers there with Kavyas, Yama with Angiras' sons, Bṛihaspati with singers.
Exalters of the Gods, by Gods exalted, aid us those Fathers in our invocations!

48 Yea, this is good to taste and full of sweetness, verily it is strong and rich in flavour.
No one may conquer Indra in the battle when he hath drunken of the draught we offer.

49 Honour the King with your oblations, Yama, Vivasvân's son, who gathers men together,
Even him who travelled o'er the mighty rivers, who searches out and shows the path to many.

---

45 *Son and progeny:* the meaning appears to be, as suggested by Prof. Ludwig, that the speaker has discharged his obligation to the Fathers by begetting a son through the favour of Vishṇu (Vishṇur yónim kalpayatu: Ṛ. V. X. 184. 1). Still *vikrámaṇam* is an unintelligible expression in this connexion. Another explanation, says Prof. Ludwig, would be to take *nápâtam* as fire and *vikrámaṇam Vishṇoḥ* [Vishṇu's striding forth] as the Sun. Prof. Grassmann translates: 'die Kinder und den höchsten Schritt des Vischnu'; the children and the highest step of Vishṇu.

46 *The earthly region:* the firmament or mid-air nearest to the earth. *The happy races:* of the Gods.

47 *Mâtalî:* a divine being, identified by the Commentators on the Ṛ. V. with Indra whose charioteer was Mâtali. *Kavyas:* a class of Manes, the spirits of a pious race of ancient time. *Angiras' sons:* the Angirases, the typical first sacrificers. *Singers:* or Ṛikvans; a class of spirits or deities who attend Bṛihaspati and sing his praises. The stanza is taken from Ṛ. V. X. 14. 3.

48 *This:* Soma juice, prepared for the sacrifice which is to be performed. The stanza is taken from Ṛ. V. VI. 47. 1.

49 This and the following stanza are taken from Ṛ. V. X. 14. 1, 2. *Mighty rivers:* that flow between the earth and the home of the Departed.

50 Yama first found for us the road to travel: this pasture never can be taken from us.
Men born on earth tread their own paths that lead them whither our ancient Fathers have departed.

51 Fathers who sit on sacred grass, come, help us: these offerings have we made for you; accept them.
So come to us with most auspicious favour: bestow on us unfailing health and plenty.

52 Bowing their bended knees and seated southward let all accept this sacrifice with favour.
Punish us not for any sin, O Fathers, which we through human frailty have committed.

53 Tvashṭar prepares the bridal for his daughter: therefore the whole of this our world assembles.
But Yama's mother, spouse of great Vivasvân, vanished as she was carried to her dwelling.

54 Go forth, go forth upon the homeward pathways whither our sires of old have gone before us.
Then shalt thou look on both the Kings enjoying their sacred food, God Varuṇa and Yama.

55 Go hence, depart ye, fly in all directions. This world for him the Fathers have provided.

---

50 *Pasture:* or dwelling.

51 Taken from Ṛ. V. X. 15. 4.

52 Taken, with a variation, from Ṛ. V. X. 15. 6. *Southward:* or on my right hand.

53 This stanza, which appears to have been inserted merely on account of the mention of Yama, is taken from Ṛ. V. X. 17. 1. The first line is found with an important variation in A. V. III. 31. 5. *Tvashṭar:* often regarded as an agent in natural phenomena. *His daughter:* Saraṇyû, the misty cloud (see stanza 4); or perhaps the dawn. *Yama's mother:* Saraṇyû. *Vanished:* or was stolen away. For the legend which has been formed out of the obscure hints contained in this and the following stanza of the original hymn, see Wilson's Translation and Muir, O. S. Texts, V. p 228.

54 This stanza, taken from Ṛ. V. X. 14. 7, is addressed to the spirit of the man whose funeral rites are being celebrated.

55 According to Sâyaṇa, this stanza, taken from Ṛ. V. X. 14. 9, is addressed to the Piśâchas and other evil spirits that haunt the place of cremation. *This world:* the home of the Departed.

Yama bestow upon this man a dwelling adorned with days and beams of light and waters.

56 We set thee down with yearning, and with yearning we enkindle thee,

Yearning, bring yearning Fathers nigh to eat the food of sacrifice.

57 We, splendid men, deposit thee, we, splendid men, enkindle thee.

Splendid, bring splendid Fathers nigh to eat the sacrificial food.

58 Our Fathers are Angirases, Navagvas, Atharvans, Bhṛigus, who deserve the Soma.

May these, the holy, look on us with favour; may we enjoy their gracious loving-kindness.

59 Come, Yama, with Angirases, the holy; rejoice thee here with children of Virûpa,

Seated on sacred grass at this oblation: I call Vivasvân too, thy father, hither.

60 Come, seat thee on this bed of grass, O Yama, accordant with Angirases and Fathers.

Let texts recited by the sages bring thee. O King, let this oblation make thee joyful.

61 He hath gone hence and risen on high mounting heaven's ridges by that path

Whereon the sons of Angiras, the conquerors of earth, went up.

---

56 *Thee:* Agni; the fire. The stanza is taken from R. V. X. 16. 12.

58 This and the two following stanzas are taken from R. V. X. 14. 6, 5, 4. *Navagvas:* the Nine; a mythical priestly race. See A. V. XIV. 1. 56.

59 *Children of Virûpa:* the Vairûpas, a sub-division of the Angirases.

60 *Angirases and Fathers:* or, perhaps, Angirases our Fathers.

61 *He:* the spirit of the dead man.

A full and excellent account of the Fathers, whose worship and sacrificial commemorations are still regarded as the most sacred and most binding of religious duties, will be found in Prof. Max Müller's India, What can it Teach us? pp. 219—242, edition of 1892. For a detailed account of Indian funeral rites, see Colebrooke's 'Miscellaneous Essays' republished from Vol. V. of the Asiatic Researches, von Roth's article in the Journal of the German Oriental Society, IV. 426, and Prof. Max Müller's paper in the same Journal, Vol. IX.

HYMN II.

FOR Yama Soma juice flows clear, to Yama is oblation paid.
To Yama sacrifice prepared, and heralded by Agni, goes.

2 Offer to Yama sacrifice most sweet in savour and draw near.
Bow down before the Ṛishis of the olden time, the ancient ones who made the path.

3 Offer to Yama, to the King, butter and milk in sacrifice.
So may he grant that we may live long days of life mid living men.

4 Burn him not up, nor quite consume him, Agni. Let not his body or his skin be scattered.
O Jâtavedas, when thou hast matured him, then send him on his way unto the Fathers.

5 When thou hast made him ready, Jâtavedas, then do thou give him over to the Fathers.
When he attains unto the life that waits him he will obey the Deities' commandment.

6 With the three jars Bṛihat alone makes pure the six wide-spreading realms.
The Gâyatrî, the Trishṭup, all metres in Yama are contained.

A funeral hymn composed mainly of verses from the Ṛigveda.

1 The first three stanzas, addressed to the priests who officiate at the ceremony, are taken, with variations, from Ṛ. V. X. 14. 13, 15, 14.

2 *Who made the path:* who have gone before us to the other world.

4 This and the following stanza are taken from Ṛ. V. X. 16. 1, 2. They are to be recited, with 7, 8, 9, 10, while the body is being partially consumed on the funeral pile.

6 This stanza, which is unintelligible to me, is taken from Ṛ. V. X. 14. 16. *Six wide-spreading realms:* or six expanses; the four cardinal points, and the spaces above and below. According to Sâyaṇa, the six earths, or the six substances, viz. heaven, earth, water, plants, the sun, and truth or reality. *Three jars:* Trikadrukas or three Soma reservoirs. According to Ludwig, 'on the Trikadruka days,' three days of the Abhiplava ceremony. *All metres:* that is, all sacrificial rites.

7 The Sun receive thine eye, the wind thy spirit; go, as thy merit is, to earth or heaven.
Go, if it be thy lot, unto the waters; go, make thy home in plants with all thy members.

8 Thy portion is the goat: with heat consume him: let thy fierce flame, thy glowing splendour, burn him.
With thine auspicious forms, O Jâtavedas, bear this man to the region of the pious.

9 Let all thy rapid flames, O Jâtavedas, wherewith thou fillest heaven and earth's mid-region,
Follow the goat as he goes on, united: then with the others, most auspicious, aid us.

10 Away, O Agni, to the Fathers send him who, offered in thee, goes with our oblations.
Wearing new life let him approach his offspring, and splendid, be invested with a body.

---

7 Taken from Ṛ. V. X. 16. 3. *The Sun receive thine eye, the wind thy spirit:* let like return to like. Cf. A. V. V. 9. 7; VIII. 2. 3.

8 Taken from Ṛ. V. X. 16. 4. *Thy portion is the goat: with heat consume him:* or, enkindle with thine heat his unborn portion. The goat (*ajá*) is identified, mystically, with the unborn (*ajá*) or immortal spirit, and in sacrificial hymns the two meanings are sometimes difficult to distinguish. See A. V. IX. 5. 16, and Muir's note, O. S. Texts, V. p. 304. From a passage in the Taittirîya-Âraṇyaka cited by Ludwig, Der Rigveda, V. p. 422, it would appear that in this place the sacrificial animal is intended: 'sovil wird richtig sein, das ajaḥ das tier bezeichnet.' According to this interpretation Agni is entreated to content himself with consuming the sacrificial goat, and to convey the spirit of the departed, uninjured, to its home. The goat, was sacred to Agni; and a goatskin was laid under the corpse on the funeral pile.

9 *The goat:* or, the soul, according to the alternative explanation. *United:* referring to the flames. *The others:* flames of domestic and sacrificial fire.

10 Taken, with two variants, from Ṛ. V. X. 16. 5. *His offspring:* *çéshaḥ*; etymologically, relict. 'Geschlecht.'—Grassman. Muir (O. S. Texts, V. p. 299) translates *çéshaḥ* in this passage by '(his) remains'; M. Müller similarly by 'die alte Hülle,' the old garb or cover; and Ludwig by 'bleibsel.' The word, which does not recur in the A. V., has the meaning of son or children in all the passages of the Ṛ. V. in which it is found: I. 93. 4; V. 12. 6; V. 70. 45; VI. 27. 4, 5; VII. 1 12; VII. 4. 7. The departed spirit is prayed to revisit, with other Fathers, the children whom he has left on earth. Cf. stanzas 28, 30, and 60.

11 Run and outspeed the two dogs, Saramâ's offspring, brindled, four-eyed, upon thy happy pathway.
Draw nigh then to the gracious-minded Fathers who take their pleasure in the feast with Yama.

12 And those two dogs of thine, Yama, the watchers, four-eyed who look on men and guard the pathway—
Entrust this man, O King, to their protection, and with prosperity and health endow him.

13 Dark-hued, insatiate, with distended nostrils, Yama's two envoys roam among the people.
May they restore to us a fair existence here and to-day that we may see the sunlight.

14 For some the Soma juice runs clear, some sit by sacrificial oil.
To those for whom the meath flows forth, even to those let him depart.

15 Let him, O Yama, go to those Ṛishis austere, of Fervour born,
First followers of Law, the sons of Law, upholders of the Law.

16 Invincible through Fervour, they who by their Fervour went to heaven,

---

11 This and the two following stanzas are taken from Ṛ. V. X. 14. 10—12. *Dogs:* See A. V. V. 30. 6. M. Müller and Ludwig take *tûbhyâm* here as an ablative: Surround him, guard him from these twain, O Sovran. *Saramâ:* the hound of Indra, mother of Yama's dogs. See Ṛ. V. I. 62. 3; A. V. IX. 4. 16.

14 This stanza and the three following are taken from Ṛ. V. X. 154. 1, 4, 2, 3.

To those let him depart: let the spirit of the dead go to the realm of the Blessed, to the Fathers who receive offerings of Soma juice and clarified butter. *Meath:* according to Sâyaṇa, honey, which is offered to the spirits of their ancestors by students of the Atharva-veda, Soma juice and *ghṛitam* or clarified butter (sacrificial oil) being offered, respectively, by students of the Sâmaveda and Yajurveda.

15 *Fervour: tápas;* literally, warmth, heat; religious fervour, asceticism, austerity, self-denial and abstracted meditation: *Of Fervour born*, meaning those whose element is such devotion.

Who practised great austerity,—even to those let him depart.

17 The heroes who contend in war and boldly cast their lives away,
Or who give guerdon thousandfold,—even to those let him depart.

18 Let him, O Yama, go to those Rishis austere, of Fervour born,
Skilled in a thousand ways and means, the sages who protect the Sun.

19 Be pleasant unto him, O Earth, thornless and lulling him to rest.
Vouchsafe him shelter broad and sure.

20 In the free amplitude of earth take roomy space to lodge thee in.
Let all oblations which in life thou paidest drop thee honey now.

21 Hither I call thy spirit with my spirit. Come thou, delighted, to these dwelling-places.
Unite thee with the Fathers and with Yama : strong and delicious be the winds that fan thee.

22 Floating in water, bringing streams, let Maruts carry thee aloft,
And causing coolness by their rush sprinkle thee with their falling rain.

23 I have recalled thy life to life, to being, power, and energy.
Let thy soul go unto its own : so to the Fathers hasten thou.

24 Let not thy soul be left behind : here let not aught of thee remain,
Of spirit, body, members, sap.

---

19 This stanza is adapted, with variations, from R. V. I. 22. 15 which is not originally a funeral verse. *O Earth :* the collected remnants of bones and ashes were buried in an urn, Cf. stanza 50.

25 Let not a tree oppress thee, nor Earth the great Goddess weigh thee down.
Among the Fathers find thy home, and thrive mid those whom Yama rules.

26 Each parted member, severed from thy body, thy vital breaths that in the wind have vanished,
With all of these, piece after piece, shall Fathers who dwell together meet and reunite thee.

27 Him have the living banished from their houses: remove him to a distance from the hamlet.
Yama's observant messenger was Mṛityu: he hath despatched men's lives unto the Fathers.

28 Those Dasyus who, not eating our oblations, come with friends' faces mingled with the Fathers,
Those who wear gross, those who wear subtile bodies,—from this our sacrifice let Agni blast them.

29 Bringing delight, prolonging our existence, here let our own, the Fathers, dwell together.
Coming with sacrifice may we assist them, living long lives through many autumn seasons.

30 Now by this cow I bring thee, by the boiled rice set in milk for thee,
Be the supporter of the folk left here without a livelihood.

31 Prolong the pleasant Dawn enriched with horses—or bearing us anew beyond the darkness.
Adjudged to die be he, the man who slew thee: this portion let him find, and not another.

---

27 *Mṛityu:* Death, the minister and messenger of the King of the Departed. *Unto the Fathers:* brought them from the Fathers, according to Hillebrandt (Vedische Mythologie, I. 510).

28 *Dasyus:* barbarians and fiends who artfully mingle with the holy company.

30 Addressed to the spirit that has just passed away to heaven. *Cow:* that supplies the milk required for the oblation.

32 Yama is higher and Vivasvân lower: nothing whatever do I see above him.
This sacrifice of mine is based on Yama. Vivasvân spread the atmosphere about us.

33 From mortal men they hid the immortal Lady, made one like her and gave her to Vivasvân.
Saraṇyû brought to him the Aṣvin brothers, and then deserted both twinned pairs of children.

34 Bring thou the Fathers one and all, Agni, to eat the sacrifice,
The buried, and the cast away, those burnt with fire, and those exposed.

35 Those, whether flames have burnt or not consumed them, who in the midst of heaven enjoy oblations—
Let them, when thou dost know them, Jâtavedas, accept with sacred food the axe and worship.

36 Burn gently, Agni, burn not up the body with too fervent heat.
Let all thy force and fury be expended on the woods and earth.

37 I give this place to him who hath come hither and now is mine, to be a home to rest in:
This was the thought of Yama when he answered: This man is mine. Let him come here to riches.

---

33 The stanza, which has no connexion with the subject of the hymn, is taken from Ṛ. V. X. 17. 2. *They:* the Gods. *The immortal Lady:* Saraṇyû, daughter of Tvashṭar and wife of Vivasvân, mother of Yama and Yamî and the twin Aṣvins. For the legend referred to, see Muir, O. S. Texts, V. 228.

34 *Cast away: páropt́ăḥ;* abandoned at death to be devoured by carnivorous beasts and birds. *Exposed: úddhitâḥ;* cast out by their kindred in extreme old age to die of hunger, as appears to have been the case with Praskaṇva (Ṛ. V. Vâlakhilya, 3. 2). This custom was sanctioned by the Old German law, and according to Strabo was followed by Iranians, Bactrians, and Massagetae See Zimmer, Altindisches Leben, p. 328.

35 *The axe:* with which sacrificial victims were slaughtered.

38 This date we settle once for all, that it may ne'er be fixt again. A hundred autumns; not before.

39 This date we order, etc.

40 This date we limit, etc.

41 This date we measure, etc.

42 This date we mete out, etc.

43 This date we stablish, etc.

44 This date we mete and measure out, that it may ne'er be fixt again. A hundred autumns; not before.

45 The period I have measured—come to heaven. I would my life were long—
Not to be measured out again; a hundred autumns, not before.

46 Inbreath and outbreath, breath diffused, life, sight to look upon the Sun—
Seek by a straight unwinding path the Fathers whom King Yama rules.

47 Unmarried men who toiled and have departed, the childless, having left their foes behind them,
Have found on high the world whereto they mounted, reflecting on the ridge of vaulted heaven.

48 The lowest is the Watery heaven, Pîlumatî the middlemost;
The third and highest, that wherein the Fathers dwell, is called Pradyaus.

49 The Fathers of our Father, his Grandfathers, those who have entered into air's wide region,
Those who inhabit earth or dwell in heaven, these Fathers will we worship with oblation.

---

38 *Hundred autumns:* regarded as the natural duration of human life.

48 *Pîlumatî:* meaning, apparently, blossoming with the Pîlu tree (the Careya Arborea, or, according to others, the Salvadora Persica). *Pradyaus: dív* or *dyaús*, heaven, + *prá*, pro or prae; the eminently bright heaven; the heaven of heavens. Cf. A. V. IV. 14. 3.

49 Apparently the great-grandfathers are in heaven, the grandfathers in the sky, and the fathers on the earth. See M. Müller, India, What can it Teach us? p. 223.

50 Thou seest now, and ne'er again shalt look upon, the Sun in heaven.
Cover him as a mother draws her skirt about her son, O Earth!

51 This once, and at no other time hereafter in a lengthened life:
Cover him, as a wife, O Earth, covers her husband with her robe!

52 Round thee auspiciously I wrap the vesture of our Mother Earth:
Be bliss among the living mine, oblation mid the Fathers thine!

53 Ye have prepared, pathmakers, Agni-Soma, a fair world for the Gods to be their treasure.
Go to that world and send us Pûshan hither to bear us on the paths the goat hath trodden.

54 Guard of the world, whose cattle ne'er are injured, may Pûshan bear thee hence, for he hath knowledge.
May he consign thee to these Fathers' keeping, and to the gracious Gods let Agni give thee.

55 Lord of all life, let Âyu guard thee, Pûshan convey thee forward on the distant pathway.
May Savitar the God conduct thee thither where dwell the pious who have gone before thee.

56 For thee I yoke these carriers twain to bear thee to the spirit world,
Hasten with them to Yama's home and join his gathered companies.

---

50 *Cover him:* cover the inurned remains of the corpse.

53 *The goat hath trodden: ajayânaiḥ;* see above stanzas 8, 9. The St. Petersburg Lexicon suggests *añjoyânaiḥ*, leading straight to the goal. Most Mss. have *ajoyânaiḥ*, which is meaningless.

54 This and the following stanza are taken from R V. X. 17. 34. *He hath knowledge:* being the guide and guardian of all travellers.

55 *Âyu:* according to Sâyaṇa, Vâyu is intended, the letter *v* being elided. Life of full vitality and duration is probably meant: 'die volle lebensdauer.'—Ludwig.

56 *These carriers:* Pûshan and Savitar.

57 This is the robe that first was wrapped about thee: cast off the robe thou worest here among us.
Go, knowing, to the meed of virtuous action, thy many gifts bestowed upon the friendless.

58 Mail thee with flesh against the flames of Agni; encompass thee about with fat and marrow;
So will the bold One eager to attack thee with fierce glow fail to girdle and consume thee.

59 From his dead hand I take the staff he carried, together with his lore and strength and splendour.
There art thou, there; and here with good men round us may we o'ercome all enemies and foemen.

60 From his dead hand I take the bow he carried, together with his power and strength and splendour.
Having collected wealth and ample treasure, come hither to the world of living beings.

---

58 Taken from Ṛ. V. X. 16. 7. *Flesh:* literally cows, here standing for sacrificial animals in general, and meaning especially the omentum of the victim with which the head and mouth of the dead were covered before cremation. *Fat and marrow:* the kidneys of the slaughtered animal were placed in the hands of the corpse. See Âṣvalâyana-Gṛihya-Sûtra, IV. 3. 20, 21.

59 Taken, with a variation, from Ṛ. V. X. 18. 9.

60 *Bow:* this stanza is to be recited only when the deceased was a Kshatriya or man of the princely and military order. *Come hither:* to protect and aid us who are left on earth.

Stanzas 9, 20—59 (with a few exceptions) which are not taken from the Ṛigveda, have been translated by Ludwig, Der Rigveda. III. pp. 482—484. Much information on the subject of the hymn will be found in Zimmer's Altindisches Leben, pp. 400—407; and further details in Colebrooke's Miscellaneous Essays, and in Prof. Max Müller's paper 'On Sepulture and Sacrificial Customs in the Veda' (Ueber Todtenbestattung und Opfergebräuche in Veda,) in Zeitschrift der Deutschen Morgenländischen Gesellschaft, Vol. IX, 1856).

HYMN III.

Choosing her husband's world, O man, this woman lays herself down beside thy lifeless body,
Preserving faithfully the ancient custom. Bestow upon her here both wealth and offspring.

2 Rise, come unto the world of life, O woman: come, he is lifeless by whose side thou liest.
Wifehood with this thy husband was thy portion, who took thy hand and wooed thee as a lover.

3 I looked and saw the youthful dame escorted, the living to the dead: I saw them bear her.
When she with blinding darkness was enveloped, then did I turn her back and lead her homeward.

4 Knowing the world of living beings, Aghnyâ! treading the path of Gods which lies before thee,
This is thy husband: joyfully receive him and let him mount into the world of Svarga.

A funeral hymn, composed partly of verses from the Rigveda.

1 Addressed to the spirit of the dead man. *Choosing her husband's world:* the widow is, or is supposed to be, ready to follow her husband, but is dissuaded by her friends. *The ancient custom:* followed, there is reason to believe, by the Âryan immigrants in the earliest times, but not generally observed when these funeral hymns were composed. Old Northern poetry contains many instances of the observance of this 'ancient custom.' Nanna was burnt with Baldr; Brynhild gave orders that she should be burnt with Sigurd; Gunnhild slew herself when Asmund died; and Gudrun was reproached with having survived her husband. See Zimmer, Altindisches Leben, pp. 329—331. *Here:* the widow is to remain in the world of life and be rewarded for her show of affection.

2 Taken from Ṛ. V. X. 18. 8. The verse is spoken by the husband's brother, a foster-son or an old family servant, who makes the widow leave the body of the dead. See Âṣvalâyana-Gṛihya-Sûtra, iv. 2.

3 *To the dead: mṛitébhyaḥ,* as given in Whitney's Index Verborum, instead of *ṛitébhyaḥ* of the MSS. and the text. If the latter reading be retained, the meaning may perhaps be, as Ludwig suggests, 'to the fires.' *Blinding darkness:* her head was probably covered with a thick veil as she was carried on her husband's bier to the funeral pile. The speaker is probably, the brother-in-law, who in some cases marries the widow. Cf. 'Who brings you homeward as the widow bedward draws her husband's brother, as the bride attracts the groom?' (Ṛ.V. X. 40. 2).

4 *Aghnyâ:* literally, Cow. *Husband:* literally, lord of the herd; bull.

5 The speed of rivers craving heaven and cane, thou, Agni, art the waters' gall.

6 Cool, Agni, and again refresh the spot which thou hast scorched and burnt.
Here let the water-lily grow, and tender grass and leafy plant.

7 Here is one light for thee, another yonder: enter the third and be therewith united.
Uniting with a body be thou lovely, dear to the Gods in their sublimest mansion.

8 Rise up, advance, run forward: make thy dwelling in water that shall be thy place to rest in.
There dwelling in accordance with the Fathers delight thyself with Soma and libations.

9 Prepare thy body: speed thou on thy journey: let not thy limbs, thy frame be left behind thee.
Follow to its repose thy resting spirit: go to whatever spot of earth thou lovest.

10 With splendour may the Fathers, meet for Soma, with mead and fatness may the Gods anoint me,
Lead me on farther to extended vision, and prosper me through life of long duration.

11 May Agni balm me thoroughly with splendour; may Vishṇu touch my lips with understanding.

---

5 *Craving heaven and cane:* eagerly consuming the dry bamboos and flaming up to the sky.

6 The stanza is taken, with a slight variation, from Ṛ. V. X. 16, 13. *Water-lily: kiyā́mbū* or *kyā́mbū;* some kind of aquatic plant. *Tender grass: sāṇḍadūrvā́;* probably the same as the *pā́kadūrvā́* of the Ṛ. V. verse, a variety of *dū́rvā* grass (Panicum Dactylon).

7 Taken, with a variation, from Ṛ. V. X. 56. 1. The spirit of the dead is addressed. *One light:* the fire of the funeral pile. *Another:* in the firmament. *The third:* the light in the highest heaven above the firmament. *A body:* a renewed body after cremation. *Mansion: sadhásthe.* The Ṛ. V. has *janítre,* birth-place.

8 *In water:* above the firmament.

9 *Of earth:* in its most comprehensive sense, including the air above it

May all the Deities vouchsafe me riches, and pleasant Waters purify and cleanse me.

12 Mitra and Varuṇa have stood about me. Âdityas, Sacrificial Posts exalt me!
May Indra balm my hands with strength and splendour. A long, long life may Savitar vouchsafe me.

13 Worship with sacrificial gift King Yama, Vivasvân's son who gathers men together,
Yama who was the first to die of mortals, the first who travelled to the world before us.

14 Depart, O Fathers, and again come hither: this sacrifice of yours is balmed with sweetness.
Enrich us here with gift of great possessions; grant blessèd wealth with ample store of heroes.

15 Kaṇva, Kakshîvân, Purumîḍha, Agastya, Ṣyâvâṣva, Sobhari, and Archanânas,
This Viṣvâmitra, Jamadagni, Atri, Kaṣyapa, Vâmadeva be our helpers!

16 Vasishṭha, Jamadagni, Viṣvâmitra, Gotama, Vâmadeva, Bharadvâja!
Atri hath won your favour with our homage. Gracious to us be ye praiseworthy Fathers.

17 They, making for themselves a new existence, wash off defilement in the brazen vessel.
May we be fragrant in our houses, ever increasing in our children and our riches.

---

12 *Sacrificial Posts:* or splinters from the stake used for sacrificial purposes, and endowed with supernatural powers.

13 *Yama:* see XVIII. 1, first note. *Of mortals:* the Gods were originally subject to death.

15 *Sobhari:* a Ṛishi of the family of Kaṇva and seer of hymns 19—22 of Book VIII. of the Ṛigveda. *Archanânas:* a Ṛishi mentioned in Ṛ. V. V. 64. 7. The rest of the names in this and the following stanza are well known and have occurred before in the A. V. *This Viṣvâmitra:* supposed to be specially present at the ceremony.

17 *In the brazen vessel: kasyé* apparently = *kâṅsye;* the word is not found elsewhere.

18 They balm him, balm him over, balm him thoroughly, caress the mighty power and balm it with the mead.
They seize the flying steer at the stream's breathing-place: cleansing with gold they grasp the animal herein.

19 Fathers, be glorious in yourselves, and follow all that is glad in you and meet for Soma.
Give ear and listen, swiftly-moving Sages, benevolent, invoked in our assembly.

20 Atris, Angirases, Navagvas, givers of liberal gifts, continual sacrificers,
Devout and pious, granting guerdon freely, sit on this holy grass and be ye joyful.

21 As in the days of old our ancient Fathers, speeding the work of sacred worship, Agni!
Sought pure light and devotion, singing praises, they cleft the ground and made red Dawns apparent.

22 Gods, doing holy acts, devout, resplendent, smelting like ore their human generation,
Brightening Agni and exalting Indra, they came encompassing the stall of cattle.

---

18 Taken from Ṛ. V. IX. 86. 43. The stanza refers to the purification and preparation of the Soma juice which is to be used in sacrifice to the Fathers. *The flying steer:* the potent Soma as it flows. *With gold:* a piece of gold was tied to the ring-finger of the officiating priest as a symbol of truth. See Ṣatapatha-Brâhmaṇa, III. 3. 2. 2. *The animal:* Soma regarded as a sacrificial victim. *Breathing-place:* where the water seems to stand still for a moment to recover breath.

21 This stanza, 22,23, and half of 24 are taken, with variations, from Ṛ. V. IV. 2. 16—19. *Cleft the ground:* burst open the cave, that is, the thick cloud, in which the Dawns were imprisoned.

22 *Gods:* the godlike Angirases. *Smelting like ore:* purifying their humanity, as ore is freed from dross by smelting. *Stall of cattle:* the enclosure that confined the cows, the days or bright rays of light that had been stolen away by the demons of darkness.

23 Strong One! he marked them, and the Gods before them, like herds of cattle in a foodful pasture.
There men moaned forth their strong desires, to strengthen even the true, the nearest One, the living.

24 We have worked for thee, we have toiled and laboured: bright Dawns have shed their light upon our worship.
All that the Gods regard with love is blessèd. Loud may we speak, with heroes, in assembly.

25 From eastward Indra, Lord of Maruts, guard me, as in her arms Earth guards the heaven above us!
Those who give room, who made the paths, we worship, you, mid the Gods, who share the gifts we offer.

26 Dhâtar with Nirṛiti save me from southward, etc. (as in stanza 25).

27 From westward Aditi with Âdityas save me! etc.

28 From westward with the All-Gods save me Soma! etc.

29 May the strong firm Sustainer bear thee upright, as Savitar bears light above the heaven.
Those who give room, who made the paths, we worship, you, mid the Gods, who share the gifts we offer.

30 Toward the eastward region I supply thee, before thou goest homeward, with oblation, as in her arms, etc. (as in stanza 25).

31 Toward the southern region, etc.

---

23 *Strong One!:* O mighty Agni. *He marked them:* Indra saw the kine or imprisoned days. *The Gods before them:* the divine Angirases standing in front of the cave. *The true, the nearest one, the living:* Agni appears to be meant.

24 The second half of this stanza is taken from Ṛ. V. II. 23. 19. *With heroes:* with brave sons about us to give us confidence.

25 *Those:* the Fathers. *Room:* freedom and comfort. *Made the paths:* prepared and showed us the way to heaven.

32 Toward the western region, etc.

33 Toward the northern region, etc.

34 Toward the stedfast region, etc.

35 Toward the upmost region I supply thee, before thou goest homeward, with oblation, as in her arms Earth bears the heaven above us.
Those who give room, who made the paths, we worship, you, mid the Gods, who share the gifts we offer.

36 Thou art the Bull, Supporter, and Upholder,

37 Who purifiest wind and mead and water.

38 From this side and from that let both assist me. As, speeding, ye have come like two twin sisters,
Religious-hearted votaries brought you forward. Knowing your several places be ye seated.

39 Sit near, sit very near beside our Soma: for you I fit the ancient prayer with homage.
The praise-song, like a chieftain on his pathway, spreads far and wide. Let all Immortals hear it.

40 Three paces hath the stake gone up, and followed her, the four-footed, with devout observance.
He with the Syllable copies the praise-song: he thoroughly purifies at Order's centre.

---

36 *Thou:* Agni.

38 This and the three following stanzas are taken, with variations and transpositions, from R̥. V. X. 13. 1—4. *Ye have come:* the verse is addressed to the two deified carts or barrows, called Havirdhânas or oblation-holders, on which the Soma plants are brought to be pressed.

40 The stanza as it stands in the text is unintelligible. Prof Ludwig (Der Rigveda, V. p. 334) suggests *yûpo* instead of *rûpó* or *rupó.* The *three paces*, stages or *padas* may, he thinks, mean the threefold aim and object of the sacrificial stake, namely the sacred duty which it performs, the lightning which it resembles (vajro vai yûpaḥ), and perhaps the institutor of the sacrifice in his sanctified and unassailable form which it represents. *Her, the four-footed:* perhaps the *vedi* or altar, representing the earth. *This: etám;* Prof. Ludwig suggests that heaven is intended, the counterpart of the praṇava or Sacred Syllable OM, as the altar is of the earth. See the corresponding stanza in the R̥igveda

41 Chose he then, death for Gods to be their portion? Why chose he not for men a life eternal?
Bṛihaspati span sacrifice, the Ṛishi; and Yama yielded up his own dear body.

42 Thou, Agni Jâtavedas, when entreated, didst bear our offerings, having made them fragrant,
And give them to the Fathers who consumed them with Svadhâ. Eat, thou God, the gifts we bring thee.

43 Lapped in the bosom of the purple Mornings, give riches to the man who brings oblation.
Grant to your sons a portion of that treasure, and, present, give them energy, O Fathers.

44 Fathers whom Agni's flames have tasted, come ye nigh: in perfect order take ye each your proper place.
Eat sacrificial food presented on the grass: grant riches with a multitude of hero sons.

(X. 13. 3.) which is equally obscure and appears to be inexplicable. It is paraphrased by Prof. Wilson, following Sâyaṇa, as follows: 'I make the five stages of the sacrifice ascend; I take four steps by pious observances: with the sacred syllable I perfect this (adoration); I purify (the Soma) on the navel of the sacrifice.' The *five stages* are, according to Sâyaṇa, the five elements of the sacrifice, grain, Soma, cows, the Puroḍâśa cake, and clarified butter. The *four steps* are the metres most commonly used.

41 The Gods are not subject to death, and immortality in another world awaits mankind. The Gods owe their eternal life to Bṛihaspati identified with Agni (cf. A. V. II. 1. 5; III. 22. 3; IV. 14. 1), and men to Yama, who died to show them the way to heaven. See Ludwig, Ueber die neuesten Arbeiten auf dem Gebiete der Ṛigveda-forschung, pp. 110 sqq.

42 Taken from R. V. X. 15 12. *With Svadhâ:* with the sacrificial exclamation Svadhâ addressed to the manes, or with their own allotted portion.

43 This and the four following stanzas are taken, with slight variations, from Ṛ. V. X. 15. 7, 11, 5, 8, 9. *Lapped in the bosom of the purple Mornings:* 'Seated in the proximity of the radiant flames (of the altar).'—Wilson. The feminine adjective *aruṇînâm* (purpurearum or rubrarum) stands without a substantiv. The Fathers are addressed.

45 May they, the Fathers who deserve the Soma, invited to their favourite oblations
Laid on the sacred grass, come nigh and listen. May they be gracious unto us and bless us.

46 Our Father's Fathers and their sires before them who came, most noble, to the Soma banquet,
With these let Yama, yearning with the yearning, rejoicing eat our offerings at his pleasure.

47 Come to us, Agni, with the gracious Fathers who dwell in glowing light, the very Sages,
Who thirsted mid the Gods, who hasten hither, oblation-winners, theme of singers' praises.

48 Come, Agni, come with countless ancient Fathers, dwellers in light, primeval, God-adorers,
Eaters and drinkers of oblation, truthful, who travel with the Deities and Indra.

49 Betake thee to the lap of Earth, our mother, of Earth far-spreading, very kind and gracious.
May she, wool-soft unto the guerdon-giver, guard thee in front upon the distant pathway.

50 Heave thyself, Earth, nor press him downward heavily : afford him easy access, pleasant to approach.
Cover him as a mother wraps her skirt about her child, O Earth !

51 Now let the heaving earth be free from motion : yea, let a thousand clods remain above him.
Be they to him a home distilling fatness : here let them ever be his place of refuge.

52 I stay the earth from thee, while over thee I place this piece of earth. May I be free from injury.
The Fathers firmly fix this pillar here for thee ; and there let Yama make thee an abiding-place.

---

49 This and the three following stanzas, to be recited during the burial of the remains of the corpse, are taken, with variations, from Ṛ. V. X. 18. 10—13. *Guerdon-giver:* the liberal rewarder of the priests.

52 *Pillar:* a mound or pile of clods raised on the place of interment.

53 Forbear, O Agni, to upset this chalice: the Gods and they who merit Soma love it.
This cup, yea this which serves the Gods to drink from,—in this let the Immortals take their pleasure.

54 The chalice brimming o'er which erst Atharvan offered to Indra, Lord of wealth and treasure,
Indu therein sets draught of virtuous action, and ever purifies himself within it.

55 What wound soe'er the dark bird hath inflicted, the emmet, or the serpent, or the jackal,
May Agni who devoureth all things heal it, and Soma who hath passed into the Brâhmans.

56 The plants of earth are rich in milk, and rich in milk is this my milk.
With all the milky essence of the Waters let them make me clean.

57 Let these unwidowed dames with goodly husbands adorn themselves with fragrant balm and unguent.
Decked with fair jewels, tearless, free from trouble, first let the dames go up to where he lieth.

58 Meet Yama, meet the Fathers, meet the merit of virtuous action in the loftiest heaven.
Leave sin and evil, seek anew thy dwelling: so bright with glory let him join his body.

---

53 Taken from Ṛ. V. X. 16. 8. *This chalice:* which holds the libation.

54 *Indu:* Soma.

55 Taken from Ṛ. V. X. 16. 6. *The dark bird:* the raven or crow.

56 Taken from Ṛ. V. X. 17, 14. *Rich in milk:* full of sap, vigour, vital and vivifying power. *My milk:* or, strength. The Ṛ. V. stanza has *vâchaḥ*, speech or prayer.

57 Taken from Ṛ. V. X. 18. 7.

58 From Ṛ. V. X. 14. 8. *Merit:* acquired by the performance of prescribed sacrifices and voluntary good works, and stored up in heaven to await the arrival of the spirits of the pious.

59 Our Father's Fathers and their sires before them, they who have entered into air's wide region,
For them shall self-resplendent Asunîti form bodies now according to her pleasure.

60 Let the hoar-frost be sweet to thee, sweetly on thee the rain descend!
O full of coolness, thou cool Plant, full of fresh moisture, freshening Herb,
Bless us in waters, female Frog: calm and allay this Agni here.

61 Vivasvân make us free from fear and peril, good rescuer, quick-pouring, bounteous giver!
Many in number be these present heroes! Increase of wealth be mine in kine and horses!

62 In immortality Vivasvân set us! Go from us Death, come to us life eternal!
To good old age may he protect these people: let not their spirits pass away to Yama.

63 The Sage of Fathers, guardian of devotions who holds thee up with might in air's mid-region,—
Praise him, ye Viṣvâmitras, with oblation. To lengthened life shall he, this Yama, lead us.

64 Mount and ascend to highest heaven, O Ṛishis: be ye not afraid.

---

59 Cf. Ṛ. V. X. 15. 14. *Asunîti:* apparently a deity presiding over funerals (see Ṛ. V. X. 59. 5, 6). The word may be a name of Yama, or may mean 'guide to (spirit) life,' or 'way to (spirit) life.' See Muir, O. S. Texts, V. 297, and Bergaigne, La Religion Védique, I. p. 96.

60 The second and third lines are taken, with variations, from Ṛ. V. X. 16. 14, following in that hymn and closely connected with stanza 6 of this hymn. 'After the fire has consumed the corpse, water is poured upon it to extinguish it. Then furthermore certain water-plants are put there. In addition to these a frog—here a female, elsewhere a male—is put upon the place where the fire has burned. These, as representatives of life in the waters, are symbolically supposed both to prevent and to extinguish fire.'—Bloomfield. See full Excursus on the subject in Contributions to the Interpretation of the Veda, Second Series. Baltimore: 1890.

63 *The Sage of Fathers:* Yama.

Soma-drinkers, to you is paid this Soma-lover's sacrifice. We have attained the loftiest light.

65 Agni is shining forth with lofty banner: the Bull is bellowing to earth and heaven.

From the sky's limit even hath he stretched near us: the Steer hath waxen in the waters' bosom.

66 They gaze on thee with longing in their spirit, as on an eagle that is mounting skyward;

On thee with wings of gold, Varuṇa's envoy, the Bird that hasteth to the home of Yama.

67 O Indra, bring us wisdom as a sire gives wisdom to his sons.

Guide us, O much-invoked in this our way: may we still living look upon the Sun.

68 Let these which Gods have held for thee, the beakers covered o'er with cake,

Be full of sacred food for thee, distilling fatness, rich in mead.

69 Grains which for thee I scatter, mixt with Sesamum, as holy food,—

May they for thee be excellent and potent: King Yama look on them as thine with favour!

70 O Tree, give back again this man who is deposited on thee,

That he may dwell in Yama's home addressing the assemblies there.

---

65 Taken, with variations, from Ṛ. V. X. 8. 1. *Lofty banner:* the lightning. *Waters' bosom:* the depth of the firmament.

66 Taken from Ṛ. V. X. 123. 6. *Thee:* Agni identified with the Sun. The original hymn is addressed to Vena, apparently the Sun as he rises in the mist and cloud of the morning. *To the home of Yama:* to the place where he sets and disappears.

67 Taken from Ṛ. V. VII. 32. 16.

68 *Gods:* the priests. *Thee:* the spirit of the dead.

70 *Tree:* the wood of the funeral pile.

The stanzas that are not taken from the Ṛigveda have been translated by Ludwig, Der Ṛigveda, III. 484—487.

71 Seize hold, O Jâtavedas; let thy flame be full of fervent heat.
Consume his body: to the world of pious ones transport this man.

72 To those, thy Fathers who have passed away at first and afterward,
Let the full brook of butter run, o'erflowing with a hundred streams.

73 Mount to this life, removing all defilement: here thine own kindred shine with lofty splendour.
Depart thou; be not left behind: go forward, first of those here, unto the world of Fathers.

HYMN IV.

RISE to your mother, flames of Jâtavedas! I send you up by paths which Fathers traverse.
With headlong speed the Oblation-bearer bore our gifts: toil ye, and place the offerer where the righteous dwell.

2 The Seasons, Deities, form and order Worship, butter, cake, ladles, sacrificial weapons.
Tread thou God-travelled paths whereby the righteous, payers of sacrifices, go to Svarga.

3 Carefully look on Sacrifice's pathway whereon the Angirases, the righteous, travel.
By those same pathways go thou up to Svarga where the Âdityas take their fill of sweetness. There make thy home in the third vault of heaven.

A funeral hymn, composed partly of verses from the Ṛigveda.

1 *To your mother:* to heaven from which ye originally came. The three fires used in the ceremony are addressed; the Âhavanîya fire placed to the south-east of the funeral pile, the Gârhapatya to the north-west, and the Dakshiṇa to the south-west. *Toil ye:* in consuming the corpse.

2 *Thou:* the spirit of the dead.

3 *Sweetness:* or, honey, in the form of libations.

4 Three eagles in the region's roar are standing high on heaven's ridge in their appointed station.
The worlds of Svarga shall, filled full of Amrit, yield food and power to him who sacrificeth.

5 Upabhṛit stablished air, Juhû the heaven, Dhruvâ supported earth securely founded.
As meed, the Svarga worlds, o'erspread with fatness, shall yield the sacrificer all his wishes.

6 Dhruvâ, ascend thou earth the all-sustainer: go thou, O Upabhrit, to air's mid-region.
Juhû, go skyward with the sacrificer; go, and with Sruva as thy calf beside thee drain all the swelling unreluctant quarters.

7 They ford the mighty rivers by the pathway which they who sacrifice, the righteous, travel.
There they gave room unto the sacrificer when they made regions and existing creatures.

8 The Angirases' pathway is the eastern Agni, the Âdityas' pathway is the Gârhapatya:

---

4 The meaning of the first line is obscure. *Roar:* or, noise; Ludwig doubtingly suggests that *māyā* may be used as a locative here. No sense can be extracted from the word as a dual.

5 The Upabhṛit, Juhû, and Dhruvâ are offering-spoons or ladles, each about a cubit long and made of a different kind of holy wood, the Dhruvâ having the largest bowl, used for pouring libations of clarified butter into the fire.

6 *Earth:* including here the air immediately above the earth. Cf. stanza 48. *Sruva:* a dipping-spoon or small ladle used for conveying the butter from the pot into one of the larger ladles. All these ladles, as well as the rest of his sacrificial implements, are deposited with the dead man on the funeral pile. The Upabhṛit is put into his left hand, the Juhû into his right, the Dhruvâ upon his chest, and the Sruva (broken in two if there is only one) on the sides of his nose.

7 *They ford the mighty rivers*: the spirits cross the great streams that flow between their own home and the world of men. Cf. XVIII. 1. 49. *When they made regions:* the ancient Rishis are often spoken of as *bhûtakṛitaḥ* or World-creators. See VI. 33. 5, and stanza 11 of this hymn.

8 *The eastern Agni:* the original domestic fire. *Gârhapatya:* the householder's western sacred fire. *Southerns:* the Fathers or Ancestral Spirits who come from the south, the abode of Yama. Cf. stanza 46.

The southward Agni is the way of Southerns.
To Agni's greatness whom the prayer divideth go powerful, unscathed, with all thy members.

9 Eastward let east fire happily consume thee, and westward happily the Gârhapatya.
Burn southern fire, thine armour and protection: from air's mid-region from the north and centre, on all sides, Agni, guard thou him from horror.

10 Do ye, with your most kindly forms, O Agni, waft, turned to rapid steeds whose ribs bear burthens,
The sacrificer to the world of Svarga where with the Gods they banquet and are joyful.

11 Happily from the rear burn this man, Agni, happily from before, above, and under.
One, triply parted, Jâtavedas, place him happily in the world that holds the righteous.

12 Happily lit, let fires, each Jâtavedas, seize on Prajâpati's appointed victim.
Let them not cast it down while here they cook it.

13 Sacrifice, duly offered, comes preparing the sacrificer for the world of Svarga.
Let all the fires, each Jâtavedas, welcome Prajâpati's completely offered victim.
Let them not cast it down while here they cook it.

14 Fain to fly up from the sky's ridge to heaven, the worshipper hath mounted visible Agni.
Lucid from out the mist to him, the pious, gleams the God-travelled path that leads to Svarga.

---

9 *Whom the prayer divideth:* who is really one, but arranged in different places for sacrificial purposes by the devotion of worshippers.

10 *Ye... ..O Agni:* one deity in sundry places; 'one, triply parted' of the next stanza.

14 *The worshipper:* the dead man, who has in his life-time offered the prescribed sacrifices.

15 On thy right hand let Indra be thy Brahman, Bṛihaspati Adhvaryu, Agni Hotar.
This ordered sacrifice goes offered thither whither presented gifts have gone aforetime.

16 Enriched with cake and milk here let the Charu rest.
World-makers, makers of the path, we worship you of the Gods who here partake oblations.

17 Enriched with cake and curds, etc. (as in stanza 16).

18 Enriched with cake and drops, etc.

19 Enriched with cake and butter, etc.

20 Enriched with cake and flesh, etc.

21 Enriched with cake and food, etc.

22 Enriched with cake and mead, etc.

23 Enriched with cake and juice, etc.

24 Here, mixt with cake and water rest the Charu!
World-makers, makers of the path, we worship those Gods of you who here partake oblations.

25 Let these which Gods have held for thee, these beakers covered o'er with cake,
Be full of sacred food for thee, distilling fatness, rich in mead.

26 Grains which for thee I scatter, mixt with Sesamum, as holy food,—
May they for thee be excellent and potent. King Yama look on them as thine with favour!

27 More immortality!

28 On all the earth, to heaven, the drop descended, on this place and on that which was before it.

---

16 *Charu:* a sacrificial caldron or pot. The word means also an oblation of rice boiled in milk, an Odana. *World-makers:* creative Rishis. See stanza 7. The second line is repeated from XVIII. 3. 25.

25 This and the following stanza are repeated from XVIII. 3. 68, 69. *Gods:* priests.

28 Taken, with variations, from R. V. X. 17. 11. The stanza is hardly intelligible. *The drop* is apparently the Soma, and not, as

I offer up, throughout the seven oblations, the drop which still to one same place is moving.

29 Those who observe men look on wealth as Vâyu with countless streams, and as light-finding Arka;
Those drain out Guerdon sprung from seven mothers, who satisfy and evermore give presents.

30 They for their weal drain out the cask, the beaker four-holed, the milch-cow Iḍâ full of sweetness.
Injure not, Agni, in the loftiest heaven Aditi heightening strength among the people.

31 On thee doth Savitar the God bestow this vesture for thy wear.
Clothe thee herein, and find meet robe in Yama's realm to cover thee.

32 The grains of corn have now become a cow, the Sesamum her calf.
He in the realm of Yama lives on her the inexhaustible.

---

elsewhere alternatively explained, Âditya or the Sun. The Ṛ V. reading of the first line is simpler: 'Through days of earliest date the drop descended, etc.' that is, Soma which originally came from heaven has been available for sacrifice at all times and in all places.

29 Taken, with variations, from Ṛ V. X. 107. 4. *Those who observe mankind:* the Maghavans, wealthy nobles and eminent householders who do not consider the cost of sacrifice, but regard it as an occasion that enables them to show their liberality and to gain the favour of Vâyu the Wind-God who brings countless showers of seasonable rain, or of the Sun who sends the light and generative warmth. *Sprung from seven mothers:* originating in, and accompanying, seven forms of sacrifice; or regulated by the seven priests.

30 *The cask, the beaker:* metaphorical expressions for the spring and source of abundance. *Four-holed*: as representing the udder of the cow of plenty. *Iḍâ;* representing the comfort and blessings which spring from sacrifice. The legend of Iḍâ as daughter of Manu is told at length in Ṣatapatha-Brâhmaṇa, I. 8. 1. 1—29. *Heightening strength:* die strotzend gedeihn verleiht [fliessen läszt] den leuten.—Ludwig.

31 This and the three following stanzas are addressed to the spirit of the dead. *This vesture:* the skin of the animal sacrificed at the ceremony.

32 *The grains:* see stanza 26.

33 Let these become thy milch-kine, man! supplying all thy heart's desires.
There, speckled, white, like-hued and various-coloured, with calves of Sesamum let them stand beside thee.

34 Let the green grains become thy white and speckled, the dusky corns become thy ruddy milch-kine.
Let those with calves of Sesamum for ever yield strength to him and never flinch from milking.

35 I offer in Vaiṣvânara this oblation, thousandfold spring that pours a hundred streamlets.
This with a swelling flow supports the Father, supports grandfathers and their sires before them.

36 Beside the spring with hundred, thousand currents, expanding on the summit of the water,
Exhaustless, yielding strength, never reluctant, the Fathers with their sacred food are seated.

37 This pile of wood, collected, heaped together, regard it, O ye kinsmen, and come near it.
To immortality this mortal goeth: prepare a home for him, all ye his kindred.

38 Be here, even here, acquiring wealth, here be thou thought, here be thou strength.
Be stronger here in manly power, life-giver, never beaten back.

39 Giving the son and grandson satisfaction, let these the present Waters full of sweetness,
Pouring forth food and Amrit for the Fathers, refresh both these and those, the Goddess Waters.

40 Waters, send Agni forward to the Fathers: let them accept the sacrifice I offer.
May they who follow Vigour that abideth there send us down wealth with full store of heroes.

---

37 *Kinsmen:* spirits of the dead man's ancestors.

38 *Be here:* as one of the Fathers, revisit and be present among those whom thou hast left on earth.

41 Lover of butter, deathless, him, Oblation-bearer, they inflame.
He knoweth well the treasured stores gone to the Fathers, far away.

42 The mingled draught, the mess of rice, the flesh which I present to thee,
May these be full of food for thee, distilling fatness, rich in sweets.

43 Grains which for thee I scatter, mixt with Sesamum, as sacred food,
May these for thee be excellent and potent. King Yama look on them, as thine, with favour.

44 This is the ancient, this the recent pathway, by which thy sires of olden time departed.
They who first travelled it, and they who followed, convey thee to the world where dwell the righteous.

45 The pious call Sarasvatî: they worship Sarasvatî while sacrifice proceedeth.
The righteous doers of good deeds invoke her: Sarasvatî send bliss to him who giveth!

46 Approaching on the south our solemn worship, the Fathers call Sarasvatî to hear them.
Sit on this holy grass and be ye joyful: give thou us strengthening food that brings no sickness.

47 Sarasvatî, who camest with them, joying in hymns and food, O Goddess, with the Fathers,
Here give the Sacrificer growth of riches, a portion, worth a thousand, of refreshment.

48 As Pṛithivî rests on earth, so do I seat thee. May the God Dhâtar lengthen our existence.

---

41 *They inflame:* men kindle Agni.

43 Repeated from XVIII. 3. 69.

45 This stanza and the two following are taken, with variations and transpositions, from Ṛ. V. X. 17. 7—9.

48 *Pṛithivî:* (earth) meaning here the air immediately above it. Cf. Stanza 6 and VII. 18. 1, note. *He who parts in turn:* the spirit of the man who goes at his appointed time to the other world.

For you may he who parts in turn find treasures, but let the Dead remain among the Fathers.

49 Depart ye two: wipe ye away whatever omens of evil fortune here have told you.
Go from this man, both Steers, to him who wills it: ye are my joys here by the giver's Fathers.

50 From a good quarter have we gained this guerdon, gift of this man, strength-giving, plenteous milker.
Bringing in youth old age unto the living, may she bear these together to the Fathers.

51 I bring this clipped grass hither for the Fathers: grass living, higher, for the Gods I scatter.
Mount this, O man, as victim: let the Fathers recognize thee when thou hast travelled yonder.

52 Set on this grass thou hast become a victim. Fathers shall know thee yonder when they meet thee.
Gather thy body, limb by limb, together: I by the power of prayer arrange thy members.

53 The royal Parṇa is the caldrons' cover: strength have we gained, force, power, and might, and vigour,
Bestowing length of life upon the living, for long existence through a hundred autumns.

54 The share of vigour which gave this man being, the stone won lordship over foods that nourish.
Hymn this with your oblations, Viṣvâmitras: may he, may Yama, lengthen our existence.

---

49 *Depart ye two:* the performer of the ceremony addresses the bullocks which he now yokes to the cart which is to take him home. The second line is obscure.

50 *Guerdon:* sacrificial fees in the shape of a milch-cow. *Bear these men together:* transport them in due time.

51 *Clipped grass:* sacrificial grass, duly trimmed, as the ritual requires.

53 *Parṇa:* the wood of the Palâṣa, as the tree was afterwards called; the Butea Frondosa. The ladle called Juhû and the covers of some sacrificial vessels were made of this wood.

54 *The stone:* representing Yama.—Ludwig.

55 As the Five Races of mankind for Yama set apart a house,
Even so I set a house apart that greater numbers may be mine.

56 Take thou and wear this piece of gold, the gold thy father used to wear.
Wipe tenderly the right hand of thy sire who goes away to heaven.

57 To all, the living and the dead, all that are born, the worshipful,
Let the full brook of fatness run, o'erflowing, with a stream of mead.

58 Far-seeing he flows on, the Bull, the Lord of hymns, promoter of the Sun, of Days, of Dawns, of Heaven.
Breath of the rivers, he hath roared into the jars, and through his wisdom entered into Indra's heart.

59 Let thy bright smoke envelop thee, spread forth, O Bright One, in the sky,
For, Purifier, like the Sun thou shinest with thy radiant glow.

60 Indu is moving forth to Indra's destined place, and slights not as a friend the promise of his friend.
Thou, Soma, comest nigh as bridegroom meets the bride, reaching the beaker by a course of hundred paths.

---

55 The meaning of the second line is not clear. Ludwig would read *te* for *me* and divide *bhūrayaḥ* into *bhūr áyaḥ*: 'that earth may be as iron unto thee.'

56 Addressed to the son of the dead.

58 Taken, with variations, from Ṛ. V. IX. 86. 19. *The Bull:* the mighty Soma.

59 Taken, with a variation, from Ṛ. V. VI. 2. 6. Addressed to Agni.

60 Taken, with variations, from Ṛ. V. IX. 86. 16. *Of his friend:* Indra. *Hundred paths:* through the interstices of the woollen filter through which the juice is strained.

61 Well have they eaten and rejoiced: their dear ones have they shaken off.
Sages, self-luminous, have praised: we who are youngest supplicate.

62 Come hither, Fathers, who deserve the Soma, by the deep pathways which the Fathers travel.
Bestow upon us life and store of children, and favour us with increase of our riches.

63 Depart, O Fathers, ye who merit Soma, by the deep pathways which the Fathers travel;
But in a month, rich in fair sons and heroes, come back into our homes to eat oblation.

64 If Agni Jâtavedas, as he bore you hence to the Fathers' world, hath left one single
Limb of your bodies, here do I restore it. Fathers, rejoice in heaven with all your members!

65 Meet for men's praises, Agni Jâtavedas was sent as envoy when the day was closing.
Thou gavest to the Fathers with oblation. They ate: eat, God, our offered sacrifices.

66 Here hast thou left thy heart; O man, as sisters leave their little pet. Do thou, O Earth, envelop him.

67 Bright be to thee those worlds where dwell the Fathers! I seat thee in that sphere which they inhabit.

---

61 Taken, with variations, from Ṛ. V. I. 82. 2. *They:* the Fathers. *Their dear ones:* their living kinsmen. The stanza is slightly out of place here, and should come after the offerings to the Manes.

62 *Deep:* far away in the interior of the lower heaven.

63 *In a month:* to attend the Piṇḍapitṛiyajña or great monthly Ancestral Sacrifice.

64 *With all your members:* Cf. XI. 3. 32, 49.

66 *Their little pet: kákutsalam;* explained in the St. Petersburg Lexicon as probably a fond name for a little child. The word (which, as a Ludwig observes, has a syllable too much for the metre) does not occur elsewhere and is suspicious here.

68 Thou art the grass whereon our Fathers seat them.

69 Loosen, O Varuṇa, the bond that binds us; loosen the bond above, between, and under.
Then under thy protection, O Âditya, may we be sinless and restored to freedom.

70 From all those bonds, O Varuṇa, release us, wherewith a man is bound at length and cross-wise.
Then may we live a hundred autumn seasons guarded by thee, O King, by thee protected.

71 To Agni, bearer of oblation to the Manes, be Hail! and homage!

72 To Soma connected with the Fathers Hail! and homage!

73 To the Fathers connected with Soma Hail! and homage!

74 To Yama connected with the Fathers Hail! and homage!

75 To thee, O Great-grandfather, and those with thee be this cry of Hail!

76 To thee, Grandfather, and to those with thee be this cry of Hail!

77 To thee, O Father, be this cry of Hail!

78 Hail to the Fathers who inhabit earth!

79 Hail to the Fathers who inhabit the firmament!

80 Hail to the Fathers who dwell in heaven!

81 Hail, Fathers, to your energy! Hail, Fathers, to your sap!

82 Hail Fathers, to your wrath! Hail, Fathers, to your ardour!

83 Hail, Fathers, to what is awful! Hail to what is terrible in you!

---

69 Taken from Ṛ. V. I. 24. 15.

71 The verses 71–74 and 76–87 are non-metrical.

84 Hail, Fathers, to all that is propitious! Hail to all that is pleasant in you!

85 Homage to you, Fathers! Hail to you, Fathers!

86 All Fathers who are here, the Fathers here are you: let them follow you. May ye be the most excellent of these.

87 All living fathers who are here are we here: let them follow us.
May we be the most excellent of these.

88 Bright Agni, we will kindle thee, rich in thy splendour, fading not,
So that this glorious fuel may send forth to heaven its light for thee. Bring food to those who sing thy praise.

89 Within the waters runs the Moon, the strong-winged Eagle soars in heaven.
Ye Lightnings with your golden wheels, men find not your abiding-place. Hear this my call, O Heaven and Earth.

---

88 The stanza is taken from Ṛ. V. V, 6. 4.

89 Taken from Ṛ. V. I, 105. 1. The original hymn is said to be an address to the Viṣvedevas by the Ṛishi Trita who had been cast into a well or pit. *Waters:* of the ocean of air. *The strong-winged Eagle:* the Sun.

The hymn has been translated by Ludwig, Der Ṛigveda III. p. 488. A full account of these ancient funeral ceremonies will be found in the Âṣvalâyana-Gṛihya-Sûtra, IV. 1—7 (Sacred Books of the East, XXIX. pp. 236 sqq). See M. Müller's India, What can it Teach us? pp. 219—228.

An excellent translation and explanation of this Book will be found in Dr. Albrecht Weber's Vedische Beiträge.

BOOK XIX.

HYMN I.

Let the streams flow together, let the winds and birds assembled come.
Strengthen this sacrifice of mine, ye singers. I offer up a duly mixt oblation.

2 O Burnt Oblations, aid, and ye, Blent Offerings, this my sacrifice.
Strengthen this sacrifice of mine, ye singers. I offer up a duly mixt oblation.

3 Each several form, each several force I seize, and compass round this man.
May the Four Quarters strengthen this my sacrifice. I offer up a duly mixt oblation.

HYMN II.

Blest be the Streams from hills of snow, sweet be spring Waters unto thee.
Sweet be swift-running Waters, sweet to thee be Water of the Rains.

The Book consists of a miscellaneous collection of hymns, chiefly prayers and charms for protection and prosperity. The MSS., which the editors of the printed text have amended, contain numerous and obvious misreadings which make utter nonsense of some parts of this and the following Book which are later additions to the original collection. The hymn is an accompaniment to the offering of an oblation.

1 Stanzas 1 and 2 are repeated, with variations, from A. V. I. 15. 1, 2. *Mixt oblation:* consisting of milk, butter, and the juice of corn (probably a sort of beer).

3 *Force:* referring to the various powers that are called upon to make the sacrifice effectual. *Compass round this man:* protect the householder who has instituted the sacrifice. The first line is taken, with variations, from A. V. I. 22. 3.

Addressed to all Waters.

2 Sweet unto thee be Waters of the waste and Waters
of the pool.
Sweet be the Waters dug from earth, to thee, and
Waters brought in jars.

3 To those who delve without a tool to dig, the wise,
the deeply moved,
To Waters better healers than physicians we address
our prayer.

4 Bathed in the Waters verily divine, in water of the
streams,
Bathed in the Waters verily, O Horses, be ye fleet
and strong.

5 Blest be the Waters unto thee, auspicious Waters,
bringing health.
They cure the injured place for thee even as thy comfort craveth it.

HYMN III.

WHITHERSOE'ER, from sky, earth, air's mid-region, from
plants and herbs, from tall trees, Jâtavedas
Is carried here and there to divers places, even thence
come thou to us with loving-kindness.

2 All majesty of thine in floods, in forests, in plants, in
cattle, in the depths of waters—
Closely uniting all thy forms, O Agni, come unto us
wealth-giving, undecaying.

3 Thy majesty among the Gods in Svarga, thy body
which hath past into the Fathers,
Thy plenty far-diffused mid human beings, even with
this, O Agni, give us riches.

4 To him the wise, the famous, swift to listen, with
words and verses I come nigh for bounty.

---

2 The stanza is taken, with variations, from I. 6. 4.

3 *Better healers than physicians:* cf. VI. 91. 3.

A prayer to Agni for protection and prosperity.

May we be safe from threatening danger. Soften by sacrifice the wrath of Gods, O Agni.

HYMN IV.

THE first oblation that Atharvan offered, earliest sacrifice paid by Jâtavedas,
Even this I, foremost, with repeated worship, now offer unto thee. May Agni carry the sacrificer's present. Hail to Agni!

2 In front I set Intention, blessèd Goddess. Mother of thought, may she be prompt to hear us.
Mine, and mine only, be the hope I fashion! May I gain this that hath possessed my spirit.

3 With Purpose, O Prajâpati, with Purpose come thou near to us.
Bestow on us a share of luck, and so be swift to hear our call.

4 Prajâpati Ângirasa with favour regard this word and this my settled purpose!
May he, whence Gods and Deities had being, Kâma attend us with his gentle guidance.

HYMN V.

KING of the living world and men is Indra, of all in varied form that earth containeth.
Thence to the worshipper he giveth riches: may he enrich even us when we have praised him.

A prayer, accompanying sacrifice, for the attainment of a wish.

1 *Thee:* Intention, Purpose, personified and worshipped as a Goddess.

2 *In front:* foremost, for adoration.

4 *Ângirasa:* connected with the ancient Ṛishi Angiras or his descendants. The name is more usually applied to Bṛihaspati. *Kâma:* Desire, Love; the Greek Erôs. Cf. 'Thereafter rose desire in the beginning, Desire the primal seed and germ of spirit' (Ṛ. V. X. 129. 4). See also A. V. IX. 2. 20—24.

A prayer for riches. The stanza is taken from Ṛ. V. VII. 27. 3.

HYMN VI.

PURUSHA hath a thousand arms, a thousand eyes, a thousand feet.

On every side pervading earth he fills a space ten fingers wide.

2 He with three quarters rose to heaven: here reappeared a fourth of him.

Thence he strode forth on every side to all that eats not and that eats.

3 So mighty is his grandeur, yea, greater than this is Purusha.

All creatures are one-fourth of him, three-fourths what dieth not in heaven.

The subject of this pantheistic hymn, which is taken, with transpositions and variations, from Ṛ. V. X. 90, is the mystical Sacrifice of Purusha.

1 *Purusha:* embodied Spirit, or Man personified and regarded as the soul and original source of the universe. Purusha is said to have *a thousand*, that is, innumerable, *arms*, *eyes*, and *feet* as being one with all created life. In the Ṛ. V. hymn a thousand heads instead of arms are ascribed to him. The transcriber seems to have substituted *arms* to agree with the number of eyes and feet. *A space ten fingers wide:* the region of the heart of man wherein the soul was supposed to reside. Although as the Universal Soul he pervades the universe, as the Individual Soul he is enclosed in a space of narrow dimensions. Cf. 'The loins of Varuṇa are both the oceans, and this small drop of water too, contains him' (A. V. IV. 16. 3). Dr. Scherman (Philosophische Hymnen aus der Ṛig-und Atharva-veda Sanhitâ, pp. 17—19) cites many passages from the Upanishads in support of this interpretation of *daçângulám*, the ten-finger space.

2 *To all that eats not and that eats:* to all inanimate and animate creation. According to Sâyaṇa and Mahîdhara, to both classes of created things, those capable of enjoyment, that is, who can taste the reward and punishment of good and evil actions, such as Gods, men, and lower animals, and those that are incapable thereof, such as mountains and rivers—*chetanam* or conscious, and *achetanam* or unconscious creation.

3 *What dieth not:* all that is exempt from the development and decay to which mere creatures or terrestrial beings are subject.

4 Purusha is in truth this All, what hath been and what yet shall be—
Lord, too, of immortality—and what hath grown with somewhat else.

5 When they divided Purusha how many portions did they make?
What was his mouth? what were his arms? what are the names of thighs and feet?

6 The Brâhman was his mouth, of both his arms was the Râjanya made.
His waist became the Vaiṣya, from his feet the Ṣûdra was produced.

7 The Moon was gendered from his mind, and from his eye the Sun had birth.
Indra and Agni from his mouth were born, and Vâyu from his breath.

8 Forth from his navel came mid-air; the sky was fashioned from his head,
Earth from his feet, and from his ear the regions. Thus they formed the worlds.

---

4 *And what hath grown with somewhat else*: 'Since he became united with another.'—Muir. The meaning is obscure. The reading of the Ṛigveda is *yád ánnenâtiróhati*, 'which (immortality, or the immortal world of the Gods) grows greater by food, that is, by the sacrificial offerings of men,' or, '[since he] far transcends what [exists] through food,' as Ludwig renders the clause.

5 *They*: the Gods. See stanza 10.

6 The Brâhman is called the mouth of Purusha as having the special privilege as a priest of addressing the Gods in prayer. The arms of Purusha became the Râjanya, the prince and soldier who wields the sword and spear. His waist or, according to the Ṛ. V., thighs, the strongest part of his body, became the agriculturist and tradesman, the chief supporters of society; and his feet, the emblems of vigour and activity, became the Ṣûdra or labouring man on whose toil and industry all prosperity ultimately rests. This is the only passage in the Ṛigveda which enumerates the four castes.

8 Cf. the creation-myth of the world-giant Ymir in Old Northern poetry. The hills are his bones, the sky his skull, the sea his blood, and the clouds his brains. See Corpus Poeticum Boreale, II. 468.

9 In the beginning rose Virâj: Purusha from Virâj was born.
As soon as he was born he spread westward and eastward o'er the earth.

10 When Gods performed the sacrifice with Purusha as their offering
Spring was the butter, summer was the fuel, autumn was the gift.

11 That sacrifice, first-born Purusha, they hallowed with the sprinkled Rains.
The Deities, the Sâdhyas, all the Vasus sacrificed with him.

12 From it were horses born, from it all creatures with two rows of teeth.
From it were generated kine, from it were goats and sheep produced.

13 From that great general sacrifice Richas and Sâma hymns were born:
Therefrom the metres were produced: the Yajus had its birth from it.

14 From that great general sacrifice the dripping fat was gathered up:
It formed the creatures fleet as wind, and animals both wild and tame.

15 Seven fencing-logs had he, thrice seven layers of fuel were prepared.
When, offering sacrifice, the Gods bound as their victim Purusha.

---

10 *The sacrifice: mânasam yajñam*, a mental or imaginary sacrifice, according to Sâyaṇa.

11 *Hallowed with the sprinkled Rains*: used the Rainy Season as holy water for aspersion. *Sâdhyas*: see IX. 10. 24, note.

13 *Metres*: or magical hymns, spells and incantations.

14 *General*: all-producing. *Dripping fat*: 'the mixture of curds and butter.'—Wilson. *Creatures fleet as wind*: or, creatures of the air.

15 *Fencing-logs*: guards, pieces of wood laid round a sacrificial fire. Sâyaṇa explains these *paridhâyaḥ* as the seven metres, or as six shallow trenches dug round the fire, and an imaginary one round the sun. Mahîdhara says that the seven oceans may be intended.

16 Forth from the head of the high God seven-and-seventy bright beams
Sprang into being, of the King Soma produced from Purusha.

HYMN VII.

THE brilliant lights shining in heaven together, which through the world glide on with rapid motion,
And Days, and Firmament with songs I worship, seeking the Twenty-eight-fold for its favour.

---

16 Instead of this stanza the Ṛigveda has: 'Gods sacrificing sacrificed the victim: these were the earliest holy ordinances. The Mighty Ones attained the height of heaven, there where the Sâdhyas, Gods of old, are dwelling.'

This hymn, which is generally called the Purusha-Sûkta or Purusha hymn, is—as is shown by its enumeration of the four castes and by the use of the word *grîshmáḥ* (summer) which does not occur in any other hymn of the Ṛigveda, and *vasantáḥ* (spring) which is found in only one other—one of the very latest pieces in that collection. It appears to be an attempt to harmonize the two ideas of sacrifice and creation. For further information regarding it, see Muir, O. S. Texts, Vol. V. pp. 367—377; Prof. Max Müller, Ancient Sanskrit Literature, pp. 570 sq; and especially Dr. Scherman who has most exhaustively discussed it in his Philosophische Hymnen aus der Rig-und Atharva-veda Sanhitâ, pp. 11—23. The Ṛigveda hymn has been translated also by Colebrooke, Miscellaneous Essays, pp. 167, 168; by Zimmer, Altindisches Leben, p. 217; by Wallis, Cosmology of the Ṛigveda, p. 87; by Sir M. Monier-Williams, in his Indian Wisdom; by Prof. Weber, Indische Studien, IX. p. 5; by Prof. Peterson, Hymns from the Ṛigveda, p. 289; and by Burnouf, Bhâgavata Purâṇa, Preface to Vol. I. Wilson's Translation should be consulted for the views of Sâyaṇa and the Indian scholars of his own and earlier times; Prof. Grassmann's version, Vol. II. p. 486, of his Rig-veda, should not be neglected; and Prof. Ludwig's Translation and commentary will, as ever, be found of the greatest service to the student.

A hymn to the Sun and various heavenly bodies for protection and prosperity.

1 *The Twenty-eight-fold:* the lunar month with its twenty-eight asterisms or lunar mansions, the places among the stars occupied by the moon in its passage.

2 Kṛittikâs, Rohiṇî be swift to hear me! Let Mṛigaṣiras bless me, help me Ardrâ!
Punarvasû and Sûnṛitâ, fair Pushya, the Sun, Âṣleshâs, Maghâ lead me onward!

3 My blissbe Svâti and benignant Chitrâ, my right First Phalgunîs and present Hasta.
Râdhas, Viṣâkhas, gracious Anurâdhâ, Jyeshṭhâ and happy-starred uninjured Mûla.

4 Food shall the earlier Ashâḍhas grant me; let those that follow bring me strength and vigour;
With virtuous merit Abhijit endow me! Ṣravaṇa and Ṣravishṭhâs make me prosper.

5 Ṣatabhishak afford me ample freedom, and both the Proshṭhapadas guard me safely.
Revatî and the Aṣvayujas bring me luck, and the Bharaṇîs abundant riches!

---

2 *Kṛittikâs:* one of the lunar mansions, the Pleiades. *Rohinî:* a lunar asterism personified as the daughter of Daksha and the favourite wife of the Moon. It is called Rohiṇi, the Red, from the colour of the constellation's principal star Aldebaran. *Mṛigaṣiras:* the Antelope's Head, a lunar asterism containing λ Orionis. *Ârdrâ:* Moist; the fourth or sixth lunar asterism. *Punarvasû:* the fifth or seventh lunar asterism. *Sûnṛitâ:* Pleasantness; a name of Ushas or Dawn. *Pushya:* the sixth, or in later times the eighth, lunar asterism. *Âṣleshâs:* the seventh lunar asterism. *Maghâ:* the tenth lunar asterism, sometimes regarded as the wife of the Moon.

3 *Svâti:* the star Arcturus, as forming the fifteenth lunar asterism. *Chitrâ:* Bright; Spica Virginis, the twelfth lunar mansion. *First Phalgunîs:* forming part of a double Nakshatra or lunar mansion called also Arjunî. *Hasta:* Hand; the thirteenth lunar asterism, identified by some with part of the constellation Corvus. *Râdhas:* Success. *Viṣâkhas:* one of the Nakshatras or lunar mansions. *Anurâdhâ:* Bringing Welfare: the seventeenth lunar mansion. *Jyeshṭhâ:* Best; the sixteenth lunar mansion, called also Jyeshṭhaghni. See A. V. VI. 110. 2. *Mûla:* the twenty-fourth lunar mansion.

4 *Earlier Ashâḍhas:* forming the eighteenth lunar mansion. *Abhijit:* the twenty-seventh lunar mansion. *Ṣravaṇa and Ṣravisṭhas:* lunar asterisms twenty-eight and one.

5 *Ṣatabhishak:* Requiring a hundred Physicians; so called because so many at least are needed to cure a person who falls ill while the moon is in this, the twenty-fifth asterism. *Proshṭhapadas:* a double Nak-

HYMN VIII.

BENIGN to me be all those Lunar Mansions to which the Moon as he moves on doth honour,
All that are in the sky, the air, the waters, on earth, on mountains, in the heavenly regions.

2 Propitious, mighty, let the eight-and-twenty together deal me out my share of profit.
Profit and wealth be mine, and wealth and profit! To Day and Night be adoration rendered!

3 Fair be my sunset, fair my morn and evening and day with lucky chase and happy omens;
With blessing and success, immortal Agni, go to the mortal and return rejoicing.

4 Excitement and invoking cry, ill-omened sneezing and reproof,
All sounds of empty pitchers send into the distance, Savitar!

5 May we escape an evil sneeze, enjoy the sneeze of happy luck,

---

shatra, the third and fourth asterisms. *Revatî:* Splendid; the fifth asterism. *Aşvayujas:* Two Horse-Harnessers; the head of Aries, forming according to one account the first and according to another the sixth asterism. *Bharaṇîs:* three stars forming the seventh asterism.

These Nakshatras or Mansions of the Moon, the asterisms in the Moon's path, were twenty-seven in number according to the earlier reckoning and twenty-eight in the later astronomy. Their names and order are somewhat differently given in the Taittirîya-Brâhmaṇa and Taittirîya-Sanhitâ. In the Veda they are considered to be the abodes of Gods, or the visible forms of the pious dead; and in the later mythology they are the daughters of Daksha and the wives of the Moon. See Weber's essay, Die Vedischen Nachrichten von den Nakshatra.

A prayer to the Lunar Mansions and other Powers for protection and prosperity.

2 *The-Eight-and-twenty:* see the preceding hymn.

4 *Excitement and invoking cry: anuhavám parihavám;* meaning, apparently, all sudden disturbing and alarming calls. *Sneezing:* regarded by the Romans also as an omen of good or evil fortune. 'Sternuit, et nobis prospera signa dedit' (Ovid. Her. 19, 151); 'Sternutamenta erunt observanda' (Cicero de Div. 2. 40). So 'God bless you' is a common benediction in England when a person sneezes.

And may our nostrils smelling what is pleasant pour forth fragrant scent.

6 These flames of Brahmaṇaspati borne to all quarters in the wind,
Turn them all hither, Indra, and make them most gracious unto me.

HYMN IX.

GENTLE be heaven, gentle be earth, gentle this spacious atmosphere,
Gentle be waters as they flow, gentle to us be plants and herbs!

2 Gentle be signs of coming change, and that which is and is not done!
Gentle be past and future, yea, let all be gracious unto us.

3 Quickened by Prayer, this Goddess Vâk who standeth in the highest place,
By whom the awful spell was made, even through her to us be peace!

4 Or, made more keen by Prayer, this mind that standeth in the highest place,
Whereby the awful spell was made, even through this be peace to us!

5 These five sense-organs with the mind as sixth, sharpened by Prayer, abiding in my heart,
By which the awful spell was made, even by these be peace to us.

6 Favour us Mitra, Varuṇa, and Vishṇu, and Prajâpati!
Gracious to us be Indra and Bṛihaspati and Aryaman.

---

5 *Fragrant scent:* cf. 'And the smell of thy nose like apples' (Solomon's Song, VII. 8).

6 *Flames:* the text has only *imâḥ*, these (feminine). *Bṛihaspati:* here meaning Agni.

A hymn or prayer for general protection and prosperity.

7 Favour us Mitra, Varuṇa, Vivasvân, and the Finisher, Portents on earth and in the air, and planets wandering in heaven!

8 Gracious to us be trembling earth, gracious the flaming meteor stroke!
Gracious be kine who yield red milk, gracious be earth when sinking down!

9 Gracious be meteor-stricken constellation, gracious to us be magic spells and witchcraft!
Gracious to us be buried charms, and gracious the meteors and the portents of the region!

10 Kind be the Powers who seize the Moon, with Râhu be Âdityas kind!
Favour us Death and Comet, and Rudras with penetrating might!

11 Rudras and Vasus favour us, Âdityas, Agnis favour us!
Favour us mighty Ṛishis, Gods, Goddesses, and Bṛihaspati!

12 Brahmâ, Dhâtar, Prajâpati, Worlds, Vedas, Agnis, Ṛishis Seven.
All these have blessed my happy way. May Indra be my guardian, may Brahmâ protect and shelter me.

---

7 *The Finisher:* Mṛityu, the God of Death.

10 *Râhu:* Seizer; mythologically a Daitya or demon who seizes and swallows the sun and moon and thus causes eclipses. According to the myth, he had four arms and his body terminated in a tail. Disguised as a God he drank some of the Amrita or nectar produced at the Churning of the Ocean (Râmâyaṇa, I. 45), but the Sun, and Moon detected his fraud and informed Vishṇu who immediately cut off his head and two of his arms. As he had secured immortality by his draught of Amrita his body was transferred to the stellar sphere, the upper part, represented by a dragon's head, being the ascending node, and revenging itself on the Sun and Moon his betrayers by occasionally swallowing them. The lower part of the body became Ketu, the descending node, which gave birth to comets and fiery meteors. *Rudras:* the sons of Rudra; Maruts or Storm-Gods.

13 May all the Gods protect me, may the Gods united shield me well.
May all alleviations in the world which the Seven Ṛishis know
Be kind and gracious unto me. Bliss and security be mine!

14 Earth alleviation, air alleviation, heaven alleviation, waters alleviation, plants alleviation, trees alleviation, all Gods my alleviation, collective Gods my alleviation, alleviation by alleviations. By these alleviations, these universal alleviations, I allay all that is terrific here, all that is cruel, all that is wicked. This hath been calmed, this is now auspicious.
Let all be favourable to us.

HYMN X.

Befriend us with their aids Indra and Agnî, Indra and Varuṇa who receive oblations!
Indra and Soma give health, wealth and comfort, Indra and Pûshan be our strength in battle!

2 Auspicious friends to us be Bhaga, Ṣańsa, auspicious be Purandhi and all Riches,
The blessing of the true and well-conducted and Aryaman in many forms apparent.

3 Kind unto us be Maker and Sustainer and the far-reaching One with godlike nature.
Auspicious unto us be Earth and Heaven, the Mountain and the Gods' fair invocations.

A prayer for general protection and prosperity. The hymn is taken from R. V. VII. 35. 1—10.

1 *Befriend us: ṣám no bhavatâm*; the indeclinable word *ṣám*, signifying happy, auspicious, pleasant, sweet, kind, agreeable, etc., is used throughout the hymn with the imperative of *bhû*, to become, *as*, to be, or other verb. I have varied the expression here and there.

2 *Ṣańsa:* Prayer or Wish personified. Or perhaps Narâṣańsa, Agni, may be intended. *Purandhi:* Plenty, or according to some, Wisdom, personified.

3 *The far-reaching One:* Earth.

4 Favour us Agni with his face of splendour, and Varuṇa and Mitra and the Asvins.
Favour us noble actions of the pious; impetuous Vâta blow on us with favour!

5 Early invoked may Heaven and Earth be friendly, and Air's mid-region good for us to look on.
To us may herbs and forest trees be gracious, gracious the Lord victorious of the region.

6 Be the God Indra with the Vasus friendly, and with Âdityas Varuṇa who blesseth.
Kind with the Rudras be the healer Rudra, and with the Dames here Tvashṭar kindly hear us.

7 Kind unto us be Soma and Devotions, kind be the Sacrifice and Stones for pressing.
Kind be the fixing of the Sacred Pillars, kind be the tender Grass, and kind the Altar.

8 May the far-seeing Sun rise up to bless us: be the four quarters of the heaven auspicious.
Auspicious be the firmly-seated Mountains, auspicious be the Rivers and the Waters.

9 May Aditi through holy works be gracious, and may the Maruts, loud in song, be friendly.
May Vishṇu give felicity, and Pûshan, and Air that cherisheth our lives, and Vâyu.

10 Prosper us Savitar, the God who rescues, and let the radiant Mornings be propitious.
Propitious to our children be Parjanya, kind to us be the field's benign Protector!

---

5 *Lord victorious of the region:* Indra the chief God of the firmament.

6 *The healer Rudra:* cf. I. 19. 3, note. *Dames:* the consorts of the Gods. Tvashṭar frequently appears as their companion and escort. Cf. R. V. II. 1. 5; 38. 10; III. 1. 9; 50. 13; X. 64. 10; 66. 3.

7 *Sacred Pillars:* the sacrificial posts to which the victims were tied.

10 *The field's benign Protector:* either Rudra or Agni.

HYMN XI.

MAY the great Lords of Truth protect and aid us: blest to us be our horses and our cattle.
Kind be the pious, skilful-handed Ṛibhus, kind be the Fathers at our invocations.

2 Kind to us be the Gods and Viṣve Devas, Sarasvatî with Holy Thoughts be gracious.
Friendly be they, the Liberal Ones, who seek us, yea, those who dwell in heaven, on earth, in waters.

3 May Aja-Ekapâd the God be gracious, gracious the Dragon of the Deep, and Ocean.
Gracious be he, the swelling Child of Waters, gracious be Pṛiṣni who hath Gods to guard her.

4 So may the Rudras, Vasus, and Âdityas accept the new hymn which we now are making.
May all the Holy Ones of earth and heaven, and the Cow's offspring hear our invocation.

5 Priests of the Gods, worthy of sacrifices, immortal, knowing Law, whom man must worship,
May these to-day give us broad paths to travel. Preserve us evermore, ye Gods, with blessings.

The hymn is a continuation of the preceding, and is taken from the remaining portion (stanzas 11—15) of Ṛ. V. VII. 35.

1 *Ṛibhus:* the three deified artificers. See VI. 47. 3, note.

3 *Aja-Ekapâd:* the Sun. Aja-Ekapâd is called in Ṛ. V. X. 65. 13 the bearer of heaven, 'and the ascription of one foot to the Sun might be due to his appearance alone in the sky as opposed to the Dawns and the Aṣvins' (Wallis, Cosmology of the Ṛigveda, p. 54). M. Bergaigne says (La Religion Védique, III. pp. 20—25): 'Aja-Ekapâd, then is 'the unborn who has only one foot,' that is to say, who dwells in the single isolated world, the place of mystery, in opposition to the God who manifests himself in divers worlds, to Agni or Soma in their various visible forms.' *Dragon of the Deep:* Ahibudhnya; a mysterious atmospheric deity, regent of the depths of the firmament. *Child of Waters:* Agni. *Pṛiṣni:* mother of the Maruts.

4 *The Cow's offspring:* the Maruts, sons of Pṛiṣni, the dappled cow or variegated cloud. According to von Roth, those who are born and live in radiant heaven.

HYMN XII.

Dawn drives away her sister's gloom, and through
her excellence makes her retrace her path.
Through her may we gain God-appointed treasure, and
with brave sons be glad through hundred winters.

HYMN XIII.

These the two sturdy, manly arms of Indra, these
that are wondrous, mighty, and successful—
First, when the need hath come will I employ them
by which the heaven of Asuras was conquered.

2 Swift, like a dread bull sharpening his weapons,
rapidly striking, stirring up the people,
Loud shouting, vigilant, the one sole Hero, Indra
subdued a hundred hosts together.

3 With him loud-roaring, ever watchful, victor, bold,
hard to overthrow, whom none may vanquish,
Indra the strong whose hand bears arrows, conquer,
ye heroes now, now vanquish in the combat.

4 He rules with those who carry shafts and quivers,
Indra who with his hand brings hosts together,
Foe-conquering, strong of arm, the Soma-drinker,
with mighty bow, shooting with well-laid arrows.

5 Conspicuous by thy strength, firm, foremost fighter,
mighty and fierce, victorious, all-subduing,
O'ercoming might, excelling men and heroes, mount
thy kine-winning conquering car, O Indra.

A prayer to Ushas or Dawn for wealth and long life.

1 The first line, in Dvipadâ Virâj metre of twenty syllables, is taken from Ṛ. V. X. 172. 4, and the second, in Trishṭup metre from Ṛ. V. VI. 17. 15. *Her sister's gloom:* the darkness of Night.

The hymn, which, with the exception of stanza 1, is taken, with transpositions and lectional variations, from Ṛ. V. X. 103. 1—9, 11, is a prayer for aid and victory in battle.

1 *Asuras:* the foes of the Gods by whom they were finally conquered, like the Titans of Grecian mythology and the rebellious Angels of Paradise Lost.

6 Troop-vanquisher, kine-winner, armed with thunder, who quells an army and with might destroys it,—
Follow him, comrades! quit yourselves like heroes, and like this Indra show your zeal and courage.

7 Piercing the cow-stalls with surpassing vigour, Indra the pitiless hero, wild with anger,
Victor in fight, unshaken and resistless,—may he protect our armies in our battles.

8 Bṛihaspati, fly with thy chariot hither, slayer of demons, driving off our foemen,
Be thou protector of our bodies, crushing our enemies, destroying those who hate us.

9 Indra guide these! Bṛihaspati, the Guerdon, and Soma, and the Sacrifice precede them!
And let the banded Maruts march in forefront of heavenly hosts that conquer and demolish.

10 Ours be the potent host of mighty Indra, King Varuṇa, and Maruts and Âdityas.
Uplifted is the shout of Gods who conquer, high-minded Gods who cause the world to tremble.

11 May Indra aid us when our flags are gathered: victorious be the arrows of our army.
May our brave men of war prevail in battle. Ye Gods, protect us in the shouts of onset.

HYMN XIV.

I HAVE attained this goodliest place to rest in Both Heaven and Earth have shown me grace and favour.
Without a foe for me be all the regions! We hate thee not. May we have peace and safety.

---

9 *Guide these:* be the leader of our troops. *The Guerdon: dákshiṇâ;* to be given to the priests who perform the sacrifice that is offered before the battle.

11 *When our flags are gathered:* 'apparently comparable with the signis collatis of the Romans.'—Ludwig.

A hymn after victory.

1 *Thee:* the conquered and submissive enemy.

HYMN XV.

INDRA, give us security from that whereof we are afraid.

Help us, O Maghavan, let thy succour grant us this: drive foes and enemies afar.

2 We call on Indra, on the liberal giver: we will be prosperous in men and cattle.

Let not the hosts of cruel fiends approach us. Drive off the Druhs to every side, O Indra.

3 Best, making household wealth increase, Indra our saviour, kills the foe.

May he from outmost point be our protector, and from the centre and from west and eastward.

4 Lead us to ample room, O thou who knowest, to happiness, security, and sunlight.

Strong, Indra, are the arms of thee the mighty: may we betake us to their lofty shelter.

5 May air's mid-region give us peace and safety, safety may both these, Heaven and Earth, afford us.

Security be ours from west, from eastward, from north and south may we be free from danger.

6 Safety be ours from friend and from the unfriendly, safety from what we know and what we know not.

Safety be ours by night and in the day-time! friendly to me be all my hopes and wishes!

A prayer for peace and security.

1 The stanza is taken from Ṛ. V. VIII. 50. 13.

2 *Druhs:* spirits of mischief.

4 Taken from Ṛ. V. VI. 47. 8.

6 *From friend:* cf. the old saying, Heaven guard me from my friend! The hymn has been translated by Ludwig, Der Rigveda, III. p. 513.

HYMN XVI.

PEACE hath been given us from the east, and from the west security.
Savitar guard me from the south, and from the north the Lord of Might!

2 May the Âdityas from the sky protect me, Agnis from the earth.
May Indra-Agni guard me from the eastward, on all sides may the Asvins give me shelter.
May Jâtavedas guard, sidelong, our cattle.
Our shield on all sides be the World-Creators!

HYMN XVII.

AGNI from eastward guard me with the Vasus! To him I go, in him I rest: this fort I seek for refuge.
May he protect me, may he be my guardian. I give my soul—All hail! into his keeping.

2 Vâyu with Air protect me from this region. To him I go, etc.

3 May Soma from the south, with Rudras, guard me. To him, etc.

4 Varuṇa with Âdityas guard me from this region! To him, etc.

5 Sûrya with Earth and Heaven from the western region guard me well. To him, etc.

A prayer for security from danger.

1 *Lord of Might: ṣáchípátiḥ;* Indra. In classical literature, Husband of Ṣachî, that is, of Might personified as his consort.

2 *World-Creators:* ancient Ṛishis who as demiurgi created the universe. See Vol. I. Index, under Bhûtakṛitas and Creative Ṛishis.

This non-metrical hymn is a prayer for protection from all dangers that may threaten the worshipper from any quarter of the earth or sky. Cf. A. V. V. 10.

6 May Waters joined with Plants protect me from this region. To them I go, in them I rest: this fort I seek for refuge.

May they protect me, may they be my guardians. I give my soul,—All hail!—into their keeping.

7 May Viṣvakarman with the Seven Ṛishis be my protector from the northern region. To him, etc.

8 May Indra, Marut-girt, protect me from this region. To him, etc.

9 Prajâpati, of generative power, with the Pratishṭhâ save me from the nadir! To him, etc.

10 Bṛihaspati, joined by the Viṣvedevas, protect me from the region of the zenith! To him I go, in him I rest: this fort I seek for refuge.

May he protect me, may he be my guardian. I give my soul—All hail!—into his keeping.

HYMN XVIII.

Let those who vex me from the eastern region, sinners, praise Agni followed by the Vasus.

2 Let those who vex me from this quarter, sinners, praise Vâyu compassed by the Air's mid-region.

3 Let those who vex me from the southern quarter, sinners, sing praise to Soma with the Rudras.

4 Let those who vex me from this quarter, sinners, praise Varuṇa connected with Âdityas.

---

7 *Viṣvakarman:* the Omnific; the Architect of the Universe; a deity resembling and sometimes identified with Prajâpati, the Lord of Creation.

9 *Pratishṭhâ:* a Sâman especially dedicated to Prajâpati.

A hymn somewhat similar to the preceding, being a prayer for security and peace on all sides. Cf. A. V. 10.

5 Let those who vex me from the western quarter, sinners, praise Sûrya linked with Earth and Heaven.

6 Let those who vex me from this quarter, sinners, give praise to plants' associates the Waters.

7 Let those who from the north side vex me, sinners, praise Viṣvakarman with the Seven Ṛishis.

8 Let those who vex me from this quarter, sinners, praise Indra with the Marut host about him.

9 Let those who vex me from the nadir, sinners, extol Prajâpati of genial power.

10 Let those who vex me from the zenith, sinners, extol Bṛihaspati with the Viṣve Devas.

HYMN XIX.

Mitra arose with Earth. To that fort I lead you: enter it, occupy it. Let it give you protection and defence.

2 Vâyu arose with Air. To that fort, etc.

3 Sûrya arose with Heaven. To that fort, etc.

4 Chandramâs arose with the Constellations. To that fort, etc.

5 Sacrifice arose with Priestly Fees. To that fort, etc.

6 Ocean arose with the Rivers. To that fort, etc.

7 Brahma arose with the Brahmachâris. To that fort, etc.

8 Indra arose with Manly Might. To that fort, etc.

9 The Gods arose with Immortality. To that fort, etc.

10 Prajâpati arose with Creatures. To that fort I lead you : enter it, occupy it. Let it give you protection and defence.

A non-metrical hymn recommending the protection of various Gods.

4 *Chandramâs :* the Moon.

7 *Brahmachâris :* religions students. See V. 17. 5 ; XI. 5.

HYMN XX.

MAY Soma, Varuṇa the King, both Asvins, Yama and Pûshan guard us well from Mṛityu—
Death caused by men, which Indra-Agni, Dhâtar, Bṛihaspati and Savitar appointed.

2 All that the World's Lord made, all that for creatures Prajâpati and Mâtarisvan fashioned,
All things within the quarters and their spaces, let all these be my manifold defences.

3 That which the Gods bound on them when they battled for their royal sway,
What Indra made his shield, may that protect us well on every side.

4 My shield is Heaven and Earth, my shield is the bright Day, my shield the Sun.
The Visve Devas made my shield. Let not misfortune fall on me.

HYMN XXI.

GÂYATRÎ, Ushṇih, Anushṭup, Bṛihatî, Trishṭup, Jagatî.

HYMN XXII.

WITH the first five chapters of the Ângirases, Hail!
2 To the sixth, Hail! 3 To the seventh and
eighth, Hail! 4 To the black-clawed ones, Hail!

A prayer for protection from Death and misfortune.

3 *That which the Gods bound on them:* an amulet or all-powerful charm; probably the Apâmârga plant. See IV. 19. 4. *What Indra made his shield:* cf. II. 27. 3.

A single line giving the names of the chief Vedic metres.

A prose hymn (with one metrical stanza) of homage to various portions of the Atharva-veda, the Ṛishis, and Brahma.

1 *Chapters:* Anuvâkas; sections or lessons. The first five of these comprise Hymns 1—28 of Book I. *Ângirases:* that is, Songs of the Angirases; a name of the Atharva-veda. See Vol. I., Preface, p. III.

2 *The sixth:* containing Hymns 29—35 of Book I. *The seventh and eighth:* Hymns 1—5, and 6 —10, respectively, of Book II.

4 *Black-clawed:* the Nilanakhas.

5 To the golden-hued ones, Hail! 6 To the small
ones, Hail! 7 To those composed in strophes, Hail!
8 To the first shells, Hail! 9 To the second shells,
Hail! 10 To the third shells, Hail! 11 To the
penultimates, Hail! 12 To the last ones, Hail!
13 To the latter ones, Hail! 14 To the Ṛishis,
Hail! 15 To those with hair in tufts, Hail! 16
To the Gaṇas, Hail! 17 To the great Gaṇas, Hail!
18 To all the Vidagaṇa Angirases, Hail! 19 To
those two with separate thousands, Hail! 20 To
Brahma, Hail!

21 Collected manly powers are topped by Brahma.
Brahma at first spread out the loftiest heaven.
Brahmâ was born first of all things existing. Who
then is meet to be that Brahmâ's rival?

HYMN XXIII.

Hail to the four-verse strophes of the Âtharvaṇas!
2 Hail to the five-versed! 3 Hail to the six-vers-
ed! 4 Hail to the seven-versed! 5 Hail to the
eight-versed! 6 Hail to the nine-versed! 7 Hail
to the ten-versed! 8 Hail to the eleven-versed! 9
Hail to the twelve-versed! 10 Hail to the thirteen-
versed! 11 Hail to the fourteen-versed! 12 Hail
to the fifteen-versed! 13 Hail to the sixteen-
versed! 14 Hail to the seventeen-versed! 15 Hail
to the eighteen-versed! 16 Hail, nineteen! 17
Hail, twenty! 18 Hail to the Great Section! 19

---

5 *Golden-hued:* the Haritas.

6 *Small ones:* the Kshudras. Various portions and hymns of the Atharva-veda, which are not clearly identifiable, are designated by these and the remaining fantastic names.

A prose hymn of homage, like the preceding hymn, to various portions of the Atharva-veda classed according the number of verses which their hymns contain. 1 *Four-versed:* chiefly in Book I. 2 *Five-versed:* in Book II. 3 *Six-versed:* in Book III. 4 *Seven-versed:* in Book IV. 5 *Eight-versed:* hymns with from eight to eighteen verses are found in Book V. Longer pieces are contained in Books VIII.—XIII. and others. 18 *Great Section:* or Book; judging by its length, num-

Hail to the triplets! 20 Hail to the single-versed
hymns! 21 Hail to the little ones! 22 Hail to
the single-non-Ṛich-versed ones! 23 Hail to the
Rohitas! 24 Hail to the two Sûryâ hymns! 25
Hail to the two Vrâtya hymns! 26 Hail to the
two Prajâpati hymns! 27 Hail to the hymn of
victory! 28 Hail to the hymns for happiness! 29
Hail to Brahma!

30 Collected manly powers are topped by Brahma. Brahma at first spread out the loftiest heaven.
Brahmâ was born first of all things existing. Who then is fit to be this Brahmâ's rival?

HYMN XXIV.

Do ye, O Brahmaṇaspati, invest for royal sway this man
With that wherewith the Deities invested Savitar the God.

2 Invest this Indra for long life, invest him for great princely power,
That I may lead him on to eld, that he may watch his princedom long.

3 Invest this Soma for long life, invest him for great hearing power,

---

ber of hymns, and the preëminence of its main subject, Book XX. must be intended. 19 *Triplets:* the three-verse hymns of Book VI. 20 *Single-versed:* found in Book VII. 22 *Non-Ṛich-versed:* consisting of one verse only, and not borrowed from the Ṛigveda. 23 *Rohitas:* the hymns of Book XIII., addressed to Rohita a form of the Sun. 24 *Sûryâ hymns:* the nuptial hymns of Book XIV. 25 *Vrâtya hymns:* of Book XV. 26 *Prajâpati hymns:* the hymns in which Prajâpati is especially honoured.

A benediction on a newly elected King.

1 *Ye:* thou and other Gods.

2 *This Indra:* this King; Indra being the type of regal power. Cf. III. 3. 2; 4. 6.

3 *This Soma:* this King, equal to Soma who is frequently called King.

That I may lead him on to eld, that he may watch o'er hearing long.

4 For us, surround him, cover him with splendour, give him long life, and death when age removes him.

This garment hath Bṛihaspati presented to Soma, to the King, to wrap about him.

5 Advance to good old age: endue the mantle. Be thou our heifers' guard from imprecation.

Live thou a hundred full and plenteous autumns, and wrap thee in prosperity of riches.

6 Thou for our weal hast clothed thee in this garment: thou hast become our cows' sure guard from curses.

Live thou a hundred full and plenteous autumns: thou living, fair thyself, shalt deal forth treasures.

7 In every need, in every fray we call, as friends, to succour us, Indra the mightiest of all.

8 Gold-coloured, undecaying, blest with heroes, dwell, dying in old age, with children round thee.

This is the spoken word of Agni, Soma, Bṛihaspati, and Savitar, and Indra.

HYMN XXV.

I YOKE thee with the mind of one unwearied still and first of all.

Be thou a bearer up the hill: run hither bearing up thy load.

---

4 Repeated from A. V. II. 13. 2. Parts of stanzas 5 and 6 are taken from verse 3 of the same hymn.

7 Taken from Ṛ. V. I. 30. 7.

The hymn has been translated by Ludwig, Der Rigveda, III., p. 458.

Apparently a charm to be used when a young ox is yoked for the first time.

HYMN XXVI.

GOLD that was born from Fire and is immortal hath been deposited with mortal creatures.
He who knows this deserves to own this jewel, and in extreme old age dies he who wears it.

2 The men of ancient time with children round them longed for this Gold, bright with the Sun's own colour.
This shall endow thee, as it shines, with splendour, and long shall be the life of him who wears it.

3 Long life and splendour let it bring, bring energy and strength to thee
That thou mayst shine among the folk with all the brightness of the Gold.

4 What Varuṇa the King knows well, and what the God Bṛihaspati,
And Indra, Slayer of the Foe, may that bestow long life on thee, may that increase thy splendid strength.

HYMN XXVII.

LET the Bull guard thee with the kine, the Stallion with the fleet-foot steeds.
Let Vâyu keep thee safe with prayer, and Indra with his mighty powers.

2 Let Soma guard thee with the plants, Sûrya protect thee with the stars;
With breath let Wind protect thee, and the Moon, foe-slayer, with the months.

A hymn accompanying investiture with an amulet of gold.

1 *Born from Fire:* or, produced from Agni whose seed it is said to be. See Sacred Books of the East, XII. 277; XXIX. 59, 390.

2 *With children:* whom the possession of the amulet brought to them.

The hymn has been translated and annotated by Dr. Grill, Hundert Lieder des Atharva-veda, pp. 49, 192.

A benedictory hymn.

3 Three are the earths, they say, and three the heavens, three are the atmospheres, and four the oceans,
Threefold the hymn of praise, threefold the Waters. Let these with triple song and triplets guard thee.

4 Three vaults of heaven, and three seas, three bright, three stationary ones,
Three Mâtariṣvans, and three suns, protectors, I arrange for thee.

5 Increasing thee with butter I, Agni! with fatness sprinkle thee.
Let not magicians harm the life of Agni or of Moon or Sun.

6 Let not magicians mar your heat, your vital or diffusive breath.
Brilliant and all-possessing Gods, run ye your course with Godlike power.

7 Fire they endow with vital breath, Wind is compact with vital breath:
With vital breath the Gods produced the Sun whose face turn every way.

8 Live with the Life-Creators' life. Die not, live on to lengthened age.
Live with the breath of men with souls. Submit not to the power of Death.

9 The secret treasure of the Gods which Indra, by pathways travelled by the Gods, discovered,
That gold the Waters with the triplets guarded. May they keep thee with threefold hymn and triplets.

10 With friendly thoughts the Deities, three-and-thirty, and three great Powers preserved it in the Waters.

---

4 *Stationary ones:* or, stablished high in heaven. The meaning of *vaishṭapắn* is uncertain.

8 *Life-Creators:* the Gods. Cf. A. V. III. 31. 8.

9 *The Waters:* into which Agni poured the gold. See Sacred Books of the East, XII. 277.

He made heroic powers with the gold that lies upon this Moon.

11 O ye eleven Gods who are in heaven, accept this sacrifice.

12 O ye eleven Gods who are in air, accept this sacrifice.

13 O ye eleven Gods who are on earth, accept this sacrifice.

14,15 repeated from XIX. 16. 1, 2.

HYMN XXVIII.

On thee I bind this Amulet for lengthened life and brilliancy,
The rival-quelling Darbha grass that burns the spirit of a foe.

2 Burning the spirit of the foe, vexing the heart of enemies,
Darbha, on every side, like heat, inflame all evil-hearted men.

3 O Darbha, burning round like heat, consuming foes, O Amulet,
Like Indra rending Vala cleave mine adversaries' hearts in twain.

4 Cleave through, O Darbha, Amulet, my foes', mine adversaries' heart.
Rise thou and batter down their heads like growth that covereth the earth.

---

10 *He:* Indra. The line is obscure.

A charm for the destruction of enemies.

1 *Darbha grass:* Sacrificial grass, especially Kuṣa grass, used for strewing the ground and other purposes in religious ceremonies. The plant is said to spring from heaven, and various sanctifying and other far-reaching supernatural powers are ascribed to it. See A. V. II. 7; VI. 43; and VIII. 7. 20, where Darbha is identified with Soma the King of Plants.

3 *Vala:* the Cave; personified as a demon who withholds the heavenly waters, and who, like his brother Vṛitra, was vanquished by Indra.

5 Cleave thou my rivals, Darbha, cleave the men who fain would fight with me.
Cleave all who wish me evil, cleave the men who hate me, Amulet!

6 Wound thou, my rivals, Darbha, etc. (as in 5, substituting 'wound' for cleave.)

7 Tear thou my rivals, Darbha, etc.

8 Hew thou my rivals, Darbha, etc.

9 Carve thou my rivals, Darbha, etc.

10 Pierce thou my rivals, Darbha, pierce the men who fain would fight with me.
Pierce those who wish me evil, pierce the men who hate me, Amulet!

HYMN XXIX.

PIERCE thou my rivals, Darbha, pierce the men who fain would fight with me.
Pierce all who wish me evil, pierce the men who hate me, Amulet!

2 Split thou my rivals, Darbha, etc. (as in 1, with 'split' for 'pierce' throughout).

3 Check thou, etc.

4 Crush thou, etc.

5 Shake thou, etc.

6 Bruise thou, etc.

7 Burn thou, etc.

8 Consume, etc.

9 Slay thou my rivals, Darbha, slay the men who fain would fight with me.
Slay all who wish me evil, slay the men who hate me, Amulet.

A charm for the destruction of enemies, a continuation of the preceding.

HYMN XXX.

Darbha, with that good shield of thine, of hundred guards till death in eld,
Arm thou this man, and with thy might strike thou his adversaries down.

2 Darbha, thou hast a hundred shields, thou hast a thousand manly powers.
All Gods have given thee to him to bear thee till extreme old age.

3 They call thee, Darbha, shield of Gods, they call thee Brahmaṇaspati.
They call thee shield of Indra: thou protectest kingdoms from attack.

4 Darbha, destroyer of the foe, vexing the hearts of enemies,
An Amulet that strengthens rule I make thee, and the body's guard.

5 What time Parjanya roared to it with lightning flashes in the sea,
Thence came the drop, the golden drop, thence Darbha into being sprang.

HYMN XXXI.

Savitar make all cattle grow and prosper in my stable with
Amulet of Udumbara, helper of him who longs for wealth!

A protective charm accompanying investiture with an amulet of Darbha grass.

5 The Darbha grass springs up at the beginning of the Rains amid the roar of the thunder-cloud and the flashes of lightning from the sea of air.

A charm to ensure general prosperity, accompanying self-investiture with an amulet of Udumbara.

1 *Udumbara*: the Glomerous Fig-tree; Ficus Glomerata; Hindî, Dumbar; a large tree, generally found in and about villages, and on the banks of rivers and water-courses where the soil is rich and moist.—Roxburgh. Besides amulets, sacrificial posts and ladles were sometimes made of the wood of this tree.

2 May he who was our Household Fire, the ruler of our cattle, strong
Amulet of Udumbara, endow us with prosperity.

3 By power of the Udumbara Charm may Dhâtar give me plenty, rich
In the kine's droppings and in fruit, and, in our dwelling, food, and drink.

4 I win great plenty, while I wear the Amulet of Udumbara,
Of quadrupeds and bipeds, of juices and food of every sort.

5 I have obtained abundant wealth of cattle, bipeds and quadrupeds, and corn in plenty.
Savitar and Bṛihaspati vouchsafe me the milk of kine and herbs' refreshing juices!

6 Fain would I be the lord of herds of cattle: may he who rules o'er riches send me riches.
May the Udumbara Amulet vouchsafe possessions unto me.

7 To me with wealth and children come the Amulet of Udumbara,
With splendour come the Amulet hastened by Indra on its way!

8 Divine, foe-quelling Amulet, wealth-winner for the gain of wealth—
May it give store of beasts and food and cause our kine to multiply.

9 As thou, O Forest Tree, wast born with increase when thy life began,
So let Sarasvatî bestow abundant growth of wealth on me.

10 Sarasvatî vouchsafe me wealth, household prosperity, and corn!
Let Sinîvâlî bring them, and this Amulet of Udumbara.

---

10 *Sinîvâlî:* see XIV. 2. 15, 21. Here she appears as a Goddess of Prosperity unconnected with her usual functions as Lucina.

11 The Lord of amulets art thou, most mighty: in thee wealth's ruler hath engendered riches.
These gains are lodged in thee, and all great treasures. Amulet, conquer thou: far from us banish malignity, and indigence, and hunger.

12 Vigour art thou, in me do thou plant vigour: riches art thou, so do thou grant me riches.
Plenty art thou, so prosper me with plenty: Householder, hear a householder's petition.

13 Amulet of Udumbara, enrich us: vouchsafe us wealth with all good men about us. I bind thee on for increase of possessions.

14 For hero is this hero bound, Amulet of Udumbara.
So may he make our offering sweetly-savoured, and grant us wealth with all good men about us.

HYMN XXXII.

For lengthened life I bind on thee the Darbha grass, the mighty plant,
Excellent, hard to overthrow, with hundred stems and thousand blades.

2 They cut not off his hair, they strike no blow upon the breast for him
To whom one gives protection by Darbha that hath uninjured leaves.

3 O Plant, thy root is in the sky, and thou art stationed on the earth:
With thee who hast a thousand stalks we strengthen all the powers of life.

4 Through all three skies the plant hath pierced, and the three regions of the earth:
With thee I split in twain the tongue and words of the bad-hearted man.

A charm, accompanying investiture with a Darbha grass amulet, to subdue enemies and win the affection of others.

2 *Cut not off his hair:* at death; that is, he will live for ever.

3 *Thy root is in the sky:* cf. II. 7. 3, note.

5 Thou art victorious in thy might: I am endowed with conquering strength:
Possessed of overpowering force we two will quell our enemies.

6 Subdue our foeman, overcome the men who fain would fight with us.
Conquer all evil-hearted ones: make many well-disposed to me.

7 With Darbha that hath sprung from Gods, stationed in heaven, full many a time,
With this have I won many men, have won and may I win them still.

8 Do thou, O Darbha, make me dear to Brâhman and Râjanya, dear to Ṣûdra, and to Ârya dear,
Yea, dear to every man we love, to every man with eyes to see.

9 He who first born fixed earth in her position, he who established heaven and air's mid-region,
Whom sinner ne'er hath known as his supporter,—this Darbha be our shelter and protection!

10 First of all plants it sprang into existence, victorious, hundred-stemmed, the foe-subduer.
So may this Darbha from all sides protect us: with this may I subdue our foes in battle.

HYMN XXXIII.

Hundred-stemmed, succulent, and worth a thousand, the Royal Rite of plants, the Waters' Agni,
Let this same Darbha guard us from all quarters. This Godlike Amulet shall with life endow us.

---

7 *Sprung from Gods*; cf. V. 4. 3, note, and 7.

A protective and benedictive charm accompanying investiture with an amulet of Darbha grass.

2 Drawn forth from butter, juicy, sweetly-flavoured, firm as the earth, unshaken, overthrowing,
Driving off foes and casting them beneath me, mount with the strength of mighty Ones, O Darbha.

3 Thou movest o'er the earth with vigour: lovely in sacrifice thou sittest on the altar.
The Ṛishis bear thee as a purifier: cleanse thou us from all evil deeds' defilement.

4 A stern and all-victorious king, foe-queller, dear to every man—
That energy of Gods and mighty power, I bind this on thee for long life and welfare.

5 Achieve heroic deeds with Darbha; wearing this Darbha never let thy soul be troubled.
In splendour and precedence over others illumine like the Sun the heaven's four regions.

HYMN XXXIV.

JANGIḌA, thou art Angiras: thou art a guardian, Jangiḍa.
Let Jangiḍa keep safely all our bipeds and our quadrupeds.

---

2 The stanza is repeated, with the final pâda altered, from V. 28. 14. *Mount:* that is, be fastened round the man's neck.

3 *Movest o'er the earth:* the grass spreads with great rapidity, re-rooting itself continually.

Lovely in sacrifice: seven bunches are used for different purposes in a sacrifice. See Haug's Aitareya-Brâhmaṇa, II. p. 79. *Sittest on the altar:* three bunches are loosened and spread over the Vedi or altar.

A protective charm addressed to the panacea called Jangiḍa.

1 *Jangiḍa:* a plant or tree which has not been identified. See II. 4. 1. note.

2 Dice-witcheries, the fifty-threes, the hundred witchcraft-practisers,
All these may Jangiḍa make weak, bereft of their effectual force.

3 Baffle the loud factitious howl, make impotent the seven decays.
As when an archer speeds the shaft, drive away want, O Jangiḍa.

4 This counteracts the sorceress, this banishes malignity:
Then may victorious Jangiḍa prolong the days we have to live.

5 Let Jangiḍa's protecting might encompass us on every side,
Wherewith he quells Vishkandha and Sanskandha, might by greater might.

6 Three times the Gods engendered thee fixt on the surface of the earth:
The Brâhmans of the olden time knew that thy name was Angiras.

7 The ancient plants surpass thee not, nor any herbs of recent days.
A potent charm is Jangiḍa, a most felicitous defence.

8 Then when thou sprangest into life, Jangiḍa of unmeasured strength,

---

2 *Dice-witcheries; akshakṛityâs* is the conjectural reading of the editors of the printed text in place of the unintelligible *jâgṛitryâs* of the MSS. *The fifty-threes:* cf. 'Merrily sports their troop, the three-and-fifty' (R̤. V. X. 34. 8).

It would appear from Sâyaṇa's Commentary that this was the usual number of dice (the nuts of the Vibhîdaka tree—Terminalia Bellerica—) employed in gambling; and yet this seems hardly probable. The points on the dice, or the winning number of points, may perhaps be intended.

3 *Seven decays:* gradual stages of increasing debility as old age comes on.

Vishkandha and Sanskandha: apparently different forms of acute rheumatic pains in the shoulder and neck *(skandha)*.

Indra, O mighty One, bestowed great power upon thee from the first.

9 To thee in truth, O Forest Tree, Indra the mighty One gave strength.
Driving away all maladies, strike thou the demons down, O Plant.

10 Lumbago and rheumatic pain, consumptive cough, and pleurisy,
And fever which each Autumn brings, may Jangiḍa make powerless.

HYMN XXXV.

While their lips uttered Indra's name the Ṛishis gave us Jangiḍa;
Which in the earliest time Gods made a remedy, Vishkandha's cure.

2 So may this Jangiḍa guard us, even as a treasurer guards wealth,
Even this which Gods and Brâhmans made a malice-quelling sure defence.

3 Hard-hearted men, the cruel eye, the sinner who hath come to is,
Destroy thou these with watchful care, O thou who hast a thousand eyes. Thou, Jangiḍa, art my defence.

4 Guard me from earth and guard me from the heavens, guard me from middle air, from plants protect me.
Protect me from the present and the future. From every region Jangiḍa preserve us!

5 All sorcerers made by the Gods, all that arise from mortal men,
These, one and all, let Jangiḍa, healer of all, make impotent.

---

10 *Which each Autumn brings:* see IX. 8. 6, note.

A protective charm addressed to the magical Jangiḍa.

HYMN XXXVI.

The Hundred-haired hath banished hence fiends and Consumptions by its might.
With splendour hath the charm that scares demons of ill-name mounted up.

2 It drives off demons with its horns and sorceresses with its root,
It stays Consumption with its waist: from this no wickedness escapes.

3 Consumptions, light and serious, and those which sounds accompany,
All these the Amulet, Hundred-haired, scarer of fiends, hath banished hence.

4 A hundred men hath it produced, hundred Consumptions chased away,
All fiends of evil-name it hath smitten, and shakes the Râkshasas.

5 The Bull that weareth horns of gold, this Amulet with hundred hairs,
Hath cleft the demons of ill-name and overcome the Râkshasas.

6 Hundred she-fiends, a hundred of Gandharvas and Apsarases,
A hundred of dog-mated nymphs, I keep away with Hundred-Hair.

A charm against disease and evil spirits.

1 *Hundred-haired:* or, Hundred-tailed; a powerful amulet made, apparently, of a great number of fibres or filaments of some magical plant, perhaps the Darbha grass of the preceding hymns. *Mounted up:* been raised up and fastened round the neck.

5 *Bull:* the potent charm.

6 *Dog-mated nymphs:* see A. V. IV. 37. 11; XI. 9. 15.

HYMN XXXVII.

To me hath come this word given by Agni, fame, force and might, and strength, and life, and lustre.
May Agni too bestow on me three-times a hundred manly powers.
2 For mighty strength, for action, I receive thee, for manly power, to last a hundred autumns.
3 For conquering strength and energy and vigour
I fasten thee, for chieftainship, for bearing royal dominion through a hundred autumns.
4 With Seasons and with Season-groups, for vigour and extended life,
With splendour of the perfect year we fasten thee about the neck.

HYMN XXXVIII.

Never Consumption, never curse touches the man, Arundhatî!
Whom the delicious odour of the healing Bdellium penetrates.
2 Consumptions flee apart from it as from a wild beast fly the deer.
If thou, O Bdellium, art produced from Sindhu or hast come from sea,
The quality of both have I taken to keep this man unscathed.

HYMN XXXIX.

Let Kushṭha from the Hill of Snow come, a divine deliverer.
Banish thou all Consumption, drive all sorceresses far away.

A charm to secure long life and dominion to a prince.

4 Cf. V. 28. 13.

A protective charm.

1 *Arundhatî:* a climbing plant. See A. V. IV. 12. 1. *Bdellium: gúggulu;* a costly fragrant gum that exudes from a tree that is said to be the vine palm (Borassus Flabelliformis). *Sindhu:* the Indus.

A protective charm.

1 *Kushṭha:* a medicinal aromatic plant, said to be the Costus Speciosus or Arabicus. See A. V. V. 4; VI. 95; 102. 3.

2 Kushṭha, three several names hast thou, Naghamâra, Naghârisha: let not mishap befall this man,
For whom I make a charm of thee at eve, at morning, and by day.

3 Jîvalâ is thy mother's name, thy father's name is Jîvala: let not mishap, etc.

4 Thou art the best amid the plants, even as the ox is best of tame, the tiger of rapacious beasts: let not mishap, etc.

5 Born thrice from the Âdityas, thrice from Bhṛigus, thrice from Angiras' sons, born from the Visve Devas thrice,
Healer of every malady, that Kushṭha stands by Soma's side.
Banish thou all Consumption, drive all sorceresses far away.

6 In the third heaven above us stands the Asvattha tree, the seat of Gods:
There is embodiment of life that dies not: thence was Kushṭha born.

7 There moved through heaven a golden ship, a ship with cordage wrought of gold:
There is embodiment of life that dies not: thence was Kushṭha born.

8 Where is the Sinking of the Ship, the summit of the Hill of Snow,
There is embodiment of life that dies not: thence was Kushṭha born.

---

2 *Naghamâra, Naghârisha:* the meaning of the words is uncertain.

3 *Jîvalâ:* Vivifier; life-giving.

6 This and the following stanza are repeated, with slight variations, from V. 4. 3, 4.

8 *The Sinking of the Ship:* or the place where the ship sank or glided down; probably the Naubandhana of the later Epos, the highest known peak of the Himâlayas, to which in the great flood Manu fastend his ship—the Ararat of the Hindûs. See the legend of the Deluge, Sacred Books of the East, XII. 216 sqq; Max Müller, Ancient Sanskrit Literature, p. 425; Muir, O. S. Texts, I. 182 sqq. *Stands by Soma's side:* 'Soma's benignant friend art thou' (A. V. V. 4. 7.)

Healer of every malady, that Kushṭha stands by Soma's side.
Banish thou all Consumption, drive all sorceresses far away.

9 Thou whom Ikshvâku's ancestor, whom he who well loved Kushṭha, knew,
Whom Vâyasa and Mâtsya knew, hence healer of all ills art thou.

10 O thou who hast all-reaching might drive away Fever, drive it down,
Head-racking Fever, tertian, continual, lasting for a year.

HYMN XL.

For each defect of mine in voice and spirit I have approached One vehement and ardent.
With all the Deities, fully approving, Bṛihaspati supply the want!

2 Disturb ye not our intellect, O Waters, nor the power of prayer.
Glide on your way, strength-giving, invocated: may I be vigorous and wise.

3 Mar not our consecrating rite, our intellect, or fervent zeal.
Gracious to us for lengthened life, propitious let the Mothers be.

---

9 *Ikshvâku:* son of Manu Vaivasvata and first King of the Solar dynasty of Ayodhyâ. *Vâyasa:* a prince of olden time. *Mâtsya:* King of the Matsyas.

10 Cf. 'Chase Fever, whether cold or hot, brought by the summer or the rains, Tertian, intermittent, or autumnal, or continual' (A. V. V. 22. 13).

A prayer for pardon of an error in sacrifice, and for wisdom, strength, and life.

1 *One vehement and ardent:* Bṛihaspati, identified with Agni.

3 *Mothers:* the maternal Waters. Cf. I. 4. 1.

4 Vouchsafe to us, ye Asvins twain, such strength as, with attendant light,
May through the darkness carry us.

HYMN XLI.

DESIRING bliss, at first, light-finding Rishis began religious rite and holy fervour.
Thence energy was born, and might, and kingship: so to this man let gathered Gods incline them.

HYMN XLII.

BRAHMA is Hotar, sacrifice: with Brahma are the stakes set up.
From Brahma was the Adhvaryu born, from Brahma hidden offering.

2 Brahma is fatness-dropping scoops: with Brahma was the altar reared.
Brahma is worship, lengthened rite, the Rishis who pay sacrifice, the victim's Immolators. Hail!

3 To him who frees from woe mine hymn I offer, to the Good Guardian, as I seek his favour.
Accept this offering of mine, O Indra. Fulfilled be all the sacrificer's wishes!

---

4 The stanza is taken from R. V. I. 46. 6. *The darkness*: in the shape of poverty or want, according to the Scholiast.

A benediction on a newly elected King.

1 *Religious rite: dikshā́m*; solemn preparation or consecration for some religious purpose. *Holy fervour: tápas*; fervent devotion, or religious austerity.

In praise of Brahma, Prayer, or Devotion.

1 *The stakes*: the sacrificial posts. *The Adhvaryu*: the priest who performs the practical part of the sacrifice, and who is associated with the Hotar or chief priest. *Hidden*: prepared in vessels covered over with Darbha grass.

2 *Fatness-dropping scoops*: sacrificial ladles from which the clarified butter is poured into the fire. *Lengthened rite: sattrám*; sacrificial session; a great Soma ceremony lasting many days and performed by many officiating priests.

4 With prayer I call on him who frees from trouble,
Prince of Gods, Splendid, chief of sacrifices,
I call the Waters' Child and both the Aṣvins.
Vigour is mine, and strength bestowed by Indra.

HYMN XLIII.

WHITHER men versed in Brahma go, with fervour and the cleansing rite,
Thither let Agni lead me, let Agni give me intelligence. All hail to Agni!

2 Whither, etc.
Thither let Vâyu lead me, let Vâyu vouchsafe me vital breath. All hail to Vâyu!

3 Whither, etc.
Thither let Sûrya lead me, let Sûrya vouchsafe me power of sight. All hail to Sûrya!

4 Whither, etc.
Thither let Chandra lead me, let Chandra vouchsafe me intellect. All hail to Chandra!

5 Whither, etc.
Thither let Soma lead me, let Soma vouchsafe me vital sap. All hail to Soma!

6 Whither, etc.
Thither let Indra lead me, let Indra bestow upon me power. All hail to Indra!

7 Whither, etc.
Thither, let Waters lead me, let the Waters give me deathless life. All hail to Waters!

---

4 *The Waters' Child:* Agni, born as lightning from the watery clouds of the sea of air.

In praise of Brahma, Prayer, or Devotion.

1 *Versed in Brahma: brahmavídaḥ;* learned in spiritual knowledge, theologians. *Cleansing rite: dîkshấ;* a preparatory or consecrating ceremony.

4 *Chandra:* the Moon.

8 Whither, etc.
Thither let Brahma lead me, let Brahma give Brahma unto me. All hail to Brahma!

HYMN XLIV.

Thou art the lengthening of life, thy name is Universal Cure:
Then, Ointment! send felicity; Waters, send happiness and peace.

2 The yellow hue, the feverish heat, the shooting pain that rends the limbs,
All the consumptive malady let the Ointment drive from out thy frame.

3 Let the Salve born upon the earth, benignant, giving life to man,
Make the swift rider on the car sinless, exempt from sudden death.

4 Preserve our breath, O Vital Breath, have mercy on our life, O Life.
From snares of Nirṛiti do thou, O Nirṛiti, deliver us.

5 Thou art the babe of Sindhu, thou art lightnings' flower, wind, breath, and Sun: thou art the eye and milk of heaven.

6 Gods' Ointment from the Three-Peaked Hill, preserve thou me on every side.
No plants of earth surpass thee, none from mountain or from cultured ground.

7 Now hath it gently crept within, fiend-slaying, chasing malady,
And driving all diseases hence, and evil omens, banished them.

A curative and protective charm.

1 *Universal Cure:* no mention is made of the plant which produces this wonderful panacea.

2 *Yellow hue:* of jaundice. *Shooting pain:* *visályaka*. Cf. IX. 8. 2.

6 *The Three-Peaked Hill:* a high mountain in the Himálaya; the modern Trikûṭa. Cf. IV. 9. 8—10.

8 Full many a falsehood, O thou King Varuṇa, man hath uttered here:
Do thou who hast a thousand powers preserve us from that misery.

9 If we have cried, O Waters! Cows! if we have cried, O Varuṇa!
For this, endowed with thousand powers! deliver us from misery.

10 Mitra and Varuṇa, O Salve, have closely followed after thee:
May they, when they have followed thee afar, restore thee for our use.

HYMN XLV.

As debt from debt repay and send sorcery to the sorcerer's house.
Split, Salve! the cruel villain's ribs whose evil eye bewitches us.

2 Whatever evil dream we have, whate'er befall our kine or home,
Be this that is salubrity, the evil-hearted's foe, applied.

3 Increasing from the Waters' strength and vigour, sprung into life from Agni Jâtavedas,
Strong as four heroes, mountain-born, this Ointment make for thee quarters and mid-points auspicious!

4 On thee is laid the Chaturvîra Ointment: let all the regions give thee peace and safety.
Secure like precious Savitar thou standest: to thee let all these regions bring their tribute.

---

9 *O Waters! Cows!:* if we have duly worshipped the celestial Waters by calling on them as sacred cows and givers of abundance.

The hymn closely resembles in parts IV. 9.

A curative and protective charm.

I *As debt from debt:* as a man returns to his creditor a part of what he owes him.

Evil eye: see note on II. 7. 5, from which this line, with a slight variation, is repeated.

4 *Chaturvîra:* 'having the strength of four heroes.'

5 Make one thy salve, thine amulet another, drink one, and with another bathe thy body.
So let the Chaturvîra keep us guarded from the four bonds of Nirṛiti and Grâhi.

6 May Agni protect me with fire for inspiration and expiration, for strength, for energy, for vigour, for weal and prosperity. All Hail!

7 May Indra protect me with his Indra-power for inspiration, etc.

8 May Soma protect me with Soma-power, etc.

9 May Bhaga with good fortune protect me, etc.

10 May the Maruts protect me with their troops for inspiration and expiration, for strength, for energy, for vigour, for weal and prosperity. All Hail!

HYMN XLVI.

For manly strength Prajâpati bound thee on first, invincible.
This for long life on thee I bind for splendour, strength, and energy. Invincible, let it guard thee well.

2 Erect, invincible, be this man's watchful keeper: let not the Paṇis or the sorcerers harm thee.
Shake off thy foes as Indra scattered Dasyus: quell all enemies. Invincible, let it guard thee well.

3 Indra hath lent the power of sight, and vital breath and strength to this,
Whom even a hundred combatants, striking, have failed to overcome. Invincible, let it guard thee well.

---

5 *One:* one portion of the precious ointment.
6 This verse and the four following are in prose.

A charm accompanying investiture with an amulet that ensures safety and victory.

2 *Paṇis:* malevolent demons. *Sorcerers:* Yâtudhânas; see A. V. I. 7. 1, note. *Dasyus:* fiends, foes of the Gods.

The hymn has been translated by Ludwig, Der Rigveda, III. p. 462.

4 Around thy limbs I place the mail of Indra who hath become the Gods' imperial Sovran.
Again let all the Deities bring thee hither. Invincible let it guard thee well.

5 One and a hundred manly powers, a thousand lives hath this Amulet, unconquered ever.
Go forth a tiger, strike down all thy foemen: let him who would oppose fall low beneath thee. Invincible, let it guard thee well.

6 Drawn forth from butter, rich in milk and sweetness, hundred-lived, thousand-homed, bestowing vigour,
Kindly, delightsome, full of sap, and mighty, invincible let it guard thee well.

7 That thou mayst be preëminent, slayer of rivals, rivalless,
May Savitar cause thee to be chief and controller of thy kin. Invincible, let it guard thee well.

HYMN XLVII.

Night! the terrestrial realm hath been filled with the Father's power and might.
Thou spreadest forth on high unto the seats of Heaven: darkness that strikes with awe comes near.

2 Each moving thing finds rest in her whose yonder boundary is not seen, nor that which keeps her separate.
O spacious, darksome Night, may we uninjured reach the end of thee, reach, O thou blessèd One, thine end.

A hymn to Night for protection from fiends, robbers, snakes, and wolves.

1 *Terrestrial realm:* the atmosphere that is immediately above the earth. *Power and might:* or, wondrous works.

3 Thy ninety-nine examiners, O Night, who look upon mankind,
Eighty-and-eight in number, or seven-and-seventy are they.

4 Sixty-and-six, O opulent, fifty-and-five, O happy One,
Forty-and-four and thirty-three are they, O thou enriched with spoil.

5 Twenty-and-two hast thou, O Night, eleven, yea, and fewer still.
With these protectors guard us well. O Daughter of the Sky, to-day.

6 Let not a fiend or spiteful man, let no ill-wisher master us.
Let not the robber seize our cows, nor the wolf take our sheep to-day.

7 Let not the thief, O Blessèd, seize our horses, nor she-fiends our men.
Let thief and robber run away on pathways most remote from us.

8 Far from us let the Rope with Fangs, far from us let the wicked flee.
Do thou make blind and headless, Night, the serpent with his pungent breath.

9 Crush the wolf's jaws in pieces, strike the robber dead against a post.
In thee, O Night, do we abide: we here will sleep. Be watchful thou.

10 Give thou protection to our kine, and to our horses, and our men.

---

3 *Examiners:* 'the sentinel stars.' The numbers, of course, are fanciful, and no reason can be given for the poet's choice of them.

5 *Daughter of the Sky:* Dawn and Night are sisters, and daughters of Dyaus or Heaven.

8 *The Rope with Fangs:* the venomous serpent. Cf. IV. 3. 2.

The hymn has been translated by Ludwig, Der Rigveda, III. p. 467; and by Zimmer, Altindisches Leben, p. 179.

HYMN XLVIII.

THEN all that we accumulate, all that the treasure-chest contains,
All this do we entrust to thee.

2 Entrust thou us to Dawn, O Mother Night.
May Dawn entrust us to the Day, and Day to thee, O splendid One.

3 Whatever flying thing be here, whatever thing that creeps and crawls.
Whatever fastens on a joint, therefrom do thou protect us, Night.

4 So guard thou us from west and east, protect us from the north and south.
O splendid One, preserve us: we, the singers of thy praise, are here.

5 They who are followers of Night, and they who watch o'er living things,
They who protect all cattle, they keep watch and ward over our lives, over our herds keep watch and ward.

6 Verily, Night, I know thy name, Dropper of Fatness art thou called.
Thee Bharadvâja knew as such: as such be watchful o'er our wealth.

A hymn to Night for protection.

1 *Treasure-chest:* the trunk or chest attached to a car or wagon. *Entrust to thee:* consign to thy guardianship during the hours of darkness when we are asleep.

5 *They who are followers of Night:* the 'examiners' or sentinels of hymn 47. 2.

6 *Dropper of Fatness:* balming the earth with gentle vivifying dew. Cf. 'Thy paths drop fatness' (Psalm 65. 11). *Bharadvâja:* a celebrated Ṛishi, to whom most of the hymns of Book VI. of the Ṛigveda are ascribed.

HYMN XLIX.

Friend of the home, the strong and youthful maiden, Night, dear to Savitar the God, and Bhaga,
All-compassing, all-glorious, prompt to listen, hath with her greatness filled the earth and heaven.

2 Over all depths hath she gone up, and mounted, most mighty One, the sky's exalted summit.
Over me now the loving Night is spreading with her auspicious Godlike ways like Mitra.

3 Excellent, high-born, blissful, meet for worship, Night, thou hast come: stay here with friendly spirit.
Guard us, the food for men that we have gotten, and all prosperity that comes of cattle.

4 With eager haste hath Night assumed the vigour of leopard, tiger, or of tawny lion,
The horse's neighing and the wild-man's bellow. Thou takest many a form when thou appearest.

5 Kind through the Night be absence of the sunshine: Mother of Frost, may she be swift to hear us.
Take notice of the hymn, thou highly favoured, wherewith I worship thee in all the regions.

6 Even as a King, O splendid Night, thou takest pleasure in our hymn.
May we through Mornings as they flush have all our good men round us, and become possessors of all wealth.

A hymn of praise and prayer to Night.

2 *Like Mitra:* as completely as the God of Day himself.

3 *Food for men:* or, manly powers.—Ludwig.

4 *Neighing: krandyám* should be read instead of *bradhnám*, splendour; 'des rosses glanz.'—Ludwig. *Wild-man's bellow: púrushasya* here probably = *kimpurushasya*, an evil being similar to man; originally perhaps, a large monkey. Ludwig translates differently: 'des menschen ruf,' the human being's call.

7 Yea, Râmyâ is the name thou hast assumed. The men who fain would spoil
My wealth do thou annoy, O Night, that not one robber may appear, none may a second time appear.

8 Thou like a well-wrought cup, O Night, art lovely: thou, a young maid, art formed in perfect beauty.
Thou lovingly, for me with eyes to see them, hast bound on thee heaven's stars as thine adornments.

9 Whatever robber comes to-day, mischievous mortal enemy,
Let Night go forth, encounter him, and smite away his neck and head;

10 His feet that he may walk no more, his hands that he may do no harm.
The robber who comes hitherward goes crushed and mutilated hence,
Goes hence, goes far away from us, goes hence and bears no spoil away.

HYMN L.

Blind him and make him headless, Night! the serpent with the pungent breath.
Strike from his head the wolf's two eyes, and dash the thief against a post.

2 Those oxen that are thine, O Night, with sharpened horns and rapid pace,
With those transport us safe to-day o'er difficulties everywhere.

3 Uninjured in our bodies may we pass through each succeeding night,
And let malignities fail to pass, as men without a boat the depth.

---

7 *Râmyâ*: Dark. The word may mean also lovely and delightful. The hymn has been translated by Ludwig, Der Ṛigveda, III. p. 466.

A hymn to Night for protection and prosperity.

2 *Those oxen*: the stars with their ever-twinkling rays: the 'many-horned and nimble oxen' of Ṛ. V. I. 154. 6.

4 As millet hurried through the air before us is beheld no more,
So cause the man to vanish, Night, who plans to do us injury.

5 The thief hast thou kept far away, the robber driver of our kine,
Even him who having covered up the horse's head would lead him off.

6 If dealing treasure thou hast come to-day, O highly favoured Night,
Cause thou us to enjoy it all so that this may not pass away.

7 Do thou entrust us to the Dawn, all of us free from sin, O Night.
May Dawn deliver us to Day, and Day to thee, O glorious One.

HYMN LI.

UNDISTURBED am I, undisturbed is my soul, undisturbed mine eye, undisturbed mine ear, undisturbed is mine in-breathing, undisturbed mine out-breathing, undisturbed my diffusive breath, undisturbed the whole of me.

2 Under the impulse of the God Savitar, sent forth from the arms of the Asvins and both hands of Pûshan I have taken thee.

---

4 *Millet: syâmâkaḥ*; Panicum Frumentaceum; a small edible grain.

5 *Covered up the horse's head:* to prevent his running away home, or neighing.

6 *This:* treasure.

The hymn has been translated by Ludwig, Der Rigveda, III. p. 465.

A sacrificial formula.

2 *Thee:* the Prâsitra or portion of Havis or sacrificial food which the Brahman eats. See Vaitâna-Sûtra, III. 9.

HYMN LII.

Thereafter rose Desire in the beginning, Desire the primal seed and germ of Spirit.
O Kâma dwelling with the lofty Kâma, give growth of riches to the sacrificer.

2 Thou, Kâma, art victorious, famous, potent, splendid, a friend to him who seeks thy friendship.
Mighty and overpowering in battle, give strength and vigour to the sacrificer.

3 They heard his prayers, and they begot, by Kâma, heavenly light for him
Who from a distance longed for it, a dealer ready to exchange.

4 O Kâma, with whatever wish we make this offering to thee,
May it be all fulfilled to us. Then taste this sacrifice. All hail!

HYMN LIII.

Prolific, thousand-eyed, and undecaying, a horse with seven reins Time bears us onward.
Sages inspired with holy knowledge mount him: his chariot wheels are all the worlds of creatures.

A hymn to Kâma.

1 *Desire:* Kâma, Erôs, Love. Sâyaṇa explains the word here by *sisṛikshâ,* desire to create. The line is taken from Ṛ. V. X. 129. 4. Cf. A. V. IX. 2.

2 See the Glorification of Kâma in IX. 2.

3 The meaning appears to be that the Gods have, through Kâma and in answer to expressed desire, given celestial light to the distant worshipper who gives prayer and praise in order to obtain the blessings of Heaven.

A hymn to Kâla or Time deified.

1 *Seven reins:* the seven solar rays. The word *raçmi* means both 'rein' and ray of light. Cf. 'Seven to the one-wheeled chariot yoke the courser; bearing seven names the single courser draws it' (Ṛ. V. I. 164. 2); where, however, *the courser* is the Sun, and the *seven* are said by Sâyaṇa to be the priests.

2 This Time hath seven rolling wheels and seven naves: immortality is the chariot's axle.
This Time brings hitherward all worlds about us: as primal Deity is he entreated.

3 On Time is laid an overflowing beaker: this we behold in many a place appearing.
He carries from us all these worlds of creatures. They call him Kâla in the loftiest heaven.

4 He only made the worlds of life, he only gathered the worlds of living things together.
Their son did he become who was their Father: no other higher power than he existeth.

5 Kâla created yonder heaven, and Kâla made these realms of earth.
By Kâla, stirred to motion, both what is and what shall be expand.

6 Kâla created land: the Sun in Kâla hath his light and heat.
In Kâla rest all things that be: in Kâla doth the eye discern.

7 In Kâla mind, in Kâla breath, in Kâla name are fixt and joined.
These living creatures, one and all, rejoice when Kâla hath approached.

---

2 *Seven rolling wheels*: perhaps the six pairs of months and the thirteenth or intercalary month; or the seven divisions of the year, solstice, season, month, fortnight, day, night, hour. *Seven naves*: perhaps the seven generic Vedic metres.

According to Dr. Ehni (Der Mythus des Yama, pp. 116, 117), the seven wheels are the seven worlds which constitute the universe; the seven naves are the seven seasons which are produced by the annual course of the Sun which is brought about by Time; and the axle represents the World of Immortality which remains firm and unmoved through all changes of Time and Season.

3 *Beaker*: the Sun, imagined as a golden urn overflowing with light.

8 Kâla embraces Holy Fire, the Highest, Brahma, in himself.
Yea, Kâla, who was father of Prajâpati, is Lord of All.

9 He made, he stirred this universe to motion, and on him it rests.
He, Kâla, having now become Brahma, holds Parameshṭhin up.

10 Kâla created living things and, first of all, Prajâpati.
From Kâla self-made Kaṣyapa, from Kâla Holy Fire was born.

HYMN LIV.

From Kâla sprang the Waters, sprang the regions, Brahma, Holy Fire.
The Sun ascends by Kâla, and in Kâla sinks again to rest.

2 By Kâla freshly blows the wind, mighty through Kâla is the Earth: on Kâla rests the mighty Sky.

---

8 *Holy Fire:* religious fervour, devotion, or austerity; 'rigorous abstraction.'—Muir. *Brahma:* 'divine knowledge.'—Muir.

9 In this stanza Muir translates *bráhma* by 'divine energy.' Scherman suggests 'heilige Wissenskraft' in this and the preceding stanza if it is thought necessary to translate the word.

10 *Self-made Kaṣyapa:* Kaṣyapa is a divine being similar to, or identified with, Prajâpati; and, as Muir observes, *svayambhûḥ*, self-born or self-made—an epithet which is elsewhere applied to Brahmâ, the derived and phenomenal demiurgus or creator—'must be regarded as not meaning anything more than one who comes into existence in an extraordinary and supernatural manner.' *Holy Fire:* see stanza 8.

The hymn has been translated by Muir, O. S. Texts, V. p. 407; Ludwig, Der Ṛigveda, III. p. 191; Sir M. Monier-Williams, Indian Wisdom, p. 25; Grill, Hundert Lieder, pp. 73, 193; and, with annotations and commentary, by Scherman, Philosophische Hymnen aus der Ṛig-und Atharva-veda Sanhitâ, p. 78.

A hymn to Kâla; a continuation of the preceding hymn.

1 Muir translates *bráhma* in the first line by 'divine knowledge,' but leaves *tápas* (Holy Fire) untranslated: Ludwig and Scherman give both words in the original form.

3 In Kâla erst the text produced what is and what is yet to be.
From Kâla sprang the Ṛichas, and from Kâla was the Yajus born.

4 They formed in Kâla sacrifice, eternal portion for the Gods.
In Kâla the Gandharvas and Apsarases and worlds abide.

5 Atharvan and this Angiras in Kâla are supreme o'er heaven.
Both this world and the world that is most lofty, the pure worlds and pure intermediate spaces,—

6 Yea, having conquered all the worlds by Brahma, Kâla as God Supreme is supplicated.

HYMN LV.

Bringing, as 'twere, with care unceasing fodder night after night to feed this stabled Courser,
Joying in food and in the growth of riches, may we thy neighbours, Agni, ne'er be injured.

2 Here is thine own desire for wealth: through this be gracious unto us.
Joying in food and in the growth of riches, may we thy neighbours, Agni, ne'er be injured.

3 Each eve that comes our household's Lord is Agni, showing his loving-kindness every morning.
Bestow upon us treasure after treasure: enkindling thee may we increase thy body.

---

3 *The text: mántraḥ*; 'the hymn.'—Muir; 'der mantra.'—Ludwig; 'der Spruch.'—Scherman. *Ṛichas:* recited verses of praise. *Yajus:* sacrificial formulas; the Yajur-veda.

This Angiras: with whom we are closely connected.

The hymn has been translated by Muir, O. S. Texts, V. p. 409, with remarks that should be consulted; and, with annotations and commentary, by Scherman, Philosophische Hymnen, p. 80.

A hymn to Agni for protection and prosperity.

2 *Desire:* the wish for rich offerings which is now being gratified.

4 Each morn that comes our household's Lord is Agni, showing his loving-kindness every evening.
Vouchsafe us treasure after treasure: kindling thee may we prosper through a hundred winters.

5 Never may I come short of food to feed me.
Glory to Agni, Rudra, the consumer and the Lord of food!

6 Protect my company, protect its courteous members, courteous God!
Only through thee, O much-invoked, may I be ever rich in kine.

7 Only to thee bringing our tribute, Agni, each day as fodder to a stabled courser,
Joying in food and in the growth of riches, may we thy neighbours, Agni ne'er be injured.

HYMN LVI.

Thou art come hither from the world of Yama: thou, resolute, affectest men with rapture.
Thou, Sleep, created in the Asura's dwelling, goest, well-knowing, with the solitary.

2 At first the all-containing depth beheld thee, ere Night was born, when only Day existed.
Thence hast thou come, thence, Sleep, hast thou come hither, concealing, deep within, all form and figure.

3 Come from the Asuras in lofty glory, he hath approached the Gods in search of greatness.
Winners of heavenly light, the Three-and-Thirty endowed this Sleep with his supreme dominion.

A hymn to Sleep.

1 *Yama:* the Ruler of the Departed. Cf. XVI. 5. 1—5, where Sleep is called Mṛityu or the God of Death himself. Homer speaks of 'Sleep and Death, those feathered twins' (Iliad, XVI. 661, Chapman's translation); so 'Death and his brother Sleep' (Shelley); 'Death's twin-brother' (Tennyson). *The Asura's dwelling:* the home of Yama.

2 *Deep within: gabhishák*; the conjectural reading of the editors of the printed text: 'with both arms.'—Ludwig.

3 *The Gods:* the Three-and-Thirty deities of heaven, middle-air and earth, as distinct from Yama.

4 Of him nor Fathers nor the Gods have knowledge, the Gods whose gentle talk is still about him.
Urged by command of Varuṇa the Âdityas, Heroes, transported Sleep to Trita Âptya.

5 Thou whose severity hath reached ill-doers, and whose reward the good have gained in slumber,
Delightest heaven with thy most lofty kinship, born from his spirit who was worn and weary.

6 Of old we know all places whence thou comest. O Sleep, we know him who is here thy ruler.
Protect us here illustrious with glory. Go, from afar, with poisons, into distance.

HYMN LVII.

As men discharge the utmost debt, collect the eighth and sixteenth part,
So to the foeman we transfer together all the evil dream.

---

4 *Have knowledge:* as subject to his power. The Âdityas who never slumber (R. V. X. 63. 4) banished Sleep from heaven to the abode of Trita Âptya, the distant limbo to which threatened calamities were consigned (A. V. VI. 46. 3, note).

5. *Severity:* punishment in the shape of tormenting dreams. *In slumber:* cf. 'For so he giveth [to] his beloved [in] sleep' (Psalm 127. 3). *His spirit:* perhaps Yama, as the setting sun, may be intended. As he was the first who died (A. V. XVIII. 3. 13) he may also be regarded as the inventor and parent of sleep.

6 *Places whence thou comest:* cf. XVI. 5. 1—5. According to Ludwig, *parijâḥ* here means 'children,' that is, I suppose, dreams. *Him who is here thy ruler:* apparently the possessor of the charm which will dominate him. *From afar:* even before thou comest near us. Here Sleep is addressed and deprecated as the sender of evil dreams.

The hymn has been translated by Ludwig, Der Rigveda, III. p. 467.

A charm against evil dreams.

1 The stanza is taken, with a variation, from R. V. VIII. 47. 17. *To the foeman:* according to the R. V. reading 'unto Âptya,' that is, to Trita Âptya.' See the preceding hymn, stanza 4, note.

2 Princes came together, debts came together, Kushṭhas came together,
Sixteenths came together. The whole evil dream that hath visited us we send away as a bad dream to the man who hates us.

3 Child of Gods' Consorts, minister of Yama is the good Dream: that which is my trouble we drive away to the enemy.

4 Thou whose name is Rough art the mouth of the Black Bird.
As such we know thee, Dream, as such we know thee well. Like a horse art thou, O Dream. As they bind girth and surcingle on a horse, so bind the alien mischief-maker, the scorner of the Gods.

5 The evil dream that threatens us, threatens our cattle or our home,
That let the scorner of the Gods, the alien mischief-maker bind as a gold jewel round his neck.

6 Having measured off nine cubits' distance from us we give away the whole of the evil dream to the man who hates us.

HYMN LVIII.

Still equal be the flow of butter ever causing the Year to prosper with oblation.
Still be our hearing, sight, and breath uninjured: let us lose nothing of our life and vigour.

---

2 *Princes:* whose presence makes the assembly complete. *Debts:* portions of a debt accumulated till repayment of the whole can be made. *Kushṭhas:* precious medicinal plants brought from the Snowy Mountains for sale (cf. V. 4. 2). These examples of gathering together are apparently intended to illustrate the collection of the parts of the evil dream and the transfer of the whole to an enemy. Stanzas 2—4, 6 are non-metrical.

4 *Black Bird:* the raven or crow, which was regarded as a bird of ill omen. Cf. XII. 3. 13.

The hymn has been translated by Ludwig, Der Rigveda, III. p. 468.

A prayer for prosperity, accompanying a sacrifice.

2 Let lively breath invite us: we call vital breath to visit us.
Earth and air's middle realm have gathered, Soma, Bṛihaspati and Dhartar gathered vigour.

3 The earth and heaven have come to be two gatherers up of vigorous might.
So let us gather vigour up and closely follow after Earth.
With glory come the cows and stand beside the master of the herd. Let us when we have gathered fame and glory closely follow Earth.

4 Prepare the cow-stall, for there drink your heroes: stitch ye the coats of armour, wide and many.
Make iron forts defying all assailants: let not your pitcher leak; stay it securely.

5 The eye of sacrifice, source and beginning with voice, ear, spirit unto him I offer.
To this our sacrifice, wrought by Viṣvakarman, may the Gods come gracious and kindly-hearted.

6 Let the Gods' Priests and those who merit worship, to whom oblation as their share is offered,
Come to this holy service with their Consorts, and all Gods revel in the food we bring them.

---

2 *Dhartar:* the Supporter; usually an appellation of Indra.

4 The stanza is taken from Ṛ. V. X. 101. 8. *The cow-stall:* a figurative expression for the place where the Soma juice is extracted. *Heroes:* the priests. *Coats of armour:* filters for straining the Soma juice. *Iron forts:* safeguards obtained by sacrifice and prayer.

5 Repeated from II. 35. 5. Viṣvakarman, the eye, source, and beginning of sacrifice, is probably an appellation of the Omnific Agni.

6 *Priests: ṛitvijoḥ:* regularly sacrificing priests. The two Celestial Hotars who are usually invoked are Agni and Âditya, or Agni and Varuṇa, or Varuṇa and Âditya (see Max Müller, Ancient Sanskrit Literature, p. 464). The Aṣvins are the Adhvaryus, Tvashṭar the Agnîdh or Fire-kindler, and Mitra the Upavaktar or Director.

HYMN LIX.

GOD among mortals, Agni, thou art guard of holy Law, thou art
To be adored in sacred rites.

2 When, ignorant, we violate the statutes of you, O Deities, with whom is knowledge,
Wise Agni shall correct our faults and failings, and Soma who hath entered into Brâhmans.

3 To the Gods' pathway have we come desiring to execute what work we may accomplish.
Let Agni—for he knows—complete the worship. He is the Priest: let him fix rites and seasons.

HYMN LX.

MAY I have voice in my mouth, breath in my nostrils, sight in mine eyes, hearing in mine ears, hair that hath not turned gray, teeth free from yellowness, and much strength in mine arms.

2 May I have power in my thighs, swiftness in my legs, stedfastness in my feet. May all my members be uninjured and my soul unimpaired.

HYMN LXI.

MAY my self remain in my body: may I enjoy the full time of life.
Rest thee pleasantly: pour forth abundance, purifying thyself in Svarga.

An expiatory hymn accompanying sacrifice.

1 The stanza is taken from Ṛ. V. VIII. II. 1.

2 Taken, with the last pâda varied, from Ṛ. V. X. 2. 4.

3 From Ṛ. V. X. 2. 4. *The Gods' pathway:* sacrifice, the path that leads to the Gods. *Seasons:* the proper times of worship.

A prayer for perfect bodily and mental health and vigour.

A prayer for long life and prosperity, and final happiness in heaven.

HYMN LXII.

MAKE me beloved among the Gods, beloved among the Princes, make
Me dear to everyone who sees, to Ṣûdra and to Âryan man.

HYMN LXIII.

RISE up, O Brahmaṇaspati; awake the Gods with sacrifice.
Strengthen the Sacrificer: aid life, breath, and offspring, cattle, fame.

HYMN LXIV.

FOR lofty Jâtavedas I have brought the fuel hither first.
May he who knoweth all bestow faith and intelligence on me.

2 With fuel and with flaming wood we, Jâtavedas, strengthen thee;
So do thou strengthen us in turn with children and with store of wealth.

3 Whatever even be the logs which, Agni, we lay down for thee,
Propitious be it all to me: accept it, O most youthful God.

4 Agni, these logs are thine: with these be, fain to burn! a flaming brand.
Vouchsafe us length of life and give us hope of immortality.

A prayer for the love of Gods and men.

The Gods: here Brâhmans, who have studied and teach sacred lore, 'human Gods' (Sacred Books of the East, XII. 309) are intended. Cf. A. V. XIX. 32. 8.

A prayer, accompanying sacrifice, for long life and prosperity.

A prayer to Agni for children, long life, and various blessings.

2 *Flaming wood:* the *samidh*, kindling-stick or fire-brand with which the fire is lighted, as distinct from the *idhmá* or fuel.

4 *A flaming brand:* the God being regarded as identical with the stick that kindles the visible flame.

HYMN LXV.

A GOLDEN Eagle thou hast soared with light to heaven. Those who would harm thee as thou fliest skyward
Beat down, O Jâtavedas, with thy fury. The strong hath feared: to heaven mount up with light, O Sûrya.

HYMN LXVI.

THE Asuras with iron nets, magicians, who roam about with hooks and bonds of iron,
With wrath I make thy thralls, O Jâtavedas. Come as a bolt foe-quelling, thousand-pointed.

HYMN LXVII.

A HUNDRED autumns may we see. 2 A hundred
autumns may we live. 3 A hundred autumns may
we know. 4 A hundred autumns may we grow. 5
A hundred autumns may we thrive. 6 A hundred
autumns may we be. 7 A hundred autumns may
we bide. 8 A hundred, yea, and even more.

HYMN LXVIII.

BOTH of the broad and narrow I with magic power unclose the mouth.
With these when we have raised the bunch of grass we pay the holy rites.

A hymn to Agni identified with the Sun.

Those who would harm thee: demons of darkness and eclipse. *The Strong:* Agni.

A hymn to Agni as the Sun.

Asuras: demons of darkness. *Iron nets:* to be used against the Sun, the Celestial Bird, the Golden Eagle.

A prayer for long life.

A preliminary sacrificial formula.

Broad and narrow: larger and smaller ladle. *Bunch of grass:* the *veda*, a bunch of Darbha grass which passes from priest to priest during the performance of a sacrifice. See Haug's Aitareya-Brahmaṇa, II. p. 79.

HYMN LXIX.

YE are alive. I fain would live. I fain would live
my complete term of life. 2 Ye live dependent.
I fain would live dependent. I fain would live
my complete term of life. 3 Ye remain alive.
I fain would remain alive. I fain would live my
complete term of life. 4 Ye are life-givers. I
fain would live. I fain would live my complete
term of life.

HYMN LXX.

LIVE, Indra. Live, Sûrya. Live, ye Gods. I fain would live. Fain would I live my complete term of life.

HYMN LXXI.

LET my libations, giving boons, adoring, further the Twice-born's song that honours Soma.

Go ye to Brahmâ's world having enriched me with life and breath, with children and with cattle, with fame and wealth, and with a Brahman's lustre.

HYMN LXXII.

WITHIN the chest whence we before extracted the bunch of grass, this do we now deposit.

Wrought is the sacrifice by power of Brahma. Through this assist me here, ye Gods, with Fervour.

A prayer or charm for long life.

1 *Ye:* the Gods are addressed. 2 *Dependent:* on the sacrifices of men, as the worshipper is dependent on the Gods.

A charm for long life.

A hymn, accompanying libations, for wealth and prosperity.

Twice-born: regenerated by investiture; men of the first three classes, especially Brâhmans. *Song that honours Soma:* a Pâvamânî verse in praise of Soma which is being strained and purified. The seven Pâvamânîs are Ṛigveda IX. 67. 21—27. *Go ye:* addressed to the libations.

A sacrificial formula.

Bunch of grass: see XIX. 68, note.

BOOK XX.

HYMN I.

THEE, Indra, we invoke, the Bull, what time the Soma hath been pressed.
Drink of the sweetly-flavoured juice.

2 The best of guardians hath the man within whose dwelling-place ye drink,
O Maruts, giants of the sky.

3 Let us serve Agni with our hymns, Sage who consumeth ox and cow,
Who beareth Soma on his back.

HYMN II.

LET the Maruts drink Trishṭups from the Potar's cup,
according to the season Soma from heaven. 2 Let
Agni from the Kindler's cup drink Trishṭups, ac-
cording to the season Soma from heaven. 3 Let

This Book, which, with Book XIX., is not a part of the original Atharva-veda, contains—with the exception of the Kuntâpa section (CXXVII—CXXXVI)—complete and composite hymns addressed almost exclusively to Indra and generally taken directly and without variants from hymns and portions of hymns of the Ṛigveda.

1 Taken from Ṛ. V. III. 40. 1.

2 Ṛ. V. I. 86. 1.

3. Ṛ. V. VIII. 43. 11. *Who beareth Soma on his back:* on whom the libation of Soma juice is poured.

This prose hymn is composed of fragments of Ṛ. V. II. 36 and 37.

1 *Drink Trishṭups:* accept hymns of praise in Trishṭup metre accompanying the libation. *The Potar's cup:* the Soma bowl of the Brahman's assistant the Potar or Purifier, one of the sixteen officiating priests at a sacrifice.

2 *Kindler:* the Agnîdh, the priest who lights the sacrificial fire.

3 *The Brahman:* this title is not given to Indra in the corresponding Ṛ. V. passage.

Indra the Brahman from the Brahman's cup drink Trishṭups, according to the season Soma from heaven. 4 Let the God, Granter of Wealth, from the Potar's cup drink Trishṭups, according to the season Soma from heaven.

HYMN III.

COME, we have pressed the juice for thee: O Indra, drink this Soma here.
Seat thee on this my sacred grass.

2 Let both thy bay steeds, yoked by prayer, long-maned, O Indra, bring thee nigh.

3 We Soma-bearing Brahmans call thee Soma-drinker with thy friend,
We, Indra, who have pressed the juice.

HYMN IV.

COME unto us who poured the juice, come hither to our eulogies.
Drink of the juice, O fair of face.

2 I pour it down within thee, so through all thy members let it run.
Take with thy tongue the pleasant drink.

3 Sweet to thy body let it be, delicious be the savoury juice.
Sweet be the Soma to thy heart.

---

4 *Granter of Wealth:* Draviṇodâs; an appellation of Agni as the mediator through whom the pious obtain riches.

The hymn is taken from Ṛ. V. VIII. 17. 1—3.

3 *With thy friend:* thy constant companion, the thunderbolt.

A continuation of the preceding hymn, taken from stanzas 4—6 of Ṛ. V. VIII. 17. 4—6.

1 *Fair of face:* or, having large, strong, or handsome jaws or cheeks.

HYMN V.

LIKE women, let this Soma juice invested with its raiment, glide
Most active Indra, close to thee.

2 Mighty in bulk, strong-necked, stout-armed, in the wild rapture of the juice
Doth Indra smite the foemen dead.

3 Indra, advance, go forward thou who by thy might art Lord of all.
Slay, Vṛitra-slayer, slay thy foes.

4 Long be thy grasping-hook wherewith thou givest treasure unto him
Who pours the juice and worships thee.

5 Here, Indra, is thy Soma draught, made pure upon the sacred grass.
Run hither, come and drink thereof.

6 Famed for thy radiance, worshipped well! this juice is shed for thy delight:
Thou art invoked, Âkhaṇḍala!

7 To Kuṇḍapâyya, grandson's son, grandson of Ṣṛingavṛish, to thee,
To him have I addressed my thought.

A continuation of the preceding hymn, taken from Ṛ. V. VIII. 17. 7—13.

1 *Like women:* who move slowly on, dressed in white garments. *Its raiment:* the milk that colours it.

4 *Grasping-hook:* Indra's bounteous power is likened to the hook with which the branches of fruit-laden trees are drawn down within reach.

6 *Famed for thy radiance, worshipped well:* the words thus rendered, *ṣâchigo* and *ṣâchipûjana*, have not been satisfactorily explained by the commentator, and their meaning is still uncertain. According to Sâyaṇa the former may mean 'thou whose cattle are strong,' or 'thou whose radiance is renowned,' and the latter 'thou of renowned adoration' or 'whose hymns are renowned.' See Professor Wilson's note.

Thou art invoked, Âkhaṇḍala!: or, Thou, O Destroyer, art invoked. This appellation of Indra does not occur again in the Ṛigveda.

7 *Kuṇḍapâyya* and *Ṣṛingavṛish* appear here to be names of men. According to Sâyaṇa *kuṇḍapâyya* is the name of a particular Soma-

HYMN VI.

THEE, Indra, we invoke, the Bull, what time the Soma is expressed.
So drink thou of the savoury juice.

2 Indra, whom many laud, accept the strength-conferring Soma juice.
Quaff, pour down drink that satisfies.

3 Indra, with all the Gods promote our wealth-bestowing sacrifice,
Thou highly-lauded Lord of men.

4 Lord of the brave, to thee proceed these drops of Soma juice expressed,
The bright drops to thy dwelling-place.

5 Within thy belly, Indra, take Soma the juice most excellent:
The heavenly drops belong to thee.

6 Drink our libation, Lord of hymns: with streams of meath thou art bedewed:
Our glory, Indra, is thy gift.

7 To Indra go the treasures of the worshipper which never fail:
He drinks the Soma and is strong.

8 From far away, from near at hand, O Vṛitra-slayer, come to us:
Accept the songs we sing to thee.

HYMN VII.

SŪRYA, thou mountest up to meet the Hero famous for his wealth,
Who hurls the bolt and works for man;

---

ceremony, and the offspring of *Sṛingavṛish* is Indra himself. '(Indra) who wast the offspring of Sṛingavṛish, of whom the *kuṇḍapāyya* rite was the protector, (the sages) have fixed (of old) their minds upon this ceremony.' See Professor Wilson's note who observes that the construction is loose, and the explanation not very satisfactory.'

The hymn is taken from Ṛ. V. III. 40, 1—8.

Stanzas 1—3 are taken Ṛ. V. VIII. 82. 1—3, and stanza 4 is repeated from the preceding hymn of this Book.

2 Him who with might of both his arms brake nine-and-ninety castles down,
Slew Vṛitra and smote Ahi dead.

3 This Indra is our gracious Friend. He sends us in a full broad stream
Riches in horses, kine, and corn.

4 Indra, whom many laud, accept the strength-conferring Soma juice.
Quaff, pour down drink that satisfies.

HYMN VIII.

Drink as of old, and let the draught delight thee: hear thou my prayer and let our songs exalt thee.
Make the Sun visible, make food abundant: slaughter the foes, pierce through and free the cattle.

2 Come to us; they have called thee Soma-lover. Here is the pressed juice: drink thereof for rapture.
Widely-capacious, pour it down within thee, and invocated hear us like a father.

3 Full is his chalice. Blessing! Like a pourer I have filled up the vessel for his drinking.
Presented on the right, dear Soma juices have brought us Indra, to rejoice him, hither.

HYMN IX.

As cows low to their calves in stalls, so with our songs we glorify
This Indra, even your wondrous God who checks attack, who joys in the delicious juice.

---

2 *Nine-and-ninety castles:* the countless cloud-fortresses of the demons of drought.

Ahi: the serpent or dragon who obstructs the seasonable rain.

Stanza 1 is taken from Ṛ. V. VI. 17. 3; 2 from I. 104. 9; and 3 from III. 32. 15.

1 *Pierce through and free the cattle:* penetrate and disperse the thick cloud and liberate the lights of day.

Stanzas 1, 2 are taken from Ṛ. V. VIII. 77. 1, 2, and stanzas 3. 4 from VIII. 3. 9, 10.

1 *Cows:* milked for sacrificial purposes, their calves being shut up during the performance of the religious ceremony.

2 Celestial, bounteous Giver, girt about with might, rich, mountain-like, in precious things—
Him swift we seek for foodful booty rich in kine, brought hundredfold and thousandfold.

3 I crave of thee that hero strength, that thou mayst first regard this prayer,
Wherewith thou holpest Bhṛigu and the Yatis and Praskaṇva when the prize was staked.

4 Wherewith thou sentest mighty waters to the sea, that, Indra, is thy hero strength.
For ever unattainable is this power of him to whom the worlds have called aloud.

HYMN X.

These songs of ours exceeding sweet, these hymns of praise ascend to thee,
Like ever-conquering chariots that display their strength, gain wealth and give unfailing aid.

2 The Bhṛigus are like suns, like Kaṇvas, and have gained all that their thoughts were bent to win.
The living men of Priyamedha's race have sung exalting Indra with their lauds.

HYMN XI.

Fort-render, Lord of Wealth, dispelling foemen, Indra with lightnings hath o'ercome the Dâsa.
Impelled by prayer and waxen great in body, he hath filled earth and heaven, the bounteous Giver.

---

3 *Yatis:* an ancient race of ascetics connected with the Bhṛigus, and, according to one legend, said to have taken part in the creation of the world. *Praskaṇva:* an ancient Ṛishi, descendant of the celebrated Kaṇva and seer of some hymns of Books I., VIII., and IX. of the Ṛigveda. *When the prize was staked:* when they fought for booty.

Taken from Ṛ. V. VIII. 3. 15, 16.

2 *Priyamedha:* a Ṛishi, of the family of Angiras, seer of several hymns of the Ṛigveda.

Taken from Ṛ. V. III. 34.

1 *Fort-render:* breaker-down of the cloud-castles of the demons who withhold the rain as well as of the strongholds of the hostile non-Âryan tribes.

2 I stimulate thy zeal, the Strong, the Hero, decking my song of praise for thee Immortal.
O Indra, thou art equally the leader of heavenly hosts and human generations.

3 Leading his band Indra encompassed Vṛitra; weak grew the wily leader of enchanters.
He who burns fierce in forests slaughtered Vyansa, and made the milch-kine of the nights apparent.

4 Indra, light-winner, days' creator, conquered, as guardian, hostile bands with those who loved him.
For man the days' bright ensign he illumined, and found the light for his great joy and gladness.

5 Forward to fiercely falling blows pressed Indra, hero-like doing many hero exploits.
These holy songs he taught the bard who praised him, and widely spread these Dawns' resplendent colour.

6 They laud the mighty acts of him the mighty, the many glorious deeds performed by Indra.
He in his strength, with all-surpassing prowess, through wondrous arts crushed the malignant Dasyus.

7 Lord of the brave, Indra who rules the people gave freedom to the Gods by might and battle.
Wise singers glorify with chanted praises these his achievements in Vivasvân's dwelling.

---

3 *He who burns fierce in forests:* perhaps the thunderbolt.

Vyansa: the name of one of the demons of drought. See Ṛ. V. I. 101. 2. and 103. 2.

Made the milch-kine of the nights apparent: according to Sâyaṇa, 'made manifest the (stolen) cows (that had been hidden) in the night;' that is, recovered the rays of light.

7 *In Vivasvân's dwelling:* in the sacrificial chamber, the abode of the sacrificer who represents Vivasvân who sacrifices for the Gods in heaven.

8 Excellent, conqueror, the victory-giver, the winner of the light and godlike waters,
He who hath won this broad earth and this heaven,—in Indra they rejoice who love devotions.

9 He gained possession of the Sun and horses; Indra obtained the cow who feedeth many.
Treasure of gold he won; he smote the Dasyus and gave protection to the race of Âryas.

10 He took the plants and days for his possession; he gained the forest trees and air's mid-region.
Vala he cleft, and chased away opponents: thus was he tamer of the overweening.

11 Call we on Maghavan, auspicious Indra, best Hero in the fight where spoil is gathered,
The Strong, who listens, who gives aid in battles, who slays the Vṛitras, wins and gathers treasures.

HYMN XII.

PRAYERS have been offered up through love of glory: Vasishṭha, honour Indra in the battle.
He who with might extends through all existence hears words which I, his faithful servant, utter.

2 A cry was raised which reached the Gods, O Indra, a cry to them to send us strength in combat.
None among men knows his own life's duration: bear us in safety over these our troubles.

3 The Bays, the booty-seeking car I harness: my prayers have reached him who accepts them gladly.
Indra, when he had slain resistless Vṛitras, forced with his might the two world-halves asunder.

---

9 *The cow who feedeth many:* both directly, with milk, and indirectly through the sacrifices for which she supplies the essential oblations.

11 *The race of Âryas:* according to Sâyaṇa, the noblest tribe or order, meaning the first three classes or castes.

Stanzas 1—6 are taken from Ṛ. V. VII. 23, and stanza 7 from V. 40. 4.

2 *A cry was raised:* I follow Professor Pischel's interpretation of this very difficult stanza. See Vedische Studien, I pp. 34—36.

3 *The two world-halves asunder:* cf. A. V. IV. 1. 4, note, and VIII. 9. 6.

4 Like barren cows, moreover, swelled the waters: the singers sought thy holy rite, O Indra.
Come unto us as with his team comes Vâyu: thou, through our solemn hymns, bestowest booty.
5 So may these gladdening draughts rejoice thee, Indra, the Mighty, very bounteous to the singer.
Alone among the Gods thou pitiest mortals: O Hero, make thee glad at this libation.
6 Thus the Vasishṭhas glorify with praises Indra, the Mighty One, whose arm wields thunder.
Praised, may he guard our wealth in kine and heroes. Ye Gods, preserve us evermore with blessings.
7 Impetuous, Thunderer, strong, quelling the mighty, King, potent, Vṛitra-slayer, Soma-drinker,
May he come hither with his yoked bay horses. May Indra gladden him at noon libation.

HYMN XIII.

Lords of great wealth, Bṛihaspati and Indra, rejoicing at this sacrifice drink Soma.
Let the abundant drops sink deep within you: vouchsafe us riches with full store of heroes.
2 Let your swift-gliding coursers bear you hitherward with their fleet pinions. Come ye forward with your arms.
Sit on the grass; a wide seat hath been made for you: delight yourselves, O Maruts, in the pleasant food.
3 For Jâtavedas, worthy of our praise, will we frame with our mind this eulogy as 'twere a car.

---

4 *Barren cows:* which are fatter than others.

Stanza 1 is taken from Ṛ. V. IV. 50. 10; stanza 2 from I. 85. 6; stanza 3 from I. 94. 1; and stanza 4 from III. 6. 9.

3 *As 'twere a car:* as a carpenter constructs a car or wain. Moreover the hymn is frequently called a chariot, as it travels swiftly to the Gods. Similarly Pindar speaks of song as a chariot, Μοισᾶν δίφρος, O. 9. 81, I. 2. 2; ἅρμα πιερίδων τετράορον, P. 10. 65; Μουσαῖον ἅρμα, I. 7. 62. *In his assembly:* among those who have met together to worship him. Or the meaning might be: good, or auspicious, is his providence or loving care of us.

For good in his assembly is this care of ours. Let us not in thy friendship, Agni, suffer harm.

4 With these, borne on one car, Agni, approach us; or borne on many, for thy steeds are able.
Bring, with their Dames, the Gods, the Three-and-Thirty, after thy Godlike nature, and be joyful.

HYMN XIV.

We call on thee, O peerless One. We, seeking help, possessing nothing firm ourselves,
Call on thee wonderful in fight:

2 On thee for aid in sacrifice. This youth of ours, the bold, the mighty, hath gone forth.
We, therefore, we thy friends, Indra, have chosen thee, free-giver, as our guardian God.

3 Him who of old hath brought to us this and that blessing, him I magnify for you,
Even Indra, O my friends, for help:

4 Borne by bay steeds, the Lord of heroes, ruling men, for it is he who takes delight.
The Bounteous Lord bestows on us his worshippers hundreds of cattle and of steeds.

HYMN XV.

To him most liberal, lofty Lord of lofty wealth, verily powerful and strong, I bring my hymn,—
Whose checkless bounty, as of waters down a slope, is spread abroad for all that live, to give them strength.

Taken from Ṛ. V. VIII. 21. 1, 2 and 9, 10.

2 *This youth of ours:* the noble, the institutor of the sacrifice, who has gone out on a warlike expedition.

4 *Cattle:* taken from the enemy.

Taken from Ṛ. V. I. 57.

2 Now all this world, for worship, shall come after thee—the offerer's libations like descending floods,
When the well-loved one seems to rest upon the hill, the thunderbolt of Indra, shatterer wrought of gold.

3 To him the terrible, most worthy of high praise, like radiant Dawn, bring gifts with reverence in this rite,
Whose being, for renown, yea, Indra-power and light, have been created, like bay steeds, to move with speed.

4 Thine, Indra, praised by many, excellently rich! are we who trusting in thy help draw near to thee.
Lover of praise, none else but thou receives our laud: as Earth loves all her creatures, love thou this our hymn.

5 Great is thy power, O Indra, we are thine. Fulfil, O Maghavan, the wish of this thy worshipper.
After thee lofty heaven hath measured out its strength: to thee and to thy power this earth hath bowed itself.

6 Thou, who hast thunder for thy weapon, with thy bolt hast shattered into pieces this broad massive cloud.
Thou hast sent down obstructed floods that they may flow: thou hast, thine own for ever, all victorious might.

---

2 *When the well-loved one:* when the lightning-laden cloud is resting on the mountain men pray to Indra that he may discharge his celestial artillery and bring down the rain.

3 *Like radiant Dawn:* as dawn brings the light. When the object compared is the person addressed, the object to which it is compared is often in the vocative case, as here. See Grassmann's Rig-veda Dictionary under *ná*. *Bring:* the worshipper addresses himself. But see Ludwig's Commentary (V. 18), who translates and explains differently, taking *ā́bharā* (ā́ bhara in the Pada text) as the first person singular.

5 *After thee:* heaven has taken thy might and majesty as a pattern for its own.

HYMN XVI.

LIKE birds who keep their watch, plashing in water, like the loud voices of the thundering rain-cloud,
Like merry streamlets bursting from the mountain, thus to Bṛihaspati our hymns have sounded.

2 The son of Angiras, meeting the cattle, as Bhaga, brought in Aryaman among us.
As Friend of men he decks the wife and husband. As for the race, Bṛihaspati, nerve our coursers.

3 Bṛihaspati, having won them from the mountains, strewed down, like barley out of winnowing-baskets,
The vigorous, wandering cows who aid the pious, desired of all, of blameless form, well-coloured.

4 As the Sun dews with meath the seat of Order, and casts a flaming meteor down from heaven,
So from the rock Bṛihaspati forced the cattle, and cleft the earth's skin as it were with water.

5 Forth from mid-air with light he drave the darkness, as the gale blows a lily from the river.
Like the wind grasping at the cloud of Vala, Bṛihaspati gathered to himself the cattle.

6 Bṛihaspati, when he with fiery lightnings cleft through the weapon of reviling Vala,

---

The hymn, addressed to Bṛihaspati, is taken from Ṛ. V. X. 68.

2 *The son of Angiras:* Bṛihaspati, especially worshipped and cherished by Angiras. *The cattle:* the imprisoned beams of light; the bright days. *Bhaga:* God of good fortune. *Aryaman:* the representative of marriage; here meaning marriage itself.

3 *Out of winnowing-baskets: sthivíbhyaḥ:* the exact meaning of the word is somewhat uncertain, but it is evidently a measure, basket, or instrument connected with corn. *Sthivimántaḥ*, 'armed with *sthivis*,' occurs in X. 27. 15, and is said by Sâyaṇa to mean 'occupants of stations.' Prof. Wilson renders *sthivíbhyaḥ* in this place by 'from the granaries.' The cows bestowed by Bṛihaspati are countless as grains of barley on the threshing-floor or winnowing-place.

4 *Cleft the earth's skin:* or surface, with the hoofs of many cattle.

5 *A lily: śîpâla:* according to Sâyaṇa the same as Śaivala, the Vallisneria Octandra, a common aquatic plant.

6 *Weapon:* I adopt Sâyaṇa's explanation of *jásum*, although in X. 33. 2 the same word means 'exhaustion.'

Consumed him as tongues eat what teeth have compassed: he threw the prisons of the red cows open.

7 That secret name borne by the lowing cattle within the cave Bṛihaspati discovered,
And drave, himself, the bright kine from the mountain, like a bird's young after the eggs' disclosure.

8 He looked around on rock-imprisoned sweetness as one who eyes a fish in scanty water.
Bṛihaspati, cleaving through with varied clamour, brought it forth like a bowl from out the timber.

9 He found the light of heaven, and fire, and Morning: with lucid rays he forced apart the darkness.
As from a joint, Bṛihaspati took the marrow of Vala as he gloried in his cattle.

10 As trees for foliage robbed by winter, Vala mourned for the cows Bṛihaspati had taken.
He did a deed ne'er done, ne'er to be equalled, whereby the sun and moon ascend alternate.

11 Like a dark steed adorned with pearl, the Fathers have decorated heaven with constellations.
They set the light in day, in night the darkness. Bṛihaspati cleft the rock and found the cattle.

12 This homage have we offered to the Cloud-God who thunders out to many in succession.
May this Bṛihaspati vouchsafe us fulness of life with kine and horses, men, and heroes.

---

8 *Sweetness:* the sweet milk; that is the cows who produced it. *Like a bowl:* which already exists potentially in the wood from which it is produced by cutting.

9 Prof. Wilson, following Sâyaṇa, paraphrases the second line:—'he seized (the cattle from the rock) of Vala surrounded by the kine as (one extracts) marrow from a bone.'

11 *The Fathers:* 'The connection of the fathers with the light, of which they are both the embodiments and the guardians, is alone sufficient to explain their action in placing the stars in the sky.'—Wallis, *Cosmology of the Ṛigveda*, p. 68.

12 *To many:* 'cows' is, apparently, understood. Sâyaṇa supplies *ṛichas*:—'who recites in order many (sacred stanzas).'—Wilson.

HYMN XVII.

In perfect unison all yearning hymns of mine that find the light of heaven have sung forth Indra's praise
As wives embrace their lord, the comely bridegroom, so they compass Maghavan about that he may help

2 Directed unto thee my spirit never strays, for I have set my hopes on thee, O much-invoked!
Sit, wonderful! as King upon the sacred grass, and let thy drinking-place be by the Soma juice.

3 From indigence and hunger Indra turns away: Maghavan hath dominion over precious wealth.
These the Seven Rivers flowing on their downward path increase the vital vigour of the Mighty Steer.

4 As on the fair-leafed tree rest birds, to Indra flow the gladdening Soma juices that the bowls contain.
Their face that glows with splendour through their mighty power hath found the shine of heaven for man, the Âryas' light.

5 As in the game a gambler piles his winnings, so Maghavan, sweeping all together, gained the Sun.
This mighty deed of thine none other could achieve, none, Maghavan, before thee, none in recent time.

6 Maghavan came by turns to all the tribes of men: the Steer took notice of the people's songs of praise.
The man in whose libations Ṣakra hath delight, by means of potent Somas vanquisheth his foes.

7 As waters flow together to the river, thus Somas to Indra flow, as rivulets to the lake.
In place of sacrifice sages exalt his might, as the rain swells the corn by moisture sent from heaven.

Stanzas 1—11 are taken from Ṛ. V. X. 43, and stanza 12 from VII. 97. 10.

3 *Turns away:* Sâyaṇa makes *vishuvṛit* transitive:—'May Indra be the remover of thirst and hunger.'—Wilson.

5 *Gained the Sun*. conquered him by taking away his moisture, that is, the water that he had absorbed.—Sâyaṇa.

8 He rushes through the region like a furious bull, he who hath made these floods the dames of worthy lords.
This Maghavan hath found light for the man who brings oblation, sheds the juice, and promptly pours his gifts.

9 Let the keen axe come forth together with the light: here be, as erst, the teeming cow of sacrifice.
Let the Red God shine pure with his refulgent ray, and let the Lord of heroes glow like heaven's clear sheen.

10 O much-invoked, may we subdue all famine and evil want with store of grain and cattle.
May we allied, as first in rank, with princes, obtain possessions by our own exertion.

11 Bṛihaspati protect us from the rearward, and from above, and from below, from sinners.
May Indra from the front, and from the centre, as friend to friends, vouchsafe us room and freedom.

12 Ye twain are Lords of wealth in earth and heaven, thou, O Bṛihaspati, and thou, O Indra.
Mean though he be, give wealth to him who lauds you. Preserve us evermore, ye Gods, with blessings.

HYMN XVIII.

THIS, even this, O Indra, we implore: as thy devoted friends,
The Kaṇvas praise thee with their hymns.

---

8 *The dames of worthy lords:* that is, subjected them to the Âryans, whereas they had been the thralls of Dâsas. See Ṛ. V. I. 32. 11.

9 *The keen axe:* Agni, who is frequently likened to an axe. See Ṛ. V. I. 127. 3, and VI. 3. 4.

The Red God: arushâḥ: according to Sâyaṇa, 'the radiant Indra'; but Agni is probably intended.

Stanzas 1—3 are taken from Ṛ. V. VIII. 2. 16—18, and stanzas 4—6 from VII. 31. 4—6.

2 Naught else, O Thunderer, have I praised in the skilled singer's eulogy:
On thy laud only have I thought.
3 The Gods seek him who presses out the Soma; they desire not sleep:
Incessantly they punish sloth.
4 Faithful to thee we loudly sing, heroic Indra, songs to thee.
Mark, gracious Lord, this act of ours.
5 Give us not up to man's reproach, to foeman's hateful calumny:
In thee alone is all my strength.
6 Thou art mine ample coat of mail, my champion, Vṛitra-slayer, thou.
With thee for Friend I brave the foe.

HYMN XIX.

O Indra, for the strength that slays the foe and conquers in the fight
We turn thee hitherward to us.
2 O Indra, Lord of Hundred Powers, may those who praise thee hitherward
Direct thy spirit and thine eye.
3 O Indra, Lord of Hundred Powers, with all our songs we invocate
Thy names for triumph over foes.
4 We strive for glory through the powers immense of him whom many praise,
Of Indra who supports mankind.
5 For the foe's slaughter I address Indra whom many invocate,
To win us booty in the wars.
6 In battles be victorious. We seek thee, Lord of Hundred Powers,
O Indra, that the foe may fall.
7 In splendid combats of the hosts, in glories where the fight is won,
Indra, be victor over foes.

Taken from Ṛ. V. III. 37. 1—7.

HYMN XX.

DRINK thou the Soma for our help, bright, vigilant, exceeding strong,
O Indra, Lord of Hundred Powers.

2 O Ṣatakratu, powers which thou mid the Five Races hast displayed—
These, Indra, do I claim of thee.

3 Indra, great glory hast thou gained. Win splendid fame which none may mar:
We make thy might perpetual.

4 Come to us either from anear, or, Ṣakra, come from far away.
Indra, wherever be thy home, come to us thence, O Thunder-armed.

5 Verily Indra, conquering all, driveth even mighty fear away;
For firm is he and swift to act.

6 Indra be gracious unto us: sin shall not reach us afterward,
And good shall be before us still.

7 From all the regions of the world let Indra send security,
The foe-subduer, swift to act.

HYMN XXI.

WE will present fair praise unto the Mighty One, our hymns to Indra in Vivasvân's dwelling-place;

Stanzas 1—4 are taken from Ṛ. V. III. 37. 8—11, and stanzas 5—7 from II. 41. 10—12.

2 *Ṣatakratu:* Lord of Hundred Powers. *Five Races:* great Âryan tribes. See A. V. III. 21. 5, note.

4 *Ṣakra:* Mighty One.

Taken from Ṛ. V. I. 53.

1 *Vivasvân's dwelling-place:* the sacrificial chamber or enclosure. See XX. 11. 7.

For he hath ne'er found wealth in those who seem to sleep; those who give wealth to men accept no paltry praise.

2 Giver of horses, Indra, giver, thou, of kine, giver of barley, thou art Lord and guard of wealth:

Man's helper from of old, not disappointing hope, Friend of our friends, to thee as such we sing this praise.

3 Indra, most splendid, powerful, rich in mighty deeds, this treasure spread around is known to be thine own.

Gather therefrom, O Conqueror, and bring to us: fail not the hope of him who loves and sings to thee.

4 Well-pleased with these bright flames and with these Soma drops, take thou away our poverty with steeds and kine.

With Indra scattering the Dasyu through these drops, freed from their hate may we obtain abundant food.

5 Let us obtain, O Indra, plenteous wealth and food, with strength exceeding glorious, shining to the sky.

May we obtain the Goddess Providence, the strength of heroes, special source of cattle, rich in steeds.

6 These our libations, strength-inspiring Soma draughts, gladdened thee in the fight with Vṛitra, Hero-Lord,

What time thou slewest for the singer with trimmed grass ten thousand Vṛitras, thou resistless in thy might.

Those who seem to sleep: Indra derives no advantage from those who are remiss in their religious duties.

6 *Ten thousand Vṛitras:* countless demons like Vṛitra.

7 Thou goest on from fight to fight intrepidly, destroying castle after castle here with strength ;
Thou Indra, with thy friend who makes the foe bow down, slewest from far away the guileful Namuchi.

8 Thou hast struck down in death Karanja, Parṇaya, in Atithigva's very glorious going forth :
Unyielding, when Ṛijiṣvan compassed them with siege, thou hast destroyed the hundred towns of Vangṛida.

9 With all-outstripping chariot wheel, O Indra, thou far-famed, hast overthrown the twice ten kings of men,
With sixty thousand nine-and-ninety followers, who came in arms to fight with friendless Suṣravas.

10 Thou hast protected Suṣravas with succour, and Tûrvayâṇa with thine aid, O Indra :
Thou madest Kutsa, Atithigva, Âyu subject unto this king, the young, the mighty.

11 May we protected by the Gods hereafter remain thy very prosperous friends, O Indra.
Thee we extol, enjoying through thy favour life long and joyful and with store of heroes.

---

7 *With thy friend* : the thunderbolt. Or *námyâ* may mean 'with Namî' as thy confederate.

Namuchi : 'non-looser (of the heavenly waters),' another demon of drought.

8 *Karanja, Parṇaya*, and *Vangṛida* are Asuras or demons ; *Atithigva* is another name of the liberal prince Divodâsa, and Ṛijiṣvan is a pious worshipper oppressed by Dasyus or barbarians. See Ṛ V. I. 51. 5, 6.

9 *Suṣravas*, and *Túrvayâṇa* in the next verse are said to be kings.

10 *Kutsa* is mentioned (Ṛ. V. I. 33. 14.) as a favourite of Indra, but is here represented, together with Atithigva and Âyu, as chastised by him.

This king : Suṣravas, or Tûrvayâṇa ; these names perhaps denote the same individual.

HYMN XXII.

Hero, the Soma being pressed I pour the juice for thee to drink :
Sate thee and finish thy carouse.

2 Let not the fools, or those who mock, beguile thee when they seek thine aid :
Love not the enemies of prayer.

3 Here let them with rich milky draught cheer thee to great munificence :
Drink as the wild bull drinks the lake.

4 Praise, even as he is known, with song Indra, the guardian of the kine,
The Son of Truth, Lord of the brave.

5 Hither his bay steeds have been sent, red steeds are on the sacred grass
Where we in concert sing our songs.

6 For Indra, Thunder-armed, the kine have yielded mingled milk and meath,
What time he found them in the vault.

HYMN XXIII.

Invoked to drink the Soma juice come with thy bay steeds, Thunder-armed !
Come, Indra, hitherward, to me.

2 Our priest is seated true to time ; the grass is regularly strewn ;
The pressing-stones were set at morn.

3 These prayers, O thou who hearest prayer, are offered. Seat thee on the grass.
Hero, enjoy the offered cake.

Stanzas 1—3 are taken from Ṛ. V. VIII. 45. 22—24, and stanzas 4—6 from VIII. 58. 4—6.

5 *Wild bull :* or Gaura ; the Bos Gaurus.

6 *In the vault :* 'in the cavity of the Soma vessel.'—von Roth ; 'on the horizon.'—Ludwig ; 'near at hand.'—Sâyaṇa.

The hymn is taken from Ṛ. V. III. 41.

4 O Vṛitra-slayer, be thou pleased with these libations, with these hymns,
Song-loving Indra, with our lauds.

5 Our hymns caress the Lord of Strength, vast, drinker of the Soma's juice,
Indra, as mother-cows their calf.

6 Delight thee with the juice we pour for thine own great munificence:
Yield not thy singer to reproach.

7 We, Indra, dearly loving thee, bearing oblation, sing thee hymns:
Thou, Vasu, dearly lovest us.

8 O thou to whom thy Bays are dear, loose not thy horses far from us:
Here glad thee, Indra, Lord Divine.

9 May long-maned coursers, dropping oil, bring thee on swift car hitherward,
Indra, to seat thee on the grass.

HYMN XXIV.

Come to the juice that we have pressed, to Soma, Indra! blent with milk:
Come, favouring us, thy bay-drawn car!

2 Come, Indra, to this gladdening drink, placed on the grass, pressed out with stones:
Wilt thou not drink thy fill thereof?

3 To Indra have my songs of praise gone forth, thus rapidly sent hence,
To turn him to the Soma-draught.

4 Hither with songs of praise we call Indra to drink the Soma juice:
Will he not come to us by lauds?

---

7 *Vasu*: or, Good Lord.

Taken from Ṛ. V. III. 42.

5 Indra, these Somas are expressed. Take them within thy belly, Lord
Of Hundred Powers, thou Prince of wealth.

6 We know thee winner of the spoil and resolute in battles, Sage!
Therefore thy blessing we implore.

7 Borne hither by thy stallions, drink, Indra, this juice which we have pressed,
Mingled with barley and with milk.

8 Indra, for thee in thine own place I urge the Soma for thy draught:
Deep in thy heart let it remain.

9 We call on thee, the Ancient One, Indra, to drink the Soma juice,
We Kuṣikas who seek thine aid.

HYMN XXV.

INDRA, the mortal man well guarded by thine aid goes foremost in the wealth of horses and of kine.
With amplest wealth thou fillest him, as round about the waters clearly seen afar fill Sindhu full.

2 The heavenly waters come not nigh the priestly bowl: they but look down and see how far mid-air is spread:
The Deities conduct the pious man to them: like suitors they delight in him who loveth prayer.

3 Praiseworthy blessing hast thou laid upon the pair who with uplifted ladle serve thee, man and wife.
Unchecked he dwells and prospers in thy law: thy power brings blessing to the sacrificer pouring gifts.

---

9 *Kuṣikas:* members of the family of Kuṣika the father or grandfather of the great Ṛishi Viṣvâmitra who is the seer of the hymn.

Stanzas 1—6 are taken from Ṛ. V. I. 83, and stanza 7 from X. 104. 3.

3 *Man and wife:* the text has only *mithunā́*, a couple. The word apparently means here the offerer of the sacrifice and his wife, who took part in the ceremony. Sâyaṇa explains it as the grain and the butter of oblation.

4 First the Angirases won themselves vital power, whose fires were kindled through good deeds and sacrifice.
The men together found the Paṇi's hoarded wealth, the cattle, and the wealth in horses and in kine.

5 Atharvan first by sacrifices laid the paths; then, guardian of the Law, sprang up the loving Sun.
Uṣanâ Kâvya drove the kine hither with him: let us with offerings honour Yama's deathless birth.

6 When sacred grass is trimmed to aid the auspicious work, or the hymn makes its voice of praise sound to the sky,
Where the stone rings as 'twere a singer skilled in laud,—Indra in truth delights when these come near to him.

7 To make thee start, a strong true draught I offer to thee the Bull, O thou whom bay steeds carry.
Here take delight, O Indra, in our voices while thou art hymned with power and all our spirit.

HYMN XXVI.

In every need, in every fray we call, as friends, to succour us
Indra the mightiest of all.

2 If he will hear us let him come with succour of a thousand kinds,
And all that strengthens, to our call.

---

4 *The Paṇi* is the illiberal demon who withholds the rain.

5 *The paths:* ways of communication between men and Gods. Uṣanâ Kâvya is the name of a celebrated ancient Ṛishi. The meaning of the latter half of the second verse is obscure. Ludwig renders it 'Seek we to win by sacrifice the immortality which has sprung from Yama.'

7 *To make thee start:* on the journey to visit us.

Stanzas 1—3 are taken from Ṛ. V. I. 30. 7—9, and stanzas 4—6 from I. 6. 1—3.

3 I call him, mighty to resist, the Hero of our ancient home,
Thee whom my sire invoked of old.

4 They who stand round him as he moves harness the bright, the ruddy steed:
The lights are shining in the sky.

5 On both sides of the car they yoke the two bay coursers dear to him,
Bold, tawny, bearers of the chief.

6 Thou, making light where no light was, and form, O Men! where form was not,
Wast born together with the Dawns.

HYMN XXVII.

If I, O Indra, were, like thee, the single sovran of all wealth.
My worshipper should be rich in kine.

2 I should be fain, O Lord of Might, to strengthen and enrich the sage,
Were I the lord of herds of kine.

3 To worshippers who press the juice thy goodness, Indra, is a cow
Yielding in plenty kine and steeds.

---

3 *Hero of our ancient home:* tutelary deity of our family.

4 *They who stand round: lokatrayavartinaḥ prâṇinaḥ,* 'the living beings of the three worlds,' is Sâyaṇa's explanation. Probably the Maruts, Indra's constant companions, are intended.

The bright, the ruddy steed (bradhnám arushám) is probably the Sun, with whom Indra is frequently connected.

5 *On both sides: vipakshasâ:* harnessed on different sides.

6 *Thou,* i. e. the Sun. *O Men!* is perhaps merely an exclamation expressive of admiration. If *maryâḥ*, men, be taken to mean the Maruts, the words *thou, making, wast born,* although in the singular number, may apply to these Gods regarded as one host or company and born at one birth. See M. Müller, Vedic Hymns, Part I., pp. 14 sqq., and cf. Ludwig, Ueber die neuesten Arbeiten auf dem Gebiete der Ṛigveda-forschung, p. 5. Prag, 1893.

Taken from Ṛ. V. VIII. 14. 1—6.

4 None is there, Indra, God or man, to hinder thy munificence,
The wealth which, lauded, thou wilt give.

5 The sacrifice made Indra strong when he unrolled the earth and made
Himself a diadem in heaven.

6 Thine aid we claim, O Indra, thine who after thou hast waxen great
Hast won all treasures for thine own.

HYMN XXVIII.

In Soma's ecstasy Indra spread the firmament and realms of light
When he cleft Vala limb from limb.

2 Showing the hidden he drave forth the cows for the Angirases,
And Vala he cast headlong down.

3 By Indra were the luminous realms of heaven established and secured
Firm and immovable in their place.

4 Indra, thy laud moves quickly like a joyous wave of water-floods.
Bright shine the drops that gladden thee.

HYMN XXIX.

For thou, O Indra, art the God whom hymns and praises magnify:
Thou blessest those who worship thee.

---

5 *Diadem: opaçám;* see Geldner, Vedische Studien, I. p. 133.

Taken from Ṛ. V. VIII. 14. 7—10, in continuation of the preceding hymn.

1 *Spread:* that is, made mid-air and heaven visible by releasing the imprisoned rays of light.

Taken, in continuation of the preceding hymn, from Ṛ. V. VIII. 14. 11—15.

2 Bay horses with their long manes bring Indra to drink the Soma juice,
The Bountiful to our sacrifice.

3 With waters' foam thou torest off, Indra, the head of Namuchi,
Subduing all contending hosts.

4 The Dasyus, when they fain would climb by magic arts and mount to heaven,
Thou, Indra, castest down to earth.

5 As Soma-drinker conquering all, thou scatteredst to every side
Their band who poured no gifts to thee.

HYMN XXX.

In the great synod will I laud thy two bay steeds: I prize the sweet strong drink of thee the Warrior-God,
His who pours lovely oil as 'twere with yellow drops.
Let my songs enter thee whose form hath golden tints.

2 Ye who in concert sing unto the gold-hued place, like bay steeds driving onward to the heavenly seat,
For Indra laud ye strength allied with tawny steeds, laud him whom cows content as 'twere with yellow drops.

---

3 *With waters' foam:* with a thunderbolt in the form of foam, according to a later legend. See Muir, O. S. Texts, V. p. 94. *Namuchi:* Non looser; Hold-fast; a demon slain by Indra. See Prof. Max Müller's remarks (Academy, Oct. 22, 1892, No. 1068) on Prof. Bloomfield's explanation of the story of Namuchi in his Contributions to the Interpretation of the Veda.

Taken from Ṛ. V. X. 96. 1—5. Throughout the hymn the poet rings the changes on words said to be derivatives of the root *hṛi* to take, as *haryatá*, delightful, *háryan*, loving, *hári*, bay or tawny, *harít*, green, yellow, or gold-coloured. These words are conjecturally explained by the Commentator, and are susceptible of various renderings.

1 *Oil:* fatness; fertilizing rain.

2 *Cows:* milked for sacrificial purposes.

3 His is that thunderbolt, of iron, golden-hued, gold-coloured, very dear, and yellow in his arms;
Bright with strong teeth, destroying with its tawny rage. In Indra are set fast all forms of golden hue.

4 As if a lovely ray were laid upon the sky, the golden thunderbolt spread out as in a race.
That iron bolt with yellow jaw smote Ahi down. A thousand flames had he who bore the tawny-hued.

5 Thou, thou, when praised by men who sacrificed of old, hadst pleasure in their lauds, O Indra golden-haired.
All that befits thy song of praise thou welcomest, the perfect pleasant gift, O golden-hued from birth.

HYMN XXXI.

THESE two dear Bays bring hither Indra on his car, thunder-armed, joyous, meet for laud, to drink his fill.
Many libations flow for him who loveth them: to Indra have the gold-hued Soma juices run.

2 The gold-hued drops have flowed to gratify his wish: the yellow drops have urged the swift Bays to the Strong.
He who speeds on with bay steeds even as he lists hath satisfied his longing for the golden drops.

3 At the swift draught the Soma-drinker waxed in might, the iron One with yellow beard and golden hair.
He, Lord of tawny coursers, Lord of fleet-foot mares, will bear his bay steeds safely over all distress.

---

3 *Tawny rage*: perhaps with reference to the effects of anger on the colour of the face.—Ludwig.

4 *The tawny-hued*: the thunderbolt wielded by Indra.

Taken, in continuation of the preceding hymn, from Ṛ. V. X. 96. 6—10.

2 *The Strong*: to Indra; that they may be harnessed and carry him to the sacrifice.

3 *The iron One*: 'iron-hearted Indra.'—Wilson.

4 His yellow-coloured jaws, like ladles, move apart, what time, for strength, he makes the yellow-tinted stir,
When, while the bowl stands there, he grooms his tawny steeds, when he hath drunk strong drink, the sweet juice that he loves.

5 Yea, to the dear one's seat in homes of heaven and earth the bay steeds' Lord hath whinnied like a horse for food.
Then the great wish hath seized upon him mightily, and the belovèd One hath gained high power of life.

HYMN XXXII.

Thou, comprehending with thy might the earth and heaven, acceptest the dear hymn for ever new and new.
O Asura, disclose thou and make visible the Cow's belovèd home to the bright golden Sun.

2 O Indra, let the eager wishes of the folk bring thee the golden-jawed, delightful, on thy car.
That, pleased with sacrifice wherein ten fingers toil, thou mayest at the feast drink of our offered mead.

3 Juices aforetime, Lord of Bays, thou drankest, and thine, and only thine, is this libation.
Gladden thee, Indra, with the mead-rich Soma: pour it down ever, Mighty One, within thee.

---

4 *For strength:* for strengthening food. *The yellow-tinted:* his yellow jaws.

5 *The dear one:* the Soma, found both in heaven and on earth, the homes of Gods and men. According to Sâyaṇa, Indra himself is meant. *The belovèd One:* Indra, whose vital vigour is quickened and increased by the Soma libations which he drinks.

Taken, in continuation of the preceding hymn, from the concluding verses, 11—13, of Ṛ. V. X. 96.

1 *The Cow's belovèd home:* the cow may be the sun, whose home is the universe which Indra will allow Sûrya to illuminate.

2 *Sacrifice:* according to Sâyaṇa, the sacrificial Soma juice which is pressed out, purified, and prepared by the fingers of the priest.

HYMN XXXIII.

DRINK of the juice which men have washed in waters and fill thee full, O Lord of tawny horses.
O Indra, hearer of the laud, with Soma which stones have mixed for thee enhance thy rapture.

2 To make thee start, a strong true draught I offer to thee the Bull, O thou whom bay steeds carry.
Here take delight, O Indra, in our voices while thou art hymned with power and all our spirit.

3 O mighty Indra, through thine aid, thy prowess, obtaining life, zealous, and skilled in worship,
Men in the house who share the sacred banquet stand singing praise that brings them store of children.

HYMN XXXIV.

HE who, just born, chief God of lofty spirit, by power and might became the Gods' protector,
Before whose breath, through greatness of his valour, the two worlds trembled, He, O men, is Indra.

2 He who fixed fast and firm the earth that staggered, and set at rest the agitated mountains,
Who measured out air's wider middle region and gave the heaven support, He, men, is Indra.

3 Who slew the Dragon, freed the Seven Rivers, and drave the kine forth from the cave of Vala,
Begat the fire between both stones, the spoiler in warriors' battle, He, O men, is Indra.

Taken from Ṛ. V. X. 104. 2—4.

True: effectual; which produces the result expected in the shape of favour. The stanza is found also in Hymn 25. 7 of this Book.

The hymn is a repetition, with three additional stanzas, of Ṛ. V. II. 12.

2 *Wider:* in consequence of the separation of heaven and earth.

3 *The Dragon:* the great serpent Ahi, the chief of the demons of drought. *Fire between both stones:* that is, the lightning between heaven and earth.

4 By whom this universe was made to tremble, who chased away the humbled brood of demons,
Who, like a gambler gathering his winnings, seized the foe's riches, He, O men, is Indra.

5 Of whom, the terrible, they ask, Where is He? or verily they say of him, He is not.
He wastes the foeman's wealth like stakes of gamblers. Have faith in him for He, O men, is Indra.

6 Stirrer to action of the poor and lowly, of priest, of suppliant who sings his praises;
Who, fair-faced, favours him who presseth Soma with stones adjusted, He, O men, is Indra.

7 He under whose supreme control are horses, all chariots, and the hamlets, and the cattle;
He who begat the Sun, begat the Morning, leader of waters, He, O men, is Indra.

---

4 *Brood of demons: dâsam várṇam;* literally, the Dâsa, demon or hostile, colour; the dusky savage inhabitants whom the Âryan immigrants classed with demons.

Cf. 'One and another say, There is no Indra. Who hath beheld him?' (R̥. V. VIII. 89. 3).

5 'Indra never commanded the permanent allegiance of all the other Gods, like Zeus and Jupiter; nay, we know from the Veda itself that there were sceptics, even at that early time, who denied that there was any such thing as Indra' (M. Müller, India, What can it Teach us? p. 180).

6 *Of the poor:* the meaning of the word *radhrá* is uncertain. Prof. M. Müller (R̥. V. II. 34. 15) translates it by 'the wretched' and (R̥. V. VII. 16. 20) 'the sluggard.' Sâyaṇa gives the double explanation, rich and righteous, and Prof. Peterson follows the authors of the Siebenzig Lieder in adopting the first of these interpretations although it will hardly suit other passages in which the word occurs. For a full discussion of *radhrá*, see Pischel, Vedische Studien, I. p. 124.

7 *The hamlets: grấmâḥ;* 'die bewaffneten scharen,' armed bands of foot-soldiers, according to Prof. Ludwig; *grâma* meaning a troop of men as well as a collection of houses. *Leader of waters:* sender of the periodical Rains.

8 To whom both armies cry in close encounter, foe against foe, the stronger and the weaker;
Whom two invoke upon one chariot mounted, each for himself, He, O ye men, is Indra.

9 He, without whom men conquer not in battle, whom, warring, they invoke for help and succour;
He, all this universe's type and image, who shakes what never shook, He, men, is Indra.

10 He who hath smitten, ere they knew their danger, with his hurled weapon many grievous sinners;
Who pardons not his boldness who provokes him, who slays the Dasyu, He, O men, is Indra.

11 He who discovered in the fortieth autumn Ṣambara dwelling in the midst of mountains;
Who slew the Dragon putting forth his vigour, the demon lying there, He, men, is Indra.

12 Who drank the juice poured at the seat of Order, subduing Ṣambara by superior prowess,
Who hoarded food within the mountain's hollow wherein he grew in strength, He, men, is Indra.

13 Who, with seven guiding reins, the Bull, the mighty, set the Seven Rivers free to flow at pleasure;
Who, thunder-armed, rent Rauhiṇa in pieces when scaling heaven, He, O ye men, is Indra.

---

8 *Both armies: krándasî;* taken by some in the same sense as *ródasî*, heaven and earth. *Two:* the warrior and the charioteer.

11 *Ṣambara:* a demon of drought. *Mountains:* thick clouds.

12 The stanza is not taken from the Ṛigveda; and the manuscripts on which the printed text is based are corrupt and unintelligible as they stand.

13 *With seven guiding reins:* 'to guide him.'—Peterson. With seven bright rays (mit siben stralen), according to Ludwig, which are explained by Sâyaṇa as seven forms of Indra. *Rauhiṇa:* regarded as a demon; originally, like the other fiends of drought, a dark purple cloud that withholds the seasonable rain.

14 Heaven, even, and the earth bow down before him,
before his very breath the mountains tremble.
Known as the Soma-drinker, armed with thunder,
the wielder of the bolt, He, men, is Indra.

15 Who aids with favour him who pours the Soma,
and him who brews it, sacrificer, singer;
Whose strength our prayer and offered Soma heighten, and this our gift, He, O ye men, is Indra.

16 Born, manifested in his Parents' bosom, He knoweth
as a son the Highest Father.
He who with vigorous energy assisted the companies
of Gods, He, men, is Indra.

17 Lord of Bay Steeds, who loves the flowing Soma,
He before whom all living creatures tremble;
He who smote Śambara and slaughtered Śushṇa, He
the Sole Hero, He, O men, is Indra.

18 Thou verily art true, strong God who sendest wealth
to the man who brews and pours libation.
So may we evermore, thy friends, O Indra, address
the synod with brave sons about us.

HYMN XXXV.

To him, to him swift, strong, and high-exalted, I
bring my song of praise as dainty viands;
My thought to him resistless, meet for praises, prayers offered most devotedly to Indra.

---

16 This and the following stanza are not taken from the Ṛigveda. *Parents:* Heaven and Earth. *Highest Father:* Dyaus or Heaven.

17 *Śushṇa:* 'the Drier up'; the demon who represents the excessive heat and drought that precedes the fall of the periodical Rains.

The hymn is a reproduction of Ṛ. V. I. 61.

1 *Thought: óham:* devout meditation in the shape of a hymn; from the root *ûh*, to reflect. According to Sâyaṇa, the meaning is 'conveyable,' from *vah*, to carry. See Bergaigne, La Religion Védique, II. p. 288, note.

2 To him I offer praise as choice refreshment, bring forth my song, with seemly laud besiege him.
For Indra, Lord of olden time, the singers shall deck their hymns with heart and mind and spirit.

3 To him then with my lips my song of praises, excellent, winning heavenly light, I offer,
To magnify with hymns of invocation and eulogies the Lord, most bounteous Giver.

4 Even for him I frame a laud—so fashions the wright a chariot for the man who needs it—
Songs for wise Indra hymned with invocation, a song composed with care and all-impelling.

5 So with my tongue I deck, to please that Indra, my hymn as 'twere a horse, through love of glory,
To reverence the Hero, bounteous Giver, famed far and wide, destroyer of the castles.

6 Even for him hath Tvashṭar forged the thunder, most deftly wrought, celestial, for the battle,
Wherewith he reached the vital parts of Vṛitra, striking—the vast, the mighty—with the striker.

7 As soon as, at libations of his mother, great Vishṇu had drunk up the draught, he plundered
The dainty cates, the cooked mess; but One stronger transfixed the wild boar, shooting through the mountain.

---

3 *With my lips:* with the service of the poet, as distinguished from that of ministering and superintending priests.

4 *For the man who needs it:* the exact meaning of *tátsinâya* is uncertain. Wilson renders it, after Sâyaṇa, by '(that the driver) may, thence, (obtain) food.' Grassmann follows the interpretation of the St. Petersburg Lexicon which I also adopt. Ludwig's explanation (Der Rigveda, V. pp. 18, 19) is different.

5 *Castles:* strongholds of the drought-demons of the air, the massive clouds which withhold the seasonable rain.

6 *The striker:* the thunderbolt; the weapon of Indra as it was of Zeus and Jupiter. Ramman, the Assyrian God of the air, is similarly armed; and Bel-Merodach bears a double trident, representing lightning, with which he overthrows the dragon Tiamat.

7 This verse is difficult. Sâyaṇa, Wilson, Benfey, and Grassmann take *víshṇuḥ* to be an appellative or epithet of Indra, and render the

8 To him, to Indra when he slew the Dragon, the Dames too, Consorts of the Gods, wove praises.
The mighty heaven and earth hath he encompassed: thy greatness heaven and earth, combined, exceed not.

9 Yea, of a truth, his magnitude surpasseth the magnitude of earth, mid-air and heaven.
Indra whom all men praise, the Sovran Ruler, waxed in his home loud-voiced and strong for battle.

10 Through his own strength with bolt of thunder Indra smote piece-meal Vṛitra, drier up of waters.
He let the floods go free, like cows imprisoned, for glory, with a heart inclined to bounty.

---

word, respectively, by *sarvasya jagato vyâpakaḥ*, the pervader of the universe, the hero, the active. Sâyaṇa explains *pachatám* (dressed, cooked) as the ripe treasure of the Asuras—an explanation which is not supported by the text and is merely founded on a later legend. Benfey understands *pachatám* to mean the thunderbolt in preparation, which, he thinks, Indra stole from the heavenly maker (*mâtúḥ*) or artist Tvashṭar. Muir (O. S. Texts, IV. 67) translates: 'Having at the libations of that great measurer [of the worlds, *i. e.* Indra], drunk the potion, and [eaten] the pleasant oblations, the impetuous Vishṇu straightway stole the cooked mess, pierced the boar and shot through the mountain.' Ludwig would prefer to read *bhrâtuḥ*, brother, instead of *mâtúḥ* (which in the first edition of my Hymns of the Ṛigveda I have rendered, according to its etymological derivation, by Maker), and thinks that if *mâtúḥ* must be retained it must mean the mother of Vṛitra. The simplest and best way is to take 'libations of his mother' to mean the Soma given by his mother to Indra at his birth Cf. Ṛ. V. III 48. 2, 3; VII. 98. 3. See Royal Asiatic Society's Journal, January, 1895, pp. 181 sqq. where the stanza and the whole legend are thoroughly discussed by Prof. A. A. Macdonell.

See also Bergaigne, La Religion Védique, III. 60, where the verse is differently translated and explained. The general meaning appears to be either that Indra strengthened himself by consuming certain sacrificial offerings, and then hurled his bolt through the mountain of cloud and pierced the wild boar, the demon Vṛitra; or that Vishṇu ate the food and left to Indra the task of slaying Vṛitra. I agree with Ludwig in preferring the latter interpretation.

8 *The Dames:* according to Sâyaṇa, the Gâyatrî and other personified metres of the Veda. The deified Waters of heaven may be intended.

11 Through his resplendent power still stood the rivers
when with his bolt on every side he stayed them.
With lordly might, favouring him who worshipped,
he made a ford, victorious, for Turvîti.

12 Vast, with thine ample power, with eager movement
against this Vṛitra cast thy bolt of thunder.
Rend thou his joints, as of an ox dissevered, with
bolt oblique that floods of rain may follow.

13 Sing with new lauds his exploits wrought aforetime,
the deeds of him, yea, him who moveth swiftly,
When, hurling forth his weapons in the battle, he
with impetuous wrath lays low the foemen.

14 When he, yea, he is born the firm-set mountains and
the whole heaven and earth tremble in terror.
May Nodhas ever lauding the protection of this dear
Friend win straightway strength heroic.

15 Now unto him of these things hath been given what
he, who rules alone o'er much, electeth.
Indra helped Etaṣa, the Soma-presser, contending in
the chariot-race with Sûrya.

---

11 *The rivers:* meaning here the waters of earth. *Turvîti:* a hero frequently mentioned in the Ṛigveda as having been protected and aided by the special intervention of Indra. Cf. 'Thou for Turvîti heldest still the flowing floods, the river-stream for Vâyya easily to pass' (Ṛ. V. II. 13. 12); and 'Thou for the sake of Vâyya, for Turvîti, didst stay the great stream, flowing, all sustaining' (Ṛ. V. IV. 19. 6). Prof. Max Müller observes (India, What can it Teach us? p. 181) "This is not very different from the Psalmist (lxxviii. 13): 'He divided the sea, and caused them to pass through; and he made the waters to stand as an heap.'"

14 *Nodhas:* the Ṛishi or inspired seer to whom the hymn was revealed.

15 Praises and sacrifice have been offered to Indra. He himself possesses all besides. Such offerings induced Indra to help Etaṣa his worshipper in a contest with Sûrya—an allusion, perhaps, to an eclipse of the sun. Or Sûrya may possibly be a man's name, and, as Sâyaṇa says, the word rendered by 'in the race of steeds' (*saúvaṣvye*) may be a patronymic, son of Svaṣva (Lord of Good Horses) qualifying *sûrya*. See Bergaigne, La Religion Védique, III. 331.

16 Thus to thee, Indra, yoker of bay coursers, the Gotamas have brought their prayers and praises.
Bestow upon them thought, decked with all beauty.
May he, enriched with prayer, come soon and early.

HYMN XXXVI.

WITH these my hymns I glorify that Indra who is alone to be invoked by mortals,
The Lord, the Mighty One, of manly vigour, victorious, Hero, true, and full of wisdom.

2 Our ancient sires, Navagvas, sages seven, while urging him to show his might, extolled him,
Dweller on heights, swift smiting down opponents, guileless in word, and in his thoughts most mighty.

3 We seek that Indra to obtain his riches that yield much food, and men, and store of heroes.
O Lord of Bay Steeds, bring, to make us joyful, celestial wealth, abundant, undecaying.

4 Declare to us—if at thy hand aforetime the earlier singers have obtained good fortune—
What is thy share and portion, strong Subduer, Asura-slayer, rich, invoked of many?

5 He who for car-borne, thunder-wielding Indra, hath a hymn, craving, deeply-piercing, fluent,

---

16 *Gotamas:* descendents of Gotama, men of the family of which the Rishi of the hymn is a member. *He, enriched with prayer:* Indra, invoked by many worshippers, or enriched by the hymn that has just been recited. This final pâda forms the burden of the hymns ascribed to Nodhas. See Vedic Hymns (Sacred Books of the East, XXXII), Part I. pp. 124, 125.

R. V. VI. 22.

2 *Navagvas:* see XIV. 1. 56; XVIII. 1. 58; 3. 20. They are here, apparently, identified with the Angirases.

4 *What is thy share and portion:* due to thee by thy worshippers. What must we offer to thee in order that we may obtain such favour as thou hast shown to our predecessors?

5 The construction of the stanza is complicated and obscure. See Ludwig, Der Rigveda, V. 108. *Comes near the mighty:* 'encounters (with confidence) the malevolent.'—Wilson.

Who sends a song effectual, firmly-grasping, and strength-bestowing, he comes near the mighty.

6 Strong of thyself! thou with this art hast shattered with thought-swift Parvata, him who waxed against thee;
And, Mightiest! rager! boldly rent in pieces things that were firmly fixed and never shaken.

7 Him will we fit for you with new devotion, the strongest, Ancient One, in ancient manner.
So may that Indra, boundless, faithful leader, conduct us o'er all places hard to traverse.

8 Thou for the people who oppress hast kindled the earthly firmament and that of heaven.
With heat, O Bull, on every side consume them: heat earth and flood for him who hates devotion.

9 Of all the heavenly folk, of earthly creatures, thou art the King, O God of splendid aspect.
In thy right hand, O Indra, grasp the thunder: Eternal! thou destroyest all enchantments.

10 Give us confirmed prosperity, O Indra, vast and exhaustless for the foes' subduing.
Strengthen therewith the Ârya's hate and Dâsa's; and let the arms of Nahushas be mighty.

11 Come with thy teams which bring all blessings, hither, disposer, much-invoked, exceeding holy!
Come to me swiftly with these teams of coursers, these which no fiend, no God may stay or hinder.

---

6 *Parvata:* the Genius of mountains and mountain-like clouds, frequently associated with Indra. According to Sâyaṇa *(bahuparvaṇâ vajreṇa)*, the many-knotted thunderbolt is intended. *Him who waxed against thee:* Vṛitra.

8 *The people who oppress:* Râkshasas and human enemies.

10 *Nahushas:* people, apparently distinct from the five Âryan tribes *par excellence*, and dwellers on or near the Indus. The St. Petersburg Lexicon explains the word as meaning men generally, but with the special sense of strangers or neighbours. See Muir, O. S. Texts, I. 179, 180.

HYMN XXXVII.

HE, like a bull with sharpened horns, terrific, singly excites and agitates all the people.
Thou givest him who largely pours libation his wealth who pours not, for his own possession.

2 Thou verily, Indra, gavest help to Kutsa, willingly lending ear to him in battle,
When, aiding Ârjuneya, thou subduedst to him both Kuyava and the Dâsa Sushṇa.

3 O Bold One, thou with all thine aids hast boldly holpen Sudâs whose offerings were accepted,
Pûru in winning land and slaying foemen, and Trasadasyu son of Purukutsa.

4 At the Gods' banquet, Hero-souled! with heroes, Lord of Bay Steeds, thou slewest many Vṛitras.
Thou sentest in swift death to sleep the Dasyu, both Chumuri and Dhuni, for Dabhîti.

5 These were thy mighty powers that, Thunder-wielder! thou swiftly crushedst nine-and-ninety castles.
Thou capturedst the hundredth in thine onslaught; thou slewest Namuchi, thou slewest Vṛitra.

Ṛ. V. VII. 19. The hymn is ascribed to the Ṛishi Vasishṭha.

1 *Excites and agitates*: as God of Battles. *Thou*: Indra. This abrupt change from the third person to the second is not unusual in the Veda.

2 *Kutsa*: a Ṛishi favoured (and sometimes persecuted) by Indra, frequently mentioned in the Ṛigveda and the seer of some of its hymns. *Ârjuneya*: Kutsa, son of Ârjuni the son of Arjuna. *Kuyava*: Spoiler of Harvest; one of the demons of drought.

3 *Sudâs*: King of the Tṛitsus. See Ṛ. V. VII. 18. *Pûru*: a protégé of Indra; King or chief of the Pûrus. *Trasadasyu*: He before whom Dasyus tremble; a prince celebrated for his liberality and favoured and protected by the Gods. See Hymns of the Ṛigveda, III. Index.

4 *In swift death*: literally, easy to slay; *suhántu* being taken as a dual qualifying *chúmurim* and *dhúnim*. See Ludwig. *Chumuri and Dhuni*: demons. *Dabhîti*: a protégé of the Aṣvins and of Indra. Cf. 'Thou with sleep whelming Chumuri and Dhuni, slewest the Dasyu, keptest safe Dabhîti' (Ṛ. V. II. 15. 9).

6 Old are the blessings, Indra, which thou gavest Sudâs the worshipper who brought oblations.
For thee, the strong, I yoke thy strong bay horses: let them approach our prayers and wealth, Most Mighty!

7 Give us not up, Lord of Bay Horses, victor, in this our time of trouble, to the wicked.
Deliver us with true and faithful succour: dear may we be to thee among the princes.

8 May we men, Bounteous Lord, the friends thou lovest, near thee be joyful under thy protection.
Fain to fulfil the wish of Atithigva, bow Turvaṣa, bow down the son of Yadu.

9 Swiftly, in truth, O Bounteous Lord, about thee men skilled in hymning sing their songs and praises.
Elect us sharers of their love and friendship who by their calls on thee despoiled the niggards.

10 Thine are these lauds, O manliest of heroes, lauds which revert to us and give us riches.
Favour these, Indra, when they strike the foemen, as Friend and Hero and the heroes' helper.

11 Now, lauded for thine aid, heroic Indra, sped by our prayer, wax mighty in thy body.
To us apportion wealth and habitations. Ye Gods, protect us evermore with blessings.

---

8 *Atithigva:* probably a descendant of Sudâs who must have lived long before the composition of this hymn, as the favour shown him by Indra is spoken of as old in stanza 6. *Turvaṣa:* the eponymous hero of one of the great Âryan tribes. He is generally mentioned in connexion with Yadu who seems to have been his father or brother.

9 *Elect us:* that is, let us share the blessings which thou withholdest from the illiberal churls who offer no oblations, and givest to those who honour thee with prayer and sacrifice.

10 *Ye Gods:* the usual conclusion of the hymns of the Vasishṭhas.

HYMN XXXVIII.

Come, we have pressed the juice for thee. O Indra, drink this Soma here.
Sit thou on this my sacred grass.

2 O Indra, let thy long-maned Bays, yoked by prayer, bring thee hitherward.
Give ear and listen to our prayers.

3 We, Soma-bearing Brahmans, call thee, Soma-drinker, with thy friend,
We, Indra, bringing juice expressed.

4 Indra the singers with high praise, Indra reciters with their lauds,
Indra the choirs have glorified.

5 Indra hath ever close to him his two bay steeds and word-yoked car,
Indra the golden, Thunder-armed.

6 Indra hath raised the Sun aloft in heaven that he may see afar.
He burst the mountain for the kine.

HYMN XXXIX.

For you, from every side, we call Indra away from other men:
Ours, and none others', let him be.

Ṛ. V. VIII. 17. 1—3, and I. 7. 1—3.

2 *Yoked by prayer:* harnessed and bringing Indra to the sacrifice when the worshipper invokes him.

3 *Thy friend:* Indra's constant companion and ally, the thunderbolt. 'With suitable praise.'—Wilson.

4 *Choirs:* referring, perhaps, both to the singers of the *stotram* and the reciters of the *śastram.*

5 *Word-yoked:* either harnessed at Indra's mere word, or at the prayer of the worshipper as in stanza 2. *Golden:* richly decorated (*sarvâbharaṇabhûshitaḥ*) according to Sâyaṇa.

6 *The mountain:* the mountain-shaped mass of thick cloud in which the cows, which are sometimes the vanished rays of light and sometimes the waters of the seasonable rain are kept imprisoned by the malignant demons of darkness or drought.

Ṛ. V. I. 7. 10; VIII. 14. 7—10.

2 In Soma's ecstasy Indra spread the firmament and realms of light,
When he cleft Vala limb from limb.

3 Showing the hidden cows he drave them forth for the Angirases,
And Vala he cast headlong down.

4 By Indra were the luminous realms of heaven established and secured,
Firm and immovable from their place.

5 Indra, thy laud moves quickly like a joyous wave of waters : bright
Have shone the drops that gladden thee.

HYMN XL.

Mayest thou verily be seen coming by fearless Indra's side :
Both joyous, equal in your sheen.

2 With Indra's well-belovèd hosts, the blameless, hastening to heaven,
The sacrificer cries aloud.

3 Thereafter they, as is their wont, threw off the state of babes unborn,
Assuming sacrificial name.

---

3 *The hidden cows:* see the preceding hymn, stanza 6.

4 *Luminous realms:* or, lucid spheres.

Ṛ. V. I. 6. 7, 8, 4.

1 *Thou:* the Marut host. *Joyous:* or bringing gladness.

2 *The sacrificer cries aloud:* this is the interpretation given by Prof. Max Müller (Vedic Hymns, Part I p. 14), but it is not thoroughly convincing. According to Prof. Ludwig the meaning is 'The Warrior (Indra) sings triumphantly.'

3 *Threw off:* see Ludwig, Ueber die neuesten Arbeiten auf dem Gebiete der Ṛgveda-forschung. Prag: 1893. *Sacrificial:* by which they are to be addressed and worshipped. The Maruts are represented as bursting forth into active life and claiming the adoration due to Gods.

HYMN XLI.

WITH bones of Dadhyach for his arms, Indra, resistless in attack,
Struck nine-and-ninety Vṛitras dead.

2 He, searching for the horse's head, removed among the mountains, found
At Ṣaryaṇâvân what he sought.

3 Then verily they recognized the essential form of Tvashtar's Bull
Here in the mansion of the Moon.

R. V. I. 84. 13—15.

1 *Dadhyach:* or, in a later form, Dadhîcha, is said to have been a Rishi, son of Atharvan, he and his father being regarded as the earliest institutors of sacrifice. He is described as having had the head of a horse given to him by the Aṣvins in the place of his own which Indra had threatened to cut off if he disclosed to any one the mystic Madhuvidyâ—the knowledge of sweetness, that is, of the true nature of the Soma—which he had taught him. Dadhyach imparted this lore to the Aṣvins; and Indra thereupon cut off the supposititious head. With the bones of Dadhyach, or, as the legend says, the bones of this horse's head, converted into a thunderbolt, Indra slew the Vṛitras or demons who withheld the rain. The Vedic legend, which was modified and amplified in later times, may have been connected in its origin with that of Dadhikrâs who is often mentioned in the Veda and described as a kind of divine horse, probably a personification of the morning sun.

Dadhyach may be the old Moon whose bones, when he dies, become the stars with which Indra slays the fiends of darkness.

2 *He:* Indra. *The horse's head:* perhaps the last crescent of the dying Moon, supposed to be given to him by the Aṣvins, the Gods of morning twilight. *Removed among the mountains:* hidden in the morning clouds. *Ṣaryaṇâvân:* according to tradition, a lake and the adjoining district in Kurukshetra, near the modern Dillî or Delhi, a holy place in ancient times where Indra may be said to have found the horse's head—the dying crescent revived—at one of the New Moon sacrifices which were celebrated there.

3 *Tvashṭar's Bull:* apparently, the Sun. The meaning may be that when, after the Rains, the bright nights of moonlight came men recognized the fact that the light was borrowed from the sun.

The best commentary on these very obscure verses may be found in Ludwig's dissertation 'Ueber die neuesten Arbeiten auf dem Gebiete der Ṛgveda-forschung.'

HYMN XLII.

From Indra have I measured an eight-footed and nine-cornered song,
Delicate, faithful to the Law.

2 Indra, both worlds complained to thee when uttering thy fearful roar,
What time thou smotest Dasyus dead.

3 Arising in thy might thy jaws thou shookest, Indra, having quaffed
The Soma poured into the bowls.

HYMN XLIII.

Drive all our enemies away, smite down the foes who press around,
And bring the wealth for which we long;

2 O Indra, that which is concealed in firm strong place precipitous:
Bring us the wealth for which we long:

3 Great riches which the world of men shall recognize as sent by thee:
Bring us the wealth for which we long,

Ṛ. V. VIII. 65 (76. M. Müller). 12, 11, 10.

1 *From Indra:* originating in him as subject or inspirer. *Eight-footed:* the original hymn consists of triplets, each of which contains nine pâdas, parts or half-lines, of eight feet or syllables each. That is, the metre is Anushṭup, and the triplet contains three stanzas in that metre or nine octosyllabic pâdas.

2 *Complained:* terrified by the furious voice of their champion.

3 *Thy jaws thou shookest:* as a sign of having finished and enjoyed the draught.

Ṛ. V. VIII. 45. 40—42.

2 *Firm strong place precipitous:* with reference, probably, to the custom of concealing treasures in deep cavities of the rocks and in the sides of wells.

HYMN XLIV.

Praise Indra whom our songs must laud, great Sovran of mankind, the Chief
Most liberal who controlleth men.

2 In whom the hymns of praise delight, and all the glory-giving songs,
Like the floods' longing for the sea.

3 Him I invite with eulogy, best King, effective in the fight,
Strong for the gain of mighty spoil.

HYMN XLV.

This is thine own. Thou drawest near, as the dove turneth to his mate.
Thou carest too for this our prayer.

2 O Hero, Lord of Bounties, praised in hymns, may power and pleasantness
Be his who sings the laud to thee.

3 Lord of a Hundred Powers, stand up to lend us succour in this fight:
In others too let us agree.

HYMN XLVI.

Him who advances men to wealth, sends light to lead them in their wars,
And quells their foemen in the fray:

Ṛ. V. VIII. 16. 1—3.

Ṛ. V. I. 30. 4—6.

1 *This is thine own:* this Soma libation belongs especially to thee.

2 *Our prayer:* neither offering nor prayer being acceptable without the other.

3 *In this fight:* the original hymn being a prayer for aid in an expected battle.

Ṛ. V. VIII. 16. 10—12.

2 May he, the saviour much-invoked, may Indra bear us in a ship
Safely beyond all enemies.

3 As such, O Indra, honour us with wealth and treasure : further us,
And lead us to felicity.

HYMN XLVII.

We make this Indra show his strength, to strike the mighty Vṛitra dead :
A vigorous Hero shall he be.

2 Indra was made for giving, most powerful, friendly in carouse,
Bright, meet for Soma, famed in song.

3 By song, as 'twere, the mighty bolt, which none may parry, was prepared :
Lofty, invincible he grew.

10 They who stand round him as he moves harness the bright, the ruddy Steed :
The lights are shining in the sky.

11 They yoke on both sides to the car the two bay coursers dear to him,
Bold, tawny, bearers of the Chief.

Ṛ. V. VIII. 82 (93, M. Müller). 7—9; I. 7. 1—3; VIII. 17. 1—3; I. 6. 1—3; I. 50. 1—9.

3 *By song:* 'in, or out of, a mountain,' according to Ludwig.

Stanzas 4—6 are repeated from Hymn 38. 4—6, and stanzas 7—9 from 1—3 of the same hymn. Stanzas 10—12 = Hymn 26. 4—6.

10 *They who stand round: lokatrayavartinaḥ prâṇinaḥ,* the living beings of the three worlds, according to Sâyaṇa's explanation. The Maruts, Indra's constant companions, are probably intended. But see Ludwig, Ueber die neuesten Arbeiten auf dem Gebiete der Ṛgvedaforschung, p. 5. *The ruddy Steed:* the Sun, with whom Indra, as God of the bright day, is intimately connected.

11 *Chief:* or Hero; Indra.

12 Thou, making light where no light was, and form, O Men! where no form was,
Wast born together with the Dawns.

13 His bright rays bear him up aloft, the God who knoweth all that is,
Sûrya, that every one may see.

14 The constellations pass away, like thieves, together with their beams,
Before the all-beholding Sun.

15 His herald rays are seen afar refulgent o'er the world of men,
Like fiery flames that burn and blaze.

16 Swift and all-beautiful art thou, O Sûrya, maker of the light,
Illuming all the radiant realm.

17 Thou goest to the troops of Gods, thou comest hither to mankind,
Hither, all light for us to see.

18 Thou with that eye of thine wherewith thou seest, brilliant Varuṇa,
The active one throughout mankind,

19 Pervadest heaven and wide mid-air, meting the days out with thy beams,
Sun, seeing all things that have birth.

20 Seven bay steeds, harnessed to thy car, bear thee, O thou far-seeing One,
God, Sûrya, thee with radiant hair.

---

12 *Thou:* the Sun. *O Men!:* perhaps, merely an exclamation expressive of admiration. If *maryâḥ*, men, be taken to mean the Maruts, the words, *thou, making, wast born*, although in the singular number, may apply to these Gods regarded as one host and born at one birth. See Max Müller, Vedic Hymns, Part I. p. 30.

13 *That every one may see:* according to Bergaigne (La Religion Védique, I. p. 8, that he may look on all.

18 *Brilliant Varuṇa:* identified with the Sun-God. The word *varuṇa* is, according to Sâyaṇa, used here as an appellative applied to Sûrya. Sâyaṇa explains it as *anishṭanivâraka*, averter of evil.

21 Sûrya hath yoked the seven bright mares, the daughters of the car: with these,
His own dear team, he travelleth.

HYMN XLVIII.

THE swiftly-moving songs of praise pour on thee streams of vital strength
As mother cows refresh the calf.

2 Swift move the bright ones while they blend the milk with vital vigour, as
A dame her infant with her heart.

3 Fair hymns bring glory to the Strong, and Indra-vigour; unto me
Fatness and milk and length of days.

4 This brindled Bull hath come and sat before the Mother in the east,
Advancing to the Father Heaven.

5 As expiration from his breath she moves along the lucid spheres:
The Bull shines forth through all the sky.

6 Song is bestowed upon the Bird. It reigns supreme through thirty realms
Throughout the days at break of morn.

---

21 *Daughters of the car*: cf. Tennyson's 'daughters of the plough' (The Princess).

Stanzas 1—3 are not taken from the Ṛigveda. The manuscripts on which the printed text is based are corrupt and unintelligible as they stand; and the translation is only a conjectural rendering of partly conjectural readings. Stanzas 4—6 are a reproduction of Ṛ. V. X. 189, which appears, with variations, in A. V. VI. 31.

4 *This brindled Bull*: the Sun. *The Mother*: Dawn.

The Bird: the Sun. His morning song, representing prayer, is supreme in power through all the regions of the world. According to Ludwig, the reference is to the thirty-three Gods, *thirty* standing for that number.

HYMN XLIX.

WHEN voices, fain to win mid-air, ascended to the Mighty One,
The vigorous God was filled with joy.

2 Praise with the voice the Mighty, praise the awful with the voice: in heaven
He, the most bounteous, hath been glad.

3 Praise with the voice the Mighty: he rules in each realm. In transport he
Hath sat upon the sacred grass.

4 As cows low to their calf in stalls, so with our songs we glorify
This Indra, even your wondrous God who checks attack, who joys in the delightful juice.

5 Celestial, bounteous Giver, God, with power and might, rich, mountain-like, in precious things,
Him soon we seek for foodful booty rich in kine, brought hundredfold and thousandfold.

6 I crave of thee that hero strength—that thou mayst first regard this prayer—
Wherewith thou holpest Bhṛigu and the Yatis and Praskaṇva when the prize was staked.

7 Wherewith thou sentest mighty waters to the sea—Indra, that manly strength of thine.
For ever unattainable is this power of him to whom the worlds have cried aloud.

Stanzas 1—3 are not taken from the Ṛigveda. The text has been conjecturally restored by von Roth and Whitney from the corrupt readings of the manuscripts. Stanzas 4, 5 are taken from Ṛ. V. VIII. 77. 1, 2; and stanzas 6, 7 from Ṛ. V. VIII. 3. 9, 10.

4 *Cows:* whose calves are shut up, while the mothers are being milked for sacrificial purposes.

6 *Bhṛigu:* see II. 5. 3; V. 19. 1. *Yatis:* an ancient family of ascetics connected with the Bhṛigus, and, according to one legend, said to have taken part in the creation of the world. *Praskaṇva:* a Ṛishi, Kaṇva's son, to whom some hymns of the Ṛigveda are ascribed.

7 *The worlds:* all men, or all living creatures.

HYMN L.

What newest of imploring hymns shall, then, the zealous mortal sing?
For have not they who laud his might and Indra-power won for themselves the light of heaven?

2 When shall they keep the Law and praise thee mid the Gods? Who counts as Ṛishi and as sage?
When wilt thou ever, Indra, Bounteous Lord, come nigh to presser's or to praiser's call?

HYMN LI.

For you will I sing Indra's praise who gives good gifts as well we know;
Praise of the Bounteous Lord who, rich in treasure, aids his singers with wealth thousandfold.

2 As with a hundred hosts he rushes boldly on, and for the offerer slays his foes.
As from a mountain flow the water-brooks, thus flow his gifts who feedeth many a one.

3 Ṣakra I praise, for victory, far-famed, exceeding bountiful,
Who gives, as 'twere in thousands, precious wealth to him who sheds the juice and worships him.

4 Arrows with hundred points, unconquerable, are this Indra's mighty arms in war.
He streams on liberal worshippers like a hill with springs, when juices poured have gladdened him.

Ṛ. V. VIII. 3. 13, 14.

2 *Mid the Gods:* or, as Ludwig takes it, 'in göttlichkeit,' in their quality of divine priests. The questions are rhetorical: now is the time to praise thee; the present singers are Ṛishis and sages; and this is the time for thee to come to the invocation of those who are pouring the Soma and offering praises to thee.

Ṛ. V. Vâlakhilya, 1. 1, 2; 2. 1, 2 (VIII. 49. 1, 2; 50. 1, 2, Max Müller).

2 *As with a hundred hosts:* 'like a weapon with a hundred edges.'—Cowell.

HYMN LII.

We compass thee like waters, we whose grass is trimmed and Soma pressed.
Here where the filter pours its stream thy worshippers round thee, O Vṛitra-slayer, sit.

2 Men, Vasu! by the Soma, with lauds call thee to the foremost place.
When comest thou athirst unto the juice as home, O Indra, like a bellowing bull?

HYMN LIII.

Who knows what vital power he wins, drinking beside the flowing juice?
This is the fair-cheeked God who, joying in the draught, breaks down the castles in his strength.

2 As a wild elephant rushes on, this way and that way, mad with heat,
None may restrain thee; yet come hither to the draught: thou movest mighty in thy power.

3 When he, the mighty, ne'er o'erthrown, stedfast, made ready for the fight,
When Indra, Bounteous Lord, lists to his praiser's call, he will not stand aloof, but come.

HYMN LIV.

Of one accord they made and formed for kingship Indra, the Hero who in all encounters overcometh,
Most eminent for power, destroyer in the conflict, fierce and exceeding strong, stalwart and full of vigour.

Ṛ. V. VIII. 33. 1, 2.

1 *Like waters:* as waters surround an islet. *Stream:* of Soma juice.

2 *Vasu:* or, Good Lord. *As home:* as familiar to thee as thine own dwelling-place in heaven.

Taken from Ṛ. V. VIII. 33. 7—9.

Taken from Ṛ. V. VIII. 86. (M. Müller, 97). 10—12.

1 *They:* the Gods.

2 Bards joined in song to Indra so that he might drink the Soma juice,
The Lord of Light, that he whose laws stand fast might aid with power and with the help he gives.
3 The holy sages form a ring, looking and singing to the Ram.
Your very bright inciters, void of all deceit, are with the chanters nigh to hear.

HYMN LV.

Oft, oft I call that Indra, Maghavan the mighty, who evermore possesses power, ever resistless.
Holy, most liberal, may he lead us on to riches, and, thunder-armed, make all our pathways pleasant for us.
2 Indra, what joys as Lord of Light thou broughtest from the Asuras,
Prosper therewith, O Maghavan, him who lauds that deed, and those whose grass is trimmed for thee.
3 The wasteless share of steeds and kine which, Indra, thou hast fast secured,
Grant to the worshipper who presses Soma and gives guerdon, not unto the churl.

HYMN LVI.

Indra, foe-slayer, hath been raised to joy and power by the men.
Him, verily, we invocate in battles whether great or small: be he our aid in fights for spoil.

---

3 *The Ram:* Indra the Warrior God; the fighting ram being the type of pugnacity. Cf. Ṛ. V. I. 10. 2; 51. 1; 52. 1. According to Sâyaṇa the reference is to a legend which says that Indra came in the form of a ram to Medhâtithi's sacrifice and drank the Soma juice which that Ṛishi had prepared. See Ṛ. V. VIII. 2. 40.

Taken from Ṛ V. VIII. 86. 13, 1, 2.

2 *Joys:* joy-giving riches. *Asuras:* from the powerful Râkshasas or demons, according to Sâyaṇa.

Taken from Ṛ. V. I. 81. 1—3. 7—9.

1 *The men:* the ministering priests who exalt and strengthen Indra with libations of Soma.

2 For, Hero, thou art like a host, art giver of abundant prey.
Strengthening even the feeble, thou aidest the sacrificer, thou givest the worshipper ample wealth.

3 When war and battles are on foot, booty is laid before the bold.
Yoke thou thy wildly rushing Bays. Whom wilt thou slay and whom enrich? Do thou, O Indra, make us rich.

4 He, righteous-hearted, at each time of rapture gives us herds of kine.
Gather in both thy hands for us treasures of many hundred sorts. Sharpen thou us, and bring us wealth.

5 Refresh thee, Hero, with the juice outpoured for bounty and for strength.
We know thee Lord of ample store, to thee have sent our hearts' desires: be therefore our protector thou.

6 These people, Indra, keep for thee all that is worthy of thy choice.
Discover thou, as Lord, the wealth of men who offer up no gifts: bring thou to us this wealth of theirs.

HYMN LVII.

As a good cow to him who milks, we call the doer of fair deeds
To our assistance day by day.

2 Come thou to our libations, drink of Soma, Soma-drinker thou!
The rich One's rapture giveth kine.

---

6 *These people:* thy worshippers here.

Taken from R. V. I. 4. 1—3; III. 37. 8—11; II. 41. 10—12; VIII. 33. 7—9, 1—3.

2 The exhilaration produced by drinking the fermented Soma juice stimulates Indra's warlike energies and disposes him to give, out of his boundless riches, liberal rewards in the shape of cattle and other wealth to those who have worshipped him.

3 So may we be acquainted with thine innermost benevolence :

Neglect us not, come hitherward.

4 Drink for our help the Soma bright, vigilant, and exceeding strong,

O Indra, Lord of Hundred Powers.

5 O Ṣatakratu, powers which thou mid the Five Races hast displayed,

These, Indra, do I claim of thee.

6 Indra, great glory hast thou gained. Win splendid fame which none may mar.

We make thy might perpetual.

7 Come to us either from anear, or, Ṣakra, come from far away.

Indra, wherever be thy home, come thence, O Caster of the Stone.

8 Verily Indra, conquering all, driveth even mighty fear away.

For firm is he and swift to act.

9 Indra be gracious unto us: sin shall not reach us afterward,

And good shall be before us still.

10 From all the regions of the world let Indra send security,

The foe-subduer, swift to act.

14 We compass thee like waters, we whose grass is trimmed and Soma pressed.

Here where the filter pours its stream thy worshippers round thee, O Vṛitra-slayer, sit.

---

4 *Vigilant*. according to Sâyaṇa, Soma prevents sleep.

7 *Caster of the Stone:* Hurler of the thunderbolt.

14 Stanzas 11—13 = A. V. XX. LIII., and 14, 15 = XX. LII. *Filter:* the woollen strainer through which the Soma juice is run to purify it.

15 Men, Vasu, by the Soma with lauds call thee to the foremost place.
When comest thou athirst unto the juice as home, O Indra, like a bellowing bull?

16 Boldly, bold Hero, bring us spoil in thousands for the Kaṇvas' sake.
O active Maghavan, with eager prayer we crave the yellow-hued with store of kine.

HYMN LVIII.

TURNING, as 'twere, to meet the Sun, enjoy from Indra all good things.
When he who will be born is born with power we look to treasures as our heritage.

2 Praise him who sends us wealth, whose bounties injure none. Good are the gifts which Indra gives.
He is not wroth with one who satisfies his wish: he turns his mind to granting boons.

3 Verily, Sûrya, thou art great; truly, Âditya, thou art great.
As thou art great indeed thy greatness is admired: yea, verily, great art thou, O God.

4 Yea, Sûrya, thou art great in fame: thou evermore, O God, art great.
By greatness thou art President of Gods, divine, far-spread, inviolable light.

---

15 *Vasu:* or, Good Lord. *As home:* as familiar and dear to thee as thine own dwelling-place in heaven.

16 *The yellow-hued:* gold; the substantive is not expressed.

Ṛ. V. VIII. 88 (M. Müller, 99). 3, 4; 90 (M. M. 101). 11, 12.

1 This stanza is difficult and obscure. Mahîdhara's explanation is: 'The gathering (rays) proceeding to the sun distribute all Indra's treasures (to living beings, sc. as rain, corn, etc.); may we too by our power leave those treasures as an inheritance to him who has been or will be born.' See Prof. Cowell's note in Wilson's Translation.

3 *Sûrya:* the Sun-God, identified with Indra.

HYMN LIX.

3 His portion is exceeding great, like a victorious soldier's spoil.
Him who is Indra, Lord of Bays, no foes subdue. He gives the Soma-pourer strength.

4 Make for the holy Gods a hymn that is not mean, but well arranged and fair in form.
Full many snares and bonds subdue not him who dwells with Indra through his sacrifice.

HYMN LX.

For so thou art the hero's Friend, a Warrior too art thou, and strong:
So may thy heart be won to us.

2 So hath the offering, wealthiest Lord, been paid by all the worshippers:
So dwell thou, Indra, even with me.

3 Be not thou like a slothful priest, O Lord of wealth and spoil: rejoice
In the pressed Soma blent with milk.

4 So also is his excellence, great, copious, rich in cattle, like
A ripe branch to the worshipper.

5 For verily thy mighty powers, Indra, are saving helps at once
Unto a worshipper like me.

6 So are his lovely gifts: let laud be said and praise to Indra sung
That he may drink the Soma juice.

R. V. VIII. 3. 15, 16; VII. 32. 12, 13. Stanzas 1, 2 = Hymn X. of this Book.

1 *His portion:* the portion of the man whom Indra befriends.

R. V. VIII. 81. 28—30; I. 8. 8—10.

HYMN LXI.

We sing this strong and wild delight of thine which conquers in the fray,
Which, Caster of the Stone, gives room and shines like gold.

2 Wherewith thou also foundest lights for Âyu and for Manu's sake:
Now joying in this sacred grass thou beamest forth.

3 This day too singers of the hymn praise, as of old, this, might of thine.
Win thou the waters, day by day, thralls of the strong.

4 Sing forth to him whom many men invoke, to him whom many laud:
Invite the potent Indra with your songs of praise;

5 Whose lofty might—for doubly strong is he—supports the heaven and earth,
And hills and plains and floods and light with manly power.

6 Such, praised by many! thou art King: alone thou smitest foemen dead,
To gain, O Indra, spoils of war and high renown.

HYMN LXII.

5 To Indra sing a Sâman, sing to the high Sage a lofty song,
To him who keeps the Law, inspired and fain for praise.

R. V. VIII. 15. 4—6, 1—3.

1 *Wild delight:* produced by draughts of Soma juice.

2 *For Âyu and for Manu's sake:* that is for Âryan men. Âyu was the son of Purûravas and Urvaşî, and Manu of Vivasvân.

3 *Thralls of the strong:* controlled and imprisoned by Vṛitra, the demon of drought.

Stánzas 5—7 are taken from R. V. VIII. 87 (M. Müller, 98). 1—3, and stanzas 8—10 from R. V. VIII. 15. 1—3. Stanzas 1—4 are repeated from A. V. XX. 14.

6 Thou, Indra, art preëminent: thou gavest splendour to the Sun.
Maker of all things, thou art mighty and All-God.

7 Radiant with light thou wentest to the sky, the luminous realms of heaven.
The Gods, O Indra, strove to win thee for their friend.

8 Sing forth to him whom many men invoke, to him whom many laud:
Invite the potent Indra with your songs of praise;

9 Whose lofty might—for doubly strong is he—supports the heaven and earth,
And hills and plains and floods and light with manly power.

10 Such, praised by many! thou art King. Alone thou smitest foemen dead,
To gain, O Indra, spoils of war and high renown.

HYMN LXIII.

We will, with Indra and all Gods to aid us, bring these existing worlds into subjection.
Our sacrifice, our bodies, and our offspring, let Indra form together with the Âdityas.

2 With the Âdityas, with the band of Maruts, may Indra be protector of our bodies;
As when the Gods came, after they had slaughtered the Asuras, keeping safe their godlike nature,

3 Brought the Sun hitherward with mighty powers, and looked about them on their vigorous God-head.
With this may we obtain strength God-appointed, and brave sons gladden us through a hundred winters.

Stanzas 1—3 are taken from R. V. X. 157; and VI. 17. 15; stanzas 4—6 from I. 84. 7—9; and stanzas 7—9 from VIII. 12. 1—3.

4 He who alone bestoweth might on mortal man who offereth gifts,
The ruler of resistless power, is Indra, sure.

5 When will he trample like a weed the man who hath no gift for him?
When verily will Indra hear our songs of praise?

6 He who with Soma juice prepared among the many harbours thee,—
Verily Indra gains thereby tremendous might.

7 Joy, mightiest Indra, known and marked, sprung most from Soma draughts, wherewith
Thou smitest down the greedy fiend, for that we pray.

8 Wherewith thou holpest Adhrigu, the great Daṣagva, and the God
Who stirs the sunlight, and the Sea, for that we pray.

9 Wherewith thou dravest forth like cars Sindhu and all the mighty floods
To go the way ordained by Law, for that we pray.

HYMN LXIV.

Come unto us, O Indra, dear, still conquering, unconcealable,
Vast as a mountain spread on all sides, Lord of heaven.

2 O truthful Soma-drinker, thou art mightier than both the worlds.
Thou strengthenest him who pours libation, Lord of heaven.

3 For thou art he, O Indra, who stormest all castles of the foe,
Slayer of Dasyus, man's supporter, Lord of heaven.

Taken from R. V. VIII. 87 (M. Müller 98). 4—6; VIII. 24. 16—18.

1 *Unconcealable:* or, from whom nothing can be concealed; one who seeth all, as identified with the Sun.

4 O ministering priest, pour out of the sweet juice what gladdens most.
So is the Hero praised who ever prospers us.

5 Indra whom tawny coursers bear, praise such as thine, preëminent,
None by his power or by his goodness hath attained.

6 We, seeking glory, have invoked this Master of all power and might
Who must be glorified by constant sacrifice.

HYMN LXV.

Come, sing we praise to Indra, friends! the Hero who deserves the laud,
Him who with none to aid o'ercomes all tribes of men.

2 To him who wins the kine, who keeps no cattle back, celestial God,
Speak wondrous speech more sweet than butter and than mead.

3 Whose hero powers are measureless, whose bounty ne'er may be surpassed,
Whose liberality, like light, is over all.

HYMN LXVI.

As Vyaṣva did, praise Indra, praise the strong unfluctuating guide
Who gives the foe's possessions to the worshipper.

2 Now, son of Vyaṣva, praise thou him who to the tenth time still is new,
The very wise, whom living men must glorify.

Taken, in continuation of the preceding hymn, from R̥. V. VIII. 24. 19—21.

Taken, in continuation of the preceding hymn, from R̥. V. VIII. 24. 22—24.

1 *Vyaṣva:* a R̥ishi frequently mentioned in the R̥. V., father of Viṣvamanas to whom some hymns are ascribed.

2 *Who keeps no cattle back:* either literally, who aids his worshippers to carry off the enemy's cattle and gives them all the booty; or, who sends forth all the kine or rays of light that he has recovered from the powers of darkness. According to Sâyaṇa, 'who rejects no praise.' *Still is new:* continually renews his liberality to us.

3 Thou knowest, Indra, thunder-armed, how to avoid destructive Powers,
As one secure from pitfalls each succeeding day.

HYMN LXVII.

The pourer of oblations gains the home of wealth, pouring his gift conciliates hostilities, yea, the hostilities of Gods.
Pouring he strives, unchecked and strong, to win him riches thousandfold.
Indra gives lasting wealth to him who pours forth gifts; yea, wealth he gives that long shall last.

2 Ne'er may those manly deeds of yours for us grow old, never may your bright glories fall into decay, never before our time decay.
What deed of yours, new every age, wondrous, surpassing man, rings forth,
Whatever, Maruts, may be difficult to gain, grant us whate'er is hard to win.

3 I think on Agni, Hotar, the munificent, the gracious, Son of strength, who knoweth all that live, as holy Sage who knoweth all.
Lord of fair rites, a God with form erected turning to the Gods,
He, when the flame hath sprung forth from the holy oil, the offered fatness, longeth for it with his glow.

Stanza 1 is taken from Ṛ. V. I. 133. 7; stanza 2 from I. 139. 8; stanza 3 from I. 127. 1; stanzas 4—6 from II. 36, 2, 4, 5; and stanza 7 from II. 37. 2. Parts of the hymn are addressed to the Maruts and Agni. Stanzas 1—3 are taken from hymns ascribed to the Ṛishi Paruchchhepa. One of the peculiarities of these hymns, which are generally obscure and frequently unintelligible is 'to reiterate a leading word which occurs the third or fourth from the end of the first line, and sometimes also of the third, and to repeat it as the last word of the line. Thus we have here [3, line 1]. *Sûnum sahaso Jâtavedasam, vipram na Jâtavedasam*; this is little else than a kind of alliterative jingle, but the scholiast thinks it necessary to assign to the repeated word a distinct signification.'—Wilson.

4 Busied with sacrifice, with spotted deer and spears, gleaming upon your way with ornaments, yea, our friends,
Sitting on sacred grass, ye sons of Bharata, drink Soma from the Potar's bowl, O Men of heaven.

5 Bring the Gods hither, Sage, and offer sacrifice. At the three altars seat thee willingly, O Priest.
Accept for thy delight the proffered Soma mead: drink from the Kindler's bowl and sate thee with thy share.

6 This is the strengthener of thy body's manly might: strength, victory for all time are laid within thine arms.
Pressed for thee, Maghavan, it is offered unto thee: drink from the chalice of this Brahman, drink thy fill.

7 Him whom of old I called on, him I call on now. He is to be invoked: his name is He who Gives.
Here brought by priests is Soma mead. Granter of Wealth, drink Soma with the Seasons from the Hotar's Cup.

---

4 Addressed to the Maruts. *Busied with sacrifice:* all natural phenomena, and especially the fall of the periodical rains, being regarded as intimately connected with the sacrifices offered on earth. *Spotted deer:* 'the recognised animals of the Maruts, originally, as it would seem, intended for the rain-clouds.'—M. Müller. *Spears:* thunderbolts. *Ornaments:* the lightning-flashes which accompany the Storm-Gods. *Bharata:* the Warrior Rudra. Ludwig translates differently, making *bharatasya* depend on *barhis:* 'einnehmend des Bharata barhis-sitz, O söhne [Rudra's und der Pṛçni].' *Potar's bowl:* the sacrificial vessel held by the Potar (Cleanser, Purifier) one of the officiating priests.

5 *Sage:* wise Agni. *Three altars:* fire-altars, hearths or receptacles for the Âhavanîya or Fire for oblations, the Gârhapatya or Householder's sacred western Fire, and the Dakshiṇa or Southern Fire. *Kindler:* the Agnîdh, the priest who lights the fire and carries a firebrand round the victim at a sacrifice. Cf. A. V. XX. 2, note.

7 Agni is invoked as Draviṇodas or Wealth-giver. *With the Seasons:* with the Ṛitus or deities who preside over the seasons of the year.

LXVIII.

4 Go to the wise unconquered One, ask thou of Indra, skilled in song,
Him who is better than thy friends.

5 Whether the men who mock us say, Depart unto another place,
Ye who serve Indra and none else;

6 Or whether, God of wondrous deeds, all our true people call us blest,
Still may we dwell in Indra's care.

7 Unto the swift One bring the swift, man-cheering, grace of sacrifice,
That to the Friend gives wings and joy.

8 Thou, Ṣatakratu, drankest this and wast the Vṛitras' slayer; thou
Holpest the warrior in the fray.

9 We strengthen, Ṣatakratu, thee, yea, thee the powerful in fight,
That, Indra, we may win us wealth.

10 To him the mighty stream of wealth, prompt Friend of him who pours the juice,
Yea, to this Indra sing your song.

11 O come ye hither, sit ye down: to Indra sing ye forth your song,
Companions, bringing hymns of praise.

Taken from R̥. V. I. 4. 4—10 (stanzas 1—3 = Hymn LVII. 1—3 of this Book), and I. 5. 1—2.

6 The general meaning of this and the two preceding verses seems to be: Indra is the best friend and protector, and so long as we enjoy his friendship and protection we care nothing for the revilings of the ungodly who mock at our faithful worship.

7 *The swift One:* Indra. The Soma juice which exhilarates men or heroes and accompanies or graces the sacrifice is also called swift both because it flows quickly and because it makes Indra hasten to the solemnity. *The Friend:* Indra whom the juice exhilarates and sends quickly to the sacrifice.

11 *Companions:* the call is addressed to the rest of the officiating priests.

12 To him the richest of the rich, the Lord of treasures excellent,
Indra, with Soma juice outpoured.

HYMN LXIX.

May he stand by us in our need and in abundance for our wealth:
With riches may he come to us;

2 Whose pair of tawny horses yoked in battles foemen challenge not:
To him, to Indra sing your song.

3 Nigh to the Soma-drinker come, for his enjoyment, these bright drops,
The Somas mingled with the curd.

4 Thou, grown at once to perfect strength, wast born to drink the Soma juice, strong Indra, for preëminence.

5 O Indra, lover of the song, may these quick Somas enter thee:
May they bring bliss to thee the Sage.

6 O Lord of Hundred Powers, our chants of praise and lauds have strengthened thee:
So strengthen thee the songs we sing!

7 Indra, whose succour never fails, accept this treasure thousandfold,
Wherein all manly powers abide.

8 O Indra, thou who lovest song, let no man hurt our bodies, keep
Slaughter far from us, for thou canst.

12 Thereafter they, as is their wont, threw off the state of babes unborn,
Taking their sacrificial name.

Taken from R. V. I. 5. 3—10: I. 6. 1—4 (Stanzas 9—11 = Hymn XXVI. 4—6 of this Book).

12 *They*: the Maruts. The stanza is repeated from A. V. XX. 40: 3.

HYMN LXX.

THOU, Indra, with the Tempest-Gods, the breakers down of what is firm,
Foundest the kine even in the cave.

2 Worshipping even as they list, singers laud him who findeth wealth,
The far-renowned, the mighty One.

3 Then, faring on by Indra's side, the fearless, let thyself be seen,
Both gracious and in splendour peers.

4 With Indra's well-belovèd hosts, the blameless, tending heavenward,
The sacrificer cries aloud.

5 Come from this place, O Wanderer, or downward from the light of heaven:
Our songs of praise all yearn for this.

6 Or Indra we implore for help from here, from heaven above the earth,
Or from the spacious firmament.

7 Indra the singers with high praise, Indra reciters with their lauds,
Indra the choirs have glorified.

Taken from Ṛ. V. I. 6. 5—10; 7. 1—10; 8. 1—4.

1 *The Tempest-Gods:* the Maruts, the constant companions and helpers of Indra. *The kine:* streams of water and the beams of light which follow their effusion. *The cave:* the thick dark cloud which holds the imprisoned waters and which Indra cleaves asunder with his thunderbolt or lightning.

3 *Thyself:* the host of Maruts. According to Benfey, the Sun.

4 *The sacrificer cries aloud:* this is the interpretation given by Prof. Max Müller, but it is conjectural and not altogether satisfactory. Benfey translates: 'Mightily shines the sacrifice'; and Ludwig: 'The warrior sings triumphantly.'

5 *Wanderer: parijman;* moving around; here applied to Indra identified with the Sun.

7 Stanzas 7—19 are repeated from A. V. XX. 38. 4—6.

8 Indra hath ever close to him his two bay steeds and word-yoked car,
Indra the golden, Thunder-armed.

9 Indra hath raised the Sun on high in heaven, that he may see afar:
He burst the mountain for the kine.

10 Help us, O Indra, in the frays, yea, frays where thousand spoils are gained,
With awful aids, O awful One.

11 In mighty battle we invoke, Indra, Indra in lesser fight,
The Friend who bends his bolt at fiends.

12 Unclose, our manly Hero, thou for ever bounteous, yonder cloud,
For us, thou irresistible.

13 Still higher, at each strain of mine, thunder-armed Indra's praises rise:
I find no laud worthy of him.

14 Even as the bull drives on the herds, he drives the people with his might,
The ruler irresistible:

15 Indra who rules with single sway men, riches, and the fivefold race.
Of those who dwell upon the earth.

16 For your sake from each side we call Indra away from other men:
Ours, and none others', may he be.

17 Indra, bring wealth that gives delight, the victor's ever-conquering wealth,
Most excellent, to be our aid;

---

15 *The fivefold race, etc.*: Benfey explains this as 'the whole inhabited world.' But the expression seems to mean the Âryan settlements or tribes only, and not the indigenous inhabitants of the country. The five tribes or settlements were probably the confederation of the Turvasas, Yadus, Anus, Druhyus, and Pûrus. Sâyaṇa's explanation is 'those who are fit for habitations,' and the phrase is said to imply the four castes and Nishâdas or indigenous barbarians. But there were no such distinctions of caste when the hymn was composed.

18 By means of which we may repel our foes in battle hand to hand,
By thee assisted with the car.

19 Aided by thee, the Thunder-armed, Indra, may we lift up the bolt,
And conquer all our foes in fight.

20 With thee, O Indra, for ally, with missile-darting heroes may
We conquer our embattled foes.

HYMN LXXI.

Mighty is Indra, yea, supreme; greatness be his, the Thunderer!
Wide as the heaven extends his power;

2 Which aideth those to win them sons who come as heroes to the fight,
Or singers loving holy thoughts.

3 His belly drinking deepest draughts of Soma like an ocean swells,
Like wide streams from the cope of heaven.

7 Come, Indra, and delight thee with the juice at all the Soma feasts,
Protector, mighty in thy strength.

8 To Indra pour ye forth the juice, the active gladdening juice to him
The gladdening omnific God.

---

18 *With the car: árvatâ*, literally, with a horse, is explained by Sâyaṇa to mean fighting on horseback. But horses seem to have been used in war as drawers of chariots only, and *árvatâ* here stands for *rathena*, with a car or chariot.

19 *May we lift up the bolt:* the thunderbolt here spoken of is sacrifice which, when employed against enemies, is as powerful a weapon as the bolt of Indra.

The hymn is a continuation of the preceding hymn, stanzas 1—6 (of which 4—6 are repeated from A. V. XX. 60. 4—6) being taken from Ṛ. V. I. 8. 4—10, and stanzas 7—16 from Ṛ. V. I. 9.

9 O Lord of all men, fair of cheek, rejoice thee in the gladdening lauds,
Present at these drink-offerings.

10 Songs have outpoured themselves to thee, Indra, the strong, the guardian Lord,
And raised themselves unsatisfied.

11 Send to us bounty manifold, O Indra, worthy of our wish,
For power supreme is only thine.

12 O Indra, stimulate thereto us emulously fain for wealth,
And glorious, O most splendid One.

13 Give, Indra, wide and lofty fame, wealthy in cattle and in strength,
Lasting our life-time, failing not.

14 Grant us high fame, O Indra, grant riches bestowing thousands, those
Fair fruits of earth borne home in wains.

15 Praising with songs the praise-worthy who cometh to our aid, we call
Indra, the Treasure-Lord of wealth.

16 To lofty Indra, dweller by each libation, the pious man
Sings forth aloud a strengthening hymn.

HYMN LXXII.

In all libations men with hero spirit urge thee, Universal, One, each seeking several light, each fain to win the light apart.

---

10 *Unsatisfied: ájoshâḥ*; that is, ever renewed, and unsatisfied with their attempts to praise him as he should be praised. Ludwig observes that the Sâmaveda has preserved the correct reading *sajóshâḥ*, 'with one accord.'

14 *Borne home in wains*: 'meaning, Sâyaṇa says, those articles of food which are conveyed in cars, carts, or waggons, from the site of their production; as rice, barley, and other kinds of grain.'—Wilson.

Taken from Ṛ. V. I. 131. 2, 3, 6. The hymn is ascribed to Paru chchhepa: see A. V. XX. 67. 1, note.

Thee, furthering like a ship, will we set to the chariot pole of strength,
As men who win with sacrifices Indra's thought, men who win Indra with their lauds.

2 Couples desirous of thine aid are storming thee, pouring their presents forth to win a stall of kine, pouring gifts, Indra, seeking thee.
When two men seeking spoil or heaven thou bringest face to face in war,
Thou showest, Indra, then the bolt thy constant friend, the bull that ever waits on thee.

3 Also this morn may he be well inclined to us, mark at our call our offerings and our song of praise, our call that we may win the light.
As thou, O Indra Thunder-armed, wilt, as the Strong One, slay the foe,
Listen thou to the prayer of me a later sage, hear thou a later sage's prayer.

HYMN LXXIII.

All these libations are for thee, O Hero: to thee I offer these my prayers that strengthen.
Ever, in every place, must men invoke thee.

2 Never do men attain, O Wonder-worker, thy greatness, Mighty One who must be lauded,
Nor, Indra, thine heroic power and bounty.

3 Bring to the Wise, the Great who waxeth mighty your offerings and make ready your devotion:
To many clans he goeth, man's Controller.

4 When, with the Princes, Maghavan, famed of old, comes nigh the thunderbolt of gold, and the Controller's car

---

2 *Couples:* sacrificers, and their wives who are associated with them in the performance of divine worship. *The bull:* the fiercely rushing thunderbolt.

The hymn is taken from Ṛ. V. VIII. 22. 7, 8; 31. 10; X. 23. 3—5.

4 *With the Princes:* accompanied by the Maruts, who are called princes, Sûris, or wealthy institutors of sacrifice in the same way as Indra

Which his two tawny coursers draw, then Indra is the Sovran Lord of power whose fame spreads far and wide.

5 With him too is this rain of his that comes like herds: Indra throws drops of moisture on his yellow beard.
When the sweet juice is shed he seeks the pleasant place, and stirs the worshipper as the wind disturbs the wood.

6 We laud and praise his several deeds of valour who, fatherlike, with power hath made us stronger;
Who with his voice slew many thousand wicked ones who spake in varied manner with contemptuous cries.

HYMN LXXIV.

O SOMA-DRINKER, ever true, utterly hopeless though we be,
Do thou, O Indra, give us hope of beauteous horses and of kine,
In thousands, O most wealthy One.

2 O Lord of strength, whose jaws are strong, great deeds are thine, the powerful:
Do thou, O Indra, give us hope of beauteous horses and of kine,
In thousands, O most wealthy One.

3 Lull thou asleep, to wake no more, the pair who on each other look:

---

is the Bounteous Lord, the Maghavan *par excellence*, and the type of human sacrificers.

5 *Drops of moisture:* meaning perhaps, as Ludwig suggests, the rain which he pours upon the lightning which may be regarded as his beard. *The pleasant place:* the sacrificial enclosure. *The worshipper:* according to Sâyaṇa, his own body. There is no word in the text here to express the object of the verb.

Taken from Ṛ. V. I. 29.

3 *The pair who on each other look:* or, who show alternately. 'The text is very elliptical and obscure. It is literally: Put to sleep the two reciprocally looking: let them sleep not being awakened. The scholiast calls them the two female messengers of Yama.'—Wilson. 'Die beiden abwechselnd schaunden [des Yama botinnen].'—Ludwig In Ṛ. V. II. 31. 5, the same epithet is applied to Night and Morning.

Do thou, O Indra, give us hope of beauteous horses and of kine,
In thousands, O most wealthy One.

4 Hero, let hostile spirits sleep, and every gentler Genius wake:
Do thou, O Indra, give us hope of beauteous horses and of kine,
In thousands, O most wealthy One.

5 Destroy this ass, O Indra, who in tones discordant brays to thee:
Do thou, O Indra, give us hope of beauteous horses and of kine,
In thousands, O most wealthy One.

6 Far distant on the forest fall the tempest in a circling course:
Do thou, O Indra, give us hope of beauteous horses and of kine,
In thousands, O most wealthy One.

7 Slay each reviler and destroy him who in secret injures us:
Do thou, O Indra, give us hope of beauteous horses and of kine,
In thousands, O most wealthy One.

HYMN LXXV.

Couples desirous of thine aid are storming thee, pouring their presents forth to win a stall of kine, pouring gifts, Indra, seeking thee.

---

5 *This ass:* our adversary, says the scholiast. 'Therefore is he called an ass, as braying, or uttering harsh sounds intolerable to hear.'

6 *On the forest:* may the cyclone or tempest expend its fury on the wood, and not come near us. The word *kuṇḍriṇâchî*, the instrumental case of which I have rendered in accordance with Sâyaṇa, means elsewhere a certain kind of animal, a lizard according to Sâyaṇa. The meaning then might be: 'may the wind fall on the forest with the *kuṇḍriṇâchî*,' whatever that may be.

Taken from Ṛ. V. I. 131. 3—5. The hymn is ascribed to Paruchchhepa: see A. V. XX. 67. 1, note.

1 This stanza is repeated from hymn 72. 2 of this Book.

When two men seeking spoil or heaven thou bringest face to face in war,
Thou showest, Indra, then the bolt, thy constant friend, the bull that ever waits on thee.

2 This thine heroic power full well the people knew, wherewith thou brakest down, Indra, autumnal forts, brakest them down with conquering might.
Thou hast chastised, O Indra, Lord of strength, the man who worships not,
And made thine own this great earth and these water-floods, with joyous heart these water-floods.

3 And they have bruited far this hero might, when thou, O Strong One, in thy joy holpest thy suppliants who sought to win thee for their Friend.
Their battle-cry thou madest sound victorious in the shocks of war.
One stream after another have they gained from thee, eager for glory have they gained.

HYMN LXXVI.

As sits the young bird on the tree rejoicing, ye, swift pair, have been roused by clear laudation,
Whose Hotar-priest through many days is Indra, earth's guardian, friend of men, the best of heroes.

2 May we, when this Dawn and the next dance hither, be thy best servants, most heroic Hero!

---

2 *The people*: *pûrávah*; or, the Pûrus, one of the Five Âryan Tribes. *Autumnal forts*: probably, strongholds on high ground, occupied as places of refuge by the non-Âryan inhabitants of the country during the heavy rains.

Taken from R. V. X. 29.

1 The meaning of the stanza is obscure, and the text of the first half line is unintelligible. I follow the reading which Sâyaṇa gives in his Commentary, *vâyo* intead of *vâ yó*. 'As (the bird) who deposits its young (in its nest) in the tree (is) eagerly looking around.'—Wilson. *Swift pair*: Aṣvins.

2 *Dance hither*: or, come dancing. Cp. Milton's 'Now the bright morning star, day's harbinger, Comes dancing from the east.' *Triple splendour*: perhaps with reference to Agni, Vâyu, and Sûrya.—Ludwig. *Hundred chiefs*: as Professor Grassmann suggests, the Maruts may be intended, 'hundred' being used indefinitely. *Kutsa*: Indra's favourite companion.

Let the victorious car with triple splendour bring hitherward the hundred chiefs with Kutsa.

3 What was the gladdening draught that pleased thee, Indra? Speed to our doors, our songs, for thou art mighty.

Why comest thou to me, what gift attracts thee? Fain would I bring thee food most meet to offer.

4 Indra, what fame hath one like thee mid heroes? With what plan wilt thou act? Why hast thou sought us?

As a true friend, Wide-Strider! to sustain us, since food absorbs the thought of each among us.

5 Speed happily those, as Sûrya ends his journey, who meet his wish as bridegrooms meet their spouses;

Men who support, O Indra strong by nature, with food the many songs that tell thy praises.

6 Thine are two measures, Indra, wide, well-meted, heaven for thy majesty, earth for thy wisdom.

Here for thy choice are Somas mixed with butter: may the sweet meath be pleasant for thy drinking.

7 They have poured out a bowl to him, to Indra, full of sweet juice, for faithful is his bounty.

O'er earth's expanse hath he grown great by wisdom, the friend of man, and by heroic exploits.

8 Indra hath conquered in his wars, the mighty: men strive in multitudes to win his friendship.

Ascend thy chariot as it were in battle, which thou shalt drive to us with gracious favour.

---

4 Indra is reminded that the protection of his worshippers is his special glory. *Wide-Strider!*: 'widely renowned,' according to Sâyana. *Food*: the hymn appears to have been 'seen' or revealed in a time of dearth or famine.'—Ludwig.

5 *Meet his wish*: satisfy his, Indra's, longing for Soma libations.

6 *Thine are two measures*: thy majesty or greatness is vast and lofty as heaven, and thy wisdom is wide as earth; or, 'with confusion of the measure and the thing measured,' thou hast measured out the heaven by thy greatness and the earth by thy wisdom. See Wallis, *Cosmology of the Ṛigveda*, p. 18.

HYMN LXXVII.

IMPETUOUS, true, let Maghavan come hither, and let his tawny coursers speed to reach us.
For him have we pressed juice exceeding potent: here, praised with song, let him effect his visit.

2 Unyoke, as at thy journey's end, O Hero, to gladden thee to-day at this libation.
Like Uṣanâ, the priest a laud shall utter, a hymn to thee, the Lord Divine, who markest.

3 When the Bull quaffing praises our libation, as a sage paying holy rites in secret,
Seven singers here from heaven hath he begotten, who e'en by day have wrought their works while singing.

4 When heaven's fair light by hymns was made apparent, (they made great splendour shine at break of morning),
He with his succour, best of heroes, scattered the blinding darkness so that men saw clearly.

5 Indra, impetuous One, hath waxed immensely: he with his vastness hath filled earth and heaven.
E'en beyond this his majesty extendeth who hath exceeded all the worlds in greatness,

6 Ṣakra who knoweth well all human actions hath with his eager friends let loose the waters.
They with their songs cleft e'en the mountain open, and willingly disclosed the stall of cattle.

Taken from Ṛ. V. IV. 16. 1—8.

1 *Impetuous:* according to Sâyaṇa, *ṛijisht*, the word in the text, means accepter, or drinker, of the spiritless Soma, of the Soma when its essence or strength has passed away. Professor Ludwig follows Sâyaṇa.

2 *Like Uṣanâ:* the Ṛishi Uṣanâ, or Uṣanâs, called also Kâvya or Kavi's son, appears in the Veda as the especial friend of Indra.

3 *The Bull:* the mighty Indra. *Seven singers:* the meaning of this line is not clear. Professor Wilson, following Sâyaṇa, translates: 'and this generates the seven efficient (rays) from heaven, which, being glorified, have made (manifest) the objects of (human) perception.'

4 *Scattered, etc:* or, 'fashioned blind turbid darkness so that men saw clearly.'

6 *His eager friends:* the Maruts.

7 He smote away the flood's obstructer Vṛitra: Earth conscious lent her aid to speed thy thunder.
Thou sentest forth the waters of the ocean as Lord through power and might, O daring Hero.

8 When, Much-invoked! the waters' rock thou cleftest, Saramâ showed herself and went before thee.
Hymned by Angirases, bursting the cowstalls, thou foundest ample strength for us as leader.

HYMN LXXVIII.

Sing this, what time the juice is pressed, to him your Hero much-invoked,
To please him as a mighty Bull.

2 He, excellent, withholdeth not his gift of power and wealth in kine
When he hath listened to our songs.

3 May he with might disclose for us the cows' stall, whosesoe'er it be,
To which the Dasyu-slayer goes.

HYMN LXXIX.

O Indra, give us wisdom as a sire gives wisdom to his sons.
Guide us, O Much-invoked, on this our foray: may we, living, still enjoy the light.

---

8 *Saramâ:* the hound of Indra, who tracked the stolen cows. Cf. Ṛ. V. I. 62. 3; 72. 8. Saramâ appears to be the Dawn or the morning breeze which guided Indra on his way.

Taken from Ṛ. V. VI. 45. 22—24.

3 *Whosesoe'er it be:* the meaning of *kuvitsasya* here is somewhat uncertain. Sâyaṇa explains it as, of Kuvitsa, a certain person who does much harm. The meaning appears to be, may Indra open for us the cow-stall and give us the cattle of any Dasyu whom he, that is, we under his guidance, may attack.

Taken from Ṛ. V. VII. 32. 26, 27.

1 *Foray:* apparently some cattle-lifting expedition. The original hymn is a prayer, with sacrifice, for success in a coming fray.

2 Grant that no mighty foes, unknown, malevolent, unhallowed, tread us to the ground.
With thine assistance, Hero! may we pass through all the waters that are rushing down.

HYMN LXXX.

Bring us, O Indra, name and fame, enriching, mightiest, excellent,
Wherewith, O wondrous God, fair-cheeked and thunder-armed, thou hast filled full this earth and heaven.

2 We call on thee, O King, mighty among the Gods, ruler of men, to succour us.
All that is weak in us, excellent God, make firm: make our foes easy to subdue.

HYMN LXXXI.

O Indra, if a hundred heavens and if a hundred earths were thine—
No, not a hundred suns could match thee at thy birth, not both the worlds, O Thunderer.

2 Thou, Hero, hast performed thy hero deeds with might, yea, all with strength, O Strongest One.
Maghavan, help us to a stable full of kine, O Thunderer, with wondrous aids.

HYMN LXXXII.

If I, O Indra, were the lord of riches ample as thine own,
I should support the singer, God who scatterest wealth! and not abandon him to woe.

2 Each day would I enrich the man who sang my praise, in whatsoever place he were.
No kinship is there better, Maghavan, than thine: a father even is no more.

Taken from Ṛ. V. VI. 46. 5, 6.

Taken from Ṛ. V. VIII. 59 (70). 5, 6.

Taken from Ṛ. V. VII. 32. 18, 19.

LXXXIII.

O INDRA, grant a happy home, a triple refuge, triply strong.
Bestow a dwelling-place on the rich lords and me, and keep thy dart afar from these.
2 They who with minds intent on spoil subdue the foe, boldly attack and smite him down,—
From these, O Indra, Bounteous Lord who lovest song, be closest guardian of our lives.

HYMN LXXXIV.

O INDRA marvellously bright, come, these libations long for thee,
Thus by fine fingers purified.
2 Urged by the holy singer, sped by song, come, Indra, to the prayers
Of the libation-pouring priest.
3 Approach, O Indra, hasting thee, Lord of Bay Horses, to the prayers:
Take pleasure in the juice we pour.

HYMN LXXXV.

GLORIFY naught besides, O friends; so shall no sorrow trouble you.
Praise only mighty Indra when the juice is shed, and say your lauds repeatedly:
2 Even him, eternal, like a bull who rushes down, men's conqueror, bounteous like a cow;
Him who is cause of both, of enmity and peace, to both sides most munificent.

Taken from Ṛ. V. VI. 46. 9, 10.

1 *Rich lords:* the nobles who institute sacrifice and liberally reward the priests.

Taken from Ṛ. V. I. 3. 4. 6.

1 *Thus:* or, still, meaning continuously.

Taken from Ṛ. V. VIII. 1. 1—4.

2 *Bounteous like a cow:* the adjective is not in the text, but must be supplied in order to make the comparison intelligible. See *Vedische Studien*, I., 103. *To both sides:* to the singers and the institutors of sacrifice.

3 Although these men in sundry ways invoke thee to obtain thine aid,
Be this our prayer, addressed, O Indra, unto thee, thine exaltation every day.

4 Those skilled in song, O Maghavan, among these men o'ercome with might the foeman's songs.
Come hither, bring us strength in many a varied form most near that it may succour us.

HYMN LXXXVI.

Those who are yoked by prayer with prayer I harness, the two fleet friendly Bays who joy together.
Mounting thy firm and easy car, O Indra, wise and all-knowing come thou to the Soma.

HYMN LXXXVII.

Priests, offer to the Lord of all the people the milked-out stalk of Soma, radiant-coloured.
No wild bull knows his drinking-place like Indra who ever seeks him who hath pressed the Soma.

2 Thou dost desire to drink, each day that passes, the pleasant food which thou hast had aforetime.
O Indra, gratified in heart and spirit, drink eagerly the Soma set before thee.

3 Thou, newly-born, for strength didst drink the Soma; thy mother told thee of thy future greatness.
O Indra, thou hast filled mid-air's wide region, and given the Gods by battle room and freedom.

4 When thou hast urged the arrogant to combat, proud in their strength of arm, we will subdue them.
Or, Indra, when thou fightest girt by heroes, we in the glorious fray with thee will conquer.

Taken from Ṛ. V. III. 35. 4.

Taken from Ṛ. V. VII. 98.

3 *Thy mother:* Aditi, who says (Ṛ. V. 18. 4):—'No peer hath he among those born already, nor among those who shall be born hereafter.'

5 I will declare the earliest deeds of Indra, and recent acts which Maghavan hath accomplished.
When he had conquered godless wiles and magic, Soma became his own entire possession.

6 Thine is this world of flocks and herds around thee, which with the eye of Sûrya thou beholdest.
Thou, Indra, art alone the Lord of cattle: may we enjoy the treasure which thou givest.

7 Ye twain are Lords of wealth in earth and heaven, thou, O Bṛihaspati, and thou, O Indra.
Mean though he be, give wealth to him who lauds you. Preserve us evermore, ye Gods, with blessings.

HYMN LXXXVIII.

HIM who with might hath propped earth's ends, who sitteth in threefold seat, Bṛihaspati, with thunder,
Him of the pleasant tongue have ancient sages, deep-thinking, holy singers, set before them.

2 Wild in their course, in well-marked wise rejoicing were they, Bṛihaspati, who pressed around us.
Preserve, Bṛihaspati, the stall uninjured, this company's raining, ever-moving birth-place.

3 Bṛihaspati, from thy remotest distance have they sat down who love the law eternal.

Taken from Ṛ. V. IV. 50. 1—6. The hymn is addressed to Bṛihaspati, Lord of Prayer.

1 *In threefold seat:* heaven, mid-air, and earth. *Set before them:* for adoration; or given them the foremost place in sacrifice.

2 *They...who pressed around us:* apparently the Maruts. *The stall:* 'the boundless stall' of Ṛ. V. III. 1. 14, the aerial home of the Maruts. *This company's:* the text has only *asya*, of this. I follow Prof. Ludwig's interpretation of this very difficult stanza and supply *gaṇasya*, troop or company, *i. e.* of the Maruts. According to Sâyaṇa, Bṛihaspati is asked to protect the worshipper or institutor of the sacrifice.

3 *Have they sat down:* probably the Maruts are intended, and not, as Sâyaṇa says, the horses of Bṛihaspati. *Wells springing from the mountains:* reservoirs of Soma juice pressed out by the stones, have been prepared: the word *ádri* signifying both mountain and stone.

For thee were dug wells springing from the mountain, which murmuring round about pour streams of sweetness.

4 Bṛihaspati, when first he had his being from mighty splendour in supremest heaven,

Strong, with his sevenfold mouth, with noise of thunder, with his seven rays, blew and dispersed the darkness.

5 With the loud-shouting band who sang his praises, with thunder, he destroyed malignant Vala.

Bṛihaspati thundering drave forth the cattle, the lowing cows who make oblations ready.

6 Serve we with sacrifices, gifts, and homage even thus the Steer of all the Gods, the Father.

Bṛihaspati, may we be lords of riches, with noble progeny and store of heroes.

HYMN LXXXIX.

Even as an archer shoots afar his arrow, offer the laud to him with meet adornment.

Quell with your voice the wicked's voice, O sages. Singer, make Indra rest beside the Soma.

2 Draw thy Friend to thee like a cow at milking: O singer, wake up Indra as a lover.

Make thou the Hero haste to give us riches even as a vessel filled brimful with treasure.

3 Why, Maghavan, do they call thee bounteous Giver? Quicken me: thou, I hear, art he who quickens.

Ṣakra, let my intelligence be active, and bring us luck that finds great wealth, O Indra.

---

4 *Sevenfold mouth:* Bṛihaspati being identified with Agni who has seven tongues of flame.

5 *The loud-shouting band:* the Angirases who accompanied Bṛihaspati.

6 *The Steer:* or Chief.

Taken from R. V. X. 42.

1 *The wicked's voice:* 'the praises of your adversaries.'—Wilson. *Sages:* wise priests.

4 Standing, in battle for their rights, together, the people, Indra, in the fray invoke thee.
Him who brings gifts the Hero makes his comrade: with him who pours no juice he seeks not friendship.
5 Whoso with plenteous juice for him expresses strong Somas as much quickly-coming treasure,
For him he overthrows in early morning his swift well-weaponed foes and slays the tyrant.
6 He unto whom we offer praises, Indra, Maghavan, who hath joined to ours his wishes—
Before him even afar the foe must tremble: low before him must bow all human glories.
7 With thy fierce bolt, O God invoked of many, drive to a distance from afar the foeman.
O Indra, give us wealth in corn and cattle, and make thy singer's prayer gain strength and riches.
8 Indra the swallower of strong libations with their thick residue, the potent Somas,
He, Maghavan, will not restrict his bounty: he brings much wealth unto the Soma-presser.
9 Yea, by superior play he wins advantage when he, a gambler, piles his gains in season.
Celestial-natured, he o'erwhelms with riches the devotee who keeps not back his money.
10 O Much-invoked, may we subdue all famine and evil want with store of grain and cattle.
May we allied, as first in rank, with princes, obtain possessions by our own exertion.
11 Bṛihaspati protect us from the rearward, and from above and from below, from sinners.
May Indra from the front and from the centre, as friend to friends, vouchsafe us room and freedom.

---

4 *The Hero*: Indra.

5 *As much quickly-coming treasure*: representing the wealth which the offering of the libations is expected to produce.

9 *When he, a gambler*: cf. 'As in the game a gambler piles his winnings, so Maghavan, sweeping all together, gained the Sun' (R. V. X. 43. 5).

10 *With princes*: with men eminent for their wealth: *rájabhirdhanánámíṣvaraiḥ*.—Sâyaṇa.

HYMN XC.

SERVED with oblations, first-born, mountain-render,
Angiras' Son, Bṛihaspati the holy,
With twice-firm path, dwelling in light, our Father,
roars loudly, as a bull, to earth and heaven.

2 Bṛihaspati who made for such a people wide room
and verge when Gods were invocated—
Slaying his foes he breaketh down their castles,
quelling his enemies and those who hate him.

3 Bṛihaspati in war hath won rich treasures, hath won,
this God, the great stalls filled with cattle.
Striving to win waters and light, resistless, Bṛihaspati with lightning smites the foeman.

HYMN XCI.

THIS holy hymn sublime and seven-headed, sprung
from eternal Law, our sire discovered.
Ayâsya, friend of all men, hath engendered the fourth
hymn as he sang his laud to Indra.

2 Thinking aright, praising eternal Order, the sons of
Dyaus the Asura, those heroes,
Angirases, holding the rank of sages, first honoured
sacrifice's holy statute.

Taken from Ṛ. V. VI. 73. The hymn is addressed to Bṛihaspati.

1 *Mountain-render:* cf. 'Bṛihaspati cleft the mountain' (Ṛ. V. I. 62. 3), that is, the thick cloud which imprisoned the rays of light.

2 *Such a people:* so good a people. *When the Gods were invocated:* in battle.

3 *With lightning:* or, with sunlight: 'with sacred prayers.'-Wilson.

Taken from Ṛ. V. X. 67. The hymn is addressed to Bṛihaspati.

1 *Seven-headed:* having seven divisions. Accompanied by the seven troops of the Maruts, or having seven metres, according to Sâyaṇa. *Sprung from:* that is, made in accordance with. *Our sire:* Angiras, the ancestor of Ayâsya to whom the hymn was revealed; or, perhaps, Ayâsya himself, as Ludwig explains. *The fourth:* or, perhaps, the strong, victorious.

3 Girt by his friends who cried with swanlike voices, bursting the stony barriers of the prison,
Bṛihaspati spake in thunder to the cattle, and uttered praise and song when he had found them.

4 Apart from one, away from two above him, he drave the kine that stood in bonds of falsehood.
Bṛihaspati, seeking light amid the darkness, drave forth the bright cows: three he made apparent.

5 When he had cleft the lairs and western castle, he cut off three from him who held the waters.
Bṛihaspati discovered, while he thundered like Dyaus, the dawn, the sun, the cow, the lightning.

6 As with a hand, so with his roaring Indra cleft Vala through, the guardian of the cattle.
Seeking the milk-draught with sweat-shining comrades he stole the Paṇi's kine and left him weeping.

7 He with bright faithful friends, winners of booty, hath rent the milker of the cows asunder.
Bṛihaspati with wild boars strong and mighty sweating with heat hath gained a rich possession.

8 They, longing for the kine, with faithful spirit incited with their hymns the Lord of cattle.

---

3 *The cattle:* the lost cows of the Angirases, representing the rays of light which had been stolen and hidden by the Paṇis or demons of darkness.

4 *Apart from one, away from two:* the meaning is uncertain; perhaps, as Ludwig suggests, at a distance from the earth, and beneath heaven and the firmament. *Falsehood:* the wickedness of the malevolent Paṇis. *Three:* heaven, firmament, and earth.

5 *Western castle:* this is obscure. Prof. Ludwig suggests that *ápâchîm* may mean 'hostile' or 'detested.' *Three:* heaven, firmament and earth, as in stanza 4. *Him who held the waters:* the demon Vala, who kept the rain, as well as the cows or rays of light, imprisoned. *The cow:* the sunlight.

6 *Comrades:* his faithful friends the Maruts. *Wild boars:* the strong fierce Maruts; according to Sâyaṇa, 'bearers of excellent water.'

7 *The Lord of cattle:* Bṛihaspati who had freed the cows from their tyrant.

Bṛihaspati freed the radiant cows with comrades self-yoked, averting shame from one another.

9 In our assembly with auspicious praises exalting him who roareth like a lion,
May we in every fight where heroes conquer rejoice in strong Bṛihaspati the victor.

10 When he had won him strength of every nature and gone to heaven and its most lofty mansions,
Men praised Bṛihaspati the mighty, bringing the light within their mouths from sundry places.

11 Fulfil the prayer that begs for vital vigour: aid in your wonted manner e'en the humble.
Let all our foes be turned and driven backward. Hear this, O Heaven and Earth, ye all-producers.

12 Indra with mighty strength hath cleft asunder the head of Arbuda the watery monster,
Slain Ahi, and set free the Seven Rivers. O Heaven and Earth, with all the Gods, protect us.

HYMN XCII.

Praise, even as he is known, with song Indra the guardian of the kine,
The Son of Truth, Lord of the brave.

2 Hither his bay steeds have been sent, red steeds are on the sacred grass
Where we in concert sing our songs.

3 For Indra thunder-armed the kine have yielded mingled milk and meath,
What time he found them in the vault.

---

10 *The light:* that is, the hymns of praise which will bring them the light of help. The stanza is obscure.

12 *The watery monster:* the fiend who dominated the sea of air. *Ahi:* or the dragon: Vṛitra or his brother.

The hymn is taken from Ṛ. V. VIII. 58 (M. Müller, 69). 4—18, and 59 (M. Müller, 70). 1—6. Stanzas 20, 21 are repeated from A. V. XX. 81

3 *In the vault:* 'in the cavity of the Soma-vessel.'—von Roth; 'on the horizon.'—Ludwig; 'near at hand.'—Sâyaṇa.

4 When I and Indra mount on high up to the bright One's place and home,
We, having drunk of meath, will reach his seat whose Friends are three-times-seven.

5 Sing, sing ye forth your songs of praise, ye Priyamedhas, sing your songs:
Yea, let young children sing their lauds: as a strong castle praise ye him.

6 Now loudly let the viol sound, the lute send out its voice with might,
Shrill be the music of the string. To Indra is the hymn upraised.

7 When hither speed the dappled cows, unflinching, easy to be milked,
Seize quickly, as it bursts away, the Soma juice for Indra's drink.

8 Indra hath drunk, Agni hath drunk: all Deities have drunk their fill.
Here Varuṇa shall have his home, to whom the floods have sung aloud as mother-kine unto their calves.

9 Thou, Varuṇa, to whom belong the Seven Streams, art a glorious God.
The waters flow into thy throat as 'twere a pipe with ample mouth.

10 He who hath made the fleet steeds spring, well-harnessed, to the worshipper,
He, the swift guide, is that fair form that loosed the horses near at hand.

---

4 *The bright One's place:* the station of the Sun. *Whose friends are three-times-seven:* Indra, the friend of the Maruts whose number is said to be seven or varying multiples of seven. See A. V. I. 1. 1, note. I follow Ludwig in making one compound word of the *triḥ saptá sákhyuḥ* of the text. Sâyaṇa's explanation is different: 'let us be united in the twenty-first sphere of the (universal) friend.' See note in Wilson's Translation.

9 Varuṇa's throat, or palate, is said to mean the sea into which the seven rivers flow.

11 Indra, the very mighty, holds his enemies in utter scorn.
He, far away, and yet a child, cleft the cloud smitten by his voice.

12 He, yet a boy exceeding small, mounted his newly-fashioned car.
He for his Mother and his Sire cooked the wild mighty buffalo.

13 Lord of the Home, with beauteous cheeks, ascend thy chariot wrought of gold.
We will attend the heavenly One, the thousand-footed, red of hue, matchless, who blesses where he goes.

14 With reverence they come hitherward to him as to a sovran lord,
That they may bring him near for this man's good success, to prosper and bestow his gifts.

15 The Priyamedhas have observed the offering of the men of old,
Of ancient custom, while they strewed the sacred grass and spread their sacrificial food.

16 He who as sovran Lord of men moves with his chariots unrestrained,
The Vṛitra-slayer, queller of all fighting hosts, preëminent, is praised in song.

17 Honour that Indra, Puruhanman! for his aid, in whose sustaining hand of old
The splendid bolt of thunder was deposited, as the great Sun was set in heaven.

---

12 *His Mother and his Sire*: Heaven and Earth. The *buffalo* is the dark rain-cloud which Indra pierces with his lightning; or perhaps the demon Vala is intended.

13 *The heavenly One*: the sun which is Indra's chariot. *Thousand-footed*: bright with countless rays of light.

14 *This man's*: who institutes the sacrifice.

17 *Puruhanman*: a Ṛishi of the family of Angiras, the seer of the hymn.

18 No one by deed attains to him who works and strengthens evermore:
No, not by sacrifice, to Indra praised of all, resistless, daring, bold in might;

19 The potent Conqueror, invincible in war, him at whose birth the mighty ones,
The kine who spread afar, sent their loud voices out, heavens, earths sent their loud voices out.

20 O Indra, if a hundred heavens and if a hundred earths were thine—
No, not a thousand suns could match thee at thy birth, not both the worlds, O Thunderer.

21 Thou, Hero, hast performed thy hero deeds with might, yea, all with strength, O Strongest One.
Maghavan, help us to a stable full of kine, O Thunderer, with wondrous aids.

HYMN XCIII.

May our hymns give thee great delight. Display thy bounty, Thunderer.
Drive off the enemies of prayer.

2 Crush with thy foot the niggard churls who bring no gifts. Mighty art thou:
There is not one to equal thee.

3 Thou art the Lord of Soma pressed, Soma unpressed is also thine.
Thou art the Sovran of the folk.

4 Swaying about, the active Ones came nigh to Indra at his birth,
And shared his great heroic might.

Taken from Ṛ. V. VIII. 53. 1—3; X. 153.

3 *Unpressed:* in its natural state in the stalks of the plant; or, as Ludwig suggests, the celestial Soma which Indra drinks in heaven may be intended.

4 The hymn from which stanzas 4—8 are taken is ascribed to Indra's Mothers, the sisters of the Gods. *The active Ones:* the Water-Goddesses may be meant.

5 Based upon strength and victory and power, O Indra is thy birth.
Thou, Mighty One, art strong indeed.
6 Thou art the Vritra-slayer, thou, Indra, hast spread the firmament:
Thou hast with might upheld the heavens.
7 Thou, Indra, bearest in thine arms the lightning that accords with thee,
Whetting thy thunderbolt with might.
8 Thou, Indra, art preëminent over all creatures in thy strength:
Thou hast pervaded every place.

HYMN XCIV.

May Sovran Indra come to the carousal, he who by holy Law is strong and active,
The overcomer of all conquering forces with his great bull-like power that hath no limit.
2 Firm-seated is thy car, thy steeds are docile: thy hand, O King, holds, firmly grasped, the thunder.
On thy fair path, O Lord of men come quickly: we will increase thy power when thou hast drunken.
3 Let strong and mighty steeds who bear this mighty Indra, the Lord of men, whose arm wields thunder,
Bring unto us, as sharers of our banquet, the Bull of conquering might, of real vigour.
4 So like a bull thou rushest to the Lord who loves the trough, the Sage, the prop of vigour, in the vat.

---

5 *Thou, Mighty One:* or, O Bull, thou art a Bull indeed.

7 *Lightning:* or, praise-song, hymn. Sâyaṇa explains *arkám* here by *stutyam:* thy laudable or adorable thunderbolt.

The hymn is taken from Ṛ. V. X. 44.

4 *The Lord:* Soma. *The trough:* the wooden vessel which receives the filtered Soma juice. *Collect them in thyself:* 'take us into thyself.' —Wilson. *Of the wise: kenipắnắm* is thus explained by the Commentators, but the meaning seems doubtful. Prof. Ludwig thinks that 'the master *of the oars,*' that is, the steersman, is intended. Prof. Grassmann translates *kenipắnắm* by 'Flutgebieter,' Controllers of the Floods,' meaning, perhaps, the demons who withhold the waters of heaven.

Prepare thine energies, collect them in thyself: be for our profit as the Master of the wise.

5 May precious treasures come to us,—so will I pray. Come to the votary's gift offered with beauteous laud.

Thou art the Lord, as such sit on this holy grass: thy vessels are inviolate as Law commands.

6 Far went our earliest invocations of the Gods, and won us glories that can never be surpassed.

They who could not ascend the ship of sacrifice sink down in desolation, trembling with alarm.

7 So be the others, evil-hearted, far away, whose horses difficult to harness have been yoked.

Here in advance men stand anear to offer gifts, by whom full many a work that brings reward is done.

8 He firmly fixed the plains and mountains as they shook. Dyaus thundered forth and made the air's mid-region quake.

He stays apart the two confronting bowls; he sings lauds in the potent Soma's joy when he hath drunk.

9 I bear this deftly-fashioned goad of thine wherewith thou, Maghavan, shalt break the strikers with the hoof.

At the libation mayst thou be well satisfied. Partake the juice, partake the banquet, Bounteous Lord.

---

6 *In desolation:* *írmáḥ* = ἔρημοι.—Ludwig. *Trembling in alarm:* doers of ill deeds, according to Yâska's interpretation of *képayaḥ*.

7 *Whose horses difficult to harness have been yoked:* whose ill-managed attempts to perform acceptable sacrifice have begun and failed. *In advance:* before death, according to Sâyaṇa.

8 *He:* Indra. *As they shook:* cf. 'He who fixed fast and firm the earth that staggered, and set at rest the agitated mountains' (Ṛ. V. II. 12. 2). *Two confronting bowls:* heaven and earth, hemispherical in appearance and seeming to meet at the horizon.

9 *Goad:* the hymn of praise which urges Indra to action. *The strikers with the hoof:* a class of Yâtudhânas or demons: cf. 'the hoof-armed demon' (Ṛ. V. X. 87. 12).

10 O Much-invoked, may we subdue all famine and evil want with store of grain and cattle.
May we allied, as first in rank, with princes, obtain possessions by our own exertions.

11 Bṛihaspati protect us from the rearward, and from above, and from below, from sinners!
May Indra from the front and from the centre, as friend to friends, vouchsafe us room and freedom.

HYMN XCV.

FROM the three jars the Great and Strong hath drunk drink blent with meal. With Vishṇu hath he quaffed the flowing Soma juice, all that he would.
That hath so heightened him the Great, the Vast, to do his mighty work.
So may the God attend the God, true Indu Indra who is true.

2 Sing strength to Indra that shall set his chariot in the foremost place.
Giver of room in closest fight, slayer of foes in shock of war, be thou our great encourager. Let the weak bowstrings break upon the bows of feeble enemies.

3 Thou didst destroy the Dragon: thou sentest the rivers down to earth.
Foeless, O Indra, wast thou born. Thou tendest well each choicest thing. Therefore we draw us close to thee. Let the weak bowstrings break upon the bows of feeble enemies.

---

10 This and the following stanza are repeated from A. V. XX. 17. 10, 11, and 89. 10, 11.

Taken from Ṛ. V. II. 22. 1; X. 133. 1—3.

1 *From the three jars:* Soma-vessels. According to Sâyaṇa, 'At the Trikadrukas,' the first three days of the religious ceremony called Abhiplava. *The God:* Indu, the deified Soma.

2 *In the foremost place:* in the van of our army, to lead us against the enemy. The original hymn, ascribed to Sudâs (see Ṛ. V. VII. 18, 19) is a prayer for victory in battle.

4 Destroyed be all malignities and all our enemy's designs.
Thy bolt thou castest at the foe, O Indra, who would smite us dead: thy liberal bounty gives us wealth.
Let the weak bowstrings break upon the bows of feeble enemies.

HYMN XCVI.

TASTE this strong draught that gives thee vital vigour: with all thy chariot here unyoke thy coursers.
Let not those other sacrificers stay thee, Indra; these juices shed for thee are ready.

2 Thine is the juice effused, thine are the juices yet to be pressed: our resonant songs invite thee.
O Indra, pleased to-day with this libation, come, thou who knowest all, and drink the Soma.

3 Whoso, devoted to the God, effuses Soma for him with yearning heart and spirit,—
Never doth Indra give away his cattle: for him he makes the lovely Soma famous.

4 He looks with loving favour on the mortal who, like a rich man, pours for him the Soma.
Maghavan in his bended arm supports him: he slays, unasked, the men who hate devotion.

5 We call on thee to come to us, desirous of booty, and of cattle, and of horses.
For thy new love and favour are we present: let us invoke thee, Indra, as our welfare.

6 For life I set thee free by this oblation from the unknown decline and from consumption;

This composite hymn is taken from R. V. X. 160. 1—5; 161. 1—5; 162; 163; 164. 1. Stanzas 6—9 have occurred, with slight variations, in A. V. III. 11. 1—4. For stanzas 17—22 cf. the similar hymn, cf. A. V. II. 33.

4 *Who hate devotion:* 'haters of Brâhmans,' according to Sâyaṇa.

6 The original hymn from which this stanza and the four following are taken is a charm to cure the disease called Râjayakshma, Consumption or Atrophy. *Unknown decline:* some insidious disease differing from pulmonary Consumption. See III. 11. 1, note.

Or, if the grasping demon have possessed him, free him from her, O Indra, thou and Agni.

7 Be his days ended, be he now departed, be he brought very near to death already,
Out of Destruction's lap again I bring him, save him for life to last a hundred autumns.

8 With thousand-eyed oblation, hundred-autumned, bringing a hundred lives, have I restored him,
That Indra for a hundred years may lead him safe to the farther shore of all misfortune.

9 Live waxing in thy strength a hundred autumns, live through a hundred springs, a hundred winters.
Through hundred-lived oblation Indra, Agni, Bṛihaspati, Savitar yield him for a hundred!

10 So have I found and rescued thee: thou hast returned with youth renewed.
Whole in thy members! I have found whole sight and all thy life for thee.

11 May Agni yielding to our prayer, the Rakshas-killer, drive away.
The malady of evil name that hath beset thy labouring womb.

12 Agni, concurring in the prayer, drive off the eater of thy flesh,
The malady of evil name that hath attacked thy babe and womb.

13 That which destroys the sinking germ, the settled, moving embryo,
That which would kill the babe at birth, even this will we drive far away.

14 That which divides thy legs that it may lie between the married pair,
That penetrates and licks thy side, even this will we exterminate.

Grasping demon: Grâhi.

9 *For a hundred:* years, understood.

11 This and the five following stanzas form an incantation designed to exorcise various evil spirits that beset women. Cf. A. V. VIII. 6.

15 What rests by thee in borrowed form of brother, lover, or of lord,
And would destroy the progeny,—even this will we exterminate.
16 That which through sleep or darkness hath deceived thee and lies down by thee,
And will destroy thy progeny,—even this will we exterminate.
17 From both thy nostrils, from thine eyes, from both thine ears and from thy chin,
Forth from thy head and brain and tongue I drive thy malady away.
18 From the neck-tendons and the neck, from the breast-bones and from the spine,
From shoulders, upper, lower arms, I drive thy malady away.
19 From viscera and all within, forth from the rectum, from the heart,
From kidneys, liver, and from spleen, I drive thy malady away.
20 From thighs, from knee-caps, and from heels, and from the forepart of the feet,
From hips, from stomach, and from groin, I drive thy malady away.
21 From what is voided from within, and from thy hair, and from thy nails,
From all thyself, from top to toe, I drive thy malady away.
22 From every member, every hair, disease that comes in every joint,
From all thyself, from top to toe, I drive thy malady away.
23 Avaunt, thou Master of the Mind! Depart and vanish far away.
Look on Destruction far from us. The live man's mind is manifold.

---

17 This and the five following stanzas are a charm against Consumption.
23 *Master of the Mind:* the spirit of evil dreams is addressed.

HYMN XCVII.

Here verily yesterday we let the Thunder-wielder drink his fill.
So in like manner offer him the juice to-day. Now range you by the Glorious One.

2 Even the wolf, the savage beast that rends the sheep, follows the path of his decrees.
So, Indra, graciously accepting this our praise, with wondrous thought come forth to us.

3 What manly deed of vigour now remains that Indra hath not done?
Who hath not heard his glorious title and his fame, the Vṛitra-slayer from his birth?

HYMN XCVIII.

That we may win us wealth and spoil we poets verily call on thee.
In war men call on thee, Indra, the hero's Lord, in the steed's race-course call on thee.

2 As such, O Wonderful whose hand holds thunder, praised as mighty, Caster of the Stone,
Pour on us boldly, Indra, kine and chariot-steeds, ever to be the conqueror's strength.

HYMN XCIX.

Men with their lauds are urging thee, Indra, to drink the Soma first.
The Ṛibhus in accord have lifted up their voice and Rudras sung thee as the First.

Taken from Ṛ. V. VIII. 55 (66). 7—9.

2 *The wolf:* according to Sâyaṇa, the robber.

Taken from Ṛ. V. VI. 46. 1, 2.

Taken from Ṛ. V. VIII. 3. 7—8.

1 *Ṛibhus:* as deities connected with the seasons which are regulated by the Sun identified with, or made to shine by, Indra. *Rudras:* the Maruts, the constant companions of Indra.

2 Indra increased his manly strength at sacrifice, in the wild rapture of this juice;
And living men to-day, even as of old, sing forth their praises to his majesty.

HYMN C.

Now have we, Indra, Friend of Song, sent our great wishes forth to thee,
Coming like floods that follow floods.

2 As rivers swell the ocean, so, Hero, our prayers increase thy might,
Though of thyself, O Thunderer, waxing day by day.

3 With holy song they bind to the broad wide-yoked car the bay steeds of the rapid God,
Bearers of Indra, yoked by prayer.

HYMN CI.

Agni we choose, the messenger, the herald, master of all wealth,
Well skilled in this our sacrifice.

2 With calls they ever invocate Agni, Agni, Lord of the House,
Oblation-bearer, much-beloved.

3 Bring the Gods hither, Agni, born for him who strews the sacred grass.
Thou art our herald, meet for praise.

---

2 *Sacrifice: vishṇavi;* 'For Vishṇu is the sacrifice.'—Ṣatapatha-Brâhmaṇa, I. 1. 2. 13.

Taken from Ṛ. V. VIII. 87 (98). 7—9.

1 *Coming like floods:* in crowds. The line is obscure. 'As men going by water (splash their friends) with handfuls'.—Wilson.

Taken from Ṛ. V. I. 12. 1—3.

1 *The messenger:* the mediator between men and Gods by wafting oblations to heaven. *The herald: devânâm âhvâtâram*, inviter or summoner of the Gods, is Sâyaṇa's explanation of *hótâram* here.

3 *Born:* newly produced by attrition for the man who has trimmed and spread the sacrificial grass as a seat for the priests and the expected deities.

HYMN CII.

MEET to be lauded and adored, showing in beauty through the dark,
Agni the Bull is kindled well.

2 Agni is kindled as a Bull, like a horse bearer of the Gods:
Men with oblations worship him.

3 Thee will we kindle as a Bull, we who are bulls ourselves, O Bull,
Thee, Agni, shining mightily.

HYMN CIII.

SOLICIT with your hymns, for aid, Agni the God with piercing flame,
For riches famous Agni, Purumîlha and ye men, Agni to light our dwelling well.

2 Agni, come hither with thy fires: we choose thee as our Hotar-priest.
Let the extended ladle full of oil balm thee, best priest, to sit on sacred grass.

3 For unto thee, O Angiras, O Son of Strength, move ladles in the sacrifice.
To Agni, Child of Force, whose locks drop oil, we seek, foremost in sacrificial rites.

HYMN CIV.

MAY these my songs of praise exalt thee, Lord who hast abundant wealth.

Taken from Ṛ. V. III. 27. 13—15.

1 *The Bull:* or, the strong.

Taken from Ṛ. V. VIII. 60 (71). 14; 49. 1, 2.

1 *Purumîlha:* an ancient sage of the family of Angiras, and one of the two Ṛishis to whom the original hymn is ascribed. The singer may be addressing himself.

3 *Angiras:* a name of Agni as first and greatest mediator between men and Gods. *Son of Strength:* as fire produced by the violent agitation of the drill. *Child of Force* has the same meaning. *Whose locks drop oil:* 'butter-haired.'—Wilson.

Taken from Ṛ. V. VIII. 3. 3, 4; 79 (90). 1, 2.

Men skilled in holy hymns, bright with the hues of fire, have sung them with their lauds to thee.

2 He, with his might enhanced by Ṛishis thousandfold, hath like an ocean spread himself.
His majesty is praised as true at solemn rites, his power where holy singers rule.

3 May Indra, who in every fight must be invoked, be near to us.
May the most mighty Vṛitra-slayer, meet for praise, come to libations and to hymns.

4 Thou art the best of all in sending bounteous gifts, true art thou, lordly in thine act.
We claim alliance with the very Glorious One, yea, with the mighty Son of Strength.

HYMN CV.

Thou in thy battles, Indra, art subduer of all hostile bands.
Father art thou, all-conquering, cancelling the curse, thou victor of the vanquisher.

2 The earth and heaven cling close to thy victorious might, as sire and mother to their child.
When thou attackest Vṛitra all the hostile bands shrink and faint, Indra at thy wrath.

3 Bring to your aid the Eternal One, who shoots and none may shoot at him,
Inciter, swift, victorious, best of charioteers, Tugrya's unvanquished strengthener;

---

1 *With the hues of fire*: or, bright as Agni is.

4 *Son of Strength*: the Strong One.

Stanzas 1—3 are from Ṛ. V. VIII. 88. 5—7 and stanzas 4, 5 from VIII. 59. 1, 2.

3 *Tugrya*: son of Tugra; Bhujyu a Râjarshi or royal sage who was miraculously rescued from drowning by the Asvins.

HYMN CVI.

THAT lofty energy of thine, thy strength and thine intelligence,
Thy thunderbolt for which we long, our wish makes keen.

2 O Indra, heaven and earth augment thy manly power and thy renown,
The waters and the mountains stir and urge thee on.

3 Vishṇu, the lofty Ruling Power, Varuṇa, Mitra sing thy praise:
In thee the Maruts' company hath great delight.

HYMN CVII.

BEFORE his hot displeasure all the peoples, all the men bow down,
As rivers bend them to the sea.

2 This power of his shone brightly forth when Indra brought together like
A skin the worlds of earth and heaven.

3 The fiercely-moving Vṛitra's head he severed with his thunderbolt,
His hundred-knotted thunderbolt.

4 In all the worlds That was the best and highest whence sprang the mighty God, of splendid valour.
As soon as born he overcomes his foemen, he in whom all who lend him aid are joyful.

Taken from Ṛ. V. VIII. 15. 7—9.

1 *Our wish:* our hopes and wishes expressed in praise, prayer, and sacrifice.

Stanzas 1—3 are taken from Ṛ. V. VIII. 6. 4—6; stanzas 4—12 from X. 120; stanza 13 from A. V. XIII. 2. 34; and 14, 15 from Ṛ. V. I. 115. 1, 2.

2 *Brought together like a skin:* that is, spread the heavens over the earth as a skin is laid on the ground for a carpet.

4 *That:* meaning, according to Sâyaṇa, Brahma the original cause of the universe. Stanzas 4—12 appear with variations, as Hymn 2 of Book V. of the Atharva-veda.

5 Grown mighty in his strength, with ample vigour, he as a foe strikes fear into the Dâsa,
Eager to win the breathing and the breathless. All sang thy praise at banquet and oblation.

6 All concentrate on thee their mental vigour, what time these, twice or thrice, are thine assistants.
Blend what is sweeter than the sweet with sweetness: win quickly with our meath that meath in battle.

7 Therefore in thee too, thou who winnest riches, at every banquet are the sages joyful.
With mightier power, bold God, extend thy firmness: let not malignant Yâtudhânas harm thee.

8 Proudly we put our trust in thee in battles, when we behold great wealth the prize of combat.
I with my words impel thy weapons onward, and sharpen with my prayer thy vital vigour.

9 Worthy of praises, many-shaped, most skilful, most energetic, Âptya of the Âptyas:
He with his might destroys the seven Dânus, subduing many who were deemed his equals.

---

5 *Eager to win*: Prof. Ludwig makes *sásni* an infinitive. *Sasnih* may be the correct reading. See Grassmann, *Wörterbuch Zum Rigveda*. *The breathing and the breathless*: the animate and the inanimate world.

6 *Mental vigour*: *krátum*: 'adoration.'—Wilson. *These*: Soma juices. *Twice or thrice*: with reference, perhaps, to the three daily libations. *What is sweeter than the sweet*: thine own celestial Soma. Sâyaṇa explains the stanza differently:—'To thee all (worshippers) offer adoration, whether those propitiators be two or three. Combine that which is sweeter than the sweet with sweetness, unite that honey with honey.'—Wilson. The 'two or three,' according to Sâyaṇa, are the sacrificer and his wife and child, and the second half of the stanza contains a reference to the propagation of children.

9 *Âptya*: the name of a class of deities of whom Trita Âptya is chief. 'Most accessible of the accessible.'—Wilson. The first line is without a verb. I praise him, may be understood. *Dânus*: a class of powerful demons.

10 Thou in that house which thy protection guardeth bestowest wealth, the higher and the lower.
Thou stablishest the two much-wandering Mothers, and bringest many deeds to their completion.

11 Bṛihaddiva, the foremost of light-winners, repeats these holy prayers, this strength to Indra.
He rules the great self-luminous fold of cattle, and all the doors of light hath he thrown open.

12 Thus hath Bṛihaddiva, the great Atharvan, spoken to Indra as himself in person.
The Mâtarisvarîs, the spotless sisters, with power exalt him and impel him onward.

13 Bright Presence of the Gods, the luminous herald, Sûrya hath mounted the celestial regions.
Day's maker, he hath shone away the darkness, and radiant passed o'er places hard to traverse.

14 The brilliant Presence of the Gods hath risen, the eye of Mitra, Varuṇa, and Agni.
The soul of all that moveth not or moveth, Sûrya hath filled the earth and air and heaven.

15 Even as a lover followeth a maiden, so doth the Sun the Dawn, refulgent Goddess:
Where pious men extend their generations before the Gracious One for happy fortune.

---

10 *The higher and the lower:* heavenly and earthly. *Mothers:* Heaven and Earth.

11 *Foremost of light-winners:* chief of Ṛishis who enjoy the light of heaven.

12 *The great Atharvan:* or Fire-priest. *As himself:* he identifies himself with the God whom he worships. *The Mâtarisvarîs:* Sâyaṇa explains *mâtariśvarî* by 'abiding in the mother earth,' *the spotless sisters* being the Rivers. Cf. A. V. V. 29., note

15 The exact meaning of the second line is somewhat uncertain. As I have rendered it, in accordance with Ludwig, it reminds one of Shelley's, 'Man, the imperial shape, then multiplied His generations under the pavilion Of the Sun's throne. Wilson, following Sâyaṇa, paraphrases, 'At which season pious men perform (the cere-

HYMN CVIII.

O INDRA, bring great strength to us, bring valour, Satakratu, thou most active, bring
A hero conquering in war.

2 For, gracious Ṣatakratu, thou hast ever been a mother and a sire to us,
So now for bliss we pray to thee.

3 To thee, Strong, Much-invoked who showest forth thy strength, O Ṣatakratu, do I speak:
So grant thou us heroic might.

HYMN CIX.

THE juice of Soma thus diffused, sweet to the taste, the bright Cows drink
Who for the sake of splendour close to mighty Indra's side rejoice, good in their own supremacy.

2 Craving his touch the dappled Kine mingle the Soma with their milk.
The milch-kine dear to Indra send forth his death-dealing thunderbolt, good in their own supremacy.

3 With veneration, passing wise, honouring his victorious might,
They follow close his many laws to win them due preëminence, good in their own supremacy.

---

monies established for) ages.' Sâyaṇa proposes an alternative rendering by taking *yugâni* (generations, ages,) to mean 'yokes for ploughs'; 'for, at this season, men seeking to propitiate the gods by the profit which agriculture yields, equip their ploughs.'

Taken from R. V. VIII. 88 (99). 10—12.

Taken from R. V. I. 84. 10—12.

1 *The bright Cows*: the waters which absorb or drink the Soma juice with which they are mixed, and which is close to, or united with, Indra when offered to and accepted by him in libation.

3 *Send forth*: the Cows, that is, the waters, exalt and strengthen Indra, and incite him to battle with the demons. The meaning of the refrain of this triad is not very clear. Wilson, following Sâyaṇa, translates it: 'abiding (in their stalls) expectant of his sovereignty.'

HYMN CX.

For Indra, lover of carouse, loud be our songs about the juice:
Let poets sing the hymn of praise.

2 We summon Indra to the draught, in whom all glories rest, in whom
The seven communities rejoice.

3 By the three Soma jars the Gods span sacrifice that stirs the mind:
Let our songs aid and prosper it.

HYMN CXI.

If, Indra, thou drink Soma by Vishnu's or Trita Âptya's side,
Or with the Maruts take delight in flowing drops;

2 Or, Sakra, if thou gladden thee afar or in the sea of air,
Rejoice thee in this juice of ours, in flowing drops.

3 Or, Lord of Heroes, if thou aid the worshipper who sheds the juice,
Or him whose laud delights thee, and his flowing drops.

HYMN CXII.

Whatever, Vritra-slayer! thou, Sûrya, hast risen upon to-day,
That, Indra, all is in thy power.

Taken from R. V. VIII. 81 (92). 19—21.

2 *The seven communities*: *saptá saṁsádaḥ*, meaning, probably, all the people: 'the seven associated priests.'—Wilson.

3 *By the three Soma jars*: according to Sâyana, 'At the Trikadrukas,' on the first three days of the Abhiplava ceremony. *Span*: sacrifice being regarded as a long unbroken thread.

Taken from R. V. VIII. 12. 16—18.

1 *Trita Âptya*: Trita (perhaps Agni as lightning) who dwells in the waters or watery clouds of the sea of air.

Taken from R. V. VIII. 82 (93). 4—6.

2 When, Mighty One, Lord of the Brave, thou thinkest, I shall never die,
That thought of thine is true indeed.

3 Thou, Indra, goest unto all Soma libations shed for thee,
Both far away and near at hand.

HYMN CXIII.

Both boons—may Indra hitherward turned, listen to this prayer of ours,
And mightiest Maghavan with thought inclined to us come nigh to drink the Soma juice.

2 For him, strong independent Ruler, Heaven and Earth have fashioned forth for power and might.
Thou seatest thee as first among thy peers in place, for thy soul longs for Soma juice.

HYMN CXIV.

O Indra, from all ancient time rivalless ever and companionless art thou:
In war thou seekest comradeship.

2 Thou findest not the wealthy man to be thy friend: those scorn thee who are flown with wine.
What time thou thunderest and gatherest, then thou, even as a father, art invoked.

---

2 *I shall never die:* cf. 'So have I heard Indrâṇî called most fortunate among these Dames, For never shall her Consort die in future time through length of days' (Ṛ. V. X. 86. 11).

Taken from Ṛ. V. VIII. 50 (61). 1, 2.

1 *Both boons:* Indra is asked to hear the prayer and to drink the libation.

Taken from Ṛ. V. VIII. 21. 13, 14.

1 *In war thou seekest comradeship:* befriendest thy worshippers when they need thy assistance in battle.

2 *Gatherest:* the clouds that bring the welcome rain.

HYMN CXV.

I FROM my Father have received deep knowledge of the holy Law:
I was born like unto the Sun.

2 After the lore of ancient time I make, like Kaṇva, beauteous songs,
And Indra's self gains strength thereby.

3 Whatever Rishis have not praised thee, Indra, or have lauded thee,
By me exalted wax thou strong.

HYMN CXVI.

NEVER may we be cast aside and strangers, as it were to thee,
We, Thunder-wielding Indra, count ourselves as trees rejected and unfit to burn.

2 O Vṛitra-slayer, we were thought slow and unready for the fray:
Yet once in thy great bounty may we have delight,
O Hero, after praising thee.

HYMN CXVII.

DRINK Soma, Lord of Bays, and let it cheer thee:
Indra, the stone, like a well-guided courser,
Directed by the presser's arms hath pressed it.

2 So let the draught of joy, thy dear companion, by which, O Lord of Bays, thou slayest foemen,
Delight thee, Indra, Lord of princely treasures.

Taken from Ṛ. V. VIII. 6. 10—12.

1 *From my Father*: from Indra the true protector, according to Sàyaṇa.

3 *Have not praised thee*: have not praised thee yet, that is, will praise thee hereafter.—Ludwig.

Taken from Ṛ. V. VIII. 1. 13, 14.

Taken from Ṛ. V. VII. 22. 1—3.

3 Mark closely, Maghavan, the words I utter, this eulogy recited by Vasishṭha :
Accept the prayers I offer at thy banquet.

HYMN CXVIII.

INDRA with all thy saving helps give us assistance, Lord of Power :
For after thee we follow even as glorious bliss, thee, Hero, finder-out of wealth.

2 Increaser of our steeds and multiplying kine, a golden well, O God, art thou ;
For no one may impair the gifts laid up in thee. Bring me whatever thing I ask.

3 Indra for worship of the Gods, Indra while sacrifice proceeds,
Indra as warriors in the battle-shock we call, Indra that we may win the spoil.

4 With might hath Indra spread out heaven and earth, with power hath Indra lighted up the Sun.
In Indra are all creatures closely held ; in him meet the distilling Soma drops.

HYMN CXIX.

AN ancient praise-song hath been sung: to Indra have ye said the prayer.
They have sung many a Bṛihatî of sacrifice, poured forth the worshipper's many thoughts.

2 In zealous haste the singers have sung forth a song distilling oil and rich in sweets.
Riches have spread among us, and heroic strength : with us are flowing Soma drops.

---

3 *Vasishṭha* : the ancient Ṛishi to whom the hymns of Book VII. of the Ṛ. V. are ascribed.

Taken from Ṛ. V. VIII. 50 (61), 5, 6 ; 3. 5, 6.

Taken from Vâlakhilya 4. 9, and 3. 10 (M. Müller Ṛ. V. VIII. 52. 9, and 51. 10).

HYMN CXX.

THOUGH, Indra, thou art called by men eastward and westward, north and south,
Thou chiefly art with Ânava and Turvaṣa, brave Champion! urged by men to come.

2 Or, Indra, when with Ruma, Ruṣama, Ṣyâvaka, and Kṛipa thou rejoicest thee,
Still do the Kaṇvas bringing praises, with their prayers, O Indra, draw thee hither: come.

HYMN CXXI.

OVER the three great distances, past the Five Peoples go thy way,
O Indra, noticing our voice.

2 Send forth thy ray like Sûrya: let my songs attract thee hitherward
Like waters gathering to the vale.

HYMN CXXII.

WITH Indra splendid feasts be ours enriched with ample spoil, wherewith,
Wealthy in food, we may rejoice.

Taken from Ṛ. V. VIII. 4. 1, 2.

1 *Ânava and Turvaṣa:* the tribes of the Anus and the Turvaṣas of the Five Âryan Nations.

2 The men mentioned in the first line appear to be princes specially favoured by Indra.

Taken from Ṛ. V. VIII. 32. 22, 23.

1 *The three great distances:* the space in front of thee, behind thee, and at thy side. *Noticing our voice:* hearing and attending to our invocations. Come to us who are thy true worshippers, and pass by others who worship thee in the hope of being avenged upon their enemies or of obtaining pardon for some sin.

2 Like thee, thyself, the singers' friend, thou movest as it were, besought,
Bold One, the axle of the car,

3 That, Ṣatakratu, thou to grace and please thy praisers, as it were,
Stirrest the axle with thy strength.

HYMN CXXIII.

THIS is the Godhead, this the might of Sûrya: he hath withdrawn what spread o'er work unfinished.
When he hath loosed his horses from their station, straight over all night spreadeth out her garment.

2 In the sky's lap the Sun this form assumeth for Mitra and for Varuṇa to look on.
His bay steeds well maintain his power eternal, at one time bright and darksome at another.

HYMN CXXIV.

WITH what help will he come to us, wonderful, ever-waxing Friend,
With what most mighty company?

2 What genuine and most liberal draught will spirit thee with juice to burst

---

2 The lines in this and the following stanza referring to the axle and the chariot or wain are somewhat obscure and have been variously interpreted. Ludwig's explanation, which I follow, appears to be the simplest and the best. The expression, movest, or stirrest, the axle, which is the firmest and strongest part of the car, is intended to signify Indra's great strength exerted at his worshippers' prayer.

Taken from Ṛ. V. I. 115. 4, 5.

1 *He hath withdrawn*: that is, says Wilson, 'the cultivator or artisan desists from his labour, although unfinished, upon the setting of the sun;' when the sun 'has withdrawn (into himself) the diffused (light which has been shed) upon the unfinished task.'

Taken from Ṛ. V. IV. 31. 1—3; X. 157; VI. 17. 15. Stanzas 4—6 are repeated from A. V. XX. 63.

1 *He*: Indra.

2 *Genuine and most liberal*: producing good results and causing

Open e'en strongly-guarded wealth?

3 Do thou who art protector of us thy friends who praise thee
With hundred aids approach us.

4 We will, with Indra and all Gods to help us, bring these existing worlds into subjection.
Our sacrifice, our bodies, and our offspring shall Indra form together with the Âdityas.

5 With the Âdityas, with the band of Maruts, may Indra be protector of our bodies.
As when the Gods came after they had slaughtered the Asuras, keeping safe their Godlike nature,

6 Brought the Sun hitherward with mighty powers, and looked about them on their vigorous Godhead.
With this may we obtain strength God-appointed, and joy with brave sons through a hundred winters.

HYMN CXXV.

DRIVE all our enemies away, O Indra, the western, mighty Conqueror, and the eastern.
Hero, drive off our northern foes and southern, that we in thy wide shelter may be joyful.

2 What then? As men whose fields are full of barley reap the ripe corn removing it in order,
So bring the food of those men, bring it hither, who come not to prepare the grass for worship.

3 Men come not with one horse at sacred seasons; thus they obtain no honour in assemblies.
Sages desiring herds of kine and horses strengthen the mighty Indra for his friendship.

---

thee to be most bountiful. *Strongly-guarded wealth:* to burst open the treasure-houses of our enemies and give us their contents; or the allusion may be to the waters shut up in the clouds.

Taken from R. V. X. 131.

3 *With one horse:* it seems to have been considered undignified and disreputable for a wealthy man to come to the sacrifice in a one-horse car; but the precise meaning of the first line is somewhat uncertain.

4 Ye, Aṣvins, Lords of Splendour, drank full draughts of grateful Soma juice,
And aided Indra in his work with Namuchi of Asura birth.

5 As parents aid a son, both Aṣvins, Indra, aided thee with their wondrous powers and wisdom.
When thou, with might, hadst drunk the draught that gladdens, Sarasvatî, O Maghavan, refreshed thee.

6 Indra is strong to save, rich in assistance: may he, possessing all, be kind and gracious.
May he disperse our foes and give us safety, and may we be the lords of hero vigour.

7 May we enjoy his favour, his the holy: may we enjoy his blessèd loving-kindness.
May this rich Indra, as our good protector, drive off and keep afar all those who hate us.

HYMN CXXVI.

MEN have abstained from pouring juice; nor counted Indra as a God,
Where at the votary's store my friend Vṛishâkapi hath drunk his fill. Supreme is Indra over all.

2 Thou, Indra, heedless passest by the ill Vṛishâkapi hath wrought;
Yet nowhere else thou findest place wherein to drink the Soma juice. Supreme is Indra over all.

---

4 The myth referred to in this and the following stanza has not been preserved. See Weber, Ueber den Râjasûya, pp. 95, 101.

Taken from R. V. X. 86.

1 Sâyaṇa ascribes this stanza to Indra; others make Indrâṇi the speaker. Vṛishâkapi is said to have monopolized the offerings that should have been presented to Indra. *Vṛishâkapi*—literally 'the strong ape,' or 'the male ape'—appears to be a sort of intermediate being between a demigod and a demon; but it is not easy to exactly determine his nature. Sâyaṇa calls him the son of Indra. He is also said to be the setting sun, and the sun who draws up vapour and irrigates with mist. According to M. Bergaigne, *La Religion Védique*, II. 270, he was a mythical sacrificer.

2 Indrâṇi blames Indra for his apathy.

3 What hath he done to injure thee, this tawny beast Vṛishâkapi,
With whom thou art so angry now? What is the votary's foodful store? Supreme is Indra over all.

4 Soon may the hound who hunts the boar seize him and bite him in the ear,
O Indra, that Vṛishâkapi whom thou protectest as a friend. Supreme is Indra over all.

5 Kapi hath marred the beauteous things, all deftly wrought, that were my joy.
In pieces will I rend his head; the sinner's portion shall be woe. Supreme is Indra over all.

6 No dame hath ampler charms than I, or greater wealth of love's delights.
None with more ardour offers all her beauty to her lord's embrace. Supreme is Indra over all.

7 Mother whose love is quickly won, I say what verily will be.
My breast, O mother, and my head and both my hips seem quivering. Supreme is Indra over all.

8 Dame with the lovely hands and arms, with broad hair-plaits and ample hips,
Why, O thou hero's wife, art thou angry with our Vṛishâkapi? Supreme is Indra over all.

---

3 Indra speaks. *What is the votary's foodful store?*: why should his appropriation of the worshipper's offerings make thee so angry?

4 Indrâṇî is the speaker of this stanza and of the two, or three, that follow.

5 *Kapi*: the ape; an abbreviation of Vṛishâkapi. *Hath marred the beauteous things*: according to Sâyaṇa, hath spoiled the oblations prepared for me by my worshippers. But it seems more probable that Vṛishâkapi has assaulted Indrâṇî and inflicted injuries on her person.

6 Indrâṇî speaks with pride of her voluptuous charms which incited Vṛishâkapi to his amorous assault.

7 This stanza is ascribed by Sâyaṇa to Vṛishâkapi. It is hardly intelligible; but, as Prof. Ludwig says, it seems to be spoken by Indrâṇî, expressing her indignation at Vṛishâkapi's audacity which makes all her body quiver with rage.

8 Indra speaks.

9 This noxious creature looks on me as one bereft of hero's love.
Yet heroes for my sons have I, the Maruts' friend and Indra's Queen. Supreme is Indra over all.

10 From olden time the matron goes to feast and general sacrifice.
Mother of heroes, Indra's Queen, the rite's ordainer is extolled. Supreme is Indra over all.

11 So have I heard Indrâṇî called most fortunate among these dames,
For never shall her Consort die in future time through length of days. Supreme is Indra over all.

12 Never, Indrâṇî, have I joyed without my friend Vṛishâkapi,
Whose welcome offering here, made pure with water, goeth to the Gods. Supreme is Indra over all.

13 Wealthy Vṛishâkapâyî, blest with sons and consorts of thy sons,
Indra will eat thy bulls, thy dear oblation that effecteth much. Supreme is Indra over all.

14 Fifteen in number, then, for me a score of bullocks they prepare,
And I devour the fat thereof: they fill my belly full with food. Supreme is Indra over all.

---

9 Indrâṇî speaks this and the following stanza. *Bereft of hero's love*: who has no brave husband to protect her.

10 *The matron goes to feast*: Indrâṇî means that Vṛishâkapi assaulted her when she was on her way to a festival, which women were accustomed to attend; and that her rank as Indra's consort did not preserve her from insult.

11 Indra speaks this and the following stanza.

13 Spoken by Vṛishâkapi to his wife Vṛishâkapâyî who is said to represent the dawn, or, by others, the gloaming which follows the setting sun Vṛishâkapi.

14 Indra speaks. *Fifteen*: sacrificers; probably Vṛishâkapi and his wife, and their sons and daughters-in-law. Sâyaṇa explains differently: 'The worshippers dress for me fifteen (and) twenty bulls.'—Wilson.

15 Like as a bull with pointed horn, loud bellowing amid the herds,
Sweet to thine heart, O Indra, is the brew which she who tends thee pours. Supreme is Indra over all.

18 O Indra, this Vṛishâkapi hath found a slain wild animal,
Dresser, and new-made pan, and knife, and wagon with a load of wood. Supreme is Indra over all.

19 Distinguishing the Dâsa and the Ârya, viewing all, I go.
I look upon the wise, and drink the simple votary's Soma juice. Supreme is Indra over all.

20 The desert plains and steep descents, how many leagues in length they spread!
Go to the nearest houses, go unto thine home, Vṛishâkapi. Supreme is Indra over all.

21 Turn thee again Vṛishâkapi; we twain will bring thee happiness.
Thou goest homeward on thy way along this path which leads to sleep. Supreme is Indra over all.

---

15 Indrâṇî speaks, endeavouring to attract him to her own libation instead of the offerings of Vṛishâkapi.

I pass over stanzas 16 and 17, which cannot be decently translated.

18 Indrâṇî speaks, but her speech is difficult to understand. *Wild animal:* Prof. Roth conjectures 'wild ass' as the meaning of *pârasvantam* here. The wild buffalo may perhaps be intended. *Dresser:* or slaughter-bench. 'A fire-place (to cook it).'—Wilson. Indrâṇî seems to speak depreciatingly of a sacrifice offered by Vṛishâkapi as consisting of an unsuitable victim, prepared with instruments and means which chance has thrown in his way. Prof. Ludwig thinks that Vṛishâkapi may represent the Moon whose spots are fancifully considered to be the objects mentioned by Indrâṇî.

19 *I look:* with favour. *The simple votary* is the worshipper who offers his libation in a sincere spirit of devotion. The stanza and the two following are spoken by Indra.

20 Vṛishâkapi appears to meditate flight into distant deserts to escape from the wrathful Indrâṇî. Indra dissuades him, and promises to reconcile Indrâṇî to him.

22 When, Indra and Vṛishâkapi, ye travelled upward to your home,
Where was that noisome beast, to whom went it, the beast that troubles man? Supreme is Indra over all.

23 Daughter of Manu, Parṣu bare a score of children at a birth.
Her portion verily was bliss although her burthen caused her grief.

---

22 The two concluding stanzas seem to be spoken by Indrâṇî. Stanza 22 is obscure, and stanza 23 has no discoverable connexion with the rest of the hymn.

23 *Daughter of Manu:* that is, of human race. Nothing more is known of *Parṣu.* Much of this hymn appears to be inexplicable. M. Bergaigne thinks that Vṛishâkapi, Indra's friend, represents Soma, and Indrâṇî the wife of Indra represents Prayer. 'This bizarre myth would symbolize the frequently expressed idea that Indra loves neither the sacred beverage without prayer nor prayer without the sacred beverage. He wishes therefore his union with Prayer to be accompanied by the union of Prayer with Soma, and he neglects sacrifice as long as this union of the two essential elements of worship remains unaccomplished.'—See *La Religion Védique*, II. 270, 271.

THE KUNTÂPA SECTION.

HYMN CXXVII.

LISTEN to this, ye men, a laud of glorious bounty shall be sung.
Thousands sixty, and ninety we, O Kaurama, among the Ruṣamas have received.

2 Camels twice-ten that draw the car, with females by their side, he gave.
Fain would the chariot's top bow down escaping from the stroke of heaven.

3 A hundred chains of gold, ten wreaths, upon the Ṛishi he bestowed,
And thrice-a-hundred mettled steeds, ten-times-a-thousand cows he gave.

4 Glut thee, O Singer, glut thee like a bird on a ripe-fruited tree.
Thy lips and tongue move swiftly like the sharp blades of a pair of shears.

5 Quickly and willingly like kine forth come the singers and their hymns:
Their little maidens are at home, at home they wait upon the cows.

Kuntâpa is said to be the name of certain organs or glands, twenty in number, supposed to be situated in the belly. The section of this Book which bears the name is a strange miscellaneous collection of hymns, sacrificial formulas, incantations, riddles, and odds and ends. These songs have no religious character, but, according to the Aitareya-Brâhmaṇa, they are to be recited by the Brâhmaṇâchchhansi after the Vṛishâkapi (Hymn 126 of this Book).

A hymn in praise of the liberality and good government of Kaurama King of the Ruṣamas, a neighbouring people.

1 *Among the Ruṣamas:* cf. Ṛ. V. V. 30. 12—15, where the poet celebrates similar liberality on the part of Ṛiṇanchaya, a King of this people.

5 *They wait upon the cows:* the girls were the milk-maids of the family. Cf. the Sanskrit *duhitar* (from *duh*, to milk), English, *daughter*; Zend *dughdhar*; Greek *thugátêr*; Gothic, *dauhtar*; Persian *dukhtar*; German, *tochter*.

6 O Singer, bring thou forth the hymn that findeth cattle, findeth wealth.
Even as an archer aims his shaft address this prayer unto the Gods.

7 List to Parikshit's eulogy, the sovran whom all people love,
The King who ruleth over all, excelling mortals as a God.

8 'Mounting his throne, Parikshit, best of all, hath given us peace and rest,'
Saith a Kauravya to his wife as he is ordering his house.

9 'Which shall I set before thee, curds, gruel of milk, or barley-brew?'
Thus the wife asks her husband in the realm which King Parikshit rules.

10 Up as it were to heavenly light springs the ripe corn above the cleft.
Happily thrive the people in the land where King Parikshit reigns.

11 Indra hath waked the bard and said, Rise, wander singing here and there.
Praise me, the strong: each pious man will give thee riches in return.

12 Here, cows! increase and multiply, here ye, O horses, here, O men.
Here, with a thousand rich rewards, doth Pûshan also seat himself.

13 O Indra, let these cows be safe, their master free from injury.
Let not the hostile-hearted or the robber have control of them.

---

7 *Parikshit's eulogy:* Parikshit appears to have been a Kauravyan or descendant of the ancient Kuru. In the Aitareya-Brâhmaṇa, VI. 32, this Parikshit (Dweller-round) is said to be Agni, or the year; for Agni 'lives round the people, and the people live round him, and the year dwells round about men, and men dwell round about the year.'

8 *A Kauravya:* one of Parikshit's subjects.

14 Oft and again we glorify the hero with our hymn of praise, with prayer, with our auspicious prayer.
Take pleasure in the songs we sing: let evil never fall on us.

HYMN CXXVIII.

The worshipper who pours the juice, for gathering and assembly fit,
And yonder foe-destroying Sun,—these have the Gods designed of old.

2 He who defiles a sister, he who willingly would harm a friend,
The fool who slights his elder, these, they say, must suffer down below.

3 Whenever any good man's son becometh bold and spirited,
Then hath the wise Gandharva said this pleasant upward-pointing word.

4 The most unprofitable churl, the wealthy man who brings no gift,
These, verily, as we have heard, are cast away by all the wise.

5 But they who have adored the Gods, and they who have bestowed their gifts,
Those liberal lords are filled with wealth like Sûrya risen up to heaven.

The hymn consists of groups of verses which are recited as sacrificial formulas. The first five are called in the Aitareya-Brâhmaṇa the *klṛiptis* or orientations, stanzas which form the directions or determine the points of the compass. For by reciting these verses—one for each cardinal point and one for the zenith or space above them—the priest forms (*kalpayati*) the directions or regions of the sky.

3 *Gandharva:* a Genius, closely connected with the Sun, who declares the secrets of heaven and divine truths. *Upward-pointing:* promising happiness in heaven, contrasted with the suffering 'down below' of stanza 2.

6 With unanointed eyes and limbs, wearing no gem or ring of gold,
No priest, no Brahman's son is he: these things are ordered in the rules.

7 With well-anointed limbs and eyes, wearing fair gem and golden ring,
Good priest is he, the Brahman's son; these things are ordered in the rules.

8 Pools with no place for drinking, and the wealthy man who giveth naught,
The pretty girl you may not touch, these things are ordered in the rules.

9 Pools with good drinking places, and the wealthy man who freely gives,
The pretty girl who may be touched, these things are ordered in the rules.

10 The favourite wife neglected, and the man who safely shuns the fight,
A sluggish horse whom none may guide, these things are ordered in the rules.

11 The favourite wife most dearly loved, the man who safely goes to war,
The fleet steed who obeys the rein, these things are ordered in the rules.

12 When, Indra, thou, as no man could, didst plunge into the Ten Kings' fight,
That was a guard for every man: for he is formed to stay disease.

---

6 Stanzas 6—11 are called the *janakalpa* verses, that is, apparently containing rules and regulations for men. The Aitareya-Brâhmaṇa explains the term differently: 'For making a footing he then repeats the *janâkalpa* verses. For children are *janakalpa* (production of men). Having made the directions in the above manner, he places people in them.'—Haug's Translation, Vol. II. p. 433.

12 Stanzas 12—16 are called the Indra-gâthâs. 'For by means of the Indra songs the Devas sang the Asuras down and defeated them. In the same way the sacrificers put down their enemies by these songs.'—Haug, *ibid. The Ten Kings' Fight:* when Indra aided King Sudâs who was attacked by ten confederate princes. See Ṛ. V. VII. 18; 83. 6—8.

13 Easily-conquering Maghavan, thou, Hero, bentest Raji down,
Rentest asunder Rauhiṇa, clavest in pieces Vṛitra's head.

14 Thou who didst separate the clouds and penetrate the water-floods,—
To thee, great slayer of the foe, be glory, Indra, yea, to thee!

15 They said to Uchchaiṣravasa running as side-horse of the Bays,
Safely to victory, O Steed, bear Indra with the beauteous wreath.

16 They yoke the white mares, on the Bay's right harness Uchchaiṣravasa.
He joyeth as he carrieth Indra the foremost of the Gods.

HYMN CXXIX.

THESE mares come springing forward to Pratîpa Prâtisutvana.

---

13 *Raji:* probably some demon. See Ṛ. V. VI. 26. 6, where it is said by Sâyaṇa to be the name of a damsel. *Rauhiṇa:* a demon of drought; originally, like other fiends of the same class, a dark purple cloud that withholds the rain. See Ṛ. V. I. 103. 2; II. 12. 12.

15 *Uchchaiṣravasa:* the king and prototype of horses produced with other treasures at the Churning of the Ocean. See Mahâbhârata, I. 366, 1094.

The Section containing Hymns CXXIX—CXXXII is called Aitaṣapralâpa, the Talk of Aitaṣa, a Muni or inspired sage of the family of Aurva a descendant of Bhṛigu. The Aitareya-Brâhmaṇa (VI. 33) says that one of Aitaṣa's sons who heard the beginning of the discourse put his hand on his father's mouth to stop it, and said that he had gone mad. Then his father cursed him for murdering his speech. All the verses have been received into the canon for use as sacrificial formulas in the ritual of the Ṛigveda; and, according to the Aitareya-Brâhmaṇa, they have the power of prolonging the life of the sacrificer, of spreading the essence of the metres over the sacrifice, and removing defects in its performance. Regarded as uninspired productions, these hymns are hardly susceptible of intelligible translation or explanation.

1 *Prâtisutvana:* son of Pratisutvana, who may be Pratiṣravas, the grandson of Parîkshit. See Zimmer, Altindisches Leben, p. 131.

3, 4 One of them is Hariknikâ. Hariknikâ, what seekest thou?

5, 6 The excellent, the golden son: where now hast thou abandoned him?

7, 8 There where around those distant trees, three Sisus that are standing there,

9, 10 Three adders, breathing angrily, are blowing loud the threatening horn.

11, 12 Hither hath come a stallion: he is known by droppings on his way,

13, 14 As by their dung the course of kine. What wouldst thou in the home of men?

15, 16 Barley and ripened rice I seek. On rice and barley hast thou fed,

17, 18 As the big serpent feeds on sheep. Cow's hoof and horse's tail hast thou.

19, 20 Winged with a falcon's pinion is that harmless swelling of thy tongue.

HYMN CXXX.

WHO carried off these stores of milk? Who took the dark cow's milk away?

3, 4 Who took away the white cow's milk? Who took the black cow's milk away?

5, 6 Question this man. Where do I ask? Where, whom that knoweth do I ask?

The mares bring the chariot forward that their master may receive the gifts of the liberal King. Cf. CXXX. 11, 12.

3 *Hariknikâ:* or little bay mare.

8 *The golden son:* meaning, apparently, her bright chestnut foal.

14 The question is addressed to the horse.

19, 20 The horse, it seems, is told that he has already eaten too greedily of hard barley and rice which have caused a swelling in his mouth (lampass), which, however, will rapidly pass away without doing any permanent injury.

The hymn has been translated by Zimmer, Altindisches Leben, p. 131

7, 8 Not to the belly comes the grain. The patient ones are angry now.

9, 10 Undecked with gems, and decked with gems: deity rivalling the Sun:

11, 12 Dapple, Harikṇikâ, and Bay ran forward to the liberal gifts.

13, 14 When the horn's blast hath sounded forth let not our friend discover thee.

15, 16 Hither to the cow's son they come. Libation hath rejoiced the God.

17, 18 Then cried they. Here he is, and, Here; again the cry was, Here is he.

19, 20 Then not defective be our steeds! A splinter so diminutive!

HYMN CXXXI.

He minishes, he splits in twain: crush it and let it be destroyed.

3, 4 Varuṇa with the Vasus goes: the Wind-God hath a hundred reins.

5, 6 A hundred golden steeds hath he, a hundred chariots wrought of gold,

7, 8 A hundred bits of golden bronze, a hundred golden necklaces.

9, 10 Lover of Kuṣa grass, Unploughed! Fat is not reckoned in the hoof.

11, 12 The ladle doth not hold apart the entrails and the clotted blood.

7, 8 Apparently the unfed and hungry horses are the subject.

11, 12 Cf. 1—4 of the preceding hymn.

13 *The horn's blast:* cf. 9, 10 of the preceding hymn.

19, 20 Cf. 19, 20 of the preceding hymn. *A splinter: salâkâ;* a tent or probe made of a pointed slip of bamboo; a pointed surgical instrument, the application of which will relieve the horse who suffers from lampass.

13, 14 This, O Maṇḍûrikâ, is mine. Thy trees are standing in a clump.

15, 16 The plain domestic sacrifice, the sacrifice with burning dung.

17, 18 Aṣvattha, Dhava, Khadira, leaf taken from the Araṭu.

19, 20 The man pervaded thoroughly lies on the ground as he were slain.

21, 22 The biestings only have they milked: one-and-a-half of the wild ass,

23 And two hides of an elephant.

HYMN CXXXII.

THEN too the single bottle-gourd, the bottle-gourd dug from the earth,

3, 4 The lute dug up from out the ground: this the wind stirs and agitates.

---

13 *Maṇḍûrikâ:* the word means rust of iron, scoria, dross. Here it appears to be the uncomplimentary name of some female.

15, 16 *Domestic sacrifice:* 'The domestic fire was lighted by each householder on his marriage, and the simple rites, the Pâkayajnas, were easily performed. "A log of wood," says Professor Max Müller, "placed on the fire of the hearth, an oblation poured out to the gods, or alms given to Brâhmaṇas, this is what constitutes a Pâkayajna."'—R. Ch. Dutt, History of Civilization in Ancient India, Book II., Chapter I. *Burning dung:* performed with dried cow-dung for fuel instead of wood.

17, 18 *Dhava:* a beautiful flowering shrub or small tree (Grislea Tomentosa). It is mentioned together with the *Aṣvattha* (Ficus Religiosa) and *Khadira* (Acacia Catechu) in A. V. V. 5. 5. *Araṭu:* a tree (Calosanthes Indica) with hard wood of which the axles of chariots and carts were made.

22 *Wild ass:* the animal called Parasvân. See A. V. VI. 72, 2; 126. 18.

---

1 *Bottle-gourd:* (Lagenaria Vulgaris Ser). The dried shell was used as a water-jar, and also as a musical instrument, a Viṇâ or kind of lute.

4 *Stirs and agitates:* making it an Aeolian harp.

5, 6 Let him prepare a nest, they say: he shall obtain it strong and stretched.

7, 8 He shall not gain it unspread out. Who among these will touch the lute?

9, 10 Who among these will beat the drum? How, if he beat it, will he beat?

11, 12 Where beating will the Goddess beat again again about the house?

13, 14 Three are the names the camel bears, Golden is one of them, he said.

15, 16 Glory and power, these are two. He with black tufts of hair shall strike.

HYMN CXXXIII.

Two rays of light are lengthened out, and the man gently touches them with the two beatings on the drum.

Maiden, it truly is not so as thou, O maiden, fanciest.

Two are thy mother's rays of light: the skin is guarded from the man.

HYMN CXXXIV.

Here are we sitting east and west and north and south, with waters. Bottle-gourd vessels.

---

16 *He with black tufts of hair:* or, He, the Dark-crested God (*nîlaśikhaṇḍaḥ*), that is, Rudra. Cf. A. V. II. 27. 6; XI. 2. 7.

There are five more stanzas, all with the refrain, Maiden, it truly is not so as thou, O maiden, fanciest. A mere literal translation of these would be unintelligible, and the matter does not deserve expansion or explanation. These six stanzas are called the Pravahlikâs or Enigmatical Verses. The Gods bewildered the Asuras by their recitation, and so defeated them; and sacrificers similarly bewilder and defeat their enemies by using them as sacrificial formulas. See Haug's Aitareya-Brâhmaṇa, Vol. II. p. 435.

These six stanzas are called the Âjijñâsenya verses, because the Gods recognised and defeated the Asuras by their means. By using them as liturgical formulas sacrificers also recognise and defeat their enemies.

2 Here east and west and north and south sit the calves sprinkling. Curds and oil.

3 Here east and west and north and south the offering of rice clings on. The leaf of the Aṣvaṭtha tree.

4 Here east and west and north and south adheres when touched. That water-drop.

5 Here east and west and north and south in iron mayst thou not be caught. The cup.

6 Here east and west and north and south fain would it clasp what would not clasp. Emmet hole.

HYMN CXXXV.

Bang! here he is. A dog.

2 Swish! it is gone. Falling of leaves.

3 Crunch! it is trodden on. A cow's hoof.

4 These Gods have gone astray. Do thou, Adhvaryu, quickly do thy work.

There is good resting for the cows. Take thy delight.

6 O singer, the Âdityas brought rich guerdon to the Angirases.

Singer, they went not near to it. Singer, they did not take the gift.

Verses 1—3 are called the Pratirâdha or Frustration, because with them the Gods frustrated the attacks of the Asuras, and sacrificers similarly frustrate the hostile attempts of their enemies by reciting them. Verse 4 is called the Ativâda, because with it the Gods abused and defeated their enemies, and sacrificers may do likewise by using it. There is no fifth verse in the text. Stanzas 6—10 are called the Devanîtha or Gods' Offering. The Aitareya-Brâhmaṇa gives the following general explanation of this last Section :—'The Añgirasas, therefore, assisted the Âdityas in their sacrifice. For this service the Âdityas gave them the earth filled with presents *(dakshiṇâ)* as reward. But when they had accepted her, she burnt them. Therefore they flung her away......That (Âditya, the sun) then assuming the shape of a white horse with bridle and harness, presented himself to the other Âdityas, who said, "Let us carry this gift to you (the Angirasas." Therefore this Devanîtha, *i. e.* what is carried by the Gods is to be recited.'—Haug's Aitareya-Brâhmaṇam, Vol. II. p. 437.

1 The lines 1—3 contain onomatopoetic riddles, and their answers.

6 *Rich guerdon : dákshiṇâm ;* in return for their assistance in the performance of sacrifice. *To it:* to the guerdon in the shape of the earth.

7 Singer, they went not near to that; but, singer, they accepted this:
That days may not be indistinct, nor sacrifices leaderless.

8 And quickly doth he fly away, the White Horse swiftest on his feet,
And swiftly fills his measure up.

9 Âdityas, Rudras, Vasus, all pay worship unto thee. Accept this liberal gift, O Angiras,
This bounty excellent and rich, this ample bounty spreading far.

10 The Gods shall give the precious boon: let it be pleasant to your hearts.
Let it be with you every day: accept our offerings in return.

11 Vouchsafe us shelter, Indra, thou to be invoked from far away.
Bring treasure hither to reward the far-famed bard who praises thee.

12 Thou, Indra, to the trembling dove whose pinions had been rent and torn
Gavest ripe grain and Pîlu fruit, gavest him water when athirst.

---

7 *That:* the earth. *This:* the White Horse, the Sun. *That days may not be indistinct:* as they would be without the Sun. As it seems impossible to force any sense out of *néta sán* of the text, I adopt Prof. Weber's conjectural emendation (Indische Studien, IX. p. 306), *ned asann.*

11 Stanzas 11—13 are called the Bhûtechhad, or Dazzling Power, from the effects produced by their employment by the Gods in their contest with the Asuras. Similarly their recitation will enable the sacrificer to overcome his enemy.

12 *Pîlu:* (Careya Arborea) 'a tree of immense size, growing on the mountains of Coromandel, etc., where it blossoms during the hot season, and the seed ripens about three or four months after.'—Roxburgh. According to others it is the Salvadora Persica, a rather uncommon middle-sized tree which produces flowers and fruit all the year round. I cannot trace the story referred to; but it somewhat resembles that of the Suppliant Dove in the Mahâbhârata. See Scenes from the Râmâyaṇa, Etc., pp. 327—331 (2nd Ed.)

13 The ready praiser loudly speaks though fastened triply with a strap.
Yea, he commends the freshening draught, deprecates languor of disease.

HYMN CXXXVI. *(See Appendix).*

END OF KUNTÂPA SECTION.

HYMN CXXXVII.

WHEN, foul with secret spot and stain, ye hastened onward to the breast,
All Indra's enemies were slain and passed away like froth and foam.

2 Indra is he, O men, who gives us happiness: sport, urge the giver of delight to win the spoil.
Bring quickly down, O priests, hither to give us aid, to drink the Soma, Indra son of Nishṭigrî.

3 So have I glorified with praise strong Dadhikrâvan, conquering steed.
Sweet may he make our mouths; may he prolong the days we have to live.

Taken from R. V. X. 155. 4; 101. 12; IV. 39. 6.; IX. 101. 4—6; VIII. 85. 13—17; 82. 7—9.

1 *Foul with secret spot and stain: maṇḍûradhânikîḥ:* the exact meaning of the word which is not found elsewhere is uncertain. See S. P. Lexicon, s. v. Prof. Ludwig translates conjecturally 'wie maṇḍûra's rufende (?),' calling out like Maṇḍûras. It seems to be a very abusive and indecent epithet applied in the original hymn to Arâyis or malignant witches. *Like froth and foam: budbudáyâçavaḥ;* frothy as a bubble, or perhaps, impotent.

2 I follow Sâyaṇa in his interpretation of the first line although its correctness is open to doubt. Professors von Roth, Ludwig, and Grassmann explain it differently. *Nishṭigrî:* said to be Aditi the mother of Indra. According to Sâyaṇa the meaning of the name is 'She who swallows up her rival Nishṭi, i. e. Diti.'

3 *Dadhikrâvan:* a mythical being described as a kind of divine horse, and probably a personification of the morning Sun. See A. V. III. 16. 6, note.

4 The Somas very rich in sweets, for which the sieve is destined, flow,
Effused, the source of Indra's joy. May your strong juices reach the Gods.

5 Indu flows on for Indra's sake—thus have the deities declared.
The Lord of Speech exerts himself, ruler of all, because of might.

6 Inciter of the voice of song, with thousand streams the ocean flows,
Even Soma, Lord of Opulence, the friend of Indra, day by day.

7 The black drop sank in Anṣumatī's bosom, advancing with ten thousand round about it.
Indra with might longed for it as it panted: the hero-hearted laid aside his weapons.

8 I saw the drop in the far distance moving, on the slope bank of Anṣumatī's river,
Like a black cloud that sank into the water. Heroes, I send you forth. Go, fight in battle.

9 And then the drop in Anṣumatī's bosom, splendid with light, assumed its proper body;
And Indra, with Bṛihaspati to aid him, conquered the godless tribes that came against him.

---

4 *The sieve*: or filter, through which the Soma juice is run to purify it.

6 *Indu*: Soma. *Lord of Speech*: as giving eloquence to those who drink it.

7 *The black drop*: the darkened moon. *Anṣumatī*: a mystical river of the air. *Ten thousand*: probably, demons of darkness; the numerals are without a substantive. *As it panted*: while striving against its assailants. *Laid aside his weapons*: after conquering the demons and restoring the darkened moon.

8 Indra addresses the Maruts.

Sâyaṇa explains stanzas 7—9 differently, in accordance with a legend which was probably suggested by this passage. He takes *drapsáḥ kṛishṇáḥ*, black drop, to mean 'the swift moving Kṛishṇaḥ,' an Asura or demon who with ten thousand of his kind had occupied the banks of the river Anṣumatî, which, he says, is the Yamunâ or Jumna, and was there defeated by Indra, Bṛihaspati, and the Maruts. See Prof. Cowell's Note in Wilson's Translation.

10 Then, at thy birth, thou wast the foeman, Indra, of those the seven who ne'er had met a rival.
The hidden pair, the heaven and earth, thou foundest, and to the mighty worlds thou gavest pleasure.

11 So, Thunder-armed! thou with thy bolt of thunder didst boldly smite that power which none might equal;
With weapons broughtest low the might of Sushṇa, and, Indra, foundest by thy strength the cattle.

12 We make this Indra very strong to strike the mighty Vṛitra dead:
A vigorous Hero shall he be.

13 Indra was made for giving, set, most mighty, o'er the joyous draught,
Bright, meet for Soma, famed in song.

14 By song, as 'twere, the powerful bolt which none may parry was prepared:
Lofty, invincible he grew.

HYMN CXXXVIII.

INDRA, great in his power and might and, like Parjanya, rich in rain,
Is magnified by Vatsa's lauds,

2 When the priests, strengthening the Son of holy Law, present their gifts,
Singers with Order's hymn of praise.

3 Since Kaṇvas with their lauds have made Indra complete the sacrifice,
Words are their own appropriate arms.

---

10 *The seven:* Kṛishṇa, Vṛitra, Namuchi, Sambara, and others.—Sâyaṇa.

11 *Sushṇa:* the Parcher, one of the chief demons of drought.

Taken from Ṛ. V. VIII. 6. 1—3.

1 *Parjanya:* the God of the rainy cloud. See A. V. I. 2. 1, note. *Vatsa:* a Ṛishi of the family of Kaṇva and seer of the original hymn.

2 *Son of holy Law:* Indra born in accordance with eternal law. *Order's hymn of praise:* song suitable to the prescribed sacrifices.

3 *Words are their own appropriate arms:* 'they declare all weapons needless.'—Wilson.

HYMN CXXXIX.

To help and favour Vatsa now, O Aṣvins, come ye hitherward.
Bestow on him a dwelling spacious and secure, and keep malignities afar.

2 All manliness that is in heaven, with the Five Tribes, or in mid-air,
Bestow, ye Aṣvins, upon us.

3 Remember Kâṇva first of all among the singers, Aṣvins, who
Have thought upon your wondrous deeds.

4 Aṣvins, for you with song of praise this hot oblation is effused,
This your sweet Soma juice, ye Lords of wealth and spoil, through which ye think upon the foe.

5 Whaṭever ye have done in floods, in the tree, Wonder-workers, and in growing plants,
Therewith, O Aṣvins, succour me.

HYMN CXL.

What force, Nâsatyas, ye exert, whatever, Gods, ye tend and heal,
This your own Vatsa gains not by his hymns alone: ye visit him who offers gifts.

Taken from Ṛ. V. VIII. 9. 1—5.

1 *Vatsa*: apparently another name of Ṣaṣakarṇa, the Ṛishi of the original hymn.

4 *Lords of wealth and spoil*: or, according to others, Lords of rapid steeds. *Think upon the foe*: meditate upon the destruction of the fiend Vṛitra.

5 *Whatever ye have done*: Prof. Wilson paraphrases, after Sâyaṇa: 'preserve me with that (healing virtue) deposited by you in the waters, in the trees, in the herbs.'

Taken, in continuation of the preceding hymn, from Ṛ. V. VIII. 9. 6—10.

1 *Nâsatyas*: a common name in the Ṛigveda for the Aṣvins, derived by the Indian commentators from *na + asatya*, 'not untrue.' *Tend and heal*: cf. 'And may the Aṣvins, the divine pair of physicians,

2 Now hath the Ṛishi splendidly thought out the Aṣvins' hymn of praise.
Let the Atharvan pour the warm oblation forth, and Soma very rich in sweets.

3 Ye Aṣvins, now ascend your car that lightly rolls upon its way.
May these my praises make you speed hitherward like a cloud of heaven.

4 When, O Nâsatyas, we this day make you speed hither with our hymns,
Or, Aṣvins, with our songs of praise, remember Kâṇva specially.

5 As erst Kakshîvân and the Ṛishi Vyaṣva, as erst Dîrghatamas invoked your presence,
Or, in the sacrificial chambers, Vainya Pṛithî, so be ye mindful of us here, O Aṣvins.

HYMN CXLI.

Come as home-guardians, saving us from foemen, guarding our living creatures and our bodies,
Come to the house to give us seed and offspring;

---

send us health' (Ṛ. V. VIII. 18. 8.); and 'the Aṣvins, leeches of the Gods, O Agni, have chased Death far from us with mighty power' (A. V. VII. 53. 1). *The Atharvan:* the priest who has special charge of the sacrificial fire and the Soma. I follow Prof. Ludwig in taking *átharvaṇi* as a nominative and not as a locative as Sâyaṇa does: 'he will sprinkle the sweet-flavoured *Soma* and the *gharma* (oblation) on the *Atharvan* fire.'—Wilson.

5 *Kakshîvân:* called Auṣija or son of Uṣij, a renowned Ṛishi of the family of Pajra and seer of several hymns of the Ṛigveda. He is mentioned in A. V. IV. 29. 5 and XVIII. 3. 15. *Vyaṣva:* a Ṛishi frequently mentioned in Ṛ. V. Book VIII. *Dîrghatamas:* son of Mamatâ, the seer of many hymns of the Ṛigveda. *Vainya Pṛithî:* Pṛithî son of Vena. See A. V. VIII. 10. 24.

Continued from Ṛ. V. VIII. 9. 11—15.

2 Whether with Indra ye be faring, Asvins, or resting in one dwelling-place with Vâyu,
In concord with the Ribhus or Âdityas, or standing still in Vishnu's striding-places.

3 When I, O Asvins, call on you to-day that I may gather strength,
Or as all-conquering might in war, be that the Asvins' noblest grace.

4 Now come, ye Asvins, hitherward: here are oblations set for you;
These Soma draughts to aid Yadu and Turvasa, these offered you mid Kanva's sons.

5 Whatever healing balm is yours, Nâsatyas, near or far away,
Therewith, great Sages, grant a home to Vatsa and to Vimada.

HYMN CXLII.

TOGETHER with the Goddess, with the Asvins' Speech have I awoke.
Thou, Goddess, hast disclosed the hymn and holy gift from mortal men.

2 Awake the Asvins, Goddess Dawn! Up, mighty Lady of Sweet Strains!
Rise straightway, priest of sacrifice! High glory to the gladdening draught!

---

2 *Vishnu's striding-places*: from which he made his three great strides his rising, culmination, and setting, as the Sun; or in his daily course through earth, air, and heaven.

3 *That*: the granting of my prayer.

4 *Yadu and Turvasa*: the eponymi of two of the Five Âryan Tribes, representing the tribes themselves.

5 *And to Vimada*: as ye did to Vimada, according to Sâyana. The ancient Rishi Vimada was specially protected and favoured by the Asvins. See R. V. I. 51. 3; 112. 19; 116. 1; 117. 20; X. 24. 4.

Continued from R. V. VIII. 9. 16—21.

1 *The Goddess*: Dawn. *The Asvins' Speech*: Vâk or Speech who glorifies the Asvins; *i. e.* the hymn that praises them.

29

3 Thou, Dawn, approaching with thy light, shinest together with the Sun,
And to this man-protecting home the chariot of the Asvins comes.

4 When yellow stalks give forth the juice as cows from udders pour their milk,
And voices sound the song of praise, the Asvins' worshippers show first.

5 Forward for glory and for strength, protection that shall conquer men,
And power and skill, most sapient Ones!

6 When, Asvins worthy of our lauds, ye seat you in the father's house
With wisdom or the bliss ye bring.

HYMN CXLIII.

We invocate this day your car, far-spreading, O Asvins, even the gathering of the sunlight,—
Car praised in hymns, most ample, rich in treasure, fitted with seats, the car that beareth Sûryâ.

---

4 *Yellow stalks:* of Soma plants.

5 *Forward for glory:* advance and come to give us glory, etc.

6 *In the father's house:* in the sacrificial hall of the father of the family, the wealthy householder who institutes the sacrifice. This stanza is a continuation of 4, although the connexion is interrupted by the intervening stanza.

A hymn to the Asvins, taken from R. V. IV. 44. 1—7; 57, 3; Vâlakhilya 9. 3 (VIII. 57. 3).

1 *The gathering of the sunlight:* Professor Wilson translates, after Sâyana, 'the associator of the solar ray,' and observes: '*Sangatim goh*, is only explained, *goh sangamayitâram*, the bringer into union, or associator, of *Go:* what the latter is intended for is not explained, and the translation is purely conjectural, founded upon the connection of the *Asvins* with light, or the sun.' Professor Grassmann translates: 'der zur Milch eilt,' 'which hastens to the milk.' *Sûryâ:* the daughter of the Sun, that is, the sunlight which the Asvins introduce. 'Sûrya, it is related, was desirous of giving his daughter Sûryâ to Soma [the Moon]; but all the gods desired her as a wife. They agreed that he who should first reach the sun, as a goal, should wed the damsel. The Asvins were victorious; and Sûryâ, well pleased by their success, rushed immediately into their chariot.'—Wilson. See R. V. I. 116. 17; 119. 5; 167. 5.

2 Asvins, ye gained that glory by your Godhead, ye Sons of Heaven, by your own might and power.
Food followeth close upon your bright appearing when stately horses in your chariot draw you.

3 Who bringeth you to-day for help with offered oblations, or with hymns to drink the juices?
Who, for the sacrifice's ancient lover, turneth you hither, Asvins, offering homage?

4 Borne on your golden car, ye omnipresent! come to this sacrifice of ours, Nâsatyas.
Drink of the pleasant liquor of the Soma: give riches to the people who adore you.

5 Come hitherward to us from earth, from heaven, borne on your golden chariot rolling lightly.
Suffer not other worshippers to stay you: here are ye bound by earlier bonds of friendship.

6 Now for us both, mete out, O Wonder-Workers, riches exceeding great with store of heroes,
Because the men have sent you praise, O Asvins, and Ajamîlhas come to the laudation.

7 Whene'er I gratified you here together, your grace was given us, O ye rich in booty.
Protect, ye twain, the singer of your praises: to you, Nâsatyas, is my wish directed.

8 Sweet be the plants for us, the heavens, the waters, and full of sweets for us be air's mid-region!
May the Field's Lord for us be full of sweetness, and may we follow after him uninjured.

9 Asvins, that work of yours deserves our wonder, the Bull of firmament and earth and heaven;
Yea, and your thousand promises in battle. Come near to all these men and drink beside us.

---

6 *Both:* priests and institutors of the sacrifice. *Ajamîlhas:* men of the Rishi's family.

8 *The Field's Lord:* said to be either Rudra or Agni; the Genius Fundi et Loci.

APPENDICES.

I. APPENDIX.

LATIN TRANSLATION OF OMITTED VERSES.

Book XX. 126. 16, 17.

16 Indrâṇî speaks. Non ille fortis (ad Venerem) est cujus mentula laxe inter femora dependet; fortis vero est ille cujus, quum sederit, membrum pilosum se extendit. Super omnia est Indra.

17 Indra speaks. Non fortis est ille cujus, quum sederit, membrum pilosum se extendit; fortis vero est ille cujus mentula laxe inter femora dependet. Super omnia est Indra.

Book XX. 136.

Si quis in hujus tenui rima præditae feminae augustias fascinum intromittit, vaccae ungularum et Sakularum piscium more pudenda ejus agitantur.

2 Quum magno pene parvula ejus pudenda vir percutit, huc et illuc illa increscunt veluti duo asini in solo arenoso.

3 Quum parvum, admodum parvum, Ziziphi Jujubae quasi granum in eam incidit, ventris ejus partes interiores, velut verno tempore arundo, extentae videntur.

Stanzas 1—10 of this hymn are called the Âhanasya Verses, that is, Erotica. By reciting them it is said (Aitareya-Brâhmaṇa, VI. 36) that the priest secures offspring for the sacrificer.

1 *Sakularum:* the Ṣakula is a small rapidly-moving fish.

2 *In solo arenoso:* where these animals still find food enough to swell them out.

3 *Ziziphi Jujubae:* the Jujube or Ber tree, which grows wild and produces a small edible fruit.

4 Si Dii mentulae intumescenti faverunt, cum femoribus suis se ostentat femina tanquam vero testi.

5 Magnopere delectata est amica: ut equus solutus adveniens vocem edidit: Vaginam, juvenis! pene percute: medium femur paratum est.

6 Amica, pilam superans, dixit: Ut tua, Arbor! (verbera) pinsunt, sic etiam nunc (hic me permolit).

7 Amica eum alloquitur: Tum etiam tu defecisti. Ut tua, Arbor! (verbera) pinsunt, sic etiam nunc (me permole).

8 Amica eum alloquitur: Tum etiam tu defecisti. Ut silvae ignis inflammatur, sic ardent mea membra.

9 Amica eum alloquitur: Fauste infixus est penis; arboris fructu celeriter fruamur.

10 Amica cum fuste gallum circumcurrit. Nos nescimus quae bestia pudendum muliebre in capite gerat.

11 Amica post currentem amatorem currit: Has ejus boves custodi tu. Me futue: coctam oryzam ede.

12 Fortunatus, Amica, te opprimit. Bona est magni viri fututio. Macrum pinguis femina obtineat. Futue me, etc.

13 Sine digito mulcta vacca *vanankaram* producit. Magna et bona est Aegle Marmelos. Futue me, etc.

---

4 *Vero testi:* the genitive *akshibhúvaḥ* appears to be used here for the dative, as in later Sanskrit. See Geldner, Vedische Studien, I. p. 281, who has given a German translation of the verse.

5 *Amica: mahánagnī;* 'quite naked'; a mistress.

6 *Pilam:* a mortar. *Arbor:* meaning here the wooden pestle. Cf. Ṛ. V. I. 28. 3, 6.

11 *Ejus boves custodi:* while the lover is otherwise engaged. These words are addressed to some bystander.

13 *Vanankaram:* the meaning of the word is uncertain. *Aegle Marmelos:* the Bilva or Bel, a kind of wood-apple, the fruit of which is used medicinally.

14 Infelix, Amica, te opprimit. Bona est magni viri fututio. Flava puellula, opere suo perfecto, procurrit.

15 Magna certe et bona est Aegle Marmelos. Bona est magna Ficus Glomerata. Magnus vir ubique opprimit. Bona est magni viri fututio.

16 Quem macrum factum puella flava pinguisque capiat sicut pollicem ex olei cado fossorem illum extrahat.

---

14 *Infelix*: *vídevaḥ*; meaning 'a feeble lover' in opposition to *sudeváḥ*, fortunatus, 'a strong or good lover,' of verse 12. See Vedische Studien, I. p. 280.

16 *Fossorem*: sensu obsceno.

By way of purification after reciting these erotic verses, the priest has to recite the Dâdhikrî verse (A. V. XX. 137. 3), and the Pâvamânî lines (R. V. IX. 67. 21—27).

II. INDEX OF HYMNS.

BOOK X.

BOOK XI.

BOOK XII.

BOOK XIII.

BOOK XIV.

BOOK XV.

BOOK XVI.

BOOK XVII.

BOOK XVIII.

BOOK XIX.

BOOK XX.

KUNTÂPA SECTION.

END OF THE KUNTÂPA SECTION.

III. GENERAL LIST OF ṚIGVEDA HYMNS AND VERSES REPRODUCED, WITH OR WITHOUT VARIATIONS, IN THE ATHARVA-VEDA.

VOL. I.

Ṛigveda. — *Atharva-veda.*

Book I.

Hymn.	Verse.	Page.
22.	17-20	340
23.	24	429
24.	9	346
25.	15	371
31.	16	103
32.	1-3	47
89.	10	330
97.		175
102.	4	350
154.	1	339
154.	2	339, 340
164.	1-22	458-464
164.	23-47	464-470
164.	26	362
164.	27	363
164.	40	363
164.	50	329
191.	4	274
191.	8	227
191.	8, 9	273

Book II.

Hymn.	Verse.	Page.
32.	6, 7	347

Book III.

Hymn.	Verse.	Page.
29.	10	111
29.	16	376
45.	1	384

Ṛigveda. — *Atharva-veda.*

Book IV.

Hymn.	Verse.	Page.
57.	4	107
57.	5	107
57.	6	107
57.	7	106
57.	8	107
58.	10	369

Book V.

Hymn.	Verse.	Page.
2.	9	375
4.	5	363
42.	4	376
46.	7, 8	349
60.	1	349
83.	8	153

Book VI.

Hymn.	Verse.	Page.
28.	1-7	161, 162
28.	7	364
28.	8	442
47.	6	366
47.	11	372
47.	12	374
47.	13	374
47.	26-28	314
47.	29-31	315
52.	2	56
54	9, 10	332
68.	10, 11	355

Ṛigveda. — *Atharva-veda.*

Hymn.	Verse.	Page.
69.	8	347
74.	2, 3	346
75.	16	110
75.	18	384
75.	19	24

Book VII.

Hymn.	Verse.	Page.
5.	58	135
15.	10	395
41.		104, 105
89.	5	273
104.		396-399
163.	1	152

Book VIII.

Hymn.	Verse.	Page.
40.	6	374
43.	11	114
47.	17	270
103.	1	152

Book IX.

Hymn.	Verse.	Page.
73.	4	197
110.	1	197

Book X.

Hymn.	Verse.	Page.
5.	6	188
9.	1-3, 5	7
9.	4, 6, 7	8

Ṛigveda.		*Atharva-veda.*	*Ṛigveda.*		*Atharva-veda.*	*Ṛigveda.*		*Atharva-veda.*
Hymn.	Verse.	Page.	Hymn.	Verse.	Page.	Hymn.	Verse.	Page.
13.	5	388	163.		74	30.	4-6	364
17.	1	127	164.	3, 4	269	30.	7	282
18.	4	389	165.		259	30.	7-9	343
19.	4	287	165.	4	261	30.	13-15	425
42.	9, 10	350	173.	4, 5	293	46.	6	298
42.	11	351	173.	6	375	50.	1-9	145, 365
56.	2	296	178.	1	372	50.	13	212
60.	12	148	179.		361	53.		337
63.	10	350	180.	2	339	57.		330
77.	4	142	180.	3, 2	371	61.		352
82.	3	42	184.	1	230	81.	1-3, 7, 9	371
83.		174	184.	2	229	82.	2	256
84.		173	189.		262	83.		342
85.	18, 19	368	191.	1	280	84.	7-9	377
87.	1-23	392-395				84.	10-12	420
87.	22	361	VOL. II.			84.	13-15	362
94.	5	272	Book I.			84.	16	216
97.	16	298	3.	4-6	396	85.	6	329
101.	3	106	4.	1-3	372	86.	1	321
101.	4	106	4.	4-10	382	94.	1	329
103.	13	110	5.	3-10	383	104.	9	325
109.	1-7	205-207	6.	1-3	343, 365	105.	1	258
120		189-191	6.	1-4	383	114.	7	60
121		131, 132	6.	4	260	115.	1	148
121.	10	368	6.	5-10	384	115.	1, 2	417
125.		171, 172	6.	7, 8, 4	361	115.	4, 5	426
128.		192, 193	7.	1-3	360, 365	127.	1	380
129.	4	433	7.	1-10	384	131.	3-5	390
131.	6	374	7.	10	360	133.	7	380
131.	7	374	8.	1-4	384	139.	8	380
137.		147, 148	8.	4-10	386	164.	17	140
141.	1-6	111	8.	8-10	375	164.	41	140
145.		108, 109	9.		386	164.	47	151
152.	1, 2-5	25	12.	1-3	414			
152.	2	403	22.	15	230	Book II.		
159.	1	34	24.	15	257	12.		349
161.	1-4	95	29.		389	22.	1	409

Ṛigveda.		Atharva-veda.
Hymn.	Verse.	Page.
23.	19	240
36.	2, 4, 5	380
36.	37	321
37.	2	380
41.	10-12	337
Book III.		
6.	9	329
27.	1-15	415
32.	15	325
33.	11	223
33.	13	174
34.		326
35.	4	397
37.	1-7	336
37.	8-11	337, 372
40.	1	321
40.	1-8	324
41.		340
42.		341
Book IV.		
2.	16-19	239
13.	4	220
16.	1-8	393
24.	1, 2	222
31.	1-3	426
39.	6	444
44.	1-7	450
50.	1-6	398
50.	10	329
57.	3	450
Book V.		
1.	1	149
6.	4	258
40.	4	328

Book VI.

Ṛigveda.		Atharva-veda.
Hymn.	Verse.	Page.
2.	6	255
17.	3	325
17.	15	273, 377, 426
22.		357
45.	22-24	394
46.	1, 2	413
46.	5, 6	395
46.	9, 10	396
47.	1	224
47.	8	275
73.		401
Book VII.		
19.		358
22.	1-3	423
22.	7, 8	353
27.	3	261
31.	4-6	335
31.	10	353
32.	12, 13	375
32.	16	246
32.	18, 19	395
32.	26, 27	394
35.	1-10	270, 271
35.	11-15	272
97.	10	334
98.		397
Book VIII.		
1.	1-4	396
1.	12	179
1.	13, 14	423
2.	16-18	335
3.	3, 4	415
3.	5, 6	424
3.	7, 8	413

Ṛigveda.		Atharva-veda.
Hymn.	Verse.	Page.
3.	9, 10	368
3.	13, 14	369
3.	15, 16	326, 375
4.	1, 2	425
6.	1, 3	446
6.	4, 6	417
6.	10-12	423
9.	1-5	447
9.	6-10	447
9.	11-15	448
9.	16-21	449
11.	1	317
12.	1-3	421
12.	16-18	421
14.	1-6	344
14.	7-10	345
14.	11-15	345
15.	1-3	376
15.	4-6, 1-3	376
15.	7, 9	417
16.	1-3	364
16.	10-12	364
17.	1-3	322, 360, 365
17.	4-6	322
17.	7-13	323
21.	1, 2, 9, 10	330
21.	13, 14	422
22.	7, 8	388
24.	16-18	378
24.	19-21	379
24.	22-24	379
31.	10	388
32.	22, 23	425
33.	1, 2	370
33.	7-9	370
33.	7-9, 1-3	372

Ṛigveda.		*Atharva-veda.*	*Ṛigveda.*		*Atharva-veda.*	*Ṛigveda.*		*Atharva-veda.*
			VÂLAKHILYA.					
Hymn.	Verse.	Page.	Hymn.	Verse.	Page.	Hymn.	Verse.	Page.
33.	13, 14	369	1.	1, 2	369	16.	4	228
43.	11	321	2.	1, 2	369	16.	5	228
45.	22	340	3.	10	424	16.	6	244
45.	40-42	363	4.	9	424	16.	7	235
47.	17	314	9.	3	450	16.	8	244
47.	18	204				16.	12	226
49.	1, 2	415	Book IX.			16.	13	237
50.	1, 2	422	86.	16	255	16.	14	245
50.	5, 6	424	86.	19	255	17.	1	225
50.	13	275	86.	43	239	17.	2	232
53.	1-3	406	101.	4-6	444	17.	7-9	253
55.	7-9	413				17.	11	250
58.	4-6	340	Book X.			17.	14	244
58.	4-18	403	2.	4	317	17.	34	234
59.	1, 2	416	8.	1	246	18.	1	105
59.	1-6	403	11.		219, 220	18.	2	106, 107
59.	5, 6	395	12.	1-8	221	18.	3	105
60.	14	415	13.	1-4	241	18.	4	105
65.	12, 11, 10	363	13.	3	241	18.	5	106
77.	1, 2	325, 368	14.	1, 2	224	18.	7	244
79.	1, 2	415	14.	3	224	18.	8	236
80.	7	1[illegible]7	14.	6, 5	226	18.	9	235
81.	19-21	417	14.	7	225	18.	10-13	243
81.	28-30	375	14.	8	244	23.	3-5	388
82.	1-3	324	14.	9	225	29.		391
82.	4-6	421	14.	10-12	229	40.	10	168
82.	7-9	365, 444	14.	13, 15, 14	227	40.	12	172
85.	13-17	444	14.	16	227	40.	13	172
86.	10-12	370	15.	1, 3, 2	223	42.		399
86.	13, 1, 2	371	15.	4	225	43.		334
87.	1-3	376	15.	6	225	44.		407
87.	4-6	378	15.	7, 11, 5		53.	8	106
87.	7-9	414		8, 9	242	56.	1	237
88.	5-7	416	15.	12	242	57.	1	142
88.	10-12	420	16.	1, 2	227	57.	2	142
90.	11	147	16.	3	228	67.		401

Ṛigveda.		*Atharva-veda.*	*Ṛigveda.*		*Atharva-veda.*	*Ṛigveda.*		*Atharva-veda.*
Hymn.	Verse.	Page.	Hymn.	Verse.	Page.	Hymn.	Verse.	Page.
68.		332	96.	1-5	346	133.	1-3	409
81.	3	146	96.	6-10	347	139.	3	41
85.		159-166	96.	11-13	348	153.		406
85.	17	179	101.	8	316	154.	1, 4, 2, 3	229
85.	18	144	101.	12	441	155.	4	444
85.	20	170	103.	1-9, 11	273	157.		377, 426
85.	22	177	104.	2-4	349	160.	1-5	410
85.	31, 32	173	104.	3	342	161.	1-5	410
85.	36	169	107.	4	251	162.		410
85.	37	177	117.	8	146, 153	163.		410
85.	38 41	171	120.		417	164.	1	410
85.	43	178	121.	2	153	172.	1	273
86.		428	123.	6	246	184.	1	224
90.		262-264	131.		427			

IV. INDEX OF NAMES, ETC.